This irresistible collection of cloned recipes is the product of years of obsessive research by self-confessed junk-food addict Todd Wilbur. Big food manufacturers and restaurant chains guard their recipes like the gold in Fort Knox, but Wilbur's dogged pursuit of taste-alike versions of his—and our—all-time favorites has paid off in this unique cookbook of over 150 scrumptious treats. Whether you're a kid or just a kid at heart, you'll have a great time making the incredible clones of a McDonald's® Big Mac®, a Burger King® Whopper®, a Tastykake® Butterscotch Krimpet®, a Yoo Hoo® Chocolate Drink, and other famous foods as well as favorite dishes from Bennigan's®, Big Boy®, Planet Hollywood®, Tony Roma's A Place for Ribs®, and more! Helpful illustrations let you re-create them to perfection. Both taste and guilty pleasures are just like the real thing.

TODD WILBUR is the bestselling author of the Top Secret Recipe books including *Top Secret Recipes—Lite!* When not taste-testing recipes on himself, his friends, or talk-show hosts, he lives in Las Vegas, Nevada.

Visit the Top Secret Recipes website at: **www.topsecretrecipes.com**

TODD WILBUR

A TREASURY OF TOP SECRET RECIPES

With Illustrations by the Author

A PLUME BOOK

PLUME
Published by the Penguin Group
Penguin Putnam Inc., 375 Hudson Street, New York, New York 10014, U.S.A.
Penguin Books Ltd, 27 Wrights Lane, London W8 5TZ, England
Penguin Books Australia Ltd, Ringwood, Victoria, Australia
Penguin Books Canada Ltd, 10 Alcorn Avenue, Toronto, Ontario, Canada M4V 3B2
Penguin Books (N.Z.) Ltd, 182–190 Wairau Road, Auckland 10, New Zealand

Penguin Books Ltd, Registered Offices: Harmondsworth, Middlesex, England

First published by Plume, a member of Penguin Putnam Inc.

This is an omnibus edition encompassing *Top Secret Recipes, More Top Secret Recipes,* and *Top Secret Restaurant Recipes.*

First Printing, July, 1999
    2   3   4   5   6   7   8   9   10

 REGISTERED TRADEMARK—MARCA REGISTRADA

LIBRARY OF CONGRESS CATALOGING-IN-PUBLICATION DATA

Wilbur, Todd.
    A treasury of top secret recipes / Todd Wilbur ; with illustrations by the author.
      p. cm.
    Includes bibliographical references and index.
    ISBN 0-452-28150-4
    1. Cookery, American. 2. Convenience foods—United States. 3. Brand name products—United States. I. Title.
    TX715 .W65873 1999
    641.5'0973—dc21

                                                                                    99-35768
                                                                                         CIP

Printed in the United States of America
Set in Gill Sans Light 2nd Machine

BOOKS ARE AVAILABLE AT QUANTITY DISCOUNTS WHEN USED TO PROMOTE PRODUCTS OR SERVICES. FOR INFORMATION PLEASE WRITE TO PREMIUM MARKETING DIVISION, PENGUIN PUTNAM INC., 375 HUDSON STREET, NEW YORK, NEW YORK 10014.

CONTENTS

A LITTLE FOREWORD   xv

PART I: BRAND-NAME CLONES

INTRODUCTION   3

CONVENIENCE FOOD: AN AMERICAN LOVE AFFAIR   10

SOME COOKING TIPS FROM A GUY WHO CARES   20

A&W® ROOT BEER   25

ARBY'S SAUCE®   27

AUNT JEMIMA® MAPLE SYRUP   28

BAILEY'S ORIGINAL IRISH CREAM®   30

BEN & JERRY'S ® HEATH® BAR CRUNCH ICE CREAM   31

BORDEN® CRACKER JACK®   33

BROWN & HALEY® ALMOND ROCA®   35

BURGER KING® WHOPPER®   38

CARL'S JR.® CHICKEN CLUB   41

CARL'S JR.® FAMOUS STAR®   43

CARL'S JR.® SANTA FE CHICKEN®   46

CARL'S JR.® WESTERN BACON CHEESEBURGER   49

CHICK-FIL-A® CHICKEN SANDWICH   52

CINNABON® CINNAMON ROLLS   55

DAIRY QUEEN® BLIZZARD®   58

DUNKIN' DONUTS®   61

EL POLLO LOCO® FLAME-BROILED CHICKEN   65

EL POLLO LOCO® SALSA   67

HARDEE'S® FRENCH FRIES   68

HARDEE'S® 1/4-POUND HAMBURGER   71

HOSTESS® TWINKIE®   73

IN-N-OUT® DOUBLE-DOUBLE   76

JACK-IN-THE-BOX® JUMBO JACK®   79

JACK-IN-THE-BOX® TACO   82

KAHLÚA® COFFEE LIQUEUR   85

KEEBLER® PECAN SANDIES®   87

KEEBLER® SOFT BATCH® CHOCOLATE CHIP COOKIES   90

KFC® BUTTERMILK BISCUITS   92

KFC® COLE SLAW   94

KFC® ORIGINAL RECIPE® FRIED CHICKEN   97

LITTLE CAESAR'S® CRAZY BREAD   100

LITTLE CAESAR'S® CRAZY SAUCE   102

LONG JOHN SILVER'S® BATTER-DIPPED FISH   103

M&M/MARS® ALMOND BAR®   106

M&M/MARS® CARAMEL TWIX® BARS   109

M&M/MARS® MILKY WAY   112

M&M/MARS® SNICKERS® BAR   115

M&M/MARS® 3 MUSKETEERS®   118

McDONALD'S® BIG MAC®   121

McDONALD'S® EGG McMUFFIN®   124

McDONALD'S® FILET-O-FISH®   127

McDONALD'S® HAMBURGER   129

McDONALD'S® McD.L.T.®   132

McDONALD'S® QUARTER POUNDER (WITH CHEESE)®   135

MRS. FIELDS® CHOCOLATE CHIP COOKIES   137

MRS. FIELDS® PEANUT BUTTER DREAM BARS   140

NABISCO® CHIPS AHOY!®   143

NABISCO® NUTTER BUTTER®   145

NABISCO® OREO® COOKIE   148

NESTLÉ® CRUNCH®   151

NESTLÉ® 100 GRAND BAR®   153

ORANGE JULIUS®   155

PANCAKES FROM INTERNATIONAL HOUSE OF
   PANCAKES®   157

PETER PAUL® MOUNDS® AND ALMOND JOY®   159

POGEN'S® GINGERSNAPS   161

POPEYE'S® FAMOUS FRIED CHICKEN®   163

POPEYE'S® RED BEANS AND RICE®   165

REESE'S® PEANUT BUTTER CUPS®   168

SARA LEE® ORIGINAL CREAM CHEESECAKE   171

SEE'S® BUTTERSCOTCH LOLLIPOP   174

SNAPPLE® ICED TEA (LEMON, DIET LEMON, ORANGE,
   STRAWBERRY, AND CRANBERRY)   177

STARK® MARY JANE®   179

SUPER PRETZELS®   182

TACO BELL® ENCHIRITO   185

TACO BELL® HOT TACO SAUCE   188

TASTYKAKE® BUTTERSCOTCH KRIMPETS®   189

TASTYKAKE® CHOCOLATE CUPCAKES   192

TASTYKAKE® PEANUT BUTTER KANDY KAKES®   195

TWIN DRAGON® ALMOND COOKIES   198

WENDY'S® CHILI   200

WENDY'S® FROSTY®   202

WENDY'S® GRILLED CHICKEN FILLET SANDWICH®   203

WENDY'S® JUNIOR BACON CHEESEBURGER®   205

WENDY'S® SINGLE®   207

WHITE CASTLE® BURGERS   210

YOO-HOO® CHOCOLATE DRINK   213

YORK PEPPERMINT PATTIE®   214

PART II: RESTAURANT CLONES

INTRODUCTION   219

TABLE FOR TWO: THE RESTAURANT TALE   227

APPLEBEE'S® NEIGHBORHOOD GRILL & BAR
    QUESADILLAS   240

APPLEBEE'S® NEIGHBORHOOD GRILL & BAR PIZZA
    STICKS®   243

APPLEBEE'S® NEIGHBORHOOD GRILL & BAR ORIENTAL
    CHICKEN SALAD   247

APPLEBEE'S® NEIGHBORHOOD GRILL & BAR CLUB HOUSE
    GRILL®   249

APPLEBEE'S® NEIGHBORHOOD GRILL & BAR TIJUANA "PHILLY"
    STEAK SANDWICH®   252

BENIHANA® HIBACHI CHICKEN AND HIBACHI STEAK   255

BENIHANA® DIPPING SAUCES   258

BENIHANA® JAPANESE FRIED RICE   260

BENNIGAN'S® BUFFALO CHICKEN SANDWICH   262

BENNIGAN'S® CALIFORNIA TURKEY SANDWICH   265

BENNIGAN'S® COOKIE MOUNTAIN SUNDAE®   268

BIG BOY® CREAM OF BROCCOLI SOUP   272

BIG BOY® ORIGINAL DOUBLE-DECKER HAMBURGER
    CLASSIC   274

BIG BOY® CLUB SANDWICH   277

CALIFORNIA PIZZA KITCHEN® ORIGINAL BBQ CHICKEN
    PIZZA   280

CALIFORNIA PIZZA KITCHEN® THAI CHICKEN PIZZA   284

CALIFORNIA PIZZA KITCHEN® SOUTHWESTERN BURRITO
    PIZZA   288

THE CHEESECAKE FACTORY® BRUSCHETTA   292

THE CHEESECAKE FACTORY® AVOCADO EGGROLLS   295

THE CHEESECAKE FACTORY® CAJUN JAMBALAYA
    PASTA   299

THE CHEESECAKE FACTORY® PUMPKIN CHEESECAKE   302

THE CHEESECAKE FACTORY® KEY LIME CHEESECAKE   305

CHI-CHI'S® NACHOS GRANDE   308

CHI-CHI'S® SWEET CORN CAKE   312

CHI-CHI'S® TWICE GRILLED BARBECUE BURRITO   314

CHI-CHI'S® MEXICAN "FRIED" ICE CREAM®   317

CHILI'S® GRILL AND BAR GRILLED CARIBBEAN
    SALAD   320

CHILI'S® GRILL AND BAR FAJITAS FOR TWO   322

CHILI'S® GRILL AND BAR PEANUT BUTTERCUP
    CHEESECAKE   325

CRACKER BARREL OLD COUNTRY STORE® HASH BROWN
    CASSEROLE   329

CRACKER BARREL OLD COUNTRY STORE® EGGS-IN-THE-
    BASKET   331

CRACKER BARREL OLD COUNTRY STORE® CHICKEN &
    DUMPLINS   334

DENNY'S® SCRAM SLAM®   337

DENNY'S® MOONS OVER MY HAMMY®   339

DENNY'S® THE SUPER BIRD®   342

DIVE!® CARROT CHIPS®   345

DIVE!® SICILIAN SUB ROSA®   348

DIVE!® BRICK OVEN MUSHROOM AND TURKEY CHEESE
    SUB®   352

DIVE!® S'MORES®   355

HARD ROCK CAFE® FILET STEAK SANDWICH   358

HARD ROCK CAFE® GRILLED VEGETABLE
    SANDWICH   361

HARD ROCK CAFE® FAMOUS BABY ROCK WATERMELON
    RIBS®   364

HARD ROCK CAFE® ORANGE FREEZE   366

HOOTERS® BUFFALO CHICKEN WINGS   367

HOOTERS® BUFFALO SHRIMP   370

HOOTERS® PASTA SALAD   373

HOULIHAN'S® HOULI FRUIT FIZZ®   375

HOULIHAN'S® 'SHROOMS®   376

HOULIHAN'S® SMASHED POTATOES®   380

INTERNATIONAL HOUSE OF PANCAKES® FRENCH
    TOAST   382

INTERNATIONAL HOUSE OF PANCAKES® CHEESE
    BLINTZ   385

INTERNATIONAL HOUSE OF PANCAKES® BANANA NUT
    PANCAKES   389

INTERNATIONAL HOUSE OF PANCAKES® FAJITA
    OMELETTE   392

LONE STAR STEAKHOUSE & SALOON® AMARILLO CHEESE
    FRIES®   395

LONE STAR STEAKHOUSE & SALOON® BLACK BEAN
    SOUP   398

LONE STAR STEAKHOUSE & SALOON® TEXAS RICE   400

LONE STAR STEAKHOUSE & SALOON® SWEET BOURBON
   SALMON   402

MARIE CALLENDER'S® FAMOUS GOLDEN CORNBREAD   404

MARIE CALLENDER'S® CHICKEN POT PIE   406

MARIE CALLENDER'S® BANANA CREAM PIE   409

THE OLIVE GARDEN® ITALIAN SALAD DRESSING   412

THE OLIVE GARDEN® HOT ARTICHOKE-SPINACH DIP   413

THE OLIVE GARDEN® TOSCANA SOUP   415

THE OLIVE GARDEN® ALFREDO PASTA   416

OUTBACK STEAKHOUSE® BLOOMIN' ONION®   417

OUTBACK STEAKHOUSE® GOLD COAST COCONUT
   SHRIMP   421

OUTBACK STEAKHOUSE® WALKABOUT SOUP®   424

OUTBACK STEAKHOUSE® ALICE SPRINGS CHICKEN®   426

PERKINS® FAMILY RESTAURANTS POTATO PANCAKES   429

PERKINS® FAMILY RESTAURANTS GRANNY'S COUNTRY
   OMELETTE®   431

PERKINS® FAMILY RESTAURANTS COUNTRY CLUB
   OMELETTE   434

PIZZA HUT® ORIGINAL STUFFED CRUST PIZZA   437

PIZZA HUT® PEPPERONI & CHEESE CRUST PIZZA   442

PIZZA HUT® TRIPLE DECKER PIZZA   443

PLANET HOLLYWOOD® PIZZA BREAD   447

PLANET HOLLYWOOD® CHICKEN CRUNCH®   450

PLANET HOLLYWOOD® POT STICKERS   453

RED LOBSTER® BROILED LOBSTER   456

RED LOBSTER® SCALLOPS AND BACON   459

RED LOBSTER® STUFFED SHRIMP AND STUFFED
   MUSHROOMS   463

RED ROBIN BURGER & SPIRITS EMPORIUM® NO-FIRE
   PEPPERS®   467

RED ROBIN BURGER & SPIRITS EMPORIUM® BBQ CHICKEN
   SALAD   470

RED ROBIN BURGER & SPIRITS EMPORIUM® MOUNTAIN HIGH
   MUDD PIE®   473

RUBY TUESDAY® POTATO CHEESE SOUP   477

RUBY TUESDAY® SMOKEY MOUNTAIN CHICKEN   479

RUBY TUESDAY® SONORA CHICKEN PASTA   482

RUBY TUESDAY® STRAWBERRY TALLCAKE® FOR
   TWO   485

RUTH'S CHRIS STEAK HOUSE® BARBECUED SHRIMP   489

RUTH'S CHRIS STEAK HOUSE® PETITE FILET   491

RUTH'S CHRIS STEAK HOUSE® CREAMED SPINACH   494

RUTH'S CHRIS STEAK HOUSE® POTATOES
   AU GRATIN   496

SHONEY'S® COUNTRY FRIED STEAK   498

SHONEY'S® SLOW-COOKED POT ROAST   500

SHONEY'S® HOT FUDGE CAKE   503

SIZZLER® CHEESE TOAST   506

SIZZLER® CHICKEN CLUB SANDWICH   507

SIZZLER® SOUTHERN FRIED SHRIMP   510

STUART ANDERSON'S BLACK ANGUS® CHEESY GARLIC
   BREAD   512

STUART ANDERSON'S BLACK ANGUS® WESTERN
   T-BONE   515

STUART ANDERSON'S BLACK ANGUS® WHISKEY PEPPER
   STEAK   517

T.G.I. FRIDAY'S® POTATO SKINS   519

T.G.I. FRIDAY'S® NINE-LAYER DIP   522

T.G.I. FRIDAY'S® CALIFORNIA CHARGRILLED TURKEY
   SANDWICH   525

T.G.I. FRIDAY'S® SPICY CAJUN CHICKEN PASTA   528

T.G.I. FRIDAY'S® FRIDAY'S SMOOTHIES®   530

TONY ROMA'S A PLACE FOR RIBS® WORLD FAMOUS
   RIBS   532

TONY ROMA'S A PLACE FOR RIBS® ORIGINAL BABY
   BACKS   534

TONY ROMA'S A PLACE FOR RIBS® CAROLINA
   HONEYS®   536

TONY ROMA'S A PLACE FOR RIBS® RED HOTS®   537

WESTERN SIZZLIN® "TERIYAKI" CHICKEN BREAST   539

BIBLIOGRAPHY   543

TRADEMARKS   545

INDEX   551

A LITTLE FOREWORD

In the laboratory (my kitchen), each of these recipes was subjected to a battering array of bakings and mixings, batch after batch, until the closest representation of the actual commercial product was finally achieved. I did not swipe, heist, bribe, or otherwise obtain any formulas through coercion or illegal means. I'd like to think that many of these recipes are the actual formulas for their counterparts, but there's no way of knowing for sure. In such cases of closely guarded secret recipes, the closer one gets to matching a real product's contents, the less likely it is that the protective manufacturer will say so.

The objective here was to match the taste and texture of the products with everyday ingredients. In most cases, obtaining the exact ingredients for these mass-produced food products is nearly impossible. For the sake of security and convenience, many of the companies have contracted confidentially with vendors for the specialized production and packaging of each of their product's ingredients. These prepackaged mixes and ingredients are then sent directly to the company for final preparation.

Debbi Fields of Mrs. Fields Cookies, for example, arranged with several individual companies to custom manufacture many of her cookies' ingredients. Her vanilla alone is specially blended from a variety of beans grown in various places around the world. The other ingredients—the chocolate, the eggs, the sugars, the flour—all get specialized attention specifically for the Mrs. Fields company. The same holds true for McDonald's, Wendy's, KFC, and most of the big-volume companies.

Even if you could bypass all the security measures and somehow get your hands on the secret formulas, you'd have a hard time executing the recipes without locating many ingredients usually impossible to find at the corner market. Therefore, with taste in mind, substitution of ingredients other than those that may be used in the actual products is necessary in many cases to achieve a closely cloned end result.

PART I

BRAND-NAME CLONES

INTRODUCTION

In 1987 I received in the mail a recipe with a letter attached, claiming it was the secret formula for Mrs. Fields Chocolate Chip Cookies. The sheet looked like a fifth- or sixth-generation photocopy. It told a curious story that went something like this: A woman had called the Mrs. Fields office in Park City, Utah, and requested the recipe for chocolate chip cookies. Someone at the office agreed to provide the recipe but told the woman it would cost her $2.50. The woman placed the fee on her credit card, and when she received her statement, was started to see a charge for $250! She was so upset about the loss that she started a chain-letter campaign, sending out dozens of copies of the recipe to friends and family members, and encouraging them to do the same.

It didn't take long to realize that this wasn't actually the recipe for Mrs. Fields Cookies, much less a recipe that even came close to the original. So what was it then? Someone's idea of a really bad prank? Or perhaps something much more devious? Whatever the reason, someone was working hard at getting this chain-letter recipe into mailboxes all over the country, and I had become one of the lucky recipients.

I would later discover that this bogus recipe had been spreading quickly across the country. And the effects of this seemingly innocent chain letter were spelling out big problems for the Mrs. Fields company.

People who had tried the recipe were disillusioned by the finished product—a cookie that did not taste at all like a Mrs. Fields cookie but more like the desk coaster I set my coffee on. And the chain letter gave the impression that the company was in the business of selling its recipe—a claim that's simply not true. Some people even responded by accusing the firm of mistreating the woman caller.

It took the company a long time to overcome the adverse effects of the chain letter. Prominent signs were placed inside each store discrediting the recipe. You may have seen them. The cookie company never did discover the chain letter's creator or the motive behind it.

Fortunately for the company, today the incident is only a bad memory. But I remained inspired by the popularity of the recipe. Thousands had seen it and passed it on, feeling privy to this "secret" that they wanted to share. Too bad they were misled.

With all of this in mind, I focused on the recipe and wondered what it might take, aside from common kitchen sense, to make the recipe a little better, more like the original; to make the cookie soft and chewy in the center but crispy around the edges; to produce that deep buttery-vanilla aroma that lures customers away from their mall shopping over to the Mrs. Fields cookie counter. What would have to change to make it taste like the original cookies that Americans can't seem to pass up? In time, with a little trial and error and flour in the eye, I had come up with a cookie that tasted just like Mrs. Fields'—it was delicious! My kitchen cloning craze had begun, and that was the day this book was born.

Within these pages you will find recipes that will help you create home clones of very well known, well respected products. But don't mistake these recipes for the actual product formulas. They probably aren't. They'll just taste like the real thing to you—if all goes well.

It may at first seem silly to spend time making any of these foods that you can simply run out and buy, but there's actually some logic at work here. For instance, there isn't one city in this country where one can buy everything in this book—many of the items are regional. And there are both economic and nutritional concerns that make this book a useful stoveside companion. These recipes will give you a degree of control you didn't have before. You can now determine for yourselves what goes into these world-famous foods and what doesn't. You'll have control over when to make the food. You'll no longer be at the mercy of slow cooks, lines, or closed doors. And you'll have something to do on rainy days when video games start to cross your eyes and blister your firing thumb.

There is a sense of satisfaction that comes from creating something in your own kitchen that tastes just like a product that has tickled the taste buds of millions. Even more exciting are the expressions of amazement from others who taste your creations—"You made this?" Humbly nod and share the recipe.

True, nothing can absolutely replace the authentic creations that have proven themselves to consumers over time. But there are some very concrete and detailed reasons why your next culinary experiment should come from these pages.

COST

With today's changing economic conditions, Americans are watching their money ever more closely. Now, instead of going out to the store or fast-food restaurant for snacks and meals, a growing number of "frugal gourmets" are staying in the household kitchen, where food can be prepared in a healthier and more cost-effective way.

At 1992 prices a McDonald's Big Mac sells for about $1.90. If you were to make four Big Macs at home, this would be your expense list:

1 package (8) sesame-seed buns	$1.09
1 pound ground beef	1.45
1 head of lettuce	.89
1 white onion	.25
1 12-ounce bottle of Kraft dressing	1.59
16 slices American cheese	2.09
1 16-ounce jar pickle slices	1.29
TOTAL	$8.65

Considering that four real Big Macs cost $7.60 to our $8.65, the economics of the home burger begin to look unfavorable. But let's not forget that after making your four burgers, you'd still have bonus food left over.

You'd be left with:

4 sesame-seed buns
¾ head of lettuce
¾ white onion
10 ounces Kraft dressing
12 slices American cheese
About 45 pickle slices

So all you'd need to buy for your next four burgers would be:

1 pound ground beef $1.45

Here's where the figures begin to come way down. Starting from scratch, if we average the numbers, eight Big Mac–style hamburgers will cost you only $1.40 apiece. That's a savings of $4.00 over buying them at the restaurant, or the equivalent of two free hamburgers and change. Plus, you'd *still* have half a head of lettuce, half an onion, two-thirds of a bottle of dressing, eight slices of American cheese, and thirty to forty sliced pickles left over.

And, as is usually the case with larger-volume production, your savings would be even more substantial if you made twelve hamburgers. Each of these sandwiches would cost you a measly $1.14, saving you a total of more than $9.00 over the retail price. That's like getting four free hamburgers and more than a dollar in change. Plus you'd *still* have lettuce, onion, dressing, cheese, and lots of pickles. At sixteen burgers you'd save close to 50 percent over the McDonald's price.

This cost-savings analysis can be applied to most of the products in the book with similar results. In fact, there's hardly an item in this book that will not cost less to produce yourself than to purchase. Perhaps you're even lucky enough to have all the ingredients for a recipe on hand, creating a currently cost-free situation, much to your satisfaction and glee.

AVAILABILITY

In the fall of 1990 I moved from California to the East Coast, leaving behind some of the local goodies I had grown to crave from time to time. The original In-N-Out Double-Double hamburger, Carl's Jr., and Jack-in-the-Box sandwiches were now all out of reach. But with this book, and some time in the kitchen, clones that quench those cravings are just minutes away.

If you live east of the Mississippi, you've no doubt enjoyed Tastykake products. The brand's popularity in the region attests to that. If you leave the area, though, you're out of luck. Tastykake has a very limited distribution, and the only way you can enjoy a fresh Tastykake treat anywhere else is to have someone send it to you. Unless you've got a recipe.

Or maybe it's raining outside, and you're dying for some Reese's Peanut Butter Cups or a Twinkie. You can get these snacks just about anywhere. But you've got a crackling fire warming the house, a great episode of *Lost in Space* on the tube, and all the ingredients handy in your kitchen. So you tie on the apron and whip up your own. It's easy, it's fresh, and you don't have to comb your hair or put on your shoes.

INGREDIENTS

Whoever first said that a Twinkie has the shelf life of uranium was wrong. After being tucked away for a few years in the darkest, most forgotten abyss of your pantry, the spongy, filled snack cake will begin to resemble a huge potato bug. At that time, eating it is highly discouraged.

Yes, Twinkies are made to sit on the store shelves for a good length of time without going stale. Consumer confidence in the manu facturer weighs heavily on the product's freshness (or appearance thereof). As with thousands of products on grocery-store shelves, brand loyalty was won over with the additives that give your favorite snack its consistent texture, color, and taste from supermarket to supermarket.

The use of additives in food dates back to 1859, when Sir William Henry Perkins found that coal-tar oil could be used to give many foods a mauve tint that was more appealing to buyers and that, coincidentally, matched the decor in some homes. The potentially harmful practice lasted some fifty years, until Teddy Roosevelt passed the Food & Drug Act in 1906, which banned many of the coal-tar dyes on the grounds that the American people were "being steadily poi-soned by the dangerous foods that were being added to food with reckless abandon," according to the Department of Agriculture.

Granted, this is not the early 1900s, and many of the additives in today's foods have been proven safer than coal tar. But some 2,000 chemical additives are in use today, and the safety of some of them is still unclear. So ask yourself, "Am I a gambler?" If you eat lots of foods with chemical additives, you can bet you are.

With this book, not only will you be able to avoid the additives and preservatives that make your food sound like a lab experiment, you will also have the freedom to substitute ingredients to your heart's desire. Now you can replace the ground beef in your favorite hamburgers with ground turkey—a substitution that, according to the *Wall Street Journal*, is already being considered by some of the largest fast-food chains. (Is there a McGobble Burger in our future?) Or you may want to use a low-calorie sweetener in place of the sugar. Or get creative and make your own original peanut-butter-and-jelly-filled Twinkies. The substitutions and variations are only limited by your imagination . . . and your courage.

CURIOSITY AND CREATIVE FULFILLMENT

Most people never considered it possible to make a Twinkie in the kitchen or taste the twin of a Big Mac they slapped together at home in less than ten minutes. You hold the proof.

As you cook, you will find that most of these recipes taste exactly like, or extremely similar to, their manufactured counterparts. I say *most* of the recipes, because:

1. Taste is an opinion subject to individual preference, and the memory of a particular taste can vary from person to person. One person might say that a hamburger tastes just like a Big Mac while another might think it ain't even close. Putting the *Top Secret Recipes* version right next to an original Big Mac, however, should help establish a consensus on the similarity.

2. Although the success of the fast-food concept lies in the security of consistency the customer receives from outlet to outlet, products created at different locations (especially franchises) are not always created equal. I've probably had four different versions of Wendy's chili—some with bigger chunks of meat, some with more onion, some spicier, some runnier.

These large companies attempt to idiot-proof their products as much as possible. While Wendy's chili is a great receptacle for the company's beef patties that break or do not sell, it is made by a kitchen chef following a recipe similar to the one in this book. In the haste of cooking for a lunch crowd, inconsistencies are not uncommon, with this or any other such designed menu item.

Developing a reasonable facsimile of a particular food depends on finding a common thread between all versions and replicating it. The recipes in this book are based on random samplings. They do not account for employee miscalculations in cooking or a manufacturer's later change in makeup of the product, nor do they account for variations in cooking time based on gas and electric ranges, or adjustments that need to be made in varying altitudes.

Although ingredient substitutions and experimentation are encouraged, you will create a more accurate clone of the original by using the exact ingredients specified and following the steps carefully.

But most of all, realize that this is a book created for enjoyment's sake, to give us fun alternatives to the foods we've made in the past.

Okay, so it may not be a book for some of the lazy snack lovers out there who feel cooking should be no more difficult than knowing how to set the timer on a microwave. But I'm convinced that most of you are of the breed motivated by the true snack lover's credo: This stuff tastes a heck of a lot better when it's fresh.

I understand that most of these recipes as written won't win a contest for nutritional awareness from the Pritikin Foundation. As health conscious as we may or may not claim to be, when our own inner Pavlov rings the bell, we're suddenly put on a mission commanded by Captain Taste Buds. That's when we walk barefoot over broken glass to satisfy the deep call for a Snickers bar. All pain and suffering is soothed by the palatal elation produced by the brand we've come to call our own, whether it's Twinkies or Snickers or a Big Mac.

So enjoy the recipes within these pages. Experiment and have fun with them.

I enjoyed writing this book, because I believe in adulation. And if what they say is true—that "imitation is the sincerest form of flattery"—then I've just paid some very big companies a darn good compliment or two.

CONVENIENCE FOOD: AN AMERICAN LOVE AFFAIR

It appears that our exposure to fast foods and snack foods has generated a notorious love/hate relationship. Major fast-food chains are opening new stores at the rate of nine a week and scooping up $70 billion a year of Americans' hard-earned cash. Our country consumes more than 3 billion pounds of candy a year; that's an average of 17 pounds per person. And while sales of snack cakes, soda, ice cream, and other sweets rise all the time, so does enrollment in Nutri-System® and Jenny Craig™.

How much we love this stuff can be clearly seen in the advertising barrage constantly reminding us that we want and need more. Escaping the media blitz is impossible if you spend any time aboveground. How do you ignore a giant corporation like McDonald's that spends more than $1 billion on advertising each year? Even if you don't succumb to the messages, you'll still find yourself humming the catchy jingles in the shower. Yes, we do deserve a break today.

The former chief nutritionist of New York City's Mount Sinai School of Medicine calls us "The McDonald's Generation." A popular and expensive advertising campaign refers to us as "The Pepsi Generation." Whatever you tag it, there's no disputing the fact that we are a generation of consumers that has come to appreciate and expect predictable quality from store to store, while embracing speed and convenience.

The sixty-one grams of fat in a Double Whopper with Cheese is going to sit like a lump in your belly until dinnertime, but when you're late for class or a one o'clock appointment, the Burger King drive-thru window is a quick and easy way to quiet a growling stomach. The advertising campaign for Snickers, America's number-one candy bar, appeals to just that sense of urgency and emptiness. A catchy jingle claims that the special blend of peanuts, caramel, and nougat, all coated with milk chocolate, will easily appease our hunger—"Snickers satisfies you." Sure, it'll stop the hunger, but we'll be left with a nutritional black hole.

The truth is, when we have an urge to graze, fulfillment is king, nutrition a pawn. Since we were children we've been conditioned to ignore nutritional value and to crave the sweet, chewy, creamy satisfaction that comes from sugar- and oil-pumped foods. At the dinner table we were told that we couldn't have dessert until all our dinner was gone. And that's what got us through the Brussels sprouts—certainly not because we liked them.

"People do not eat foods because they are good for them—rather because they appeal to their appetite, to their emotions, to their soul," wrote Dr. Robert S. Harris, professor of nutritional biochemistry at the Massachusetts Institute of Technology. Let's face it, food is one of the most powerful emotional stimuli in our lives.

In his *Complete Junk Food Book*, Michael S. Lasky states, "Behavioral psychologists tell us that flavor is probably the most important characteristic in satisfying our appetites—the instinctive craving. The flavors we like best are not necessarily found in those foods that form part of a well-balanced, nutritious diet. We seem to be born junk food junkies. Well, not quite. But we are ideal candidates for the blitz of external brainwashing stimuli that will convince us the sweetened, the oily, and the salted provide the greatest pleasure."

When we satisfy our cravings with goodies like those found in this book, we practically get high on the oral gratification—much as we did when we were nursing infants, or when we were kids, and our parents treated us to a drive down to the local hamburger joint on a Saturday night.

Convenience foods are as popular as ever and will probably remain so. But the foods our taste buds guided us to in the past are now being reevaluated by our brains. An evolving nutritional awareness is altering fast-food menus to include more health-conscious fare. Salad bars, extra-lean burgers, and lower-cholesterol ingredients are in demand, and corporate fast-food giants are delivering. Of course they are. They'll do whatever it takes to ensure that we continue to spend an average of one out of every two of our restaurant dollars on their food.

After all, that's the American way.

Convenience products are a twentieth-century phenomenon. Their roots go back centuries, but most of our popular prepackaged sweets and made-to-order foods didn't gain much ground until the 1900s rolled around.

In the late nineteenth century the French first discovered a special process of canning foods using heat that would preserve them for a greater length of time. The method also made storage, sale, and shipping much easier.

Soon, large canneries spread from Europe into America during what would be called the Industrial Revolution. More factories were built to box, bottle, and bag varieties of fruits, grains, vegetables, meats, and spices that formerly were sold only in bulk.

Then today's popular brand names began to emerge: Milton Hershey was making chocolate, Clarence Birdseye was packaging precooked fruits and vegetables, the National Biscuit Company (now Nabisco) was making crackers and cookies, druggist Charles Pemberton was bottling Coca-Cola, and F. W. Rueckheim was perfecting his Cracker Jack caramel-coated popcorn.

It was also around that time that the German contribution to our fast-food concept took hold. Some say it was at the Chicago World's Fair—some say it was on Coney Island—that the first frankfurter was introduced. The beef sausage slapped into a custom-made bun and dressed up with mustard and sauerkraut was perfect for carry-out eating at sidewalk carts and at baseball games. American cartoonist Tad Dorgan supplied the wiener with a head, tail, and legs in one of his drawings, and it has been called a hot dog ever since.

During the First World War, new methods of packaging and preservation of food were developed to help supply the American armies in Europe. We began to see the emergence of restaurants that focused on quicker service than what people had become used to around the turn of the century. Joseph Monninger wrote in *American Heritage* magazine, "It may have started in 1921 at the Royce Hailey's Pig Stand in Dallas when drivers began pulling up for barbecue sandwiches. Doubtless it started with cars, a population pushing out of the cities into the suburbs, and a volume of business based on large production at minimal costs: hamburger factories with retail outlets."

The hot dog begat the hamburger.

Later that year, in Wichita, Kansas, a bright man named E. W. Ingram opened his first restaurant. His concept was to sell steam-broiled hamburgers by the sack for five cents apiece. The concept caught on quickly. Some years later, Ingram's White Castle stores had spread into eleven other states.

The dawn of the automobile age gave birth to other successful drive-in restaurants. In 1922 Roy Allen and Fred White lent the initials of their last names to the first of the A&W root beer outlets. In 1925 Howard Johnson bought a money-losing drugstore, where he served his homemade ice cream at the soda fountain. Eventually he added hot dogs and hamburgers to the menu. When he began to turn a profit, he turned the store into a restaurant and expanded into other regions. Howard Johnson's was the first to establish the mass-market menu. And thus the fast-food chain was born.

It was during World War II that Americans found an even bigger need for convenience foods. The military required food that could be carried in small lightweight packages and that could be prepared and eaten easily. Advances were made in food freezing, dehydration, and fabrication. Vending machines were developed, and central commissaries provided mass-produced food. Supermarkets began to fill with greater numbers of packaged products, and fast-food restaurants—both drive-up and self-service—were multiplying.

By the end of the war, candy companies such as Hershey, Mars, Peter Paul, and Nestlé were all well established and putting smiles on the faces of millions of chocolate lovers. The snack-cake companies that produced the Hostess and Tastykake lines were enjoying huge success, while cookie and cracker manufacturers Keebler, Nabisco, and Pepperidge Farm were busy developing new products to boost their growing businesses.

TOP-SELLING CHOCOLATE BARS IN THE U.S.

RANK	CANDY	MANUFACTURER
1	Snickers	Mars
2	Reese's Peanut Butter Cups	Hershey
3	M&M's Peanut	Mars
4	M&M's Plain	Mars
5	Kit Kat	Hershey
6	Hershey's Almond	Hershey
7	Hershey's Milk Chocolate	Hershey
8	Milky Way	Mars
9	Butterfinger	Nabisco
10	Nestlé Crunch	Nestlé

In the forties, two Americans hungry for thicker wallets set out to satisfy the hunger of others. Carl Karcher and Glen Bell started their careers in convenience food in much the same way—each by selling hot dogs in southern California. They had witnessed the success of earlier quick-service start-up shops such as Dairy Queen, Orange Julius, and the White Tavern Shoppes (which would later become Long John Silver's Seafood Shoppes). They would each move into selling hamburgers and eventually find tremendous success in the fast-food industry, Karcher with his Carl's Jr. hamburger outlets and Bell with Mexican-style fast food at Taco Bell.

When these two first started flipping burgers, just around the corner were two brothers doing some flipping of their own. The brothers never thought these humble beginnings would give birth to a chain making the single biggest impact on American convenience food and marketing. Dick and Mac McDonald would see theirs become a household name.

It seems odd that today the McDonald's Corporation celebrates Founder's Day in honor of Ray Kroc, who died in 1984. The McDonald brothers had sold twenty-one restaurant franchises and had opened nine restaurants in California when Ray Kroc was still a Chicago-based milkshake-machine salesman. It was only in 1954 that Kroc entered the picture. His curiosity had been aroused when the brothers ordered eight milkshake machines for their growing enterprise. No other restaurant needed to make that many milkshakes at once. So Kroc went to California to investigate. What he saw he liked. And wanted.

Kroc pressured the brothers to let him in on their success. A year later he became a franchisor with his first restaurant in Des Plaines, Illinois. Six years after that, Kroc convinced the brothers to sell their shares to him and his associates for $2.7 million—not much when you consider that McDonald's now has sales averaging $50 million a day.

It was Kroc who perfected what came to be known as "the system," for ensuring consistent, dependable service from outlet to outlet. But it was Dick and Mac McDonald who had the vision to replace the carhops that were widely used at drive-in hamburger stands at that time. It was the brothers who drew the layout of their new self-service concept in chalk on a tennis court and who would knock service time down from twenty minutes to twenty seconds. It was the brothers who decided to start using plastic utensils instead of metal and to serve the meal on paper plates and in bags.

"Up until the time we sold, there was no mention of Kroc being the founder," the surviving brother, eighty-two-year-old Dick McDonald, told the *Wall Street Journal.* "If we had heard about it, he would have been back selling milkshake machines." McDonald says today that the company history begins in 1955, "and everything before that is wiped out."

Another huge chain that was developing at the same time would compete with McDonald's for the number-one spot in fast food. Harland Sanders, christened a Kentucky colonel by the state governor, had set out across the country to share his secret blend of herbs and spices with restaurant owners for a small royalty on each piece of chicken they sold. His "finger lickin' good" recipe was a hit.

But in 1964 Sanders made a deal with some Nashville businessmen that he would later regret, much as the McDonald brothers did after making their deal with Kroc. Jack C. Massey and John Brown, Jr., convinced Sanders to sell the rights to his product for $2 million. In the contract, the Colonel was obligated to travel around the world over a quarter of a million miles a year as a PR man for the company—its human trademark. This made Sanders angry. But what bothered him most was that with the company out of his control, his recipes were being altered, such as the one for his tasty gravy—and there was nothing he could do about it. Just seven years later, Massey and Brown sold

Kentucky Fried Chicken to Heublein, a liquor and food conglomerate, for $275 million. The Colonel had been deep-fried.

In the seventies women's move from the home into the office made convenience food even more of an American fixation. As a growing number of Moms joined Dads in the work force, there was less time for cooking. Families could depend on their local burger joint to sell them security. A sandwich bought today would taste like one bought yesterday, from location to location.

Grocery stores and supermarkets were tuned into this appetite for speed and convenience. More items were hitting the shelves that took less or no time to prepare. One-step TV dinners were a big hit in the fifties and sixties. Then microwave ovens came along, and manufacturers had another million-dollar market open up wide for them.

Today there are 160,000 fast-food restaurants in the United States. McDonald's is the country's largest owner of real estate, and one person out of five eats at a fast-food restaurant on an average day, according to *Consumer Reports*.

Convenience stores can be found on every other corner, and supermarkets stock more than 11,000 items, many of which are backed by expensive advertising campaigns and packaged in containers that are their own billboards. Marketing studies quoted in Michael Lasky's *The Complete Junk Food Book* show that "70 to 90 percent of the time the purchase of such junkie favorites as candy, cookies, snacks, and frozen desserts is the result of an in-store decision. As it happens, they are all products with high profit margins."

High profit margins are typical of convenience food. Fast-food restaurants usually mark up their products by about 400 percent over cost: A hamburger that costs you $2.00 at the pick-up window costs only around 50 cents to make. Fast food is not always cheap food. You will undoubtedly pay less for the same food you buy at the drive-thru if you make it yourself. Yes, convenience is gonna cost you.

LEADING FAST-FOOD CHAINS IN THE U.S.

1991 RANKING	COMPANY	UNITS	1991 SALES IN $ MILLIONS
1	McDonald's	12,418	19,928.2
2	Burger King	6,409	6,200.0
3	KFC	8,480	6,200.0
4	Pizza Hut	9,000	5,300.0
5	Hardee's	3,727	3,431.0
6	Wendy's	3,804	3,223.6
7	Taco Bell	3,670	2.800.0
8	Domino's Pizza	5,550	2,400.0
9	Dairy Queen	5,329	2,352.1
10	Little Caesars	3,650	1,725.0
11	Arby's	2,500	1,450.0
12	Subway	6,106	1,400.0
13	Dunkin' Donuts	2,203	990.8
14	Jack-in-the-Box	1,089	978.0
15	Baskin Robbins	3,533	829.7
16	Carl's Jr.	630	614.0
17	Long John Silver's Seafood	1,450	555.0
18	Popeye's Fried Chicken	808	540.2
19	Sonic Drive-Ins	1,112	518.0
20	Church's Chicken	1,136	506.6
21	Captain D's	636	420.8
22	Chick-fil-A	460	324.6
23	TCBY	1,850	321.0
24	Round Table Pizza	575	320.0
25	Whataburger	475	318.4

SOURCE: *Restaurants & Institutions*

What'll cost you even more is healthy convenience. KFC's Skin-Free Crispy chicken introduced in 1991 costs nearly 20 percent more than its greasier predecessor. TastyLights Creme Filled Cup Cakes, which are 94 percent fat free, cost 10 cents more a box than the regular Tastykake version. Hostess Twinkies Lights Low Fat Snack Cakes cost 60 cents more a box than regular Twinkies—that means you pay close to 25 percent more a box. There appears to be a new-math formula these days that applies to the healthier line of foods: Less costs more.

A new trend emerged in 1989, when an Omaha businessman named Phil Sokolof began running full-page ads in major newspapers denouncing the saturated-fat content of McDonald's food. Those ads echoed the concerns of a public whose chant—"We are what we eat"—was growing louder. In 1990 it had an effect. McDonald's and Wendy's switched from beef fat to vegetable oil for cooking french fries and hash browns. Other fast-food restaurants soon followed suit.

The move toward healthier fare spread through the world of convenience food. Soon we were seeing more grilled and roasted chicken sandwiches, leaner milkshakes, nonfat yogurt, bran muffins, side salads, lighter mayonnaise, baked potatoes, and the heralded McLean Deluxe—McDonald's 91 percent fat-free hamburger. There's even a new candy bar that's easier on the fat and calories, called Milky Way II.

And when health-minded America led to ecology-minded America, McDonald's and other chains found themselves at the center of controversy again. A movement to discourage the use of Styrofoam cartons and other environmentally damaging materials for packaging succeeded in convincing convenience-food companies that using recycled materials was the only way to go.

These are smart companies. They know that the best way to make a buck is to keep the customer happy. Keep the bathrooms clean, give service with a smile, keep prices down, and most of all, avoid controversy. They also know that it's a good idea to introduce a lot of new products—new products that may include the next Dairy Queen Blizzard, which now outsells all other Dairy Queen products. Or it could be the next Egg McMuffin, which revolutionized breakfast out of the home. These companies hope to unveil new products that will grab hold of a customer's palate and wring the money right out of his or her wallet.

Of course, you'll get your losers. Nobody wanted KFC's Barbecued Ribs, or Carl's Jr.'s Chicken Fried Steak Sandwich. Even McDonald's McD.L.T. got canned. You can't say the American palate isn't honest. Just because we need a quick fix doesn't mean we'll continue buying snack food and fast food we don't like. There's too much out there to choose from. The menus get bigger, the lights on the LIMITED TIME ONLY signs get brighter, the supermarket aisles get longer, and the prices for all this convenience keep creeping higher and higher.

Certainly there's a multitude of newly inspired products to look forward to in our even faster-paced future. At fast-food outlets we'll likely see more chicken and turkey products and items with international roots customized for American taste buds. In snacks we'll see more "sequels" to already existing products as manufacturers develop lines that appeal to health-conscious, label-scanning eaters. All those huge corporations will wrestle with one another for market shares, for shelf space, and for our attention wherever a message can be relayed.

As advertising millions become billions, as national becomes global, it is hard not to see where the beef is. There's big money to be made in convenience food. It is an industry that bears responsibility for changing the way we live. What was once a world of home-cooked meals is now a world of prescribed and proven secret formulas.

This book is an occasion to combine the best of those two worlds.

SOME COOKING TIPS FROM A GUY WHO CARES

Sometimes I can be a real idiot in the kitchen. I've wasted as many as four eggs when separating the whites by accidentally dropping in specks of yolk. I've often burned chocolate when melting it for dipping candy, and I've squandered hours on making dough for a simple recipe just because I forgot to look at the date on the package of yeast.

It was on these days that I determined there is a hard way to pick up little cooking hints, and there's an easy way. The hard way is by doing what I did—screwing up, then having to throw away your mistakes and run to the store in the pouring rain with a fistful of change to buy more ingredients so you can start the whole thing over again.

Then there is the easy way, which is to get cooking tips from somebody who learned the hard way.

SOME WORDS ABOUT CHOCOLATE

First off, some words about that delicate substance we call chocolate. Everybody's eaten it, but if you've cooked with it, you know it can be a pain—especially when the recipe requires that you melt it, as some of the recipes in this book do.

There are several different types of chocolate: sweet, semisweet, bittersweet, unsweetened, milk chocolate, and white chocolate (which actually isn't chocolate at all).

You will be using only semisweet and milk chocolate. Both are called for in the form of chocolate chips, which you buy by the bag. The most common are Nestlé and Hershey. Each company makes both milk chocolate and semisweet, and each works equally well.

I have found that the best place to melt chocolate is in the microwave. Semisweet chocolate is much easier to work with than milk chocolate, because it contains more chocolate liquor and no milk solids. Semisweet will melt to a much smoother, thinner consistency, and will not scorch as easily. This means that semisweet lends itself much more readily to dipping.

When melting either type of chocolate, use a microwave-safe glass or ceramic bowl that will retain heat. Set your microwave on half power and melt the chips for 1 minute. Stir. Rotate the bowl and microwave for another minute. Stir again. After 2 minutes, if the chocolate needs to melt more, heat it in 30-second intervals.

With milk chocolate, you have to find a delicate balance between microwaving and stirring. If you heat the chips too much, the chocolate will scorch. If you stir too much, the chocolate won't set up properly when you dip. Perfectly melted milk chocolate should set nearly as firm as it was in its original form at room temperature (68 to 70°F).

If you can't use a microwave to melt your chocolate, use a double boiler. You want to set the heat very low so that the water in the double boiler is only simmering and not boiling. Boiling water will scorch chocolate. Grease the inside of your double boiler lightly before you put the chocolate in and you'll be able to get practically all melted chocolate out of the pan.

For some of the recipes in this book, you may feel like substituting dark, semisweet chocolate instead of milk chocolate or even using white chocolate. It may be worth a try. How about a white-chocolate–covered Milky Way? Hmm.

And here's another tip to remember when making anything with chocolate. You can intensify the chocolate flavor by adding some vanilla to the recipe. You'll notice that this is what I've done with the recipes in the book for chocolate icings.

SOME WORDS ABOUT YEAST DOUGH

There are some recipes in this book that call for yeast dough, and I thought it was important to supply you with some pointers that will help you here and in the rest of your dough-making life.

The only yeast you'll need to use with this book is Fleischmann's— the type that comes in the three-envelope packages. That's the only kind I ever use. Always check to be sure the yeast you're using has not expired. Every package of yeast is stamped with an expiration date—usually eight to twelve months from the date you purchased it. Store your unopened yeast packages in the refrigerator.

When kneading dough, use your hands. This is much better than a wooden or plastic spoon because the warmth of your hands will help the yeast start rising (and it brings you back to those carefree Play-Doh days). When the dough pulls away from your hands easily, it has been kneaded enough.

One good way to get the dough rising is to put it in its bowl, uncovered, in the oven (the oven should be off) with a pan of boiling water. The hot water will start the dough rising right away, and the moisture from the water will keep the dough's surface from getting hard and dry.

You can tell when the dough has risen enough by sticking your finger into it up to the first knuckle. If the dough does not bounce back, it's ready. If it giggles, you're in a Pillsbury commercial.

SOME WORDS ABOUT SEPARATING EGGS

For the recipes that require egg whites, I've found that one of the easiest ways to separate the white from the yolk is to crack the egg with one hand into the other hand cupped over a small bowl. The egg whites will run out between your fingers, and you will be holding just the yolk in your hand. You can also use a small funnel. Just crack the egg into the funnel, and the egg white will run through, leaving the yolk. Use a container other than the bowl you will be beating the whites in. You don't want to risk ruining all the whites if some yolk should fall through.

If an accident should happen and you do get some yolk into the whites, use one of the egg shells to scoop out the yolk. Strangely, the shells act like a magnet for the specks of stray yolk.

To save your yolks for another recipe, slide them into a small bowl or cup, pour some cold water over them, and store them in the refrigerator. When you want to use the yolks, just pour off the water and slide the yolks into your recipe.

By the way, as a general rule in this book and any other cookbook, when a recipe calls for eggs and does not specify size, always use large eggs. Medium or extra-large eggs could throw off your measurements.

SOME WORDS ABOUT BAKING

Every once in a while, you should check your oven thermostat with an oven thermometer. I did and found out that my oven was off by twenty-five degrees. That's normal. It can be off by twenty-five degrees in either direction, but if it's any more than that, you should make adjustments when cooking, and get it fixed.

When baking, allow at least fifteen minutes for your oven to preheat. This is especially important if you do not have an indicator light that tells you when your oven is ready.

Several recipes in this book call for baking on cookie sheets. I highly recommend using two cookies sheets and alternating them, putting one sheet in the oven at a time. This will allow you to let one sheet cool before loading it up for the next run. If you don't let the sheet cool, your cooking time may be inaccurate because the dough will start to heat before you put the sheet into the oven.

If you absolutely must bake more than one cookie sheet at a time, you'll have to extend the cooking time. It will take the oven longer to reach the proper temperature with more dough to heat.

If you're baking cookies, you can very easily make them all uniform in size by rolling the dough into a tube with the diameter you need, then slicing it with a very sharp knife.

Keep in mind, especially with cookies, that baked goods will continue to cook for a while even after they've come out of the oven unless you remove them to a rack. The cookie sheet or baking pan will still be hot, and the sugar in the recipe will retain heat. This is why many people tend to overcook their cookies. I know the feeling. When you follow suggested cooking times, it sometimes seems as though the cookies aren't done when they come out of the oven—and they probably aren't. But they'll be fine after sitting for some time on the cookie sheet.

SOME WORDS ABOUT HAMBURGER PATTIES

Just about every backyard hamburger cookout I've attended included hamburger patties that tipped the scale in size and weight. Most home-made burgers are way too thick to cook properly, and the added thickness doesn't add anything to the taste of the sandwich. In fact, if we cut the amount of beef we use in the hamburger patties, we're cutting out excess fat and calories, decreasing the chance that the burgers may not cook thoroughly, while not compromising anything in overall taste. At the same time, thicker patties tend to shrink up as they cook into unmanageable mutant forms, bulging in the middle, and stacking poorly onto buns and lettuce.

You'll notice that every hamburger recipe in this book requires a very thin patty. This is the way the experts in the business do it—the Dave Thomases, the Carl Karchers, the McDonald Brothers—for concerns over cost, taste and a thorough, bacteria-free cooking process. But just how do we get our patties so thin like the big boys, and still make them easy to cook without breaking? We freeze 'em, folks.

Plan ahead. Hours, even days, before you expect to make your hamburgers, pat the patties out onto waxed paper on a cookie sheet with a diameter slightly larger than the buns you are using, and about ⅛ to ¼ inch thick (with consistent thickness from center to edge). Thickness depends on the burger. If you're making a small hamburger, like the one at McDonald's, which is only about ⅛ ounce before cooking, make the patties ⅛ inch thick. If you're going for the Quarter Pounder, make your patty ¼ inch thick—never more than that. Lay waxed paper over the top of your patties and put them in the freezer.

When your patties are completely frozen, it's time to cook. You can cook them straight out of the freezer on a hot grill or frying pan for 3 to 7 minutes per side, without worrying about thorough cooking. And the patties will flip easily without falling apart.

A & W
ROOT BEER

☆ ♥ ☎ ✎ ✈ ✉ ✂ ☛ ✿

On a hot summer afternoon in 1919, Roy Allen came up with a plan. He set up a roadside stand to sell cool drinks to spectators of a Veterans Day Parade in Lodi, California. For a nickel, thirsty parade-goers could knock back a tall glass of what would eventually become America's favorite root beer. The success of Allen's unique blend of roots, herbs, and berries led to three root beer concessions in Sacramento, California, all featuring carhop service—the first of the drive-in fast-food chains. Allen expanded his business further in 1922 when he formed a partnership with entrepreneur Frank Wright. This led to the name that would become famous, A&W, the country's best-selling root beer. In 1993 Cadbury Schweppes PLC, a British candy and beverage company, bought A&W Brands, Inc., for $334 million.

The root beer you'll make here is a simplified version of Roy Allen's method from the early 1900s. Instead of harvesting roots, herbs, and berries, you have the luxury of using a root beer concentrate that can be found in most grocery stores.

¾ cup granulated sugar
¾ cup hot water
1 liter cold seltzer water

½ teaspoon plus ⅛ teaspoon root beer concentrate (McCormick is best)

1. Dissolve the sugar in hot water.
2. Add the root beer concentrate and let cool.
3. Combine the root beer mixture with the cold seltzer water, drink immediately, or store in refrigerator in tightly covered container.

- MAKES 5 CUPS

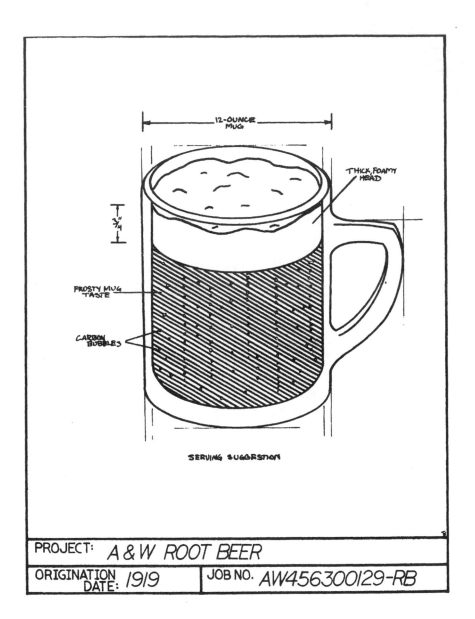

12-OUNCE MUG

THICK, FOAMY HEAD

3/4"

FROSTY MUG TASTE

CARBON BUBBLES

SERVING SUGGESTION

PROJECT:	A & W ROOT BEER	
ORIGINATION DATE:	1919	JOB NO. AW456300129-RB

ARBY'S
SAUCE

In 1964, when the Arby's concept was created by brothers Leroy and Forrest Raffel, the name was supposed to be R.B., for Raffel Brothers, but that was expanded to the more familiar Arby's. Having marked its 30th year in 1994, Arby's is celebrating more than $1.5 billion in sales from 2,603 outlets. Arby's Miami headquarters took a big hit in 1992 from Hurricane Andrew, the most damaging hurricane to hit Florida in decades, but the company bounced back and continued growing.

The company's unique sliced beef sandwiches offer customers a departure from hamburgers made of ground beef. This special barbecue sauce enhances a roast beef sandwich, as well as many other homemade and store-bought creations.

1 cup catsup	1/4 teaspoon pepper
2 teaspoons water	1/4 teaspoon salt
1/4 teaspoon garlic powder	1/2 teaspoon hot pepper sauce
1/4 teaspoon onion powder	(Tabasco is best)

1. Combine all the ingredients in a small saucepan and cook over medium heat, stirring constantly, until the sauce begins to boil, 5 to 10 minutes.
2. Remove the sauce from the heat. Cover and allow to cool.
3. Pour into a covered container for storage in your refrigerator. Keeps for a month or two.

   • MAKES 1 CUP

AUNT JEMIMA MAPLE SYRUP

☆　♥　☎　✎　✈　✉　✂　☞　✿

The year 1989 marked the 100th anniversary of the Aunt Jemima trademark. The name was conceived in 1889 by Chris Rutt while he was attending a vaudeville show and watching a New Orleans–style dance number performed to a jazzy tune called "Aunt Jemima." Rutt liked the music so much he stuck the name on his products. The maple syrup came along much later, in 1964, and is now the country's largest-selling syrup.

Today some folks tell the story of how their friends or relatives once met Aunt Jemima many years ago and how she was a kind and cordial woman. Little do they realize these people were fooled by a promotional campaign for the products back in the forties and fifties that used actresses traveling from town to town dressed up and acting like the "famous woman." There never really was an Aunt Jemima.

2 cups water
1 cup granulated sugar
2 cups dark corn syrup

¼ teaspoon salt
1 teaspoon maple flavoring

1. Combine the first four ingredients in a saucepan over medium heat.
2. Stir occasionally, until the mixture comes to a full boil. Let it boil for 7 minutes.
3. Turn the heat off and let the syrup cool for 15 minutes.
4. Add the maple flavoring and stir.
5. When completely cool, transfer the syrup to a covered plastic or glass container.

   • MAKES 1 QUART

TIDBITS

For syrup with a butter flavor, just add 3 tablespoons of butter to the mixture before heating.

For a lighter syrup, use a sugar substitute instead of the granulated sugar.

The absence of natural maple syrup in this recipe is not unusual. In fact, there is no real maple syrup in any Aunt Jemima syrups.

BAILEY'S ORIGINAL IRISH CREAM

☆ ♥ ☎ ✎ ✈ ✉ ✂ ☞ ✿

Bailey's launched its Irish Cream Liqueur in 1974, after years of development. The cream liqueur is based on an old Irish recipe using all-natural ingredients, including cream that is produced just for the Bailey's company. In fact, because the product line has become so successful, Bailey's accounts for one-third of Ireland's entire milk production. More than 4,000 farmers supply the 40 million gallons of milk used annually in producing cream for the liqueur. Bailey's now ranks number one among all liqueur brands in the world.

1 cup light cream (not heavy cream)
One 14-ounce can Eagle sweetened
    condensed milk
1⅔ cups Irish whiskey
1 teaspoon instant coffee

2 tablespoons Hershey's chocolate
    syrup
1 teaspoon vanilla extract
1 teaspoon almond extract

1. Combine all the ingredients in a blender set on high speed for 30 seconds.
2. Bottle in a tightly sealed container and refrigerate. The liqueur will keep for at least 2 months if kept cool. Be sure to shake the bottle well before serving.

   • MAKES 4 CUPS

TIDBITS

If you can't find light cream, use half-and-half or whole milk (rather than heavy cream, which will tend to separate).

BEN & JERRY'S HEATH BAR CRUNCH ICE CREAM

☆   ♥   ☎   ✎   ✈   ✉   ✂   ☛   ✿

When Ben Cohen and Jerry Greenfield first met in their seventh-grade gym class, they quickly became good friends. After college, the two decided they wanted to try their hand at selling ice cream. With $12,000 to invest, they moved from New York to Burlington, Vermont, where they purchased an abandoned gas station as the first location for their ice cream store.

After passing a five-dollar correspondence course on ice cream making from Pennsylvania State University and spending their life savings on renovating the gas station, the two were officially in the ice cream business. Ben and Jerry opened the doors to their first ice cream parlor in 1978. The pair's ice cream was such a big hit that they soon moved to a much larger facility. Today, just fifteen years after opening day, they produce more than 500,000 gallons of ice cream each month.

Heath Bar Crunch was one of the earliest flavors on the menu and is still the most popular of the thirty original chunky ice cream creations that made them famous.

5 Heath candy bars	3 cups whipping cream
3 eggs	1 ½ cups half-and-half
1 cup granulated sugar	3 teaspoons vanilla extract

1. Freeze the candy bars.
2. Beat the eggs by hand until fluffy.
3. Slowly beat in the sugar.
4. Add the cream, half-and-half, and vanilla and mix well.
5. Pour the mixture into an ice cream maker and freeze.

6. While the ice cream is freezing, place the frozen candy bars in a plastic bag and break them into small pieces with a knife handle.

7. When the ice cream is done, remove it from the ice cream maker and add the candy pieces. Mix well with a large spoon and store in the freezer.

• MAKES 1 QUART

TIDBITS

The real secret to Ben & Jerry's ice cream is its consistency. It is a thick and creamy ice cream developed with special equipment that keeps a great deal of air out of the mixture. The less air in the ice cream, the thicker the consistency. Therefore, you may find the above recipe fills your ice cream maker a little more than other ice cream recipes.

It's also important to get the right consistency of Heath bar chunks. Most of the candy bar should be crushed into crumbs, but stop breaking the candy when there are still several 1- and ½-inch chunks remaining.

I hope you enjoy experimenting with this recipe and that you try substituting other ingredients for the Heath bar chunks, just as Ben and Jerry have. Try Reese's Peanut Butter Cups, Oreo cookies, Kit Kat bars, Rollo cups, M&Ms, and chunks of raw cookie dough.

BORDEN
CRACKER JACK

☆ ♥ ☎ ✎ ✈ ✉ ✂ ☛ ✿

In 1871 a German immigrant named F. W. Reuckheim came to Chicago with $200 in his pocket. He used all of his money to open a small popcorn shop in the city and started selling a sweet caramel-and molasses–coated popcorn confection. Rueckheim's big break came in 1893, when the treat was served at Chicago's first world's fair. From then on the popcorn's popularity grew enormously. In 1896 a salesman tasting the treat for the first time said, "That's a cracker jack," and the name stuck. Shortly after Cracker Jack's debut another customer commented, "The more you eat, the more you want," and that's still the slogan today.

In 1912 the Cracker Jack Company started adding toy surprises, ranging from small books to miniature metal toy trains. To date they have given away more than 17 billion toy surprises. In 1964 Borden, Inc. bought the Cracker Jack Company, and today the Cracker Jack division is the largest user of popcorn in the world, popping more than twenty tons of corn a day.

4 quarts popped popcorn (or
   1 1/3 bags microwave popcorn)
1 cup Spanish peanuts
4 tablespoons (1/2 stick) butter

1 cup brown sugar
1/2 cup light corn syrup
2 tablespoons molasses
1/4 teaspoon salt

1. Preheat the oven to 250°F.
2. Combine the popcorn and peanuts in a metal bowl or on a cookie sheet and place in the preheated oven.
3. Combine all of the remaining ingredients in a saucepan.
4. Stirring over medium heat, bring the mixture to a boil.
5. Using a cooking thermometer, bring the mixture to the hard-crack stage (290°F, or the point at which the syrup, when

dripped into cold water, forms a hard but pliable ball). This will take about 20 to 25 minutes (or until you notice the mixture turning a slightly darker brown).

6.   Remove the popcorn and peanuts from the oven and, working quickly, pour the caramel mixture in a fine stream over them. Then place them back in the oven for 10 minutes.

7.   Mix well every five minutes, so that all of the popcorn is coated.

8.   Cool and store in a covered container to preserve freshness.

• MAKES 4 QUARTS

BROWN & HALEY ALMOND ROCA

☆　♥　☎　✎　✈　✉　✂　☞　✿

Founded in 1914 by Harry Brown and J. C. Haley in Tacoma, Washington, the Brown & Haley Candy Company is one of the oldest confectioners in the country. In 1923 the company hit the jackpot when Harry Brown and the former cook from what would eventually become M&M/Mars, created a chocolate-coated butter candy, sprinkled with California almonds. They took the sweet to Tacoma's head librarian, and she named it *Almond Roca—roca* means "rock" in Spanish. In 1927 the two men decided to wrap the little candies in imported gold foil and pack them into the now-familiar pink cans to extend their shelf life threefold. In fact, because of the way the candy was packaged, it was carried by troops in World War II, the Korean War, the Vietnam War, and the Gulf War.

The Brown & Haley candy company is still housed in the former shoe factory that it has occupied since 1919. Almond Roca is so popular today that it can be found in sixty-four countries and is a market leader in Hong Kong, Singapore, Korea, Taiwan, the Philippines, and Japan. The company sells more than 5 million pounds of Almond Roca each year and is the United States's leading exporter of packaged confections.

1 cup (2 sticks) butter	1 teaspoon light corn syrup
1 cup granulated sugar	1 cup finely chopped toasted almonds
3 tablespoons water	1 cup milk-chocolate chips

1. Melt the butter in a saucepan.
2. Add the sugar, water, and corn syrup.
3. Cook the mixture over medium heat, stirring.

4. When the sugar dissolves and the mixture begins to boil, raise the heat and bring the mixture to 290°F on a cooking thermometer. (This is called the *soft-crack stage*.) It will be light brown in color, and syrup will separate into threads that are not brittle when dribbled into cold water.
5. Quickly stir in ½ cup chopped almonds.
6. Immediately pour the mixture onto an ungreased baking sheet.
7. Wait 2 or 3 minutes for the candy surface to firm, then sprinkle on the chocolate chips.
8. In a few minutes, when the chips have softened, spread the chocolate evenly over the surface.
9. Sprinkle the remaining almonds over the melted chocolate.
10. When the chocolate hardens, crack the candy into pieces. Store covered.

- MAKES 1½ POUNDS

Heath Bar or Hershey's® Skor®

These two candy bars are very similar, and both are composed of ingredients similar to those in Almond Roca. One obvious difference is that there are no almonds on top of these bars. To make these candy bars, simply follow the same directions for Almond Roca, omitting step 9.

TIDBITS

These recipes taste very much like the candies they clone, but you may notice right away that the finished products don't *look* like their corporate counterparts. This is largely due to the fact that the chocolate is only a top coating, surrounding the almond candy centers. This was done in the interest of simplicity—to make the recipes easier on the chef (that's you, right?). You could make your almond candy center first, then crack it into smaller pieces and dip those into chocolate. But is it really worth the trouble?

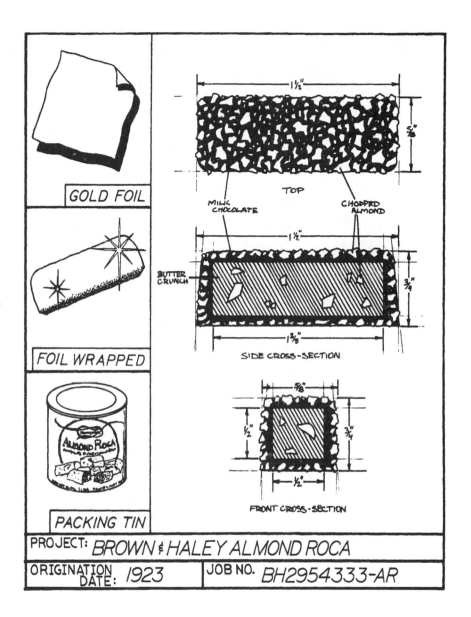

GOLD FOIL

FOIL WRAPPED

PACKING TIN

TOP

1½"

⅝"

MILK CHOCOLATE

CHOPPED ALMOND

SIDE CROSS-SECTION

1½"

3/4"

1⅜"

BUTTER CRUNCH

FRONT CROSS-SECTION

⅝"

½"

3/4"

½"

PROJECT: BROWN & HALEY ALMOND ROCA

ORIGINATION DATE: 1923

JOB NO. BH2954333-AR

BURGER KING WHOPPER

☆　♥　☎　✎　✈　✉　✂　☞　✿

In 1954, in Miami, Florida, James McLamore and David Edgerton built the first Burger King Restaurant. By 1991 more than 6,400 Burger King outlets could be found in forty countries and all fifty states. That gives this burger giant more than $6 billion in sales each year, making it the country's second-largest fast-food chain. (McDonald's is the largest.)

For many, the favorite item on the menu is a flame-broiled hamburger conceived by the partners on a business trip from Orlando to Miami in 1957. Dubbed the "Whopper," this sandwich is overwhelmingly popular; figures show that Burger King sells more than 540 million annually, or nearly 2 million each day. And with more than 1,023 different combinations of the eight-or-so ingredients, including a vegetarian version, you really can "have it your way."

1 sesame-seed hamburger bun
¼ pound ground beef
Dash salt
3 dill pickle slices
1 teaspoon catsup

3 to 4 onion rings
2 tomato slices
¼ cup chopped lettuce
1 tablespoon mayonnaise

1. Preheat a barbecue grill on high.
2. Toast both halves of the bun, face down, in a hot skillet. Set aside.
3. Form the beef into a thin patty slightly larger than the bun.
4. Lightly salt the hamburger patty and cook on the barbecue grill for 2 to 3 minutes per side.
5. Build the burger in the following stacking order from the bottom up:

bottom bun
hamburger patty
pickles
catsup
onion rings

tomatoes
lettuce
mayonnaise
top bun

• MAKES 1 HAMBURGER

TIDBITS

It's important that your barbecue grill be clean so that the hamburger will not pick up the taste of any food that was previously cooked there. Some foods, such as fish, are especially potent.

Also, be sure your grill is good and hot before cooking.

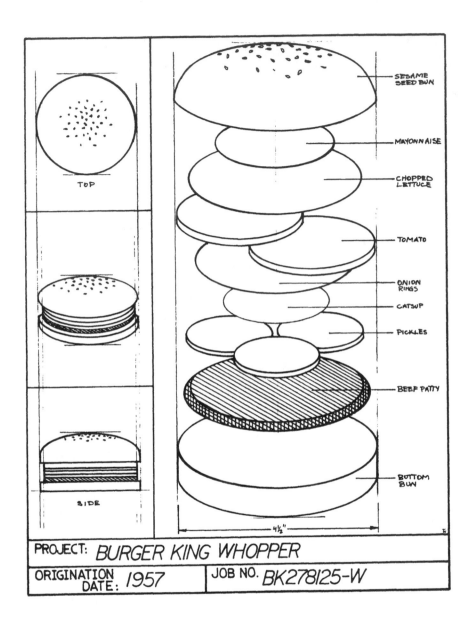

TOP

SIDE

SEDAME SEED BUN

MAYONNAISE

CHOPPED LETTUCE

TOMATO

ONION RINGS

CATSUP

PICKLES

BEEF PATTY

BOTTOM BUN

4½"

PROJECT: *BURGER KING WHOPPER*

ORIGINATION DATE: *1957*

JOB NO. *BK278125-W*

CARL'S JR.
CHICKEN CLUB

☆ ♥ ☎ ✎ ✈ ⊠ ✄ ☛ ✿

The first day's receipts at Carl Karcher's just-purchased hot-dog cart in 1941 totaled $14.75. Peanuts, right? But Karcher was determined to make it big. So during the next two years he purchased several more stands throughout the Los Angeles area, later expanding into restaurants and diversifying the menu. In 1993, what had once been a business of one tiny hot-dog cart had become a multi-million-dollar company with 642 outlets. From $14.75 on the first day to today's $1.6 million in daily receipts, old Carl was on the right track.

2 whole chicken breasts, skinned,
    boned, and halved
1 cup teriyaki marinade (Lawry's is best)
4 whole-wheat hamburger buns
8 slices bacon

1/4 cup mayonnaise
1 cup alfalfa sprouts, loosely packed
4 lettuce leaves
4 large tomato slices
4 slices Kraft Swiss Cheese Singles

1. Marinate the chicken in the teriyaki marinade in a shallow bowl for 30 minutes.
2. Preheat a clean barbecue to medium grilling heat.
3. Brown the faces of each bun in a frying pan on the stove. Keep the pan hot.
4. Cook the bacon in the pan until crisp, then set aside.
5. Grill the chicken breasts 5 to 8 minutes per side, or until cooked through.
6. Spread about 1/2 teaspoon of mayonnaise on the face of each bun, top and bottom.
7. Divide the sprouts into 4 portions and mound on each bottom bun.
8. On the sprouts, stack a lettuce leaf, then a slice of tomato.
9. Place one chicken breast half on each of the sandwiches, atop the tomato.

10. Next, stack a slice of Swiss cheese on the chicken, and then the 2 pieces of bacon, crossed over each other.
11. Top off the sandwich with the top bun.
12. Microwave for 15 seconds on high.

- MAKES 4 SANDWICHES

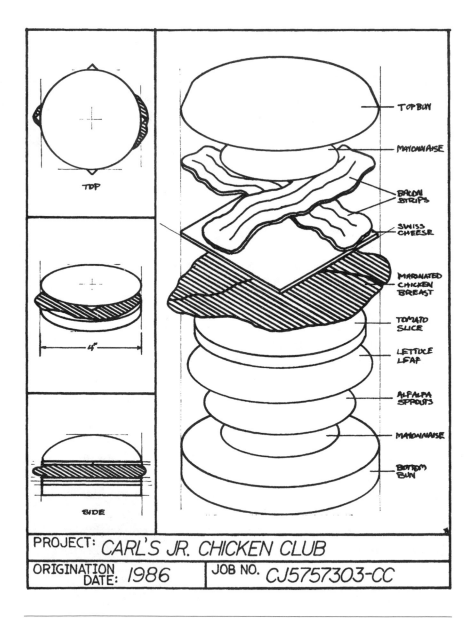

PROJECT: CARL'S JR. CHICKEN CLUB

ORIGINATION DATE: 1986   JOB NO. CJ5757303-CC

CARL'S JR.
FAMOUS STAR

☆   ♥   ☎   ✎   ✈   ✉   ✂   ☞   ✿

It was in Los Angeles in 1941 that Carl Karcher and his wife, Margaret, found a hot-dog cart on Florence and Central for sale for $326. They borrowed $311 on their Plymouth, added $15 of their own, and bought the brightly colored stand. Although the sign on this first stand read HUGO'S HOT DOGS, Karcher began purchasing more carts, painting on them CARL'S HOT DOGS. In 1945 Karcher opened his first drive-thru restaurant, which he named Carl's Drive-In Barbecue. In 1956 he opened two smaller restaurants in Anaheim and Brea, California, and used the Carl's Jr. name for the first time.

With 642 units as of 1993, the chain's trademark smiling star can be seen throughout the West and Southwestern United States, as well as in Mexico, Japan, and Malaysia. The chain has come a long way from the days when Karcher used to mix the secret sauce in twenty-gallon batches on his back porch. Carl's Jr. takes credit for introducing salad bars to fast-food restaurants back in 1977. Today, salads are regular fare at most of the major chains.

Carl's top-of-the-line hamburger is still the flame-broiled Famous Star, one of several products that has made Carl's Jr. famous.

1 sesame-seed hamburger bun
2 onion rings
½ teaspoon sweet pickle relish
1½ teaspoons catsup
¼ pound ground beef
Dash salt

2 teaspoons mayonnaise
3 dill pickle slices
¼ cup coarsely chopped lettuce
2 tomato slices

1. Preheat a clean barbecue grill on high. (The cleaner the barbecue, the less likely the beef patty will pick up other flavors left on the grill.)

2. Toast both halves of the bun, face down, in a skillet over medium heat. Set aside.
3. Cut each of the 2 onion rings into quarters.
4. Mix the catsup and relish together. This is your "secret sauce."
5. Form the ground beef into a thin patty slightly larger than the bun.
6. Grill the meat for 2 or 3 minutes per side. Salt lightly.
7. Build the burger in the following stacking order from the bottom up:

bottom bun	onion
half of the mayonnaise	beef patty
pickles	remainder of mayonnaise
lettuce	special sauce (catsup and relish)
tomato slices	top bun

• MAKES 1 HAMBURGER

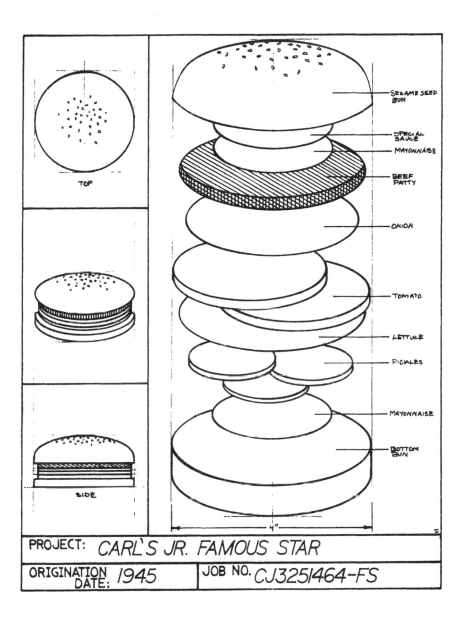

TOP

SIDE

SESAME SEED BUN

SPECIAL SAUCE

MAYONNAISE

BEEF PATTY

ONION

TOMATO

LETTUCE

PICKLES

MAYONNAISE

BOTTOM BUN

4"

PROJECT: *CARL'S JR. FAMOUS STAR*

ORIGINATION DATE: *1945*

JOB NO. *CJ325I464-FS*

CARL'S JR. SANTA FE CHICKEN

☆ ♥ ☎ ✎ ✈ ✉ ✂ ☛ ✿

This has to be one of my favorite fast-food sandwiches of all time. It's only been around since March of 1991, but has become a favorite for those familiar with Carl's Jr. outlets dotting the western United States. Today Carl's Jr. outlets can be found in California, Arizona, Utah, Nevada, Oregon, Mexico, Malaysia, China, Japan, and the Mideast. For all of you who live elsewhere, this is the only way you're going to get to try this fast-food treat. And it is worth trying.

2 whole chicken breasts, skinned, boned, and halved
1 cup teriyaki marinade (Lawry's is best)
¼ cup mayonnaise
¼ teaspoon paprika
⅛ teaspoon cayenne pepper

¼ teaspoon curry powder
Pinch salt
4 whole-wheat hamburger buns
4 lettuce leaves
One 4-ounce can mild green chili peppers, well drained
4 slices American cheese

1.   Marinate the chicken in the teriyaki marinade in a shallow bowl for 30 minutes.
2.   Preheat a clean barbecue to medium grilling heat.
3.   Prepare the sauce in a small bowl by mixing the mayonnaise with the paprika, cayenne pepper, curry powder, and salt.
4.   Grill the chicken for 5 to 8 minutes per side, or until done.
5.   Brown the faces of each bun in a hot frying pan.
6.   Spread a tablespoon of sauce on the faces of each bun, top and bottom.
7.   On each bottom bun place a lettuce leaf, then a green chili pepper. You want the pepper to be spread over most of the lettuce.

To do this, slice the pepper down the middle and spread it open so that it covers more territory. When sliced open like this, some peppers are big enough for 2 sandwiches. Some are much smaller and enough for only one sandwich.

8.   Place one chicken breast half on each of the sandwiches, on top of the chili pepper.

9.   Place a slice of American cheese on the chicken.

10.   Top it all off with the top bun.

- MAKES 4 SANDWICHES

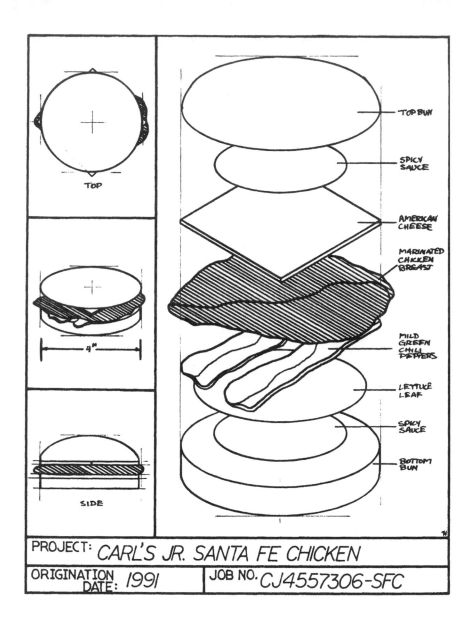

TOP

4"

SIDE

TOP BUN

SPICY SAUCE

AMERICAN CHEESE

MARINATED CHICKEN BREAST

MILD GREEN CHILI PEPPERS

LETTUCE LEAF

SPICY SAUCE

BOTTOM BUN

PROJECT: *CARL'S JR. SANTA FE CHICKEN*

ORIGINATION DATE: *1991*

JOB NO. *CJ4557306-SFC*

CARL'S JR. WESTERN BACON CHEESEBURGER

In 1989, Carl's Jr. became the first fast-food chain to allow customers to use their ATM cards to make purchases. Not only can customers buy a Western Bacon Cheeseburger and fries to go without using cash, they can get up to forty bucks out of their account.

The Western Bacon Cheeseburger is definitely up there on my list of favorite burgers. Onion rings, bacon, and cheese combine to make a tasty gut-grinder that can be thoroughly enjoyed when you're taking time off from the saturated-fat watch. The sandwich was introduced in 1983, and has since become so successful that it has spawned variations, from a junior version to the monstrous double, both of which are included here.

2 frozen onion rings
1/4 pound ground beef
1 sesame-seed hamburger bun
2 slices bacon
Salt to taste
1 slice American cheese

2 tablespoons Bull's-Eye Hickory Smoke barbecue sauce (you must use this brand and variety to make it taste just like Carl's; other brands will produce different, but still tasty, results)

1.   Preheat a clean barbecue to medium grilling heat.
2.   Bake the onion rings in the oven according to the directions on the package.
3.   Form the ground beef into a flat burger the same diameter as the bun. It's best to premake your burger and store it in the freezer, then cook it frozen.
4.   Grill the faces of the top and bottom bun in a frying pan on the stove over medium heat. Keep the pan hot.

5. Cook the bacon slices in the pan.
6. Grill the burger for 3 to 4 minutes per side, or until done. Salt each side.
7. Spread 1 tablespoon of the barbecue sauce on the faces of each bun, top and bottom.
8. Place both onion rings on the sauce on the bottom bun. Next stack the burger, then the cheese and the 2 bacon slices, crossed over each other.
9. Top off the sandwich with the top bun.

- MAKES 1 SANDWICH

Carl's Jr. Junior Western Bacon Cheeseburger®

For about a buck, Carl's Jr. sells this smaller version of the preceding sandwich. It's made with a slightly smaller bun, a smaller portion of beef, half the bacon, and half the onion rings.

Here's what you do: Pat out ⅛ pound of ground beef to the same diameter as the bun. Use only one slice of bacon, broken in two, with the pieces crossed over each other. Use only one big onion ring, and build the burger in the same stacking order as the larger, original version.

Carl's Jr. Double Western Bacon Cheeseburger®

For real cholesterol fans, Carl's Jr. has designed a supersize version of this very popular burger. It is essentially the same as the original, with an additional ¼-pound patty of beef and an additional slice of American cheese stacked on top of the other cheese and beef. Everything else is made the same as in the original. If you try it you'll like it. Just remember to jog an extra mile.

TIDBITS

As I was experimenting, I discovered a variation of this sandwich that I think is pretty darn good. I called it a Western Bacon Chicken Sandwich, and it goes something like this:

Prepare your chicken by marinating and cooking it the same way as in the Carl's Jr. Chicken Club or Santa Fe Chicken recipe. Then stack the sandwich as you would for a Western Bacon Cheeseburger, but using the chicken instead. Tastes great, less filling.

Carl, are you paying attention?

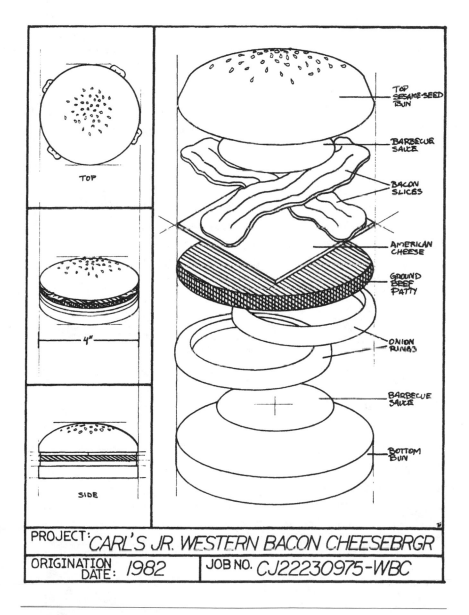

PROJECT: *CARL'S JR. WESTERN BACON CHEESEBRGR*

ORIGINATION DATE: *1982*   JOB NO. *CJ22230975-WBC*

CHICK-FIL-A CHICKEN SANDWICH

☆   ♥   ☎   ✎   ✈   ✉   ✂   ☛   ✿

In 1946 twenty-five-year-old S. Truett Cathy and his younger brother, Ben, opened a restaurant called The Dwarf House in Hapeville, Georgia. In the early sixties Cathy began experimenting with different seasonings and a faster cooking method for his original chicken sandwich. The finished product is the famous pressure-cooked chicken sandwich now served at all 460 Chick-fil-A outlets in thirty-one states.

Annual sales for the chain topped $324 million in 1991. That makes Chick-fil-A the fourth largest fast-food chicken restaurant in the world. And Cathy still adheres to the deeply religious values that were with him in the days of the first Dwarf House. That is why you won't find any Chick-fil-A restaurants open on Sundays.

3 cups peanut oil
1 egg
1 cup milk
1 cup flour
2½ tablespoons powdered sugar
½ teaspoon pepper

2 tablespoons salt
2 skinless, boneless chicken breasts, halved
4 plain hamburger buns
2 tablespoons melted butter
8 dill pickle slices

1. Heat the peanut oil in a pressure cooker over medium heat to about 400°F.
2. In a small bowl, beat the egg and stir in the milk.
3. In a separate bowl, combine the flour, sugar, pepper, and salt.
4. Dip each piece of chicken in milk until it is fully moistened.
5. Roll the moistened chicken in the flour mixture until completely coated.
6. Drop all four chicken pieces into the hot oil and close the pres-

sure cooker. When steam starts shooting through the pressure release, set the timer for 3½ minutes.

7. While the chicken is cooking, spread a coating of melted butter on the face of each bun.

8. When the chicken is done, remove it from the oil and drain or blot on paper towels. Place two pickles on each bottom bun; add a chicken breast, then the top bun.

- MAKES 4 SANDWICHES

TIDBITS

Since my recipe was created, most manufacturers of pressure cookers have discouraged frying in their products, and warn that doing so could be hazardous. For that reason you should NEVER use a pressure cooker to fry anything unless the manufacturer has specifically designed the cooker for this use. I understand that there are now only a few cookers available that you can fry in, and finding one may now be difficult. The alternative is to pan fry or deep fry the chicken for roughly double the specified cooking time, until the chicken is golden brown.

It is very important that your oil be hot for this recipe. Test the temperature by dropping some of the flour coating into the oil. If it bubbles rapidly, your oil is probably hot enough. It should take about 20 minutes to heat up.

To make a "deluxe" chicken sandwich, simply add two tomato slices and a leaf of lettuce. Mayonnaise also goes well on this sandwich—it is a side order at the restaurant.

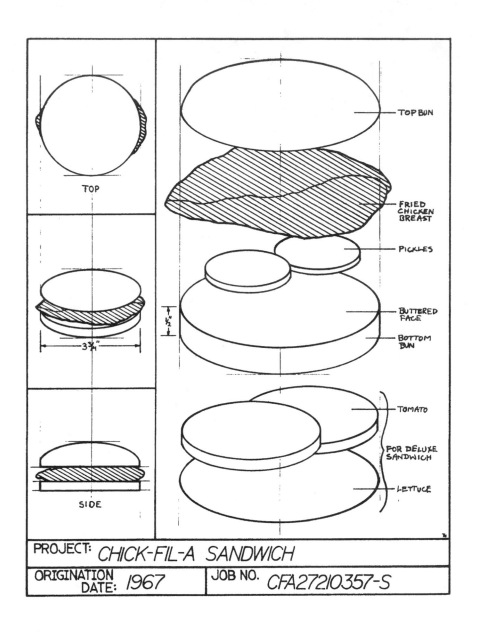

TOP

SIDE

3¾"

½"

TOP BUN

FRIED CHICKEN BREAST

PICKLES

BUTTERED FACE

BOTTOM BUN

TOMATO

FOR DELUXE SANDWICH

LETTUCE

PROJECT: CHICK-FIL-A SANDWICH

ORIGINATION DATE: 1967

JOB NO. CFA27210357-S

CINNABON CINNAMON ROLLS

☆ ♥ ☎ ✎ ✈ ✉ ✂ ☞ ✿

In early 1985, restaurateur Rich Komen decided there was a specialty niche in convenience-food service just waiting to be filled. His idea was to create an efficient outlet that could serve freshly made cinnamon rolls in shopping malls throughout the country. It took nine months for Komen and his staff to develop a cinnamon roll he knew customers would consider the "freshest, gooiest, and most mouthwatering cinnamon roll ever tasted." The concept was tested for the first time in Seattle's Sea-Tac mall later that year, with workers mixing, proofing, rolling, and baking the rolls in full view of the customers. Now, more than 200 outlets later, Cinnabon has become the fastest-growing cinnamon roll bakery in the country.

ROLLS

1 ¼-ounce package active dry yeast
1 cup warm milk (105 to 110°F)
½ cup granulated sugar
⅓ cup margarine, melted

1 teaspoon salt
2 eggs
4 cups all-purpose flour

FILLING

1 cup packed brown sugar
2½ tablespoons cinnamon

⅓ cup margarine, softened

ICING

8 tablespoons (1 stick) margarine, softened
1½ cups powdered sugar

¼ cup (2 ounces) cream cheese
½ teaspoon vanilla extract
⅛ teaspoon salt

1. For the rolls, dissolve the yeast in the warm milk in a large bowl.

2. Mix together the sugar, margarine, salt, and eggs. Add flour, and mix well.

3. Knead the dough into a large ball, using your hands dusted lightly with flour. Put in a bowl, cover, and let rise in a warm place about 1 hour, or until the dough has doubled in size.

4. Roll the dough out on a lightly floured surface. Roll the dough flat until it is approximately 21 inches long and 16 inches wide. It should be about ¼ inch thick.

5. Preheat oven to 400°F.

6. For the filling, combine the brown sugar and cinnamon in a bowl. Spread the softened margarine evenly over the surface of the dough, and then sprinkle the cinnamon and sugar evenly over the surface.

7. Working carefully from the top (a 21-inch side), roll the dough down to the bottom edge.

8. Cut the rolled dough into 1¾-inch slices and place 6 at a time, evenly spaced, in a lightly greased baking pan. Let the rolls rise again until double in size (about 30 minutes). Bake for 10 to 15 minutes, or until light brown on top.

9. While the rolls bake, combine the icing ingredients. Beat well with an electric mixer until fluffy.

10. When the rolls come out of the oven, coat each generously with icing.

- MAKES 12 ROLLS

TIDBITS

These rolls can be frozen after baking. Just pop one into the microwave for 20 to 30 seconds to reheat.

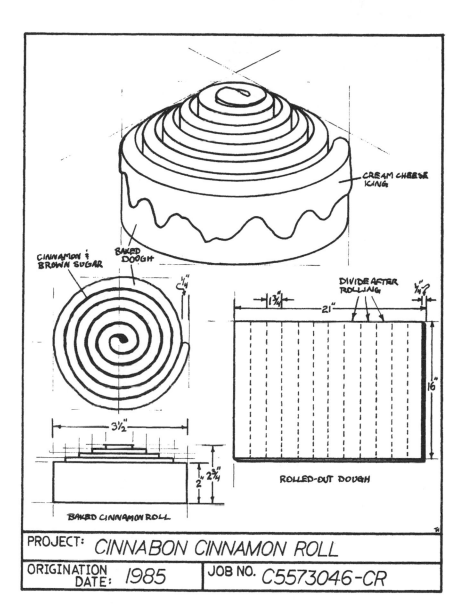

CREAM CHEESE
KING

CINNAMON &
BROWN SUGAR

BAKED
DOUGH

DIVIDE AFTER
ROLLING

1¾"

21"

¼"

16"

3½"

2¾"
2"

ROLLED-OUT DOUGH

BAKED CINNAMON ROLL

| PROJECT: | CINNABON CINNAMON ROLL |
| ORIGINATION DATE: *1985* | JOB NO. *C5573046-CR* |

DAIRY QUEEN BLIZZARD

☆　♥　☎　✎　✈　✉　✂　☞　❀

When the United States was emerging from the Great Depression in 1938, J. F. McCullough was experimenting with the idea of creating a new frozen dairy product. McCullough felt ice cream tasted better when it was soft and dispensed fresh from the freezer, not frozen solid. To test his theory with the public, McCullough held an "All-the-Ice-Cream-You-Can-Eat-for-Only-10-Cents" sale at a friend's ice cream store. More than 1,600 people were served the soft ice cream in the course of two hours. Convinced that the new product was a big hit, McCullough had to find a machine that could dispense the product at the right consistency. It wasn't long before he found Harry Oltz, the inventor of a freezer that could do the job. In 1940 McCullough opened the first Dairy Queen in Joliet, Illinois.

As of 1991 the company claimed to have more than 5,300 retail stores in the United States and twelve other countries. Since its creation in 1985, the Blizzard has shot to the top as the most popular Dairy Queen product, with more than 200 million of the treats sold each year. This is my version of the treat with Heath bar added.

1 Heath candy bar	2½ cups vanilla ice cream
¼ cup milk	1 teaspoon fudge topping

1. Freeze the Heath bar.
2. Break the candy into tiny pieces with a knife handle before removing from wrapper.
3. Combine all of the ingredients in the blender and blend for 30 seconds on medium speed. Stop the blender to stir the mixture with a spoon; repeat until well mixed.
4. Pour into a 16-ounce glass.

- MAKES 1 SERVING

TIDBITS

You can also make this treat with a variety of other candy ingredients. Some of the more popular Dairy Queen add-ins include pieces of Butterfinger candy bars, Reese's Peanut Butter Cups, and Oreo cookies. Now's your chance to be creative.

Also, corporate procedure dictates that when a customer is served a Blizzard in a Dairy Queen outlet, the server must turn the cup upside down quickly to confirm the thickness of the treat before handing it over. If everything is in order, the Blizzard won't "kerplop" onto the counter in front of you.

After using a conventional blender in this recipe (not a commercial mixer as found in Dairy Queens), your Blizzard may not be quite as thick as its commercial counterpart.

If you would like a thicker treat, after pouring the mixture into your cup, simply place it in the freezer for 5 to 10 minutes, or until it reaches the desired consistency. Then give it your own thickness test. Cross your fingers and turn the cup upside down. Have a towel handy.

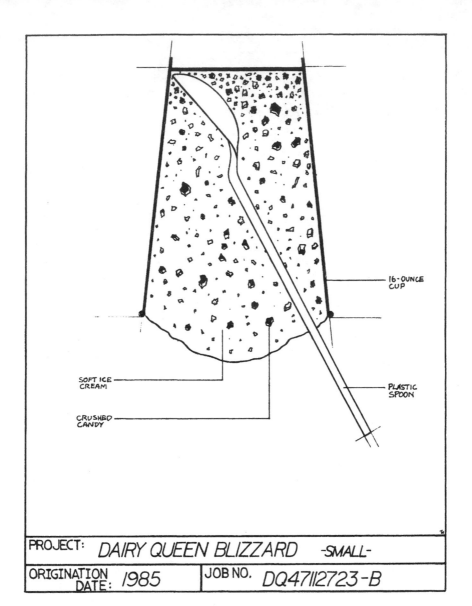

16-OUNCE
CUP

PLASTIC
SPOON

SOFT ICE
CREAM

CRUSHED
CANDY

PROJECT: *DAIRY QUEEN BLIZZARD* -SMALL-

ORIGINATION
DATE: 1985

JOB NO. *DQ47112723-B*

DUNKIN' DONUTS

☆ ♥ ☎ ✎ ✈ ⌧ ✄ ☛ ✿

As he worked long, hard days at a shipyard in Hingham, Massachusetts, during World War II, William Rosenberg was struck with an idea for a new kind of food service. As soon as the war ended, Rosenberg started Industrial Luncheon Services, a company that delivered fresh meals and snacks to factory workers. When Rosenberg realized that most of his business was in coffee and donuts, he quit offering his original service. He found an old awning store and converted it into a coffee-and-donut shop called The Open Kettle. This name was soon changed to the more familiar Dunkin' Donuts, and between 1950 and 1955 five more shops opened and thrived. The company later spread beyond the Boston area and has become the largest coffee-and-donut chain in the world.

Today, Dunkin' Donuts offers fifty-two varieties of donuts in each shop, but the most popular have always been the plain glazed and chocolate-glazed yeast donuts.

DONUTS

One ¼-ounce package active dry yeast
2 tablespoons warm water (98°F)
¾ cup warm milk (30 seconds in the microwave does the trick)
2½ tablespoons margarine or butter

1 egg
⅓ cup granulated sugar
1 teaspoon salt
2¾ cups all-purpose flour
3 cups vegetable oil

GLAZE

5⅓ tablespoons (⅓ cup) margarine or butter
2 cups powdered sugar

½ teaspoon vanilla extract
⅓ cup hot water

61

1 cup semisweet chocolate chips

1. In a medium bowl, dissolve the yeast in the warm water.
2. Add the milk, margarine or butter, egg, sugar, and salt, and blend with an electric mixer until smooth.
3. Add half the flour and mix for 30 seconds.
4. Add the remaining flour and knead the dough with flour-dusted hands until smooth.
5. Cover the bowl of dough and leave it in a comfy, warm place until the dough doubles in size, about 1 hour. You can tell that the dough has risen enough when you poke it with your finger and the indentation stays.
6. Roll out the dough on a heavily floured surface until it's about ½ inch thick.
7. If you don't have a donut cutter, and don't intend to buy one, here's a way to punch out your dough: Empty a standard 15-ounce can of whatever you can find—vegetables, refried beans, even dog food. Be sure to wash out the can very well, and punch a hole in the opposite end so that the dough won't be held inside the can by a vacuum.
8. When you've punched out all the dough (you should have about a dozen unholed donuts), it's time for the holes. Find the cap to a bottle of lemon juice or Worcestershire sauce, or any other small cap with a diameter of about 1¼ inches. Use this to punch out holes in the center of each of your donuts.
9. Place the donuts on plates or cookie sheets, cover, and let stand in the same warm, comfy place until they nearly double in size. This will take 30 to 45 minutes.
10. Heat the vegetable oil in a large frying pan over medium heat. Bring the oil to about 350°F. It is easily tested with scrap dough left over from punching out the donuts. The dough should bubble rapidly.
11. Fry each donut for about 30 seconds per side, or until light golden brown. Cool 5 minutes on paper towels.
12. For either the plain or the chocolate glaze, combine the mar-

garine or butter with the powdered sugar in a medium bowl and blend with an electric mixer.

13. Add the vanilla and hot water. Mix until smooth.

14. If you're making the chocolate glaze, melt the chocolate chips in a microwave-safe bowl in the microwave for 30 to 40 seconds. Stir, then microwave another 30 seconds and stir again until completely melted. Add to the plain glaze mixture. Blend until smooth.

15. When the donuts have cooled, dip each top surface into the glaze and then flip over and cool on a plate until the glaze firms up, about 15 minutes.

- MAKES 1 DOZEN DONUTS

TIDBITS

You can also make "donut holes" as they do at Dunkin' Donuts by cooking and glazing the holes you've punched out the same way you prepared the donuts.

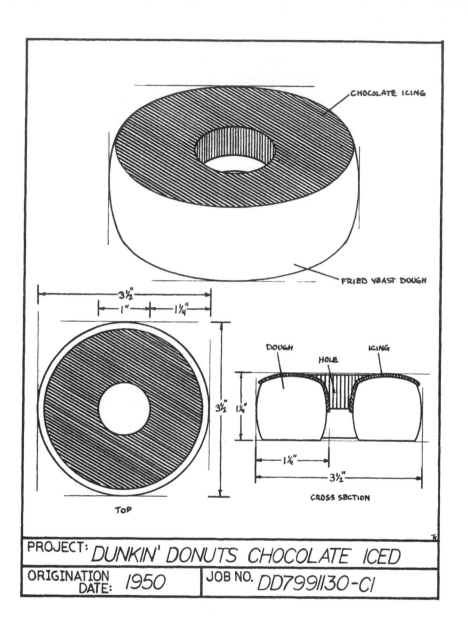

CHOCOLATE ICING

FRIED YEAST DOUGH

3½"
1"
1¼"

3½"

TOP

DOUGH   HOLE   ICING

1¼"

1¼"

3½"

CROSS SECTION

PROJECT: DUNKIN' DONUTS CHOCOLATE ICED

ORIGINATION DATE: 1950

JOB NO. DD7991130-C1

EL POLLO LOCO
FLAME-BROILED
CHICKEN

☆　♥　☎　✎　✈　✉　✂　☛　✿

Okay, time to brush up on your Spanish.

El Pollo Loco, or "The Crazy Chicken," has been growing like mad since it crossed over the border into the United States from Mexico. Francisco Ochoa unknowingly started a food phenomenon *internacional* in 1975 when he took a family recipe for chicken marinade and opened a small roadside *restaurante* in Gusave, Mexico. He soon had 90 stores in 20 cities throughout Mexico. The first El Pollo Loco in the United States opened in Los Angeles in December of 1980 and was an immediate success. It was only three years later that Ochoa got the attention of bigwigs at Denny's, Inc., who offered him $11.3 million for his U.S. operations. Ochoa took the deal, and El Pollo Loco grew from 17 to more than 200 outlets over the following decade. *¡Muy bien!*

2 cups water
4 teaspoons salt
2 teaspoons pepper
1 garlic clove
1 teaspoon yellow food coloring (or a
　　pinch of ground saffron)

2 tablespoons pineapple juice
1 teaspoon lime juice
1 whole frying chicken with skin,
　　halved or quartered

1. In a blender, combine the water, salt, pepper, garlic, and food coloring (or saffron). Blend on high speed for 15 seconds. Add pineapple juice and lime juice to marinade blend for 5 seconds.
2. Marinate the chicken in the liquid in a bowl or pan for 45 minutes. Turn and marinate for 30 minutes more.
3. Preheat a clean barbecue to medium-low grilling heat.

4. Cook the chicken on the open grill for 45 minutes to 1 hour, or until the skin is golden brown and crispy. Be sure the flames are not scorching the chicken, or the skin may turn black before the center is done. Lower the heat if necessary. (If you do not have a gas grill, you can spray a little water on the charcoal to keep the flames at bay.) Turn the chicken often as it cooks.

5. Cut the chicken into 8 pieces, with a large, sharp knife, cutting the breast in half and cutting the thighs from the legs.

• MAKES 8 PIECES

EL POLLO LOCO
SALSA

☆ ♥ ☎ ✎ ✈ ✉ ✄ ☛ ✿

El Pollo Loco's success is based on its unique approach to fast food. The marinated, flame-broiled chicken is served with flour or corn tortillas and a fresh tomato salsa, so that hungry customers can strip the chicken from the bones and make their own soft tacos, smothered in spicy salsa. It's actually a very low-fat, low-calorie version of the fried chicken you normally find at a fast-food chain.

Use this salsa with the marinated chicken from the previous recipe wrapped in tortillas, or with other dishes.

2 medium tomatoes
1 fresh jalapeño pepper, stemmed, or
    10 slices canned jalapeños, or
    "Nacho Slices"

½ teaspoon salt

1. Chop the tomatoes and jalapeños together until they have the consistency of a coarse puree. You can use a food processor, but stop chopping when the mixture is still quite coarse. There will be a lot of liquid, which you want to use as well. Pour everything into a medium bowl.
2. Add the salt to the mixture and stir.
3. Pour the salsa into a covered container and let it sit for several hours to allow the flavor to develop. Overnight is best.

- MAKES ABOUT 2 CUPS

HARDEE'S
FRENCH FRIES

☆　♥　☎　✎　✈　✉　✄　☛　❀

Led by CEO Leonard Rawls, the Hardee's Company opened its first hamburger restaurant in 1961 at the corner of Church Street and Falls Road in Rocky Mount, North Carolina. Hardee's has grown steadily through the years, with a number of well-planned acquisitions: first, the purchase of the 200-unit Sandy's chain in 1972, then the buyout of the 650-unit Burger Chef chain in 1983. The company's latest acquisition was the 1990 buyout of the 648 Roy Rogers restaurants. This latest purchase made Hardee's the third largest hamburger chain in the world, just behind McDonald's and Burger King. With that acquisition, the company claimed to be operating close to 3,800 restaurants in forty-one states and nine foreign countries.

Hardee's was the first major hamburger chain to switch to all-vegetable oil to cook its fried products. One of those products is french fries, the most popular item on the Hardee's menu.

6 cups vegetable oil
⅓ cup granulated sugar
2 cups warm water

2 large russet potatoes, peeled
Salt

1.　Heat the oil in a deep saucepan over low-medium heat for about 20 minutes.
2.　In a medium bowl, mix the sugar into the water until dissolved.
3.　Cut the potatoes in half lengthwise, and then into ¼-inch strips.
4.　Put the potatoes into the sugar solution and soak for 15 minutes.
5.　Remove the potatoes and dry them thoroughly on paper towels.
6.　The right oil temperature is crucial here. To test the oil, fry a couple of potato slices for 6 minutes. Remove and cool, then taste. The fries should not get too dark too soon and should be

soft in the middle. If the oil is too hot, turn it down and test again. The fries should not be undercooked, either. If they are, turn up the heat.

7. When the oil temperature is just right, put all the potato slices in the oil for 1 minute. This is the blanching stage.
8. Take the fries out of the oil and let them cool.
9. When the fries have cooled, place them into the oil again for 5 minutes, or until golden brown.
10. Remove from the oil and place on a paper towel–covered plate.
11. Salt to taste.

- MAKES 4 TO 5 DOZEN FRENCH FRIES

TIDBITS

Oil temperature is crucial in cooking these french fries. Be sure to test the oil on several potato slices before cooking massive portions. And keep in mind that the more you cook at once, the longer your cooking time may be.

The blanching stage may seem to be a nuisance, but it is crucial if you want your fries to come out right. Blanching allows the fries to soak up a little oil while cooling, and will make them crispy when done.

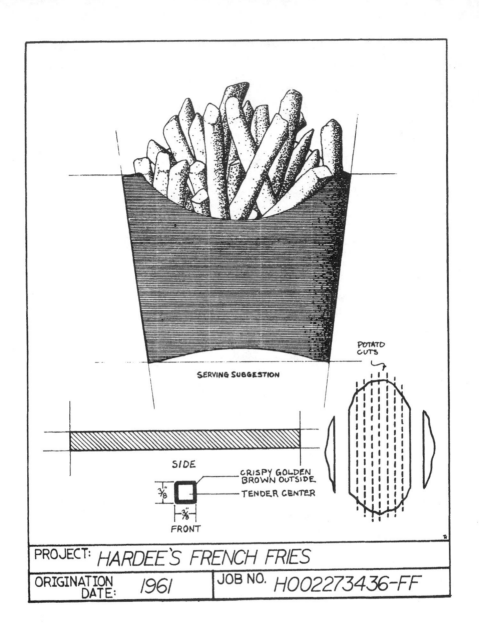

SERVING SUGGESTION

POTATO CUTS

SIDE

CRISPY GOLDEN BROWN OUTSIDE
TENDER CENTER

⅜"

⅜"

FRONT

PROJECT: *HARDEE'S FRENCH FRIES*

ORIGINATION DATE: *1961*

JOB NO. *H002273436-FF*

HARDEE'S
¼-POUND
HAMBURGER

☆　♥　☎　✎　✈　✉　✂　☛　✿

In 1975 Hardee's opened its 1,000th restaurant. The 2,000th unit was opened in 1983, and shortly after that, in 1988, the 3,000th unit opened its doors. This pattern of expansion has continued: A new Hardee's restaurant now opens on the average of one each workday. With the acquisition of the Roy Rogers chain in 1990, Hardee's neared the 4,000-unit mark, racking up systemwide sales of more than $3 billion. This is a chain that has come a long way since its first menu in 1961, which contained only eight items, including fifteen-cent hamburgers and ten-cent soft drinks.

As part of its continuing effort to offer nutrition-conscious customers a range of menu choices, Hardee's was one of the first of the "Big Four" burger chains to switch to low-calorie mayonnaise for its sandwiches.

1 sesame-seed hamburger bun	1 large tomato slice
¼ pound ground beef	1 leaf lettuce
Dash salt	1 teaspoon low-calorie mayonnaise
2 onion rings	1 teaspoon catsup
3 sliced dill pickles	

1. Preheat a griddle or frying pan to medium temperature.
2. Toast both halves of the hamburger bun, face down. Set aside.
3. Form the ground beef into a patty slightly larger than the bun. Salt it lightly.
4. Cook the patty for 2 to 3 minutes on each side.
5. Build the burger in the following stacking order from the bottom up:

bottom bun
beef patty
onion rings
pickles
tomato slice

lettuce leaf
mayonnaise
catsup
top bun

- MAKES 1 HAMBURGER

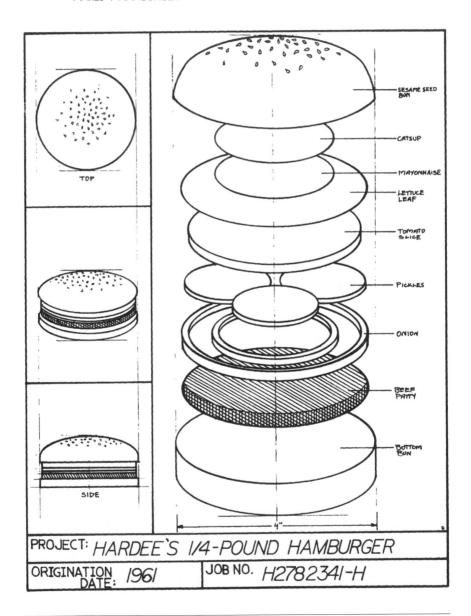

HOSTESS TWINKIE

☆ ♥ ☎ ✎ ✈ ✉ ✂ ☛ ✿

The Twinkie was invented in 1930 by the late James A. Dewar, then the Chicago-area regional manager of Continental Baking Company, the parent corporation behind the Hostess trademark. At the time, Continental made "Little Short Cake Fingers" only during the six-week strawberry season, and Dewar realized that the aluminum pans in which the cakes were baked sat idle the rest of the year. He came up with the idea of injecting the little cakes with a creamy filling to make them a year-round product and decided to charge a nickel for a package of two.

But Dewar couldn't come up with a catchy name for the treat—that is, until he set out on a business trip to St. Louis. Along the road he saw a sign for TWINKLE TOE SHOES, and the name TWINKIES evolved. Sales took off, and Dewar reportedly ate two Twinkies every day for much of his life. He died in 1985.

The spongy treat has evolved into an American phenomenon, from which nearly everyone has slurped the creamy center. Today the Twinkie is Continental's top Hostess-line seller, with the injection machines filling as many as 52,000 every hour.

You will need a spice bottle (approximately the size of a twinkie), ten 12 × 14-inch pieces of aluminum foil, a cake decorator or pastry bag, and a toothpick.

CAKE

Nonstick spray
4 egg whites
One 16-ounce box golden pound
     cake mix
2/3 cup water

FILLING

2 teaspoons very hot water
Rounded 1/4 teaspoon salt
2 cups marshmallow creme (one
     7-ounce jar)
1/2 cup shortening
1/3 cup powdered sugar
1/2 teaspoon vanilla

1. Preheat the oven to 325°F.
2. Fold each piece of aluminum foil in half twice. Wrap the folded foil around the spice bottle to create a mold. Leave the top of the mold open for pouring in the batter. Make ten of these molds and arrange them on a cookie sheet or in a shallow pan. Grease the inside of each mold with a light coating of nonstick spray.
3. Disregard the directions on the box of cake mix. Instead, beat the egg whites until stiff. In a separate bowl combine cake mix with water, and beat until thoroughly blended (about 2 minutes). Fold egg whites into cake batter, and slowly combine until completely mixed.
4. Pour the batter into the molds, filling each one about ¾ inch. Bake in the preheated oven for 30 minutes, or until the cake is golden brown and a toothpick stuck in the center comes out clean.
5. For the filling, combine the salt with the hot water in a small bowl and stir until salt is dissolved. Let this mixture cool.
6. Combine the marshmallow creme, shortening, powdered sugar, and vanilla in a medium bowl and mix well with an electric mixer on high speed until fluffy.
7. Add the salt solution to the filling mixture and combine.
8. When the cakes are done and cooled, use a toothpick or skewer to make three small holes in the bottom of each one. Move the toothpick around the inside of each cake to create space for the filling.
9. Using a cake decorator or pastry bag, inject each cake with filling through all three holes.

- MAKES 10

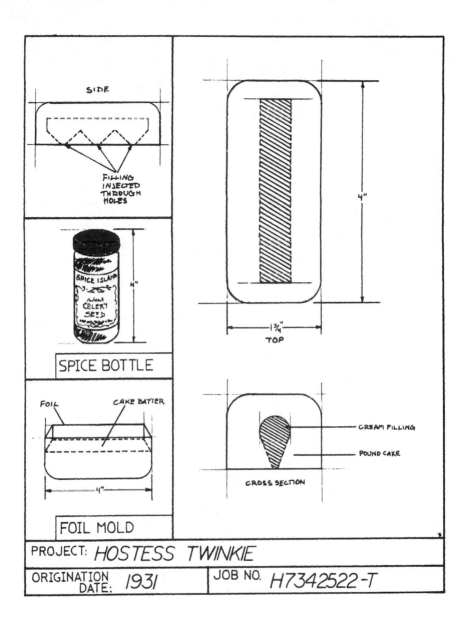

SIDE

FILLING INJECTED THROUGH HOLES

4"

1 3/4"

TOP

SPICE BOTTLE

4"

SPICE ISLAND

CELERY SEED

FOIL MOLD

FOIL

CAKE BATTER

4"

CROSS SECTION

CREAM FILLING

POUND CAKE

PROJECT: HOSTESS TWINKIE

ORIGINATION DATE: 1931

JOB NO. H7342522-T

IN-N-OUT
DOUBLE-DOUBLE

☆ ♥ ☎ ✎ ✈ ✉ ✂ ☛ ✿

In 1948 Harry and Esther Snyder opened In-N-Out Burger in Baldwin Park, the first drive-thru restaurant in southern California. When Harry Snyder died in 1976, his son Richard took over the helm of the company, being sure to keep intact the simplicity that was so important to his father. The outlet still has a very small menu—only eight items. The french fries are made from fresh potatoes in each store, all the burgers are made to order, the lettuce is hand-leafed, and the milkshakes are made from fresh ice cream. All of this special treatment means that service is much slower than at most fast-food outlets—an average of twelve minutes per order. The experience is reminiscent of hamburger drive-ins of the fifties.

The company now has more than seventy-one outlets, each of which sells more than 52,000 hamburgers a month. Among these are the increasingly popular Double-Double hamburgers—quite a handful of sandwich.

1 plain hamburger bun	1 large tomato slice (or 2 small slices)
⅓ pound ground beef	1 large lettuce leaf
Dash salt	4 slices American cheese (singles) OR
1 tablespoon Kraft Thousand Island	2 slices real American cheese
dressing	1 onion slice

1. Preheat a frying pan over medium heat.
2. Lightly toast both halves of the hamburger bun, face down. Set aside.
3. Separate the beef into two even portions, and form each half into a thin patty slightly larger than the bun.
4. Lightly salt each patty and cook for 2 to 3 minutes on the first side.

5. Flip the patties over and place two slices of cheese on top of each one. Cook for 2 to 3 minutes.
6. Build the burger in the following stacking order from the bottom up:

bottom bun	beef patty with cheese
dressing	onion slice
tomato	beef patty with cheese
lettuce	top bun

- MAKES 1 HAMBURGER

TIDBITS

The recipe requires 4 slices of cheese if you are using the common individually wrapped American cheese slices; also known as "cheese food." However, if you would like to use thicker, real American cheese slices, use only 1 slice on each beef patty.

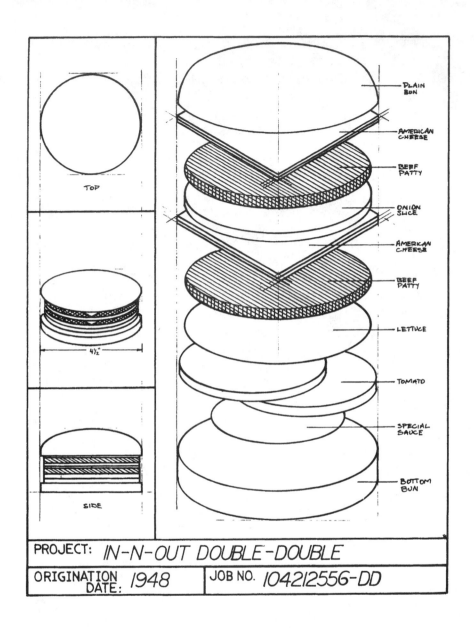

TOP

SIDE

4½"

PLAIN BUN

AMERICAN CHEESE

BEEF PATTY

ONION SLICE

AMERICAN CHEESE

BEEF PATTY

LETTUCE

TOMATO

SPECIAL SAUCE

BOTTOM BUN

PROJECT: IN-N-OUT DOUBLE-DOUBLE

ORIGINATION DATE: 1948

JOB NO. 104212556-DD

JACK-IN-THE-BOX
JUMBO JACK

☆　♥　☎　✎　✈　✉　✂　☛　✿

In 1950 a man named Robert O'Petersen built the first Jack-in-the-Box restaurant at El Cahon and 63rd streets in San Diego, California. The restaurant was originally built for drive-thru and walk-up service only—customers would speak into a clown's mouth to order their food. The clown was blasted to smithereens with explosives in a 1980 advertising campaign, however, signifying a shift toward a more diverse adult menu.

The Jumbo Jack hamburger has been on the menu since 1974.

1 sesame-seed hamburger bun	2 tomato slices
⅕ pound ground beef	1 large lettuce leaf
Dash salt	2 dill pickle slices
2 teaspoons mayonnaise	1 tablespoon chopped onion

1. Preheat a frying pan over medium heat.
2. Lightly toast both halves of the hamburger bun, face down. Set aside.
3. Form the ground beef into a thin patty slightly larger than the hamburger bun.
4. Cook the patty in the hot pan for 2 to 3 minutes per side. Lightly salt.
5. Build the burger in the following stacking order from the bottom up:

bottom bun	tomatoes
half of mayonnaise	lettuce leaf
beef patty	pickles

onion   top bun
remainder of mayonnaise

- MAKES 1 HAMBURGER

TIDBITS

If you want to add a slice of American cheese, it should go on top of the beef patty.

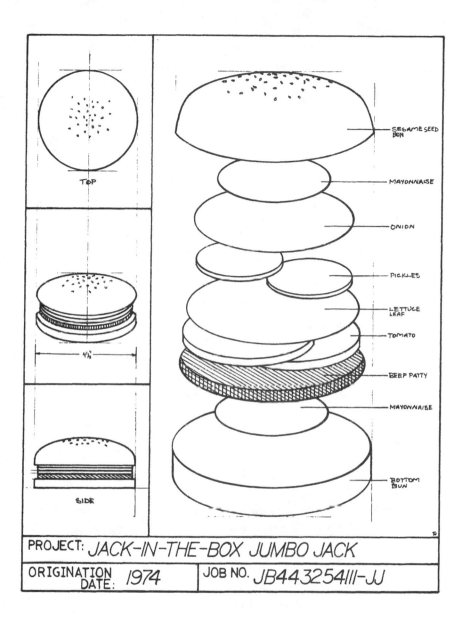

TOP

SIDE

4½

SESAME SEED BUN

MAYONNAISE

ONION

PICKLES

LETTUCE LEAF

TOMATO

BEEF PATTY

MAYONNAISE

BOTTOM BUN

PROJECT:	JACK-IN-THE-BOX JUMBO JACK	
ORIGINATION DATE:	1974	JOB NO. JB443254III-JJ

JACK-IN-THE-BOX TACO

☆ ♥ ☎ ✎ ✈ ✉ ✄ ☛ ✿

Older than both McDonald's and Burger King, Jack-in-the-Box is the world's fifth-largest hamburger chain, with 1,089 outlets (by the end of 1991) in thirteen states throughout the West and Southwest. The restaurant, headquartered in San Diego, boasts one of the largest menus in the fast-food world—a whopping forty-five items.

Now taste for yourself the homemade version of Jack's most popular item. The Jack-in-the-Box Taco has been served since the inception of the chain, with very few changes over the years.

1 pound ground beef
⅓ cup refried beans
¼ teaspoon salt
2 tablespoons chili powder
¼ cup Ortega or Pico Pica brand mild taco sauce

3 cups cooking oil (Crisco brand preferred)
12 soft corn tortillas
6 slices American cheese
1 head finely chopped lettuce

1. Slowly brown the ground beef over low heat, using a wooden spoon to chop and stir the meat, keeping it very fine and smooth.
2. When the beef is brown, drain the fat.
3. Add the refried beans and use the wooden spoon to smash the whole beans into the mixture, creating a smooth texture.
4. Add the salt, chili powder, and 2 tablespoons of the taco sauce to the mixture. Remove from the heat.
5. In another skillet, heat ¼ inch of oil until hot. (Test with a small piece of tortilla—it should bubble when dropped into the oil.) Crisco oil will give the food a taste closest to the original.
6. Spread ½ of the beef mixture on the center of each corn tortilla.

7. Fold the tortillas over and press so that the beef filling acts as an adhesive and holds the sides together.
8. Drop each taco into the pan of hot oil and fry on both sides until crispy.
9. When cooked, remove the tacos from the oil and place them on a rack or some paper towels until they are a little cooler.
10. Pry open each taco slightly. Add ½ slice of American cheese (cut diagonally) and some lettuce. Top with about 1½ teaspoons of the remaining taco sauce.

- MAKES 12 TACOS

TIDBITS

Try to use very thin tortillas for this recipe so that they won't crack when you fold the filled tacos in half before frying. It's best to use warm tortillas and even moisten them along the middle where you will be folding, for additional flexibility.

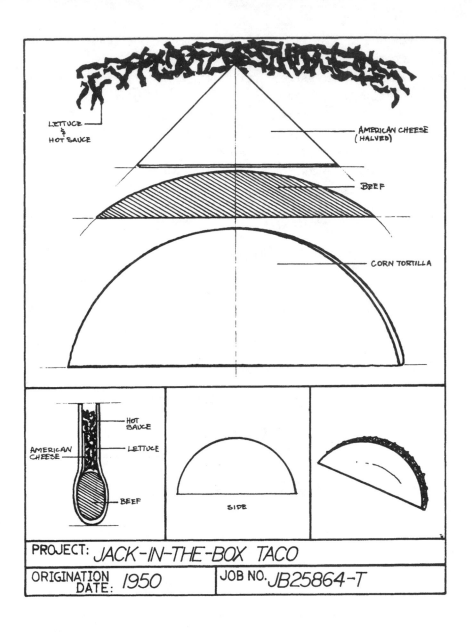

LETTUCE & HOT SAUCE

AMERICAN CHEESE (HALVED)

BEEF

CORN TORTILLA

HOT SAUCE

AMERICAN CHEESE

LETTUCE

BEEF

SIDE

PROJECT: JACK-IN-THE-BOX TACO

ORIGINATION DATE: 1950

JOB NO. JB25864-T

KAHLÚA
COFFEE LIQUEUR

☆　♥　☎　✎　✈　✉　✂　☞　✿

No one knows for sure the true origin of Kahlúa, the largest-selling imported liqueur in America, but we do have a few clues. The oldest proof of Kahlúa's date of origin is a bottle found by Maidstone Co., a former distributor of the liqueur. The bottle came from Mexico, where the drink is now made, and is dated 1937. The world *Kahlúa* was discovered to have ties to ancient Arabic languages, and the old label, which bears a similarity to the current label, shows a turbaned man smoking a pipe beneath a Moorish archway. The only obvious change in the current label is that the man has become a sombrero-wearing Mexican napping beneath the same Moorish archway.

In 1959 Jules Berman discovered Kahlúa in Mexico and started importing it to the United States. In 1991 Kahlúa had annual worldwide sales of more than 2½ million cases, or the equivalent of 750 million drinks a year.

You will need an empty 750-ml. liquor bottle with a top for storing the liqueur.

2 cups water
1½ cups granulated sugar
1½ tablespoons instant coffee

2 cups 80-proof vodka
1½ tablespoons vanilla extract

1.	Combine water, sugar, and coffee in a covered saucepan over high heat. Bring mixture to a boil, and continue to boil for 10 minutes. Be sure mixture does not boil over.
2.	Remove the mixture from the heat and let it cool for 5 minutes.
3.	Add vodka and vanilla. Stir.
4.	Store in an empty 750-ml. liquor bottle with a screw top or another bottle with a resealable lid.

- MAKES 750 ML.

It is very important that you use a covered saucepan when making this drink. The alcohol will boil away if the solution is not covered when it gets hot.

Also, the longer this drink is bottled and stored in a dark, cool place, the better it will taste. For the best flavor, store it for at least thirty days before drinking. Probably the hardest part of making this simple recipe is not drinking the stuff before it matures!

KEEBLER
PECAN SANDIES

☆　♥　☎　✎　✈　✉　✂　☛　✿

This company was founded as the United Biscuit Company of America back in 1927. It was made up of sixteen bakeries from Philadelphia to Salt Lake City, marketing cookies and crackers under a variety of brand names. That system lasted for twenty-two years, and eventually the name Keebler was adopted for the entire conglomerate. Keebler was linked with the United Biscuit name once again after it was bought in 1974 by a British company of that name.

Today the company makes 50 billion cookies and crackers each year; among them are the popular Pecan Sandies, first sold in 1955. The Toffee variety came thirty-eight years later.

1 ½ cups vegetable shortening
¾ cup granulated sugar
1 ½ teaspoons salt
2 eggs

4 cups all-purpose flour
¼ teaspoon baking soda
2 tablespoons water
1 cup shelled pecans

1. Preheat the oven to 325°F.
2. In a large bowl, cream together the shortening, sugar, and salt with an electric mixer on medium speed.
3. Add the eggs and beat well.
4. While mixing, slowly add the flour, baking soda, and add extra water as necessary to make the dough stick together.
5. Chop the pecans into very small bits using a food processor or blender on low speed. Be careful not to overchop; you don't want to make pecan dust. The pieces should be about the size of rice grains.
6. Add the pecans to the dough and knead with your hands until the pecans are well blended into the mixture.

7. Roll the dough into 1-inch balls and press flat with your hands onto ungreased baking sheets. The cookies should be about 2 inches in diameter and ½ inch thick.
8. Bake for 25 to 30 minutes, or until the edges of the cookies are golden brown.

- MAKES 4 DOZEN COOKIES.

Keebler® Toffee Sandies®

Follow the Pecan Sandies recipe, above, replacing the chopped pecans with one 6-ounce package of Heath® Bits 'o Brickle®.

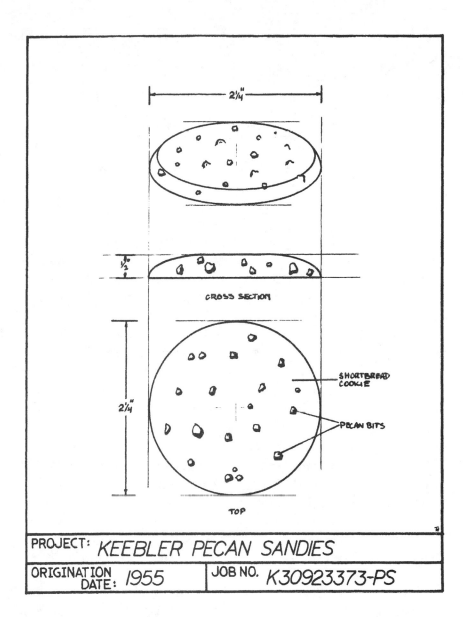

2¼"

½"

CROSS SECTION

SHORTBREAD
COOKIE

PECAN BITS

2¼"

TOP

PROJECT:	KEEBLER PECAN SANDIES	
ORIGINATION DATE: 1955	JOB NO. K30923373-PS	

KEEBLER SOFT BATCH CHOCOLATE CHIP COOKIES

☆ ♥ ☎ ✎ ✈ ✉ ✂ ☛ ✿

In pre–Civil War Philadelphia, Godfrey Keebler earned a reputation for baking the best cookies and crackers around. Keebler joined in a federation with sixteen local and regional bakeries to help form the United Biscuit Company in 1927. This system lasted for twenty-two years, until 1949, when the conglomerate chose to operate under a single name. *Keebler* was judged to be the most sound and memorable. In 1983 Keebler expanded its distribution to the West Coast, making the conglomerate a national concern.

Today Keebler manufactures more than 200 different products from its 83,000-square-foot facility in Elmhurst, Illinois. Those products, including the chewy Soft Batch cookie, are sold in some 75,000 retail outlets nationwide. Total annual sales for the company are in excess of $1.5 billion, making Keebler the second-largest cookie and cracker manufacturer in the United States, with popular products that have been enjoyed by five generations of Americans.

1 pound (4 sticks) butter, softened	1 teaspoon baking powder
2 eggs	1 ½ teaspoons baking soda
2 tablespoons molasses	1 teaspoon salt
2 teaspoons vanilla extract	5 cups all-purpose flour
⅓ cup water	1 ½ twelve-ounce packages semisweet
1 ½ cups granulated sugar	chocolate chips
1 ½ cups packed brown sugar	

1. Preheat the oven to 375°F.
2. Cream the butter, eggs, molasses, vanilla, and water in a medium-size bowl.

3. In a large bowl, sift together the sugars, baking powder, baking soda, salt, and flour.
4. Combine the moist mixture with the dry mixture. Add the chocolate chips.
5. Shape the dough into 1-inch balls, and place them 1 inch apart on an ungreased cookie sheet.
6. Bake for 8 minutes, or until light brown around edges.

- MAKES 4 DOZEN COOKIES

Pepperidge Farm® Chesapeake® and Sausalito® Cookies
Pepperidge Farm products bear the name of the farm where Margaret Rudkin lived and created her first product. It was on that farm in Fairfield, Connecticut, in 1937 that Mrs. Rudkin baked her first loaf of homemade bread for her children. Her first few loaves turned out terribly, but she was persistent and eventually came up with a loaf of bread so delicious that friends began requesting it. Soon Mrs. Rudkin was baking as a commercial venture and adding new products. In 1961 Pepperidge Farm was purchased by the Campbell Soup Company. Six years later Margaret Rudkin passed away at the age of sixty-nine.

But Mrs. Rudkin's kitchen enterprise lives on and is bigger than ever. Today Pepperidge Farm has more than 300 products in distribution. One of them is the crispy Chesapeake cookie.

Simply follow the recipe for the Keebler Soft Batch cookie with these exceptions: Omit the water and molasses. Add 3 cups of chopped pecans. (For the Sausalito cookie, substitute macadamia nuts.) Bake at the same temperature, but for 10 to 11 minutes rather than 8 minutes. This will make the cookies crispier.

KFC
BUTTERMILK
BISCUITS

In 1991 Kentucky Fried Chicken bigwigs decided to improve the image of America's third-largest fast-food chain. As a more health-conscious society began to affect sales of fried chicken, the company changed its name to KFC and introduced a lighter fare of skinless chicken. The company is now working hard on developing a new line of baked and roasted chicken.

In the last forty years KFC has experienced extraordinary growth. Five years after first franchising the business, Colonel Harland Sanders had 400 outlets in the United States and Canada. Four years later there were more than 600 franchises, including one in England, the first overseas outlet. In 1964 John Y. Brown, Jr., twenty-nine, a young Louisville lawyer, and Jack Massey, sixty, a Nashville financier, bought the Colonel's business for $2 million. Only seven years later, in 1971, Heublein, Inc., bought the KFC Corporation for $275 million. Then in 1986, for a whopping $840 million, PepsiCo added KFC to its conglomerate, which now includes Pizza Hut and Taco Bell. That means PepsiCo owns more fast-food outlets than any other company including McDonald's—totaling over 20,000.

At each KFC restaurant, workers blend real buttermilk with a flour mixture to create the well-known buttermilk biscuits that have been a popular menu item since their introduction in 1982.

½ cup (1 stick) butter
2½ tablespoons granulated sugar
1 beaten egg
¾ cup buttermilk

¼ cup club soda
1 teaspoon salt
5 cups Bisquick biscuit mix

1. Preheat the oven to 450°F.
2. Combine all of the ingredients. Knead the dough by hand until smooth.
3. Flour your hands. Pat the dough flat to ¾-inch thickness on waxed paper and punch out biscuits with a biscuit cutter.
4. Bake on a greased baking sheet for 12 minutes, or until golden brown.

- MAKES 18 BISCUITS

TIDBITS

To produce biscuits that most closely resemble the KFC variety, it is best to use a biscuit cutter for this recipe, as specified above. If you don't have a biscuit cutter, the lid of an aerosol can will suffice—just be sure it's not from a product that is toxic. A lid from a can of nonstick cooking spray, for example, works great.

If all you have is a lid from a can of Raid bug spray, I would say that you should form the biscuits as best you can with your bare hands.

KFC
COLE SLAW

☆　♥　☎　✎　✈　✉　✂　☛　✿

In 1935, shortly after the first Kentucky Fried Chicken restaurant had opened, Governor Ruby Laffoon made Harland Sanders a Kentucky colonel in recognition of his contribution to the state's cuisine. In 1952, at the age of sixty-six, Colonel Sanders began to franchise his fried chicken business. Traveling through Ohio, Indiana, and Kentucky, he met with restaurant owners, cooking his chicken for them and their employees. If the restaurant owners liked the chicken, they would agree with a handshake that the Colonel would supply the "secret blend" of spices in exchange for a nickel on each piece of chicken sold. As of 1991 there were more than 8,000 Kentucky Fried Chicken stores worldwide, with sales of more than $5 billion.

The recipe for the Colonel's cole slaw, which is made from scratch in each store, is kept as secret as that for the herbs and spices in the fried chicken. Now taste our "top-secret" version of the Colonel's well-known favorite slaw.

8 cups very finely chopped cabbage (1 head)
1/4 cup shredded carrot (1 medium carrot)
2 tablespoons minced onions
1/3 cup granulated sugar
1/2 teaspoon salt
1/8 teaspoon pepper
1/4 cup milk
1/2 cup mayonnaise
1/4 cup buttermilk
1 1/2 tablespoons white vinegar
2 1/2 tablespoons lemon juice

1.   Be sure that the cabbage, carrots, and onion are chopped up into very fine pieces (about the size of rice kernels).
2.   Combine the sugar, salt, pepper, milk, mayonnaise, buttermilk, vinegar, and lemon juice, and beat until smooth.

3. Add the cabbage, carrots, and onions. Mix well.
4. Cover and refrigerate for at least 2 hours before serving.

- SERVES 8

TIDBITS

The critical part of this cole slaw recipe is the flavor-enhancement period prior to eating. Be absolutely certain the cole slaw sits in the refrigerator for at least a couple of hours prior to serving for a great-tasting slew of slaw.

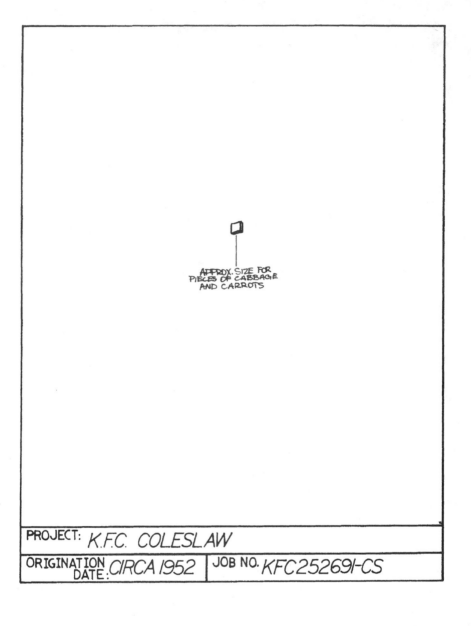

APPROX. SIZE FOR
PIECES OF CABBAGE
AND CARROTS

PROJECT: K.F.C. COLESLAW

ORIGINATION
DATE: CIRCA 1952

JOB NO. KFC252691-CS

KFC
ORIGINAL RECIPE
FRIED CHICKEN

☆   ♥   ☎   ✎   ✈   ⊠   ✂   ☞   ✿

Since 1952, when Colonel Harland Sanders opened his first franchise, only a select few have been privy to the secret "herbs and spices" contained in the billion-dollar blend. To protect the top-secret recipe, the company claims, portions of the secret blend are premixed at two confidential spice companies and then distributed to KFC's offices, where they are combined. In 1983, in his book *Big Secrets*, author William Poundstone hired a laboratory to analyze a dry sampling of the spice mixture. The surprising discovery was that instead of identifying "eleven herbs and spices," the analysis showed only four ingredients: flour, salt, pepper, and monosodium glutamate, a flavor enhancer.

The cooking procedure is believed to be the other half of the secret. Colonel Sanders became famous for using a pressure cooker shortly after its invention in 1939. He discovered that hungry travelers greatly appreciated the ten-minute pressure-cooking process (compared to the half hour it used to take for frying chicken), and the new process made the chicken juicy and moist inside.

KFC is the third-largest fast-food chain in the country, and uses around 500 million chickens every year.

6 cups Crisco cooking oil
1 egg, beaten
2 cups milk
2 cups all-purpose flour
4 tablespoons salt
2 teaspoons black pepper

1 teaspoon MSG (monosodium
    glutamate—you can use Accent
    Flavor Enhancer)
2 frying chickens with skin, each cut
    into 8 pieces

1. Pour the oil into the pressure cooker and heat over medium heat to about 400°F.
2. In a small bowl, combine the egg and milk.
3. In a separate bowl, combine the remaining four dry ingredients.
4. Dip each piece of chicken into the milk until fully moistened.
5. Roll the moistened chicken in the flour mixture until completely coated.
6. In groups of four or five, drop the covered chicken pieces into the oil and lock the lid in place.
7. When steam begins shooting through the pressure release, set the timer for 10 minutes.
8. After 10 minutes, release the pressure according to manufacturer's instructions, and remove the chicken to paper towels or a metal rack to drain. Repeat with the remaining chicken.

• MAKES 16 PIECES

TIDBITS

If you prefer not to use MSG, you may substitute an additional ½ tablespoon of salt. Be aware, however, that using MSG produces the best clone of KFC's Fried Chicken.

Since my recipe was created, most manufacturers of pressure cookers have discouraged frying in their products, and warn that doing so could be hazardous. For that reason you should NEVER use a pressure cooker to fry anything unless the manufacturer has specifically designed the cooker for this use. I understand that there are now only a few cookers available that you can fry in, and finding one may now be difficult. The alternative is to pan fry or deep fry the chicken for roughly double the specified cooking time, until the chicken is golden brown.

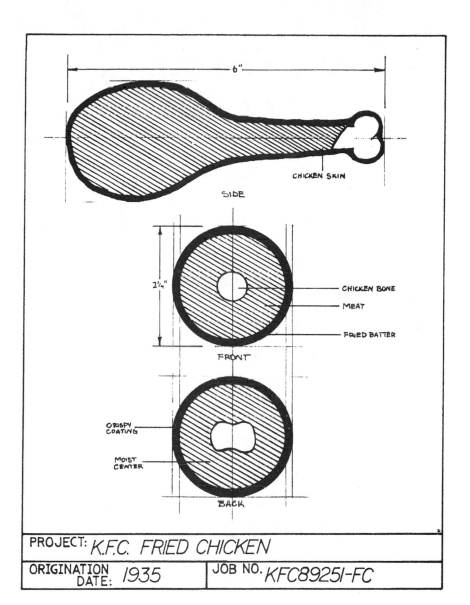

6"

CHICKEN SKIN

SIDE

2¼"

CHICKEN BONE

MEAT

FRIED BATTER

FRONT

CRISPY COATING

MOIST CENTER

BACK

PROJECT: *K.F.C. FRIED CHICKEN*	
ORIGINATION DATE: *1935*	JOB NO. *KFC89251-FC*

LITTLE CAESAR'S CRAZY BREAD

☆ ♥ ☎ ✎ ✈ ✉ ✂ ☞ ✿

In 1959, Michael Ilitch and his wife, Marian, opened the first Little Cae-sar's restaurant in Garden City, Michigan, fifteen miles west of Detroit. Encouraged by their success, the couple opened a second restaurant two years later, and soon Little Caesar's Pizza was a household name in the Detroit area. Biographical material provided by the company claims that Ilitch "thinks pizza," and that when he designed the Little Caesar's conveyor oven, the company was able to serve hot pizza faster than anyone else in the industry.

One of the most popular products available from Little Caesar's is the Crazy Bread, first served in 1982. It's just a pizza crust cut into eight pieces, then coated with garlic salt, butter, and Parmesan cheese.

One 10-ounce tube Pillsbury pizza
    dough
2 tablespoons (¼ stick) butter

1 teaspoon garlic salt
Kraft 100% grated parmesan cheese
    for topping

1. Preheat the oven to 425°F.
2. Unroll the dough on a cutting board. Position it lengthwise (longer from left to right than from top to bottom). With a sharp knife, cut the dough in half down the middle. Then cut each of those halves vertically in half, and then in half once more so that you have 8 even strips of dough.
3. Being careful not to stretch the dough, place each strip on a lightly greased cookie sheet and bake for 6 to 8 minutes, or until the top just turns golden brown.
4. While the dough bakes, melt the butter (on the stove or in the microwave on high for 15 to 20 seconds), then add the garlic salt and stir until it dissolves.
5. Remove the browned dough from the oven and with a pastry

brush or spoon spread a coating of garlic butter over each piece.

6. Sprinkle a generous amount of Parmesan cheese on each.

- MAKES 8 PIECES

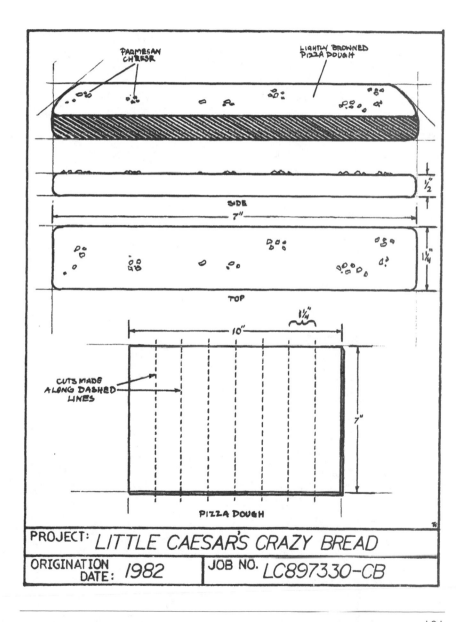

PARMESAN CHEESE

LIGHTLY BROWNED PIZZA DOUGH

SIDE
7"
½"

TOP
1¼"

1¼"
10"
7"

CUTS MADE ALONG DASHED LINES

PIZZA DOUGH

PROJECT: LITTLE CAESAR'S CRAZY BREAD

ORIGINATION DATE: 1982

JOB NO. LC897330-CB

LITTLE CAESAR'S CRAZY SAUCE

☆ ♥ ☎ ✎ ✈ ✉ ✂ ☞ ✿

From 1990 to 1993, Little Caesar's sales growth ranked in the top five in the restaurant industry, according to *Nation's Restaurant News* magazine. As of 1993, the company had more than 4,800 outlets raking in $2.3 billion. It's no wonder that founder Michael Ilitch was able to purchase the Detroit Red Wings hockey team in 1982, and then the Detroit Tigers in 1992. Ilitch also owns several arenas and theaters, including the Second City comedy theater in Detroit.

The Crazy Sauce at Little Caesar's is usually served with the Crazy Bread, for dipping. It's a version of pizza sauce, heated in a microwave before you buy it. The sauce can be used with the preceding Crazy Bread recipe, or as a great, fresh sauce for any homemade pizza.

One 15-ounce can tomato puree
½ teaspoon salt
¼ teaspoon pepper
¼ teaspoon garlic powder

¼ teaspoon dried basil
¼ teaspoon dried marjoram
¼ teaspoon dried oregano
¼ teaspoon ground thyme

1. Combine all the ingredients in an uncovered saucepan over medium heat.
2. When the sauce begins to bubble, reduce the heat and simmer for 30 minutes, stirring often.
3. Remove the sauce from the heat and let it cool. Store in a tightly sealed container in the refrigerator; it will keep for 3 to 4 weeks. Serve hot.

- MAKES 1 ½ CUPS

LONG JOHN SILVER'S BATTER-DIPPED FISH

☆ ♥ ☎ ✎ ✈ ✉ ✂ ☞ ✿

Jerrico, Inc., the parent company for Long John Silver's Seafood Shoppes, got its start in 1929 as a six-stool hamburger stand called the White Tavern Shoppe. Jerrico was started by a man named Jerome Lederer, who watched Long John Silver's thirteen units dwindle in the shadow of World War II to just three units. Then, with determination, he began rebuilding.

In 1946 Jerome launched a new restaurant called Jerry's, and it was a booming success, with a growth across the country. Then he took a chance on what would be his most successful venture in 1969, with the opening of the first Long John Silver's Fish 'n' Chips. The name was inspired by Robert Louis Stevenson's *Treasure Island*.

In 1991 there were 1,450 Long John Silver Seafood Shoppes in thirty-seven states, Canada, and Singapore, with annual sales of more than $781 million. That means the company holds about 65 percent of the $1.2-billion quick-service seafood business.

3 cups soybean oil
2 pounds fresh cod fillets
1⅓ cups self-rising flour
1 cup water

1 egg
2 teaspoons granulated sugar
2 teaspoons salt

1. Heat the oil in a deep pan to about 400°F.
2. Cut the fish into approximately 7 × 2-inch wedges.
3. With a mixer, blend the flour, water, egg, sugar, and salt.
4. Dip each fillet into the batter, coating generously, and quickly drop into the oil.
5. Fry each fillet until dark golden brown, about 5 minutes.

6.   Remove from the oil and place on paper towels or a metal rack to drain.

• MAKES 4 TO 6 FILLETS

TIDBITS

Soybean oil is what your local Long John Silver's uses to fry their fish, and you will best duplicate the real thing by using the same oil. But any other oil may be substituted. You might want to try canola oil. It is the oil lowest in saturated fat, and the taste difference is only slight.

It's crucial that your oil be hot before frying the fish. To test the temperature, drip some batter into the oil. It should bubble rapidly. After 5 minutes, the test batter should become golden brown. If so, fry away, fish fiends.

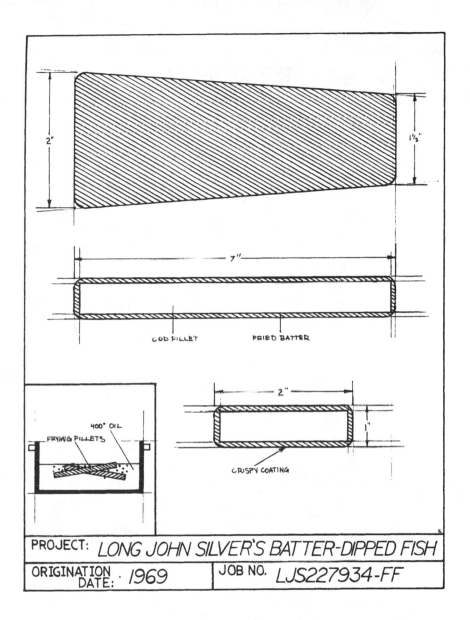

2"

1½"

7"

COD FILLET   FRIED BATTER

2"

1"

CRISPY COATING

400° OIL

FRYING FILLETS

PROJECT: LONG JOHN SILVER'S BATTER-DIPPED FISH

ORIGINATION DATE: 1969   JOB NO. LJS227934-FF

M&M/MARS ALMOND BAR

☆　♥　☎　✎　✈　✉　✂　☛　✿

What started in Tacoma, Washington, in 1911 as a small home-based candy shop has now grown to be one of the largest privately held companies in the world. Mars products are found in more than 100 countries, and the Mars family pulls in revenues in the range of a sweet $11 billion each year.

The Mars Almond Bar was first produced in 1936, when it was known as the Mars Toasted Almond Bar. It was reformulated in 1980 and the name was changed to Mars Bar; in 1990 it was renamed once again, becoming Mars Almond Bar.

You'll need a heavy-duty mixer to handle the nougat in this recipe.

2 cups granulated sugar
½ cup light corn syrup
½ cup plus 2 tablespoons water
Pinch salt
2 egg whites

⅔ cup whole roasted almonds
35 unwrapped Kraft caramels
Two 12-ounce bags milk chocolate
   chips

1. In a large saucepan over medium heat, combine the sugar, corn syrup, ½ cup of the water, and the salt. Heat to boiling, then cook using a candy thermometer to monitor the temperature.
2. Beat the egg whites until they are stiff and form peaks. Don't use a plastic bowl for this.
3. When the sugar mixture reaches 270°F, or the *soft-crack stage*, remove from the heat and pour the mixture in thin streams into the egg whites, blending completely with an electric mixer set on low.
4. Continue to mix about 20 minutes, or until the nougat begins

to harden and thickens to the consistency of dough. Mix in the almonds.

5. Press the nougat into a greased 9 × 9-inch pan and chill until firm, about 30 minutes.

6. Melt the caramels with the remaining 2 tablespoons water in a small saucepan over medium heat.

7. Pour the caramel over the nougat and return the pan to the refrigerator.

8. When the caramel and nougat are firm (about 30 minutes), slice down the middle of the pan with a sharp knife, and then slice across into 7 segments to make a total of 14 bars.

9. Melt the milk chocolate chips in a microwave for 2 minutes on half power, stirring halfway through the cooking time. Melt completely, but be careful not to overheat.

10. Resting the bar on a fork (and using your fingers if needed), dip each bar into the chocolate to coat completely and tap the fork against the side of the bowl to knock off the excess chocolate. Place on waxed paper and let cool at room temperature until the chocolate is firm, 1 to 2 hours.

• MAKES 14 CANDY BARS

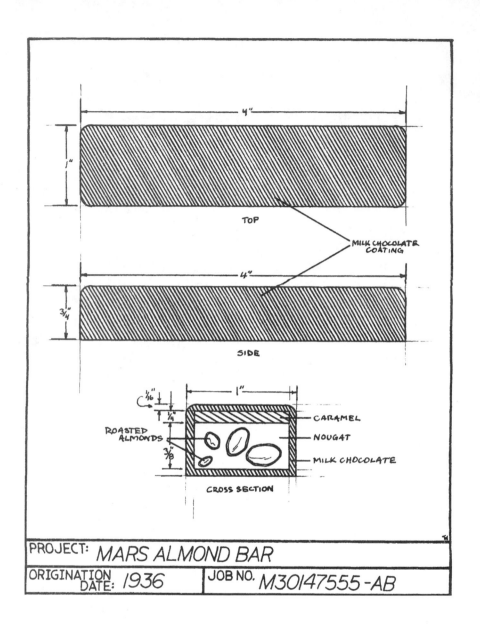

4"

1"

TOP

MILK CHOCOLATE COATING

4"

3/4"

SIDE

1/16"

1/4"

ROASTED ALMONDS

3/8"

1"

CARAMEL

NOUGAT

MILK CHOCOLATE

CROSS SECTION

PROJECT:	*MARS ALMOND BAR*	
ORIGINATION DATE: *1936*	JOB NO.	*M30147555-AB*

M&M/MARS CARAMEL TWIX BARS

☆ ♥ ☎ ✎ ✈ ⊠ ✂ ☛ ✿

The process by which M&M/Mars and other candy companies smoothly chocolate-coat their confections is called *enrobing*. Enrobing was created in 1900 to protect the interiors from drying out. The process begins when the uncoated centers pass through a curtain of liquid chocolate on a continuous stainless-steel belt. The top and sides of each bar are coated. The process is repeated a second time, and then the fully coated bar is quickly cooled and wrapped.

Enrobing is the least expensive way for manufacturers to coat their chocolates. At M&M/Mars, the enrobing machines run around the clock to meet the high demand for their products. Unfortunately, traditional kitchen appliances don't include among them an enrobing machine, so in our case, dipping will have to suffice.

The caramel Twix was introduced in 1977, and peanut butter Twix came along in 1982. Other variations of the bar, including cookies & cream and fudge, were introduced in the early nineties.

35 unwrapped Kraft caramels
2 tablespoons water
1 box (40) Nabisco Lorna Doone
  shortbread cookies

Two 12-ounce bags milk-chocolate
  chips

1. Combine the caramels with the water in a small pan and melt over low heat.
2. Place the shortbread cookies side by side on an ungreased cookie sheet.
3. Spoon a dab of caramel onto each cookie. Then place all the cookies in the refrigerator until the caramel firms up.

4. In the meantime, in a double boiler over low heat, melt the chocolate chips. You may also use the microwave for melting the chocolate. Just zap the chips for 1 minute on high, stir, then zap 'em for another minute.

5. Remove the cookies from the refrigerator. Rest each one on a fork and dip it into the chocolate. Tap the fork on the side of the pan or bowl to knock off any excess chocolate. Then place each one on a sheet of waxed paper and let them cool at room temperature (65 to 70°F). This could take several hours, but the bars will set best this way. If you want to speed up the process, put the candy in the refrigerator for 30 minutes.

- MAKES 40 BARS

M&M/Mars Peanut Butter Twix® Bars

Substitute 1 cup of peanut butter sweetened with ½ cup powdered sugar for the caramels. The peanut-butter mixture will be of a consistency that allows you to spread it on the shortbread cookies with your fingers. Follow the rest of the directions exactly.

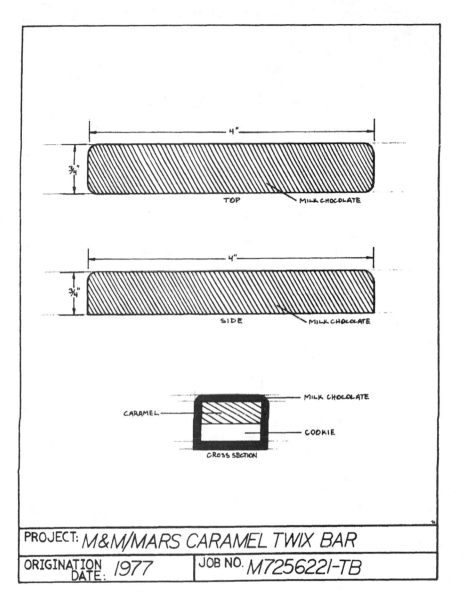

4"

3/4"

TOP

MILK CHOCOLATE

4"

3/4"

SIDE

MILK CHOCOLATE

MILK CHOCOLATE

CARAMEL

COOKIE

CROSS SECTION

PROJECT: M&M/MARS CARAMEL TWIX BAR

ORIGINATION DATE: 1977

JOB NO. M7256221-TB

M&M/MARS
MILKY WAY

☆　　♥　　☎　　✎　　✈　　⊠　　✂　　☞　　❀

I find that some people are confused by the brand name M&M/Mars. The company is actually a snack division within the parent company Mars, Incorporated, which produces food products around the world as diverse as Uncle Ben's rice and Kal Kan dog food. When the founder's son, Forrest E. Mars, Sr., returned from England (where he had established the first canned pet food business in that country), he formed a company in Newark, New Jersey, to make small chocolate candies that could be sold throughout the year, not melting in the hot summer months. Those were the first M&M's. The company, called M&M Limited, consolidated with other Mars confectionery businesses in the United States in 1967 to form M&M/Mars as it exists today.

The Mars Milky Way bar was the first chocolate-covered candy bar to find widespread popularity in the United States. It was developed in 1923 by the Mars family, and became so successful so quickly that the company had to build a new manufacturing plant in Chicago just to keep up with demand.

You'll need a heavy-duty mixer for this recipe.

2 cups granulated sugar
½ cup light corn syrup
½ cup plus 2 tablespoons water
Pinch salt
2 egg whites

¼ cup semisweet chocolate chips
35 unwrapped Kraft caramels
Two 12-ounce bags milk chocolate
    chips

1.　In a large saucepan over medium heat, combine the sugar, corn syrup, ½ cup of the water, and the salt. Stir often until the mixture begins to boil, then continue to cook, using a candy thermometer to monitor the temperature.

2. While the candy boils, beat the egg whites until they are stiff and form peaks. Don't use a plastic bowl for this.

3. When the sugar mixture reaches 270°F, or the *soft-crack stage*, remove from the heat and pour the mixture in thin streams into the egg whites, blending with a mixer set on low speed.

4. Continue to mix for 15 minutes or so. The mixture will thicken as you mix, until it reaches the consistency of cookie dough. At this point, add the semisweet chocolate chips. Be warned; the mixture will not get any thicker after the chocolate is added, so be sure the candy is very thick and fluffy before adding the chips.

5. When the chocolate chips are completely blended into the candy, press the mixture into a greased 9 × 9-inch pan and refrigerate until cool, about 30 minutes.

6. Heat the caramels with the remaining 2 tablespoons water in a small saucepan until thoroughly melted. Pour the caramel over the refrigerated candy.

7. While the candy cools, melt the milk chocolate chips in the microwave for 2 minutes on medium power. Stir halfway through the heating time. Melt completely, but be careful not to overheat.

8. When the caramel is set, use a sharp knife to cut down the center of the pan. Then cut the candy across into 7 segments, making a total of 14 bars.

9. Resting a bar on a fork (and using your fingers if needed), dip each bar into the chocolate to coat completely, then tap the fork against the side of the bowl to knock off the excess chocolate.

10. Place each bar on waxed paper and cool until firm at room temperature, 1 to 2 hours.

• MAKES 14 CANDY BARS

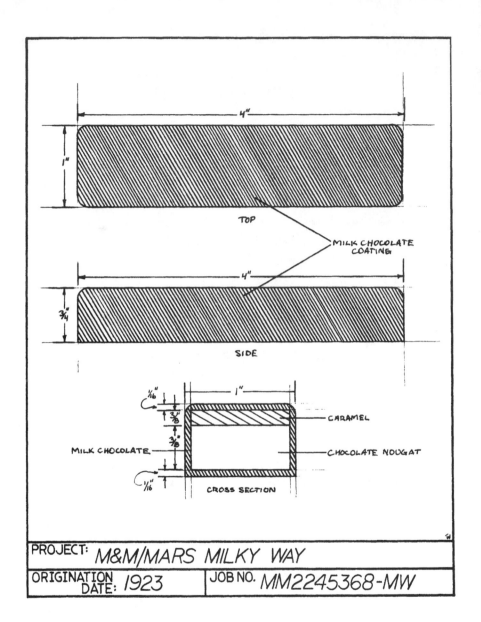

TOP

MILK CHOCOLATE COATING

SIDE

CARAMEL

MILK CHOCOLATE

CHOCOLATE NOUGAT

CROSS SECTION

PROJECT:	M&M/MARS MILKY WAY	
ORIGINATION DATE: 1923	JOB NO.	MM2245368-MW

M&M/MARS
SNICKERS BAR

☆　♥　☎　✎　✈　✉　✄　☛　✿

In 1992 *Fortune* magazine estimated the Mars family's personal worth at somewhere around $12.5 billion—quite a fistful of peanuts. This solid foundation of wealth, built on the country's undying passion for chocolate and other sweets, has made this clan the richest family in America—and the most reclusive. A family rule prohibits photographs to be taken of the Mars family and corporate executives. According to *Fortune*, a photographer who once tried to get a shot of Forrest Mars, Sr., found himself enveloped in a cloth that was thrown as he was about to snap the picture.

The empire started in 1902, when nineteen-year-old Franklin C. Mars began selling homemade candy. In 1910 he started a wholesale candy business in Tacoma, Washington. Ten years later Frank moved to Minneapolis, where he used the family kitchen to make buttercreams, which were personally delivered to retailers in the city by his wife, Ethel. Business grew steadily, and in 1940 Frank's son Forrest established M&M Limited in Newark, New Jersey.

By 1967 the family's confectionery business in the United States had been consolidated into M&M/Mars. The fortune grew steadily larger as the corporation routinely kept four brands in the top-ten-selling chocolates in the country: Milky Way, M&M's Plain and Peanut, and, in the number-one spot, Snickers.

1 tablespoon plus 2 tablespoons water
¼ cup light corn syrup
2 tablespoons butter
1 teaspoon vanilla extract
2 tablespoons peanut butter
Dash salt

3 cups powdered sugar
35 unwrapped Kraft caramels
1 cup (or two 3.5-ounce packages)
　dry-roasted unsalted peanuts
Two 12-ounce bags milk-chocolate
　chips

1. With the mixer on high speed, combine 1 tablespoon water, corn syrup, butter, vanilla, peanut butter, and salt until creamy. Slowly add the powdered sugar.

2. When the mixture has the consistency of dough, remove it from the bowl with your hands and press it into a lightly greased 9 × 9-inch pan. Set in the refrigerator.

3. Melt the caramels in a small pan with 2 tablespoons water over low heat.

4. When the caramel is soft, mix in the peanuts. Pour the mixture over the refrigerated nougat in the pan. Let this cool in the refrigerator.

5. When the refrigerated mixture is firm, melt the chocolate over low heat in a double boiler or in a microwave oven set on high for 2 minutes. Stir halfway through cooking time.

6. When the mixture in the pan has hardened, cut it into 4 × 1-inch sections.

7. Set each chunk onto a fork and dip into the melted chocolate. Tap the fork against the side of the bowl or pan to knock off any excess chocolate. Then place the chunks on waxed paper to cool at room temperature (less than 70°F). This could take several hours, but the bars will set best this way. You can speed up the process by placing the bars in the refrigerator for 30 minutes.

- MAKES ABOUT 2 DOZEN BARS

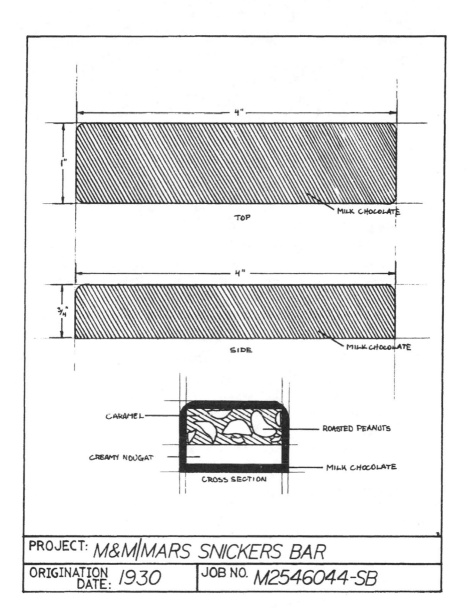

4"

1"

MILK CHOCOLATE

TOP

4"

3/4"

MILK CHOCOLATE

SIDE

CARAMEL

ROASTED PEANUTS

CREAMY NOUGAT

MILK CHOCOLATE

CROSS SECTION

PROJECT: M&M/MARS SNICKERS BAR

ORIGINATION DATE: 1930

JOB NO. M2546044-SB

M&M/MARS
3 MUSKETEERS

☆　♥　☎　✎　✈　✉　✂　☞　✿

Nougat is an important ingredient in the 3 Musketeers Bar, as well as in many other candy bars created by M&M/Mars. Nougat is made by mixing a hot sugar syrup with whipped egg whites until the solution cools and stiffens, creating a *frappe*. Other ingredients may be added to the nougat during this process to give it different flavors. In this recipe, you'll add chocolate chips to create a dark, chocolaty nougat.

But the 3 Musketeers Bar wasn't always filled with just a chocolate nougat. In fact, when the candy bar was created back in 1932, it was actually three pieces with three flavors: vanilla, strawberry, and chocolate. After World War II, the product was changed to a single chocolate bar because that was the favorite flavor, and customers wanted more of it. Thankfully they didn't decide to change the name to 1 Musketeer!

You'll need a heavy-duty electric mixer for this recipe.

3 cups granulated sugar
¾ cup light corn syrup
¾ cup water
⅛ teaspoon salt

3 egg whites
⅓ cup semisweet chocolate chips
Two 12-ounce bags milk chocolate
　chips

1.　In a large saucepan over medium heat, combine the sugar, corn syrup, water, and salt. Heat, stirring, to boiling, then continue to cook, using a candy thermometer to monitor the temperature.
2.　Beat the egg whites until they are stiff and form peaks. Don't use a plastic bowl for this.
3.　When the sugar solution comes to 270°F, or the *soft-crack stage*, remove from the heat and pour the mixture in thin streams into the egg whites, blending completely with a mixer set on low speed.

4. Continue to mix until the candy begins to harden to the consistency of dough. This may take as long as 20 minutes. At this point, add the semisweet chocolate chips. Remember that the candy *must* already be at the consistency of dough when you add the chocolate; the nougat will thicken no more after the chocolate is added.

5. When the chocolate is thoroughly blended and the nougat has thickened, press it into a greased 9 × 9-inch pan. Refrigerate until firm, about 30 minutes.

6. With a sharp knife, cut the candy in half down the middle of the pan. Then cut across into 7 segments to create a total of 14 bars.

7. Melt the milk chocolate chips in the microwave for 2 minutes on half power, stirring halfway through the heating time. Melt completely, but be careful not to overheat.

8. Resting a bar on a fork (and using your fingers if needed), dip each bar into the chocolate to coat completely and place on waxed paper. Cool till firm at room temperature, 1 to 2 hours.

• MAKES 14 CANDY BARS

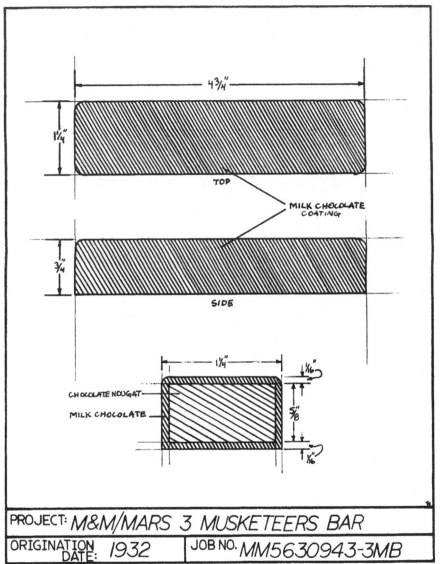

TOP

MILK CHOCOLATE
COATING

SIDE

CHOCOLATE NOUGAT

MILK CHOCOLATE

PROJECT: M&M/MARS 3 MUSKETEERS BAR

ORIGINATION DATE: 1932

JOB NO. MM5630943-3MB

McDONALD'S
BIG MAC

☆   ♥   ☎   ✎   ✈   ✉   ✂   ☛   ✿

Brothers Dick and Mac McDonald opened the first McDonald's drive-in restaurant in 1948, in San Bernardino, California. When the brothers began to order an increasing amount of restaurant equipment for their growing business, they aroused the curiosity of milkshake-machine salesman Ray Kroc. Kroc befriended the brothers and became a franchising agent for the company that same year, opening his first McDonald's in Des Plaines, Illinois. Kroc later founded the hugely successful McDonald's Corporation and perfected the fast-food system that came to be studied and duplicated by other chains over the years.

The first day Kroc's cash register rang up $366.12. Today the company racks up about $50 million a day in sales in more than 12,000 outlets worldwide, and for the past ten years a new store has opened somewhere around the world an average of every fifteen hours.

The double decker Big Mac was introduced in 1968, the brainchild of a local franchisee. It is now the world's most popular hamburger.

1 sesame-seed hamburger bun	1 teaspoon finely diced onion
Half of an additional hamburger bun	1/2 cup chopped lettuce
1/4 pound ground beef	1 slice American cheese
Dash salt	2 to 3 dill pickle slices
1 tablespoon Kraft Thousand Island dressing	

1.   With a serrated knife, cut the top off the extra bun half, leaving about a 3/4-inch-thick slice. This will be the middle bun in your sandwich.
2.   Place the three bun halves on a hot pan or griddle, face down, and toast them to a light brown. Set aside, but keep the pan hot.

3. Divide the ground beef in half and press into two thin patties slightly larger than bun.
4. Cook the patties in the hot pan over medium heat for 2 to 3 minutes on each side. Salt lightly.
5. Build the burger in the following stacking order from the bottom up:

bottom bun	remainder of dressing
half of dressing	remainder of onion
half of onion	remainder of lettuce
half of lettuce	pickle slices
American cheese	beef patty
beef patty	top bun
middle bun	

- MAKES 1 HAMBURGER

TIDBITS

To build a Big Mac Jr.® (it is sold on a "limited time only" basis), follow this stacking order from the bottom up:

bottom bun	½ teaspoon finely diced onion
beef patty	½ tablespoon Kraft
American cheese slice	Thousand Island dressing
2 pickle slices	top bun
¼ cup chopped lettuce	

Using real American cheese slices, not processed cheese food, will yield the best "taste-alike" results. Since the beef patties must be very thin, you may find it easier to cook them slightly frozen (like the real thing).

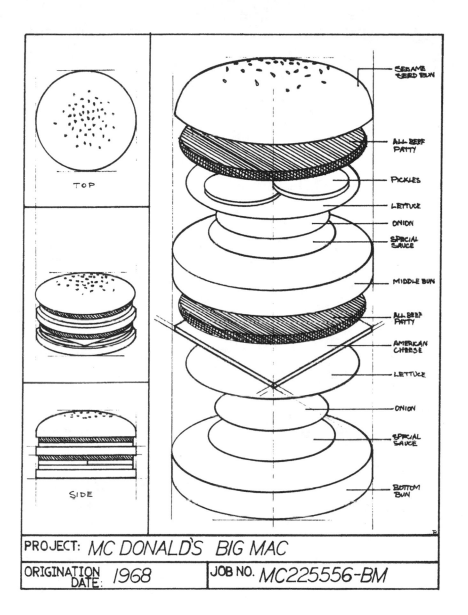

TOP

SIDE

SESAME SEED BUN

ALL BEEF PATTY

PICKLES

LETTUCE

ONION

SPECIAL SAUCE

MIDDLE BUN

ALL BEEF PATTY

AMERICAN CHEESE

LETTUCE

ONION

SPECIAL SAUCE

BOTTOM BUN

PROJECT: *MC DONALD'S BIG MAC*

ORIGINATION DATE: *1968*

JOB NO. *MC225556-BM*

McDONALD'S EGG McMUFFIN

☆   ♥   ☎   ✎   ✈   ⊠   ✂   ☛   ✿

In March 1988 the first McDonald's in Belgrade, Yugoslavia, set an all-time opening-day record by running 6,000 people under the arches. And in early 1990, when a Moscow McDonald's opened, it became the busiest in the world by serving more than 20,000 people in just the first month of operation. The McDonald's Rome franchise racks up annual sales of more than $11 million. And in August of 1992, the world's largest McDonald's opened in China. The Beijing McDonald's seats 700 people in 28,000 square feet. It has over 1,000 employees, and parking for 200 employee bicycles. McDonald's outlets dot the globe in fifty-two countries today, including Turkey, Thailand, Panama, El Salvador, Indonesia, and Poland. In fact, about 40 percent of the McDonald's that open today stand on foreign soil—that's more than 3,000 outlets.

Back in the United States, McDonald's serves one of every four breakfasts eaten out of the home. The Egg McMuffin sandwich was introduced in 1977 and has become a convenient breakfast-in-a-sandwich for millions. The name for the sandwich was not the brainstorm of a corporate think tank as you would expect, but rather a suggestion from ex-McDonald's chairman and CEO Fred Turner. He says his wife Patty came up with it.

You will need an empty clean can with the same diameter as an English muffin. (A 6½-ounce tuna can works best.)

1 English muffin	1 egg
1 slice Canadian bacon	1 slice American cheese

1. Split the English muffin and brown each face in a hot pan. Set aside. Keep the pan on medium heat.
2. In a frying pan of boiling water, cook the Canadian bacon for 10 minutes.

3.   Grease the inside of the can with shortening or coat with a non-stick spray.
4.   Place the greased can in the hot pan over medium heat and crack the egg into the center.
5.   Break the yolk. Lightly salt the egg.
6.   When the surface of the egg begins to firm, cut around the inside of the can with a butter knife to free the edges.
7.   Pull the can off the egg; turn the egg over and cook for 1 minute more.
8.   Build the sandwich in the following stacking order from the bottom up:

bottom English muffin	Canadian bacon
American cheese	top English muffin
egg	

9.   Microwave for 15 to 20 seconds on high for uniform heating, if desired.

- MAKES 1 SANDWICH

TIDBITS

For a closer clone, use real American cheese slices, not processed cheese food.

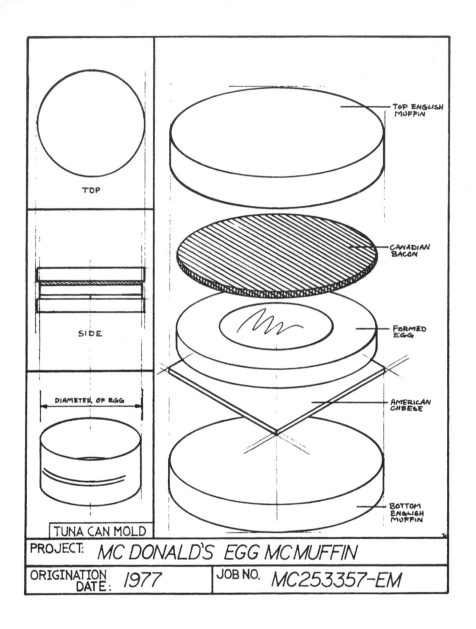

TOP

SIDE

DIAMETER OF EGG

TUNA CAN MOLD

TOP ENGLISH MUFFIN

CANADIAN BACON

FORMED EGG

AMERICAN CHEESE

BOTTOM ENGLISH MUFFIN

PROJECT: MC DONALD'S EGG MC MUFFIN

ORIGINATION DATE: 1977

JOB NO. MC253357-EM

McDONALD'S FILET-O-FISH

☆   ♥   ☎   ✎   ✈   ✉   ✂   ☛   ✿

The year 1963 was a big one in McDonald's history. The 500th McDonald's restaurant opened in Toledo, Ohio, and Hamburger University graduated its 500th student. It was in that same year that McDonald's served its one billionth hamburger in grand fashion on *The Art Linkletter Show*. Ronald McDonald also made his debut that year in Washington, D.C. (one of Willard Scott's earlier jobs—he hasn't changed much). And the Filet-O-Fish sandwich was introduced as the first new menu addition since the restaurant chain opened in 1948.

2 tablespoons mayonnaise
2 teaspoons sweet relish
2 teaspoons minced onion
Pinch salt

2 plain hamburger buns
2 Mrs. Paul's breaded fish portions
   (square)
1 slice American cheese

1. In a small bowl, mix together the mayonnaise, relish, minced onion, and salt and set aside. This is your tartar sauce.
2. Lightly grill the faces of the buns.
3. Cook the fish according to the package instructions. You can bake the fish, but your sandwich will taste much more like the original if you fry it in oil.
4. Divide the tartar sauce and spread it evenly on each of the top buns.
5. Slice the cheese in half and place a piece on each of the bottom buns.
6. Place the cooked fish on top of the cheese slice on each sandwich, and top off the sandwiches with the top buns.
7. Microwave each sandwich on high for 10 seconds.

- MAKES 2 SANDWICHES

If you can find fish only in wedge shapes, just use two wedges on each sandwich, fitting them together side by side to form a square.

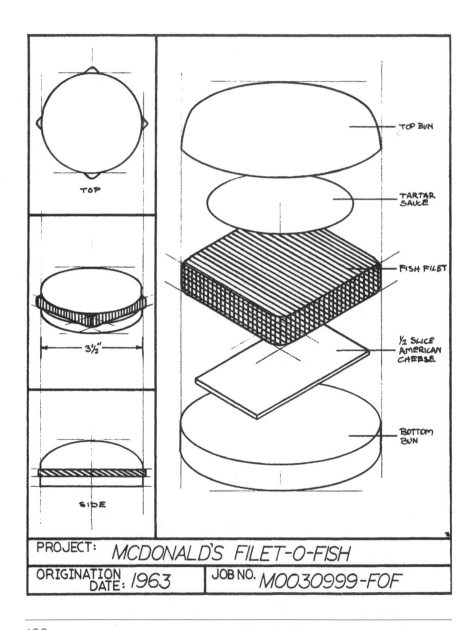

TOP

3½"

SIDE

TOP BUN

TARTAR SAUCE

FISH FILET

½ SLICE AMERICAN CHEESE

BOTTOM BUN

PROJECT: *MCDONALD'S FILET-O-FISH*

ORIGINATION DATE: *1963*

JOB NO. *M0030999-FOF*

McDONALD'S HAMBURGER

☆   ♥   ☎   ✎   ✈   ⊠   ✄   ☛   ✿

Yes, Ronald McDonald is truly an international hero and celebrity. In Japan, since the "R" sound is not part of the Japanese language, everyone knows the burger-peddling clown as "Donald McDonald." And in Hong Kong, where people place a high value on family relationships, he is called Uncle McDonald, or in their language, "McDonald Suk Suk."

These burgers were the original hallmark of the world's largest fast-food chain. In 1948, when brothers Dick and Mac McDonald opened their first drive-in restaurant in San Bernardino, California, it was this simple sandwich that had hundreds of people driving in from miles around to pick up a sackful for just 15 cents a burger.

⅛ pound ground beef
1 plain hamburger bun
Salt to taste
1 tablespoon catsup

½ teaspoon prepared mustard
½ teaspoon finely minced onion
1 dill pickle slice

1.   Roll the ground beef into a ball and then press flat on waxed paper until about ⅛ inch thick. You can also prepare the burger ahead of time and freeze it for easier cooking. The burger need not be defrosted before cooking.
2.   Brown the faces of the bun in a frying pan over medium heat.
3.   Remove the bun and cook the burger in the same pan for 2 minutes per side. Salt both sides during the cooking.
4.   On the top bun, spread the catsup, mustard, and onion, in that order, and top with the pickle slice.

5.   Put the beef patty on the bottom bun and slap the top and bottom together.
6.   Microwave the burger on high for 10 to 15 seconds.

   • MAKES 1 HAMBURGER

McDonald's Cheeseburger

Follow the recipe above, but add a slice of American cheese (not processed cheese food) on top of the beef patty in the final assembly. Microwave for 15 seconds on high to get that "just out from under the heat lamp" taste.

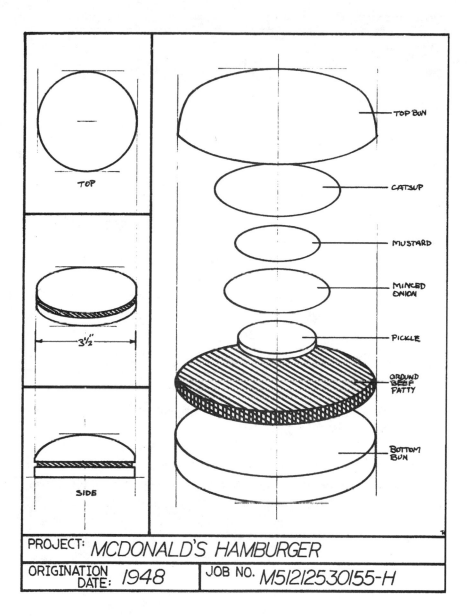

TOP

TOP BUN

CATSUP

MUSTARD

MINCED ONION

PICKLE

GROUND BEEF PATTY

BOTTOM BUN

3½"

SIDE

PROJECT: MCDONALD'S HAMBURGER

ORIGINATION DATE: 1948

JOB NO. M51212530155-H

McDONALD'S
McD.L.T.

☆ ♥ ☎ ✎ ✈ ✉ ✂ ☞ ✿

And how about this ...?

In 1963 the busiest clown in America, Ronald McDonald, made his debut in Washington, D.C. But beneath that red wig and 14½-inch shoes was someone who would later become the portly weatherman on NBC's "Today" show. You got it, Willard Scott.

Future Ronald McDonald wanna-bes get their training at McDonald's so-called college, just as many of the chain's managers and franchise owners do. It is a surprisingly busy institution. By 1991 the 40,000th student was granted a Hamburgerology Degree from McDonald's Hamburger University in Oak Brook, Illinois. (Hamburger University was set up to provide instruction for McDonald's personnel in the various aspects of their business—equipment, controls, human relations skills, and management skills.)

Nearly 3,000 students pass through the halls of the school each year as they continue to grow in their McDonald's careers. And the American Council on Education has approved eighteen of the university's courses for college credit.

One more chapter in the studies of H.U. graduates came in 1985, when the "hot side" and "cool side" of the McD.L.T. found their way onto McDonald's menu. It lives on only in this book, for five years after it was introduced, the McD.L.T. was dropped and replaced with the McLean Deluxe.

1 sesame-seed hamburger bun	1 tablespoon mayonnaise
⅛ teaspoon prepared mustard	1 slice American cheese
1 teaspoon catsup	2 tomato slices
2 medium onion rings, chopped	¼ pound ground beef
3 dill pickle slices	Dash salt
¼ cup chopped lettuce	

1. Lightly brown both halves of the hamburger bun, face down, in a hot pan. Set aside; keep the pan hot.
2. Build the "cool side" of the McD.L.T. in the following stacking order from the bottom up:

bottom bun	chopped lettuce
mustard	mayonnaise
catsup	American cheese slice
chopped onion	tomato slices
pickle slices	

3. With your hands, form the ground beef into a thin patty slightly larger in diameter than the bun.
4. Cook the patty in the hot pan for 2 to 3 minutes per side. Salt lightly.
5. Build the "hot side" in the following stacking order from the bottom up:

   top bun
   beef patty
6. When you are ready to eat, slap the "cool side" and the "hot side" together.

   • MAKES 1 HAMBURGER

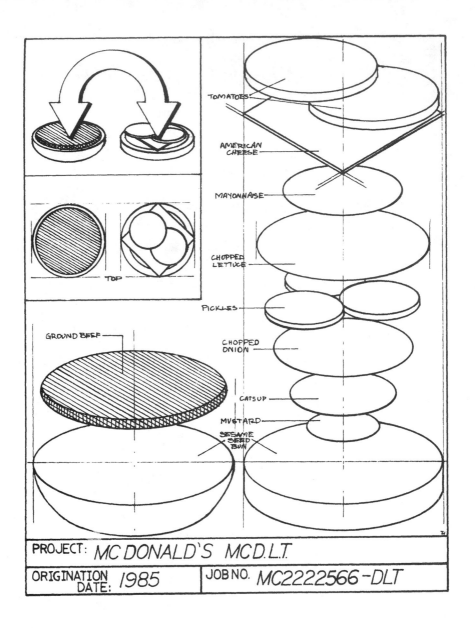

TOMATOES

AMERICAN CHEESE

MAYONNAISE

CHOPPED LETTUCE

PICKLES

CHOPPED ONION

CATSUP

MUSTARD

SESAME SEED BUN

GROUND BEEF

TOP

PROJECT: MC DONALD'S MCD.L.T.

ORIGINATION DATE: 1985

JOB NO. MC2222566-DLT

McDONALD'S QUARTER POUNDER (WITH CHEESE)

☆ ♥ ☎ ✎ ✈ ⊠ ✂ ☛ ✿

What is McDonald's sign referring to when it says "Over 100 billion served"? That's not the number of customers served, but actually the number of beef patties sold since McDonald's first opened its doors in the forties. A hamburger counts as one patty. A Big Mac counts as two.

McDonald's sold its 11 billionth hamburger in 1972, the same year that this sandwich, the Quarter Pounder, was added to the growing menu. That was also the year large fries were added and founder Ray Kroc was honored with the Horatio Alger Award (the two events were not related). In 1972, the 2,000th McDonald's opened its doors, and by the end of that year McDonald's had finally become a billion-dollar corporation.

1 sesame-seed bun	½ teaspoon prepared mustard
¼ pound ground beef	1 teaspoon chopped onion
Salt to taste	2 dill pickle slices
1 tablespoon catsup	2 slices American cheese

1. Brown the faces of the bun in a large frying pan over medium heat.
2. Roll the ground beef into a ball and then flatten on waxed paper until about ¼ inch thick.
3. Cook the burger for 3 to 4 minutes per side. Salt each side during the cooking.
4. Spread catsup and then the mustard on the top bun; then add the onion and pickle.
5. Place 1 slice of cheese on the bottom bun, then the beef patty, then the other slice of cheese.

6. Top off the sandwich with the top bun.
7. Microwave on high for 15 seconds.

- MAKES 1 BURGER

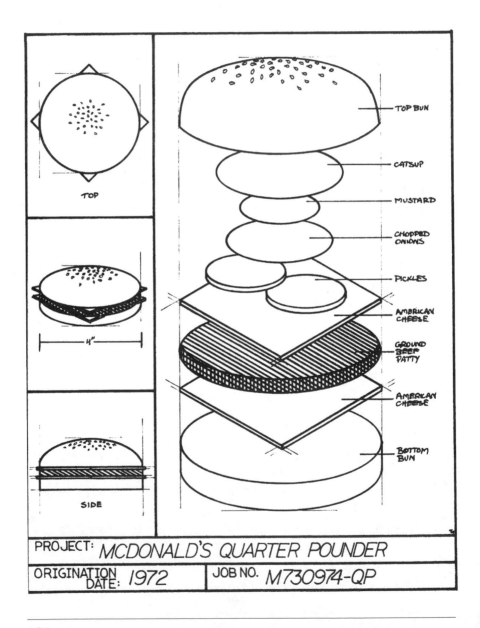

TOP

SIDE

PROJECT: MCDONALD'S QUARTER POUNDER

ORIGINATION DATE: 1972   JOB NO. M730974-QP

MRS. FIELDS CHOCOLATE CHIP COOKIES

☆　♥　☎　✎　✈　✉　✂　☛　✿

In 1975 eighteen-year-old Debbi Sivyer perfected the chocolate chip cookies she had been making since the age of twelve. Little did she know then that her delicious cookies would soon launch her into a successful career with her own multi-million-dollar business. It happened two years later, when her new husband, financial consultant Randy Fields, noticed that his clients couldn't resist the batches of cookies that Debbi sent to work with him. With the help of Randy and a banker who lent her $50,000 because he loved her chocolate chip cookies so much, she opened her first cookie store in Palo Alto, California, in 1977. The second store opened two years later in San Francisco.

Without spending a dollar on advertising, the Mrs. Fields Company is now listed on the London Stock Exchange, claims more than 600 stores worldwide, and has purchased the 113-unit bakery chain, La Petite Boulangerie, from PepsiCo.

1 cup (2 sticks) softened butter	¾ teaspoon salt
½ cup granulated sugar	1 teaspoon baking powder
1½ cups packed brown sugar	1 teaspoon baking soda
2 eggs	1½ twelve-ounce bags semisweet
2½ teaspoons vanilla extract	chocolate chips
2½ cups all-purpose flour	

1.　Preheat the oven to 350°F.
2.　In a large mixing bowl, cream the butter, sugars, eggs, and vanilla.
3.　Mix together the flour, salt, baking powder, and baking soda.
4.　Combine the wet and dry ingredients.

5. Stir in the chocolate chips.
6. With your fingers, place golf-ball-size dough portions 2 inches apart on an ungreased cookie sheet.
7. Bake for 9 minutes, or until edges are light brown.

- MAKES 30 COOKIES

TIDBITS

It's very important that you not exceed the cooking time given above, even if the cookies appear to be underbaked. When the cookies are removed from the oven, the sugar in them will stay hot and continue the cooking process. The finished product should be soft in the middle and crunchy around the edges.

For variations of this cookie, substitute milk chocolate for the semisweet chocolate and/or add 1½ cups of chopped walnuts or macadamia nuts to the recipe before baking. Although you can substitute margarine for butter in this recipe, you will have the best results from butter. The cookie will have a richer taste and will be crispier around the edges like the original.

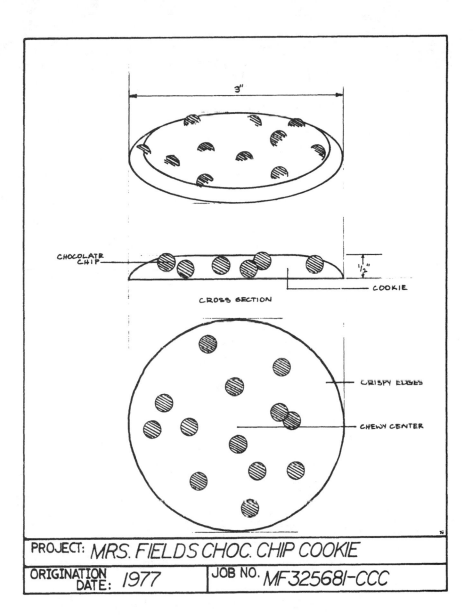

3"

CHOCOLATE CHIP

CROSS SECTION

½"

COOKIE

CRISPY EDGES

CHEWY CENTER

PROJECT: MRS. FIELDS CHOC. CHIP COOKIE

ORIGINATION DATE: 1977

JOB NO. MF325681-CCC

MRS. FIELDS PEANUT BUTTER DREAM BARS

☆ ♥ ☎ ✎ ✈ ✉ ✂ ☞ ✿

In 1987 the Mrs. Fields Corporation devised a rather clever treat called the Peanut Butter Dream Bar—a delicious combination of peanut butter, chocolate, and a cookie-crumb crust. It was not only a tasty product but an economical one. Mrs. Fields has always had the policy of removing cookies that are more than two hours old from outlet display cases. Now, instead of being thrown away, the cookies are crumbled up and mixed with melted butter to form the Dream Bar Crust.

8 Mrs. Fields Chocolate Chip Cookies
    (see previous recipe)
5 tablespoons melted butter
¾ cup peanut butter

1 ½ cups powdered sugar
One 12-ounce bag milk-chocolate
    chips

1. Preheat the oven to 350°F.
2. Crumble the cookies into a medium mixing bowl.
3. Add the melted butter; stir until the mixture darkens and the butter is evenly mixed in.
4. Pour the mixture into an ungreased 9 × 9-inch baking pan.
5. Press the dough down solidly into the pan and bake for 10 minutes, or until firm around edges. When done, cool in the refrigerator.
6. Mix the peanut butter and sugar until blended. The mixture should have a doughy texture that allows you to knead it with your hands.
7. Melt the chocolate chips in a double boiler over low heat, stir-

ring often. You may also melt them in a microwave oven set on high for 2 minutes, stirring halfway through the heating time.

8. When the dough is cool, spread half of the melted chocolate over the surface.
9. Cool in the refrigerator for 20 to 30 minutes, or until hardened.
10. Spread the peanut butter mixture evenly over the surface of the chocolate.
11. Spread the remaining chocolate over the peanut butter, covering to the edges of the pan.
12. Cool the finished product in the refrigerator or let it sit at room temperature until hardened.
13. Slice into five even rows and then once down the middle.

- MAKES 10 BARS

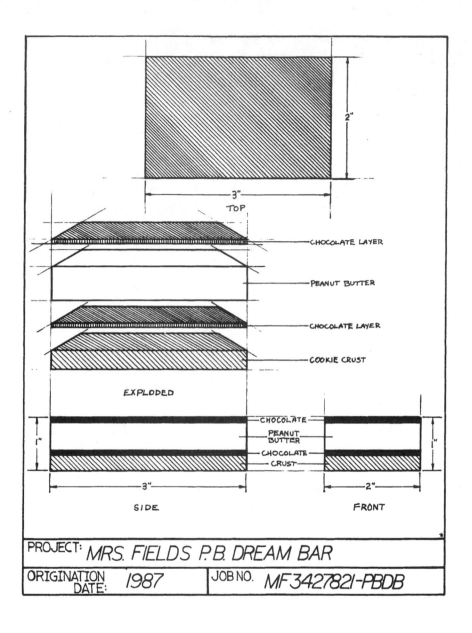

TOP

2"

3"

CHOCOLATE LAYER

PEANUT BUTTER

CHOCOLATE LAYER

COOKIE CRUST

EXPLODED

CHOCOLATE
PEANUT BUTTER
CHOCOLATE
CRUST

1"

3"

SIDE

2"

1"

FRONT

PROJECT: MRS. FIELDS P.B. DREAM BAR

ORIGINATION DATE: 1987

JOB NO. MF3427821-PBDB

NABISCO CHIPS AHOY!

☆ ♥ ☎ ✎ ✈ ✉ ✂ ☛ ✿

As you bake these cookies, imagine producing a quarter of a million cookies and crackers every minute. That's what Nabisco does—which is why the conglomerate is the largest manufacturer of cookies and crackers in the world. Chips Ahoy! Chocolate Chip Cookies were developed in 1964, along with Chicken In A Biscuit Crackers and Mister Salty Pretzels. But Chips Ahoy! became the big winner for the company. Today it's the world's top-selling chocolate-chip cookie, with more than 6 billion sold every year.

1 ½ cups vegetable shortening
1 cup packed light brown sugar
1 cup granulated sugar
2 teaspoons salt
1 ½ teaspoons vanilla extract

1 teaspoon baking soda
4 cups all-purpose flour
¼ cup water
One 12-ounce bag mini semi-sweet
    chocolate chips

1. Preheat the oven to 325°F.
2. In a large mixing bowl, combine the shortening and sugars and blend with an electric mixer until smooth.
3. Add the salt, vanilla, and baking soda.
4. While beating at low speed, slowly add the flour. Then add the water. Mix thoroughly, adding more water as necessary to make the dough stick together. Stir in the chocolate chips. Add extra water to dough if needed to make it stick together.
5. Form the cookies by breaking off bits of dough and patting them out with your fingers into 2-inch rounds about ⅛ inch thick.
6. Place the cookies on ungreased cookie sheets and bake for 12 to 18 minutes, or until golden brown on the top and around the edges.

- MAKES ABOUT 3 DOZEN COOKIES

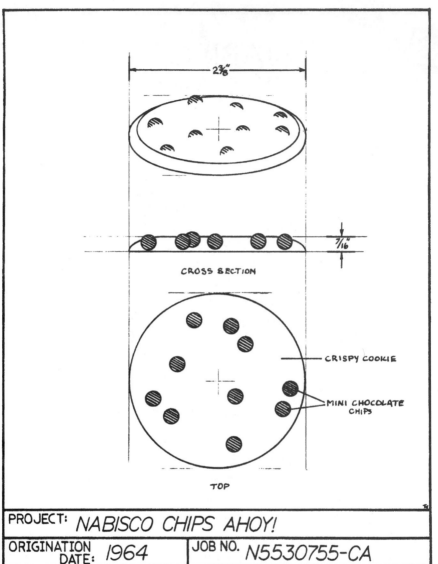

2⅜"

7/16"

CROSS SECTION

CRISPY COOKIE

MINI CHOCOLATE CHIPS

TOP

PROJECT: *NABISCO CHIPS AHOY!*

ORIGINATION DATE: *1964*   JOB NO. *N5530755-CA*

NABISCO NUTTER BUTTER

☆ ♥ ☎ ✎ ✈ ✉ ✄ ☛ ✿

Formerly called the National Biscuit Company, Nabisco was formed in the late 1800s by several bakeries that joined together to meet a growing demand. In the 1870s Nabisco's forefathers had introduced the first individually packaged baked goods. Before this, cookies and crackers had been sold from open barrels or biscuit boxes. The company has become the world's largest manufacturer of cookies and crackers, selling some 42 million packages of Nabisco products each day to retail outlets on every continent.

Nutter Butter Cookies were introduced in 1969 and have quickly taken their place alongside Nabisco's most popular products, including Oreos, Chips Ahoy!, and Fig Newtons.

COOKIES

½ cup vegetable shortening
⅔ cup granulated sugar
1 egg
½ teaspoon salt

3 tablespoons peanut butter
½ cup old-fashioned Quaker oats
1 cup all-purpose flour

FILLING

½ cup peanut butter
¾ cup powdered sugar

1 tablespoon fine graham cracker
    crumbs

1. Preheat the oven to 325°F.
2. In a large bowl, cream together the shortening and sugar with an electric mixer.
3. Add the egg, salt, and peanut butter and beat until well blended.
4. Put the oats in a blender and blend on medium speed until they are almost as finely ground as flour.

5. Add the oats and flour to the mixture and blend well.

6. Pinch out small portions of dough and roll into 1-inch balls in the palm of your hand. Press these flat on ungreased cookie sheets so that they form 2-inch circles. If you're a stickler for a cookie that looks just like the original, you can form the dough into flat peanut shapes similar to those illustrated.

7. Bake for 8 to 10 minutes, or until light brown around the edges.

8. While the cookies bake, combine the filling ingredients in a small bowl.

9. When the cookies are cool, use a butter knife to spread a thin layer of filling on the flat side of a cookie and press another on top. Repeat.

- MAKES 2 DOZEN COOKIES

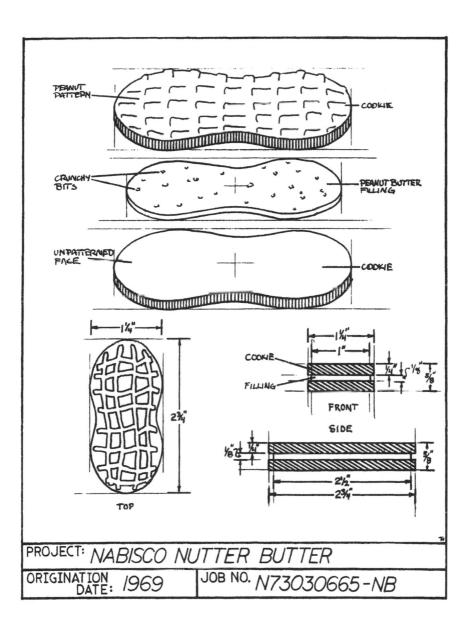

PEANUT PATTERN

COOKIE

CRUNCHY BITS

PEANUT BUTTER FILLING

UNPATTERNED FACE

COOKIE

1¼"

2¾"

TOP

COOKIE

FILLING

1¼"

1"

¼" ⅛" ⅝"

FRONT

SIDE

⅛" ¼" ⅝"

2½"

2¾"

PROJECT: *NABISCO NUTTER BUTTER*

ORIGINATION DATE: *1969*

JOB NO. *N73030665-NB*

NABISCO OREO COOKIE

☆　♥　☎　✎　✈　✉　✂　☛　✿

At one time Nabisco actually conducted a study that determined that 50 percent of Oreo consumers twist the cookie apart before eating it. I guess this is important information, since it concerns the world's top-selling cookie. Historians at Nabisco aren't sure who came up with the idea for this sandwich cookie back in 1912, but they do know that it was introduced along with two other cookie creations that have long since died. The name may have come from the Greek word for mountain, *oreo,* which would once have made sense because the first test version was hill-shaped. When the Oreo was first sold to the public, it was much larger than today's cookie, but it kept shrinking over the years until Nabisco realized it had become much too small and had to enlarge it again to today's current 1¾-inch diameter.

In 1975, Nabisco figured we couldn't have too much of a good thing, so the company gave us Double Stuf Oreos, with twice the filling. A smart move. Today Double Stuf holds its own rank as the fifth most popular cookie in America.

COOKIE

One 18.25-ounce package Betty
    Crocker chocolate fudge cake mix
3 tablespoons shortening, melted
½ cup cake flour, measured
    then sifted

1 egg
3 tablespoons water
2 tablespoons brown-paste food
    coloring (optional)*

FILLING

3¾ cup powdered sugar
⅓ tablespoon granulated sugar
½ teaspoon vanilla extract

½ cup shortening
2 tablespoons hot water

1. Combine the cookie ingredients in a large bowl. Add the water a little bit at a time until the dough forms. Cover and chill for 2 hours.
2. Preheat the oven to 350°F.
3. On a lightly floured surface, roll out a portion of the dough to just under 1/16th of an inch thick. To cut, use a lid from a spice container with a 1 1/2-inch diameter (Schilling brand is good). Arrange the cut dough rounds on a cookie sheet that is sprayed with a light coating of nonstick spray. Bake for 10 minutes. Remove wafers from the oven and cool completely.
4. As the cookies cool, combine the filling ingredients well with an electric mixer.
5. With your hands form the filling into balls about 1/2 to 3/4 inch in diameter.
6. Place a filling ball in the center of the flat side of a cooled cookie and press with another cookie, flat side down, until the filling spreads to the edge. Repeat with the remaining cookies.

- MAKES 60 COOKIES

TIDBITS

If the cookie dough seems too tacky, you can work in as much as 1/4 cup of flour as you pat out and roll the dough. Use just enough flour to make the dough workable, but not tough.

This may be obvious to you, but you can expand your own homemade line of Oreos by creating your own versions of Double Stuf® or the giant Oreos called Oreo Big Stuf®. Just add twice the filling for Double Stuf, or make the cookie twice the size for Big Stuf. Go crazy. Try Triple Stuf or Quadruple Stuf or Quintuple Stuf ... somebody stop me.

---

*This is an optional step to help re-create the color of the original cookie. If you do not use the paste food coloring be sure to change the amount of water added to the wafer cookies from 3 tablespoons to 1/4 cup. The food coloring gives the cookies the dark brown, almost black color. The coloring can be found with cake decorating supplies at art supply and craft stores.

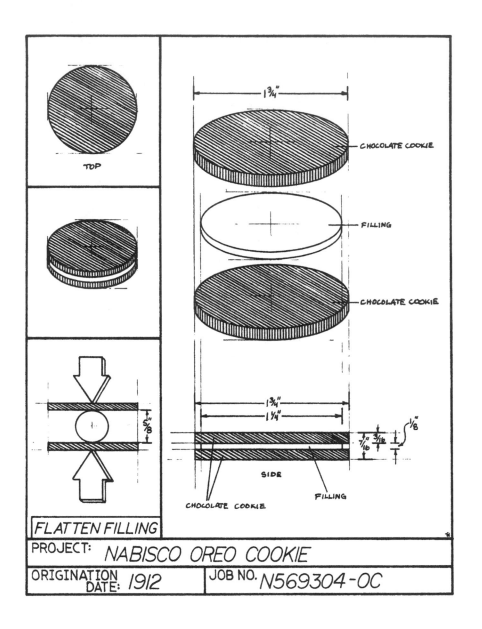

TOP

SIDE

CHOCOLATE COOKIE

FILLING

CHOCOLATE COOKIE

CHOCOLATE COOKIE

FILLING

FLATTEN FILLING

PROJECT: NABISCO OREO COOKIE

ORIGINATION DATE: 1912

JOB NO. N569304-OC

NESTLÉ CRUNCH

☆　♥　☎　✎　✈　✉　✂　☞　✿

In 1867, infant mortality rates in Vevey, Switzerland, had been climbing and Henri Nestlé was working hard on a concoction of concentrated milk, sugar, and cereal for babies who were refusing their mother's milk. Eventually he discovered a formula that helped infants to stay strong and healthy. He called his new product Farine Lactée and merged with two American brothers, Charles and George Page, who had come to Switzerland to capitalize on Swiss canned milk technology. Their new company was called Nestlé & Anglo-Swiss Condensed Milk Company, and quickly expanded into fifteen other countries. Seven years later, Nestlé sold the company to three local businessmen for one million francs.

The new company kept the Nestlé name and started selling chocolate in 1904. In 1929, the company acquired Cailler, the first company to mass-produce chocolate bars, and Swiss General, the company credited with inventing milk chocolate. This company was the core of the chocolate business as we know it today. The Nestlé Crunch bar was introduced in 1928 and is now the company's top-selling candy bar.

Two 12-ounce bags milk chocolate　　　1 ½ cups Rice Krispies
　chips (Nestlé is best)

1.　Melt the chocolate chips in a microwave-safe bowl in a microwave set on medium for 2 minutes. Stir halfway through the heating time. Melt thoroughly, but be careful not to overheat.
2.　Gently mix the Rice Krispies into the chocolate and pour into a greased 9 × 12-inch pan.
3.　Slam the pan on the counter or floor to level the chocolate.
4.　Refrigerate until firm, about 30 minutes.

5. Cut the candy in half widthwise and then cut it twice lengthwise, making 6 bars.

    • MAKES 6 KING-SIZE BARS

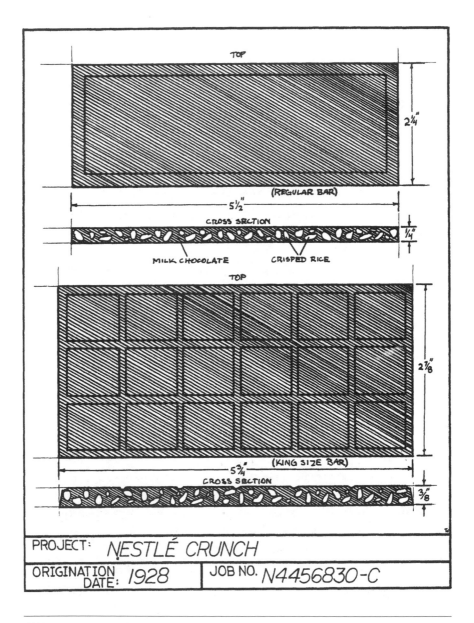

NESTLÉ
100 GRAND BAR

☆　♥　☎　✎　✈　✉　✂　☛　✿

Nestlé is the world's largest packaged food manufacturer, coffee roaster, and chocolate maker. It is the largest single company in Switzerland today, but Nestlé derives only 2 percent of its revenue from its home country.

The company is quite diverse. Nestlé's product lines include beverages and drinks, chocolate and candy, dairy products, and frozen foods. The company also operates more than thirty Stouffer Hotels and owns 25 percent of the French cosmetics giant L'Oréal. In the United States, where the company is called Nestlé USA, it ranks third behind Mars, Inc., and Hershey USA in chocolate sales.

This candy bar was introduced in 1966 as the $100,000 Bar, then its name was changed to 100 Grand Bar in 1985.

30 unwrapped Kraft caramels, at room temperature
One 12-ounce bag milk chocolate chips

¾ cup Rice Krispies

1. With your fingers, flatten each caramel into a rectangle about ¼ inch thick.
2. Melt the chocolate chips in a microwave-safe bowl in a microwave set on half power for 2 minutes. Stir halfway through the heating time. Melt thoroughly, but do not overheat.
3. Add the Rice Krispies and stir just until blended.
4. Dip each caramel into the chocolate to coat completely and then place on waxed paper. Cool until firm at room temperature, 1 to 2 hours.

• MAKES 30 CANDY BARS

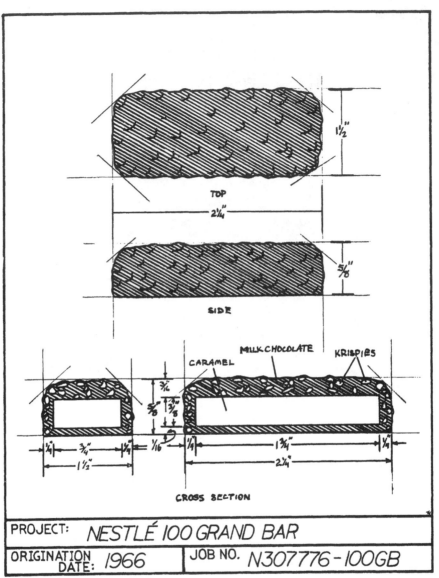

TOP

1½"

2¼"

SIDE

5/8"

CARAMEL MILK CHOCOLATE KRISPIES

CROSS SECTION

PROJECT:	*NESTLÉ 100 GRAND BAR*
ORIGINATION DATE: *1966*	JOB NO. *N307776-100GB*

ORANGE JULIUS

☆　♥　☎　✎　✈　✉　✂　☛　❀

In 1926 a man named Julius Freed opened a fresh-orange-juice shop in downtown Los Angeles, initially ringing up sales of $20 a day. The real estate agent who helped locate his first store just so happened to be an ex-chemist named Bill Hamlin. The two became good friends. One day Hamlin, drawing on his chemistry background, presented Freed with an idea for a compound, using all natural ingredients, that would give his orange juice a creamy, frothy texture. When the two began selling the new drink, response was so tremendous that sales skyrocketed to $100 a day. An increasing number of customers would come by the store saying, "Give me an orange, Julius," and so the name was born. By 1929 the chain had opened 100 stores across the United States.

In 1987 International Dairy Queen bought the Orange Julius chain, and today you'll find more than 500 Orange Julius outlets nationwide serving the drink in a variety of natural flavors, including strawberry and pineapple.

I cup orange juice
I cup water
2 egg whites

¾ teaspoon vanilla extract
¼ cup granulated sugar
I heaping cup ice

Combine all of the ingredients in a blender set on high speed for 15 to 30 seconds.

Strawberry Julius and Pineapple Julius

1 cup frozen sliced strawberries,
    thawed, or one 8-ounce can
    crushed pineapple in juice
1 cup water

2 egg whites
¾ teaspoon vanilla extract
¼ cup granulated sugar
1 heaping cup crushed ice

Combine all the ingredients in a blender set on high speed for exactly 1 minute.

• MAKES 2 DRINKS

TIDBITS

For the Strawberry Julius, sweetened sliced strawberries work best. They can often be found in 16-ounce boxes in the frozen-food section of the supermarket. Make sure to thaw them first.

If you don't like the idea of raw egg whites, you can substitute ¼ cup whole milk, but the flavor and texture will no longer match exactly.

PANCAKES FROM INTERNATIONAL HOUSE OF PANCAKES

☆　♥　☎　✎　✈　✉　✀　☛　✿

Al Lupin opened the first International House of Pancakes in Toluca Lake, California, in 1958. Now, more than thirty years later, the company has added 490 restaurants, which together serve more than 400,000 pancakes on an average day. That's enough pancakes to make a stack 8,000 feet tall! For comparison, the huge stack of flapjacks would dwarf Chicago's Sears Tower, the world's tallest building, which rises a mere 1,454 feet.

Nonstick spray
1 1/4 cups all-purpose flour
1 egg
1 1/2 cups buttermilk
1/4 cup granulated sugar

1 heaping teaspoon baking powder
1 teaspoon baking soda
1/4 cup cooking oil
1/4 teaspoon salt

1.　Preheat a skillet over medium heat. Use a pan with a nonstick surface or apply a little nonstick spray.
2.　In a blender or with a mixer, combine all of the remaining ingredients until smooth.
3.　Pour the batter by spoonfuls into the hot pan, forming 5-inch circles.
4.　When the edges appear to harden, flip the pancakes. They should be light brown.
5.　Cook on the other side for same amount of time, until light brown.

• MAKES 8 TO 10 PANCAKES

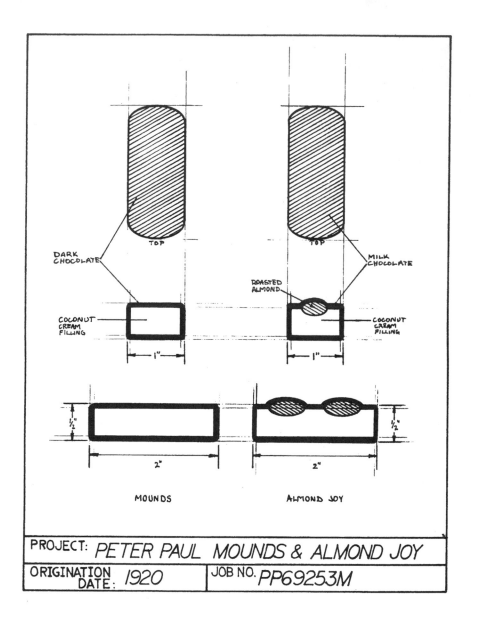

DARK CHOCOLATE

MILK CHOCOLATE

ROASTED ALMOND

TOP

TOP

COCONUT CREAM FILLING

COCONUT CREAM FILLING

1"

1"

½"

½"

2"

2"

MOUNDS

ALMOND JOY

PROJECT: *PETER PAUL MOUNDS & ALMOND JOY*

ORIGINATION DATE: *1920*

JOB NO. *PP69253M*

PETER PAUL
MOUNDS AND
ALMOND JOY

☆   ♥   ☎   ✎   ✈   ✉   ✂   ☛   ✿

At the train station in Naugatuck, Connecticut, candy and ice cream shop owner Peter Paul Halajian used to meet the commuter trains carrying baskets full of fresh hand-made chocolates. The most popular of his candies was a blend of coconut, fruits, nuts, and chocolate that he called *Konabar*.

In 1919, when demand for his confections grew, Halajian and five associates, all of Armenian heritage, opened a business in New Haven to produce and sell his chocolates on a larger scale. Because there were no refrigerators, they made the chocolate by hand at night, when the air was the coolest, and sold the candy during the day. In 1920 the first Mounds bar was introduced.

Peter Paul merged with Cadbury U.S.A. in 1978, and in 1986 Cadbury U.S.A. merged with the Hershey Foods Corporation, now the world's largest candy conglomerate.

Today the recipes for Mounds and Almond Joy are the same as they were in the roaring twenties.

5 ounces Eagle sweetened
   condensed milk
1 teaspoon vanilla extract
2 cups powdered sugar

14 ounces premium shredded or
   flaked coconut
One 24-ounce package semisweet
   chocolate chips

1.   Blend the condensed milk and vanilla.
2.   Add the powdered sugar to the above mixture a little bit at a time, stirring until smooth.
3.   Stir in the coconut. The mixture should be firm.

4. Pat the mixture firmly into a greased 9 × 13 × 2-inch pan. Chill in the refrigerator until firm.
5. In a double boiler over hot (not boiling) water, melt the chocolate, stirring often. You may also use a microwave oven. Place the chips in a bowl and heat for 1 minute on high; stir, then heat for 1 minute more.
6. Remove the coconut mixture from the refrigerator and cut it into 1 × 2-inch bars.
7. Set each coconut bar onto a fork and dip into the chocolate. Tap the fork against the side of the pan or bowl to remove any excess chocolate.
8. Air-dry at room temperature on waxed paper. This could take several hours, but chocolate sets best at cool room temperature (below 70°F). You may speed up the process by placing the bars in the refrigerator for about 30 minutes.

• MAKES ABOUT 3 DOZEN BARS

Peter Paul Almond Joy
And if you feel like a nut, follow the above recipe with these changes:

1. Add 1 cup dry-roasted almonds to the list of ingredients.
2. Substitute milk-chocolate chips for semisweet chocolate.
3. In step 7, place two almonds atop each bar before dipping.

POGEN'S GINGERSNAPS

☆ ♥ ☎ ✎ ✈ ✉ ✂ ☞ ✿

Back in the 1870s, in the coastal city of Malmö, Sweden, a man named Anders Pahlsson baked the first of his soon-to-be famous gingersnaps in a bakery he named Pogen's. In 1970 Pogen's, Inc., opened in the United States, expanding the line of baked goods that Pahlsson developed in the nineteenth century.

A legend that dates back many years says that if you place a gingersnap in the palm of your hand, press down in the middle, and it breaks into three pieces, good luck will follow. Today, more than 100 years later, good luck and hard work have made Pogen's the third-largest supplier of cookies to the growing vending business.

1/4 cup (1/2 stick) butter
1/2 cup vegetable shortening
1 cup packed brown sugar
1/4 cup molasses
1 egg
2 1/4 cups sifted all-purpose flour

2 teaspoons baking soda
1/2 teaspoon salt
1 teaspoon powdered ginger
2 teaspoons ground cinnamon
1/2 teaspoon ground cloves

1. Preheat the oven to 350°F.
2. Cream the butter, shortening, brown sugar, molasses, and egg until light and fluffy.
3. Sift together the dry ingredients; combine both mixtures.
4. Form the dough into walnut-size balls. With floured fingers, press the balls into flat circles on an ungreased cookie sheet.
5. Bake for 8 minutes, or until golden brown.
6. Remove the gingersnaps from the cookie sheet as soon as they are cool and seal in a covered container to preserve their crunch.

• MAKES 4 DOZEN

If you follow the above recipe, you will be making gingersnaps in a simple circular form. However, Pogen's gingersnaps are made in a smattering of animal shapes. If you would like a more accurate clone of the Pogen's variety, simply sprinkle the dough with flour and roll it flat. Then use animal-shaped cookie cutters to form the dough before baking.

POPEYE'S FAMOUS FRIED CHICKEN

☆　♥　☎　✎　✈　✉　✂　☞　✿

Popeye's Famous Fried Chicken & Biscuits has become the third largest quick-service chicken chain in the world in the twenty-two years since its first store opened in New Orleans in 1972. (KFC has the number-one slot, followed by Church's Chicken.) Since then, the chain has grown to 813 units, with many of them overseas in Germany, Japan, Jamaica, Honduras, Guam, and Korea.

I picked this recipe because the chicken has a unique Cajun-style spiciness. See what you think.

6 cups vegetable oil
⅔ cup all-purpose flour
1 tablespoon salt
2 tablespoons white pepper

1 teaspoon cayenne pepper
2 teaspoons paprika
3 eggs
1 frying chicken with skin, cut up

1. Heat the oil over medium heat in a deep frying or in a wide, deep pan on the stove.
2. In a large, shallow bowl, combine the flour, salt, peppers, and paprika.
3. Break the eggs into a separate shallow bowl and beat until blended.
4. Check the oil by dropping in a pinch of the flour mixture. If the oil bubbles rapidly around the flour, it is ready.
5. Dip each piece of chicken into the eggs, then coat generously with the flour mixture. Drop each piece into the hot oil and fry for 15 to 25 minutes, or until it is a dark golden brown.
6. Remove the chicken to paper towels or a rack to drain.

- MAKES 8 PIECES

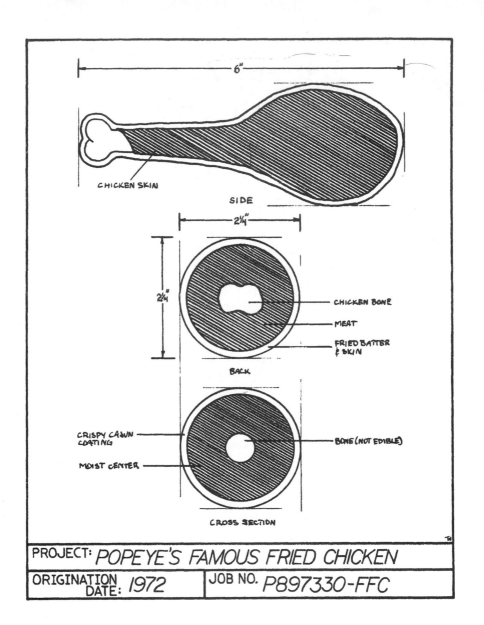

6"

CHICKEN SKIN

SIDE

2¼"

2¼"

CHICKEN BONE

MEAT

FRIED BATTER & SKIN

BACK

CRISPY CAJUN COATING

BONE (NOT EDIBLE)

MOIST CENTER

CROSS SECTION

PROJECT: *POPEYE'S FAMOUS FRIED CHICKEN*

ORIGINATION DATE: *1972*

JOB NO. *P897330-FFC*

POPEYE'S RED BEANS AND RICE

☆ ♥ ☎ ✎ ✈ ✉ ✄ ☞ ✿

If there isn't a Popeye's Famous Chicken & Biscuits outlet near you, there probably will be sometime soon. Popeye's now has restaurants in thirty-eight states and is growing impressively. With a name like Popeye's, you would expect something with spinach in it, but instead you'll find a selection of Cajun-spiced fare including this tasty combination of white rice and red beans. I know many people who go to Popeye's just for a sixteen-ounce cup of Red Beans and Rice, and I've now become one of them.

BEANS

One 30-ounce can or two 15-ounce cans small red beans
1½ teaspoons white pepper
¼ teaspoon paprika

4 tablespoons (½ stick) butter
¼ teaspoon garlic powder
¼ teaspoon salt

RICE

1½ cups quick-cooking white rice (Minute Rice or Uncle Ben's)
1½ cups water

2 tablespoons (¼ stick) butter
½ teaspoon garlic salt

1. Pour the beans with their liquid into a large saucepan. Turn the heat to medium.
2. Add the pepper, paprika, butter, garlic powder, and salt.
3. When the beans begin to boil, use a fork to mash some of them against the side of the pan. Stir the mixture constantly. In about

20 minutes, the beans will reach the consistency of refried beans (in other words, they will have a smooth, creamy texture with some whole beans still swimming around).

4. Prepare the rice, using the 2 tablespoons butter and ½ teaspoon garlic salt instead of the butter and salt amounts specified on the box for 4 servings.

5. To serve, pour ½ cup of beans into a bowl and scoop the same amount of rice on top of the beans.

• SERVES 4

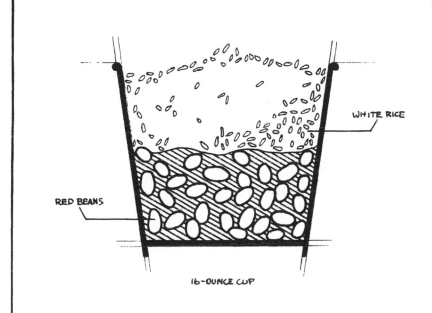

WHITE RICE

RED BEANS

16-OUNCE CUP

PROJECT:	*POPEYE'S RED BEANS & RICE -LARGE-*	
ORIGINATION DATE: *1972*	JOB NO. *P578307-RBR*	

REESE'S PEANUT BUTTER CUPS

In south central Pennsylvania, in 1917, a thirty-eight-year-old man named H. B. Reese moved to Hershey, Pennsylvania, to operate one of Milton Hershey's dairy farms. Inspired by Hershey's success, and possibly urged on by his growing family (he was to have six sons and seven daughters), Reese soon left the dairy to make his living in the candy business. Then in 1923, after achieving a small success with a few products, Reese produced a candy consisting of specially processed peanut butter covered with Hershey's milk chocolate. It changed a struggling candy plant into a solid business concern. During World War II conditions prompted Reese to discontinue his other products and focus on the peanut butter cup. He thereby developed something unique in America's food industry—a major company built and thriving on one product.

In 1963 the names Hershey and Reese were linked once again when the Hershey Foods Corporation purchased the successful H. B. Reese Candy Company. Today the Reese's Peanut Butter Cup often tops the list of America's best-selling candies.

You will need a muffin tin with shallow cups.

1 cup peanut butter	One 12-ounce package Hershey's
¼ teaspoon salt	milk-chocolate chips
½ cup powdered sugar	

1. In a small bowl, mix the peanut butter, salt, and powdered sugar until firm.
2. Slowly melt the chocolate chips in a double boiler over hot, not

boiling, water. You may also melt them in a microwave oven set on high for 2 minutes, stirring halfway through the heating time.

3. Grease the muffin-tin cups and spoon some chocolate into each cup, filling halfway.

4. With a spoon, draw the chocolate up the edges of each cup until all sides are coated. Cool in the refrigerator until firm.

5. Spread about a teaspoon of peanut butter onto the chocolate in each cup, leaving room for the final chocolate layer.

6. Pour some chocolate onto the top of each candy and spread it to the edges.

7. Let sit at room temperature, or covered in the refrigerator. Turn out of the pan when firm.

- MAKES 12 PIECES

TIDBITS

It is best to use a shallow muffin tin or candy tin for this recipe. But if you only have the larger, more common, muffin tin, it will work just fine—simply fill each tin only halfway with the chocolate and peanut butter. Unless, that is, you want to make giant-size, mutant peanut butter cups. In that case, fill those cups up all the way!

For even better clones, make your Peanut Butter Cups inside paper baking cups. Cut each baking cup in half horizontally to make it shallower, and "paint" your first layer of chocolate onto the inside of each cup with a spoon. Put the cups into a muffin tin so that they hold their shape, and then put the tin into the refrigerator to set. Add your peanut butter and the top layer of chocolate according to the instructions in the recipe.

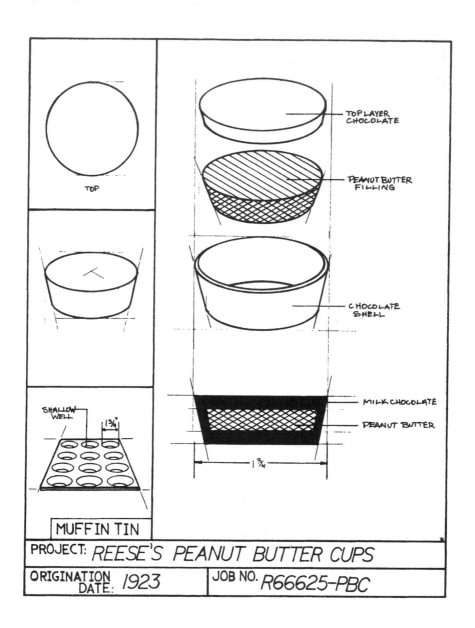

TOP

TOP LAYER CHOCOLATE

PEANUT BUTTER FILLING

CHOCOLATE SHELL

MILK CHOCOLATE

PEANUT BUTTER

SHALLOW WELL

1¾"

1¾"

MUFFIN TIN

PROJECT: *REESE'S PEANUT BUTTER CUPS*

ORIGINATION DATE: *1923*

JOB NO. *R66625-PBC*

SARA LEE ORIGINAL CREAM CHEESECAKE

☆　♥　☎　✎　✈　⊠　✄　☛　✿

In 1949 a bakery owner named Charles Lubin pioneered in the frozen-foods business when he invented a top-quality cream cheesecake for sale in supermarkets and restaurants. He named the cheesecake after his daughter, Sara Lee. Though skeptics believed that a frozen bakery item could not be sold in large grocery stores, Lubin's cheesecake was such a success that only two years later, in 1951, he opened the Kitchens of Sara Lee and began to add other items to his line. In the early 1950s Lubin experimented with, and introduced, the aluminum foil pan, which allowed his products to be baked, quickly frozen, and sold in the same container.

Today the Kitchens of Sara Lee produce more than 200 varieties of baked goods. And few people know that this diverse company has also been successful in manufacturing and marketing coffee, meats, and even pantyhose under the Hanes and Liz Claiborne labels.

CRUST

1 ½ cups fine graham-cracker crumbs (11 crackers, rolled)

¼ cup granulated sugar
½ cup (1 stick) butter, softened

FILLING

16 ounces cream cheese
1 cup sour cream
2 tablespoons cornstarch

1 cup granulated sugar
2 tablespoons butter, softened
1 teaspoon vanilla extract

TOPPING

¾ cup sour cream   *¼ cup powdered sugar*

1. Preheat the oven to 375°F.
2. For the crust, combine the graham-cracker crumbs, sugar, and butter, and mix well.
3. Press the mixture firmly into an ungreased 9-inch pie plate. Press flat onto bottom only.
4. Bake for 8 minutes, or until the edges are slightly brown. Reduce the oven temperature to 350°F.
5. For the filling, combine the cream cheese, sour cream, corn-starch, and sugar in the bowl of a mixer. Mix until the sugar has dissolved.
6. Add the butter and vanilla and blend until smooth. Be careful not to overmix, or the filling will become too fluffy and will crack when cooling.
7. Pour the filling over the crust.
8. Bake for 30 to 35 minutes, or until a knife inserted 1 inch from the edge comes out clean.
9. Cool for 1 hour.
10. For the topping, mix the sour cream and powdered sugar. Spread the mixture over the top of the cooled cheesecake. Chill or freeze until ready to eat.

TIDBITS

If you decide to freeze this cheesecake, defrost it for about an hour at room temperature before serving. You may also defrost slices in the microwave oven if you're in a hurry. (Impatience is a common cheesecake-craving affliction.) Set the microwave on high and zap as follows:

1 slice—15 seconds
2 slices—25 seconds
3 slices—40 seconds
Be sure to refreeze the remaining cheesecake after slicing.

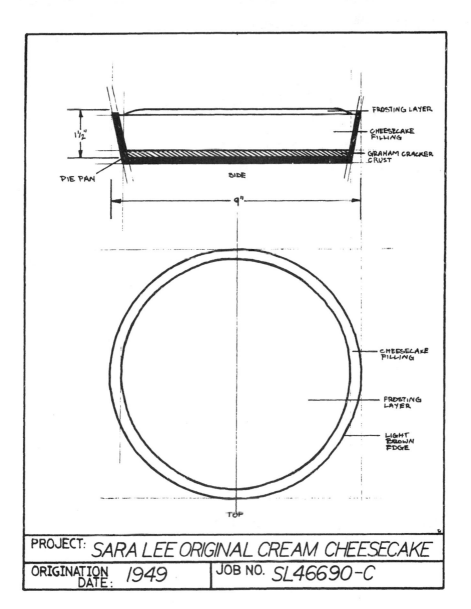

FROSTING LAYER

CHEESECAKE FILLING

GRAHAM CRACKER CRUST

1½"

PIE PAN

SIDE

9"

CHEESECAKE FILLING

FROSTING LAYER

LIGHT BROWN EDGE

TOP

PROJECT: *SARA LEE ORIGINAL CREAM CHEESECAKE*

ORIGINATION DATE: *1949*   JOB NO. *SL46690-C*

SEE'S BUTTERSCOTCH LOLLIPOP

☆　♥　☎　✎　✈　✉　✄　☞　❀

The first See's Candy shop was opened in Los Angeles in 1921 by Charles A. See. He used his mother's candy recipes, and a picture of her at the age of seventy-one embellished every black-and-white box of chocolates. Mary See died in 1939 at the age of eighty-five, but her picture went on to become a symbol of quality and continuity. See's manufacturing plants are still located in California, but because the company will ship anywhere in the United States, it has become a known and respected old-fashioned-style chocolatier across the country.

In an age of automation, many companies that manufacture chocolate have resorted to automated enrobing machines to coat their chocolates. But See's workers still hand-dip much of their candy.

One of the company's most popular sweets isn't dipped at all. It's a hard, rectangular lollipop that comes in chocolate, peanut butter, and butterscotch flavors. The latter, which tastes like caramel, is the most popular flavor of the three, and this recipe will enable you to clone the original, invented more than fifty years ago.

You will need twelve shot glasses, espresso cups, or sake cups for molds, and twelve lollipop sticks or popsicle sticks.

1 cup granulated sugar	2 tablespoons butter or margarine
1 cup heavy cream	1 teaspoon vanilla extract
3 tablespoons light corn syrup	Nonstick spray

1. Combine the first four ingredients in a saucepan over medium heat. Stir until the sugar has dissolved.
2. Let the mixture boil until it reaches 310°F on a cooking ther-

mometer (this is called the *hard-crack stage*), or until a small amount dropped in cold water separates into hard, brittle threads.

3. Stir in the vanilla, then remove from the heat.

4. Coat the molds with nonstick spray and pour the mixture in. (If you are using shot glasses, be sure to cool the mixture first so that the glass won't crack.)

5. Place a small piece of aluminum foil over each mold and press a lollipop stick or popsicle stick in the center.

6. When cool, remove from molds.

• MAKES 1 DOZEN LOLLIPOPS

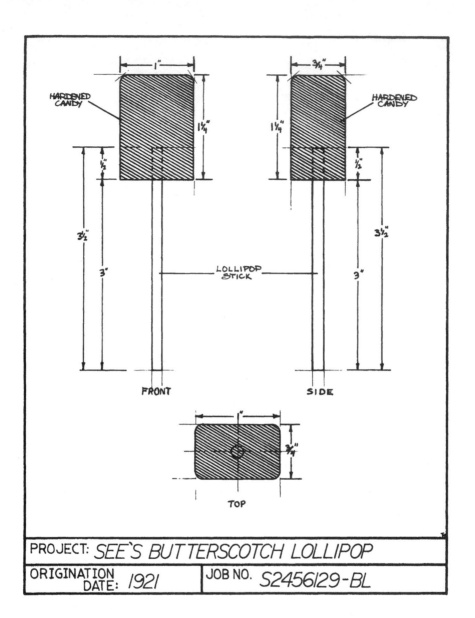

PROJECT: *SEE`S BUTTERSCOTCH LOLLIPOP*

ORIGINATION DATE: *1921*   JOB NO. *S2456129-BL*

SNAPPLE
ICED TEA

☆ ♥ ☎ ✎ ✈ ⊠ ✀ ☞ ✿

In 1972, brothers-in-law Leonard Marsh and Hyman Golden had become tired of running a window-washing business. They contacted their friend Arnold Greenberg and told him they wanted to start selling bottled fruit juices. Greenberg had a health-food store and thought their idea for all-natural beverages was a good one, so together they started selling pure fruit juices under the name Unadulterated Food Products. It took the trio about a decade to acquire the name they really wanted, Snapple, for $500 from a guy in Texas who had used it on an apple soda that bombed. Snapple's big break came in 1988, when the company started bottling ready-to-drink iced teas. It took only five years for Snapple to become the leader in the iced tea market, blowing away giants Lipton and Nestea. The Snapple iced tea phenomenon helped the company increase sales between 1988 and 1992 by nearly 1,300 percent. Whew.

LEMON

2 quarts (8 cups) water
3 Lipton tea bags (orange pekoe and
　　pekoe cut black tea blend)

¾ cup granulated sugar or one
　16-ounce bottle light corn syrup
⅓ cup plus 1 tablespoon lemon juice

DIET LEMON

2 quarts (8 cups) water
3 Lipton tea bags (orange pekoe and
　　pekoe cut black tea blend)

Twelve 1-gram envelopes Sweet'n Low
　or Equal sweetener
⅓ cup plus 1 tablespoon lemon juice

ORANGE

2 quarts (8 cups) water
3 Lipton tea bags (orange pekoe and
    pekoe cut black tea blend)
¾ cup granulated sugar or one
    16-ounce bottle light corn syrup

⅓ cup lemon juice
⅛ teaspoon orange extract

STRAWBERRY

2 quarts (8 cups) water
3 Lipton tea bags (orange pekoe and
    pekoe cut black tea blend)
¾ cup granulated sugar or one
    16-ounce bottle light corn syrup

⅓ cup plus 1 tablespoon lemon juice
1 tablespoon strawberry extract

CRANBERRY

2 quarts (8 cups) water
3 Lipton tea bags (orange pekoe and
    pekoe cut black tea blend)
¾ cup granulated sugar or one
    16-ounce bottle light corn syrup

⅓ cup plus 2 tablespoons lemon juice
2 tablespoons Ocean Spray cranberry
    juice cocktail concentrate

1. For any of the flavors, boil the water in a large saucepan.
2. When the water comes to a rapid boil, turn off the heat, put the tea bags into the water, and cover.
3. After the tea has steeped about 1 hour, pour the sugar or sweetener into a 2-quart pitcher; then add the tea. The tea should still be warm, so the sugar or sweetener will dissolve easily.
4. Add the flavoring ingredients (plus additional water if needed to bring the tea to the 2-quart line). Chill.

    • MAKES 2 QUARTS

STARK
MARY JANE

☆　♥　☎　✎　✈　✉　✂　☛　❀

In 1914, Charles H. Miller came up with this molasses and peanut butter candy and named it after his favorite aunt. His candy company flourished, selling many confections, but none as popular as the Mary Jane. Eventually all the other candies were eliminated and Mary Janes came to be the only candy produced by the Miller company. Miller tried playing with the formula to improve the candy, but none could compare to the original. In 1985, Stark Candy Company bought the Miller company and added the Stark name to the wrapper. The candy is much the same today as it was eighty years ago.

1 cup granulated sugar	3 tablespoons molasses
1 cup light corn syrup	1/2 cup peanut butter
1/2 cup water	1/4 cup powdered sugar
1 egg white	Cornstarch for dusting

1. Combine the sugar, corn syrup, and water in a saucepan over medium heat.
2. Heat, stirring, until the sugar begins to boil, then continue to cook, using a candy thermometer to monitor the temperature.
3. When the sugar reaches 240°F, or the *soft-ball* stage, beat the egg white in a microwave-safe bowl until it is stiff and forms peaks. Divide the beaten egg white, and throw out half. (We only need 1/2 egg white for this recipe, and it is easier to divide when beaten.)
4. When the sugar reaches 265°F, or the *hard-ball stage*, stir in the molasses, then pour the mixture in thin streams into the egg white while beating with an electric mixer on low speed.
5. Beat for 3 to 4 minutes and then pour half the mixture into a

9 × 9-inch greased pan and let it firm up in the refrigerator for 5 to 10 minutes.

6. Combine the peanut butter and powdered sugar.
7. When the candy is firm, spread a thin layer of the peanut butter mixture on top.
8. Microwave the remaining candy mixture for 1 minute on high, or until it becomes soft again.
9. Pour the softened candy over the peanut butter layer.
10. When the candy is cool but still pliable (about 20 minutes later), turn it out onto a surface dusted lightly with cornstarch. Use a cornstarch-dusted rolling pin to roll the candy about ¼ inch thick.
11. Use kitchen scissors or a sharp knife to cut the candy into 1½ × ½-inch rectangles.

- MAKES 30 CANDIES

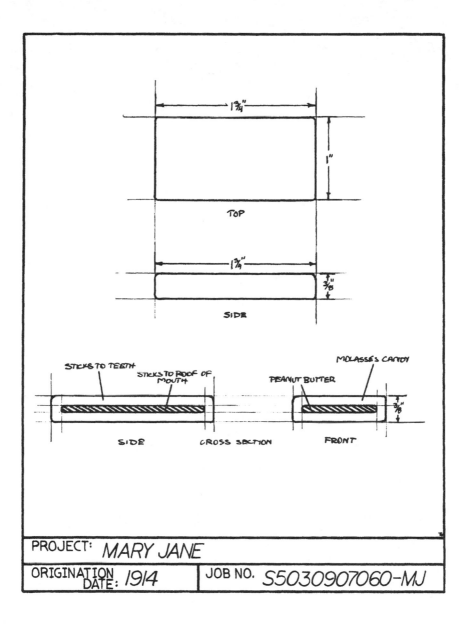

TOP

SIDE

STICKS TO TEETH

STICKS TO ROOF OF MOUTH

PEANUT BUTTER

MOLASSES CANDY

SIDE

CROSS SECTION

FRONT

PROJECT: MARY JANE

ORIGINATION DATE: 1914

JOB NO. S5030907060-MJ

SUPER PRETZELS

☆ ♥ ☏ ✎ ✈ ✉ ✄ ☛ ✿

Gerry Shreiber, a college dropout, wasn't happy with the metal-working business he had been operating for about seven years with a friend, so the two decided to sell out. Shreiber's take was about $60,000, but he needed a new job. By chance one day, he wandered into a Philadelphia waterbed store and struck up a conversation with an investor in a troubled soft pretzel company. After touring the run-down plant, Shreiber thought he could turn the company around, so he put his money to work and bought J&J Soft Pretzels for $72,100. That was in 1971. At the time, J&J had at least ten competitors in the soft pretzel business, but over the years Shreiber devised a strategy that would eliminate this competition and help his company grow—he simply bought most of them out.

Today J&J Super Pretzels are uncontested in the frozen soft pretzel market, and they currently constitute about 70 percent of the soft pretzels that are sold in the country's malls, convenience stores, amusement parks, stadiums, and movie theaters.

One ¼-ounce package active dry
    yeast
1 cup warm water (105 to 110°F)
3¾ cups all-purpose flour
3 tablespoons light corn syrup
2 tablespoons (¼ stick) butter,
    softened

1 teaspoon salt
4 cups cold water
⅓ cup baking soda
Coarse pretzel salt (such as
    kosher salt)

1.   Dissolve the yeast in the warm water in a large bowl.
2.   Add 2 cups of the flour and beat until smooth.
3.   Add the corn syrup, butter, and salt, and mix well, about 2 minutes.

4. Add the remaining flour and knead with your hands until all the flour is worked into the dough.

5. Cover the bowl and set the dough in a warm, cozy place where it can ponder the meaning of "Rise, you gooey glob!" Allow the dough to double in size, from 1 to 1½ hours.

6. Remove the dough from the bowl and divide into 10 equal pieces.

7. With your hands, roll each piece of dough out on a flat surface until it's about 2 feet long.

8. Holding the dough at both ends, give each strip of dough a twist. Lay the twists well spaced on greased cookie sheets (refer to the illustration for design specifics). Let these rise for another 30 to 45 minutes.

9. When the dough has nearly doubled again, combine the cold water and baking soda in a large saucepan and bring to a boil. This will be your browning solution (a.k.a. *caustic bath*).

10. Preheat the oven to 350°F.

11. Drop each pretzel, one at a time, into the boiling solution. Soak each pretzel for 1 minute, carefully turning after 30 seconds. Return to the cookie sheets.

12. Bake the pretzels for 12 to 15 minutes, or until they are golden brown.

13. Eat the pretzels hot or allow them to cool and freeze them. If you want salt, lightly moisten the surface of the pretzel with a pastry brush and apply a generous sprinkling of coarse salt.

14. Frozen pretzels can be reheated in a microwave set on high for about 30 seconds.

- MAKES 10 PRETZELS

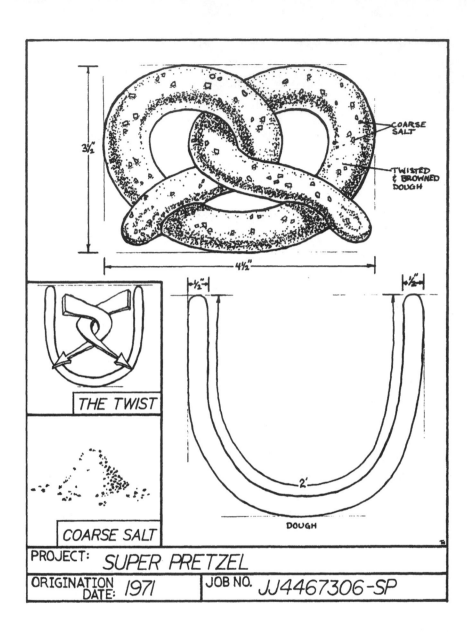

COARSE SALT

TWISTED & BROWNED DOUGH

3½"

4½"

½"

½"

2'

THE TWIST

COARSE SALT

DOUGH

PROJECT: *SUPER PRETZEL*

ORIGINATION DATE: *1971*

JOB NO. *JJ4467306-SP*

TACO BELL
ENCHIRITO

☆ ♥ ☎ ✎ ✈ ✉ ✂ ☞ ✿

An enterprising young man named Glen Bell was fresh out of the Marines in 1946 and was looking for something to do. He worked at a couple of odd jobs, then eventually scraped together $400 in 1947 to buy a hot-dog stand in San Bernardino, California. By 1952 business was so good at Bell's Drive-In that he decided to add hamburgers, just as two brothers named McDonald were starting their own hamburger business in the same city.

Bell soon realized that he needed to expand his menu to differentiate his restaurant from the McDonald brothers'. A fan of Mexican food, Bell devised a way to make tacos and other Mexican specialties quickly and inexpensively. The business grew rapidly, and the name Taco Bell was officially established in 1962, when Bell sold forty company shares to family members at $100 apiece. In 1969, to take his corporation public, he split those original stocks 30,000 to 1.

There are now more than 3,600 Taco Bell units dotting the globe, with total sales in 1991 of $2.8 billion. The company, owned by PepsiCo, Inc., plans to have more than 10,000 outlets by the year 2001.

Today this is the only place you will find the Enchirito. When the product's popularity waned in early 1992, the company said adios.

1 pound ground beef
1/4 teaspoon salt
1 teaspoon chili powder
1/2 tablespoon dried minced onion
One 30-ounce can refried beans
1 package 10- or 12-inch flour tortillas

1/4 onion, diced
One 10-ounce can La Victoria
   enchilada sauce
2 1/2 cups shredded cheddar cheese
One 2-ounce can sliced black olives

1. Slowly brown the ground beef in a skillet, using a wooden spoon or spatula to separate the beef into pea-size pieces.

2.   Add the salt, chili powder, and minced onion.
3.   With a mixer or a potato masher, beat the refried beans until smooth.
4.   Heat the refried beans in a small saucepan or in a microwave oven.
5.   Warm the tortillas all at once in a covered container, or wrapped in moist towel in microwave. Set on high for 40 seconds, or warm individually in a skillet over low heat for 2 to 3 minutes each side.
6.   Spoon 3 tablespoons of beef into the center of each tortilla. Sprinkle on ½ teaspoon diced fresh onion. Add ⅓ cup refried beans.
7.   Fold the sides of each tortilla over the beans and meat. Flip the tortilla over onto a plate.
8.   Spoon 3 tablespoons of enchilada sauce over the top of the tortilla.
9.   Sprinkle on ¼ cup shredded cheese.
10. Top with 3 olive slices.

• MAKES 10

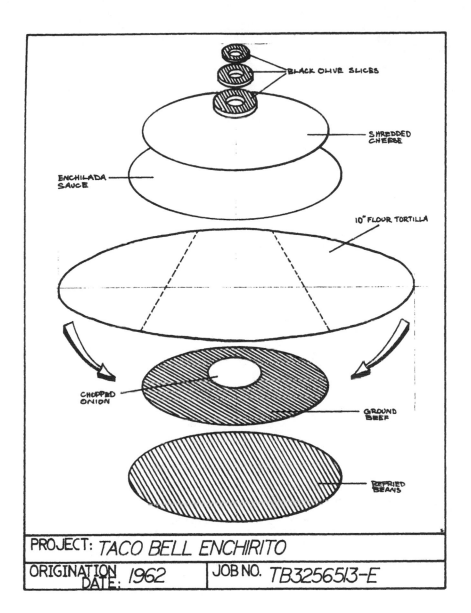

BLACK OLIVE SLICES

SHREDDED CHEESE

ENCHILADA SAUCE

10" FLOUR TORTILLA

CHOPPED ONION

GROUND BEEF

REFRIED BEANS

PROJECT: *TACO BELL ENCHIRITO*	
ORIGINATION DATE: *1962*	JOB NO. *TB3256513-E*

TACO BELL
HOT
TACO SAUCE

☆ ♥ ☎ ✎ ✈ ✉ ✂ ☛ ✿

You can't buy it in grocery stores, so if you want a substantial portion of Taco Bell's great Taco Sauce to smother your own creations in, you'll have to collect pocketfuls of those little blister packs. But that would be mooching. So here's a way to make plenty of hot sauce just like the stuff people are pouring over the 4 million tacos served at 4,200 Taco Bell restaurants in forty states and around the world every day.

One 6-ounce can tomato paste
3 cups water
2 teaspoons cayenne pepper
1 ½ tablespoons chili powder
2 teaspoons cornstarch

2 teaspoons distilled white vinegar
1 tablespoon minced dried onion
2½ teaspoons salt
2 tablespoons canned jalapeño slices
     ("nacho slices"), finely chopped

1. Combine the tomato paste with the water in a saucepan over medium heat. Stir until smooth.
2. Add the cayenne pepper, chili powder, salt, cornstarch, vinegar, and dried onion and stir.
3. Chop the jalapeño slices very fine. You can use a food processor, but don't puree. The best kind of jalapeños to use are those bottled for nachos or pizza. Add them to the mixture.
4. Heat the mixture to boiling. Continue to stir about 3 minutes and remove from the heat.
5. Let the sauce stand until cool, and then put in a tightly sealed container and refrigerate. This will last for 1 to 2 months.

• MAKES 3½ CUPS

TASTYKAKE BUTTERSCOTCH KRIMPETS

☆　♥　☎　✎　✈　✉　✂　☞　✿

In 1914 Pittsburgh baker Philip J. Baur and Boston egg salesman Herbert T. Morris decided that there was a need for prewrapped, fresh cakes that were conveniently available at local grocers. The two men coined the name *Tastykake* for their new treats and were determined to use only the finest ingredients, delivered fresh daily to their bakery.

The founders' standards of freshness are still maintained. Tastykakes baked tonight are on the shelves tomorrow. That philosophy has contributed to substantial growth for the Tasty Baking Company. On its first day, the firm's sales receipts totaled $28.32; today the company boasts yearly sales of more than $200 million.

Among the top-selling Tastykake treats are the Butterscotch Krimpets, first created in 1927. Today, approximately 6 million Butterscotch Krimpets are baked each and every week.

CAKE

4 egg whites
One 16-ounce box golden pound
　　cake mix

⅔ cup water

FROSTING

⅛ cup Nestlé Butterscotch Morsels
　　(about 40 chips)

½ (1 stick) cup butter, softened
1½ cups powdered sugar

1.　Preheat the oven to 325°F.
2.　Beat the egg whites until thick.
3.　Blend the egg whites with the cake mix and water.

4. Pour the batter into a greased 9 × 12-inch baking pan. Bake for 30 minutes, or until the top is golden brown and a toothpick inserted in the center comes out clean. Cool.
5. For the frosting, melt the butterscotch morsels in a microwave oven on high for 45 seconds. If you don't have a microwave oven, use a double boiler over hot, not boiling, water.
6. Mix the butter with the melted butterscotch. Add the powdered sugar. Blend with a mixer until the frosting has a smooth consistency.
7. Spread the frosting on top of the cooled pound cake.
8. Cut the cake into nine rows. Then make two cuts lengthwise. This should divide cake into twenty-seven equal pieces.

• MAKES 27 CAKES

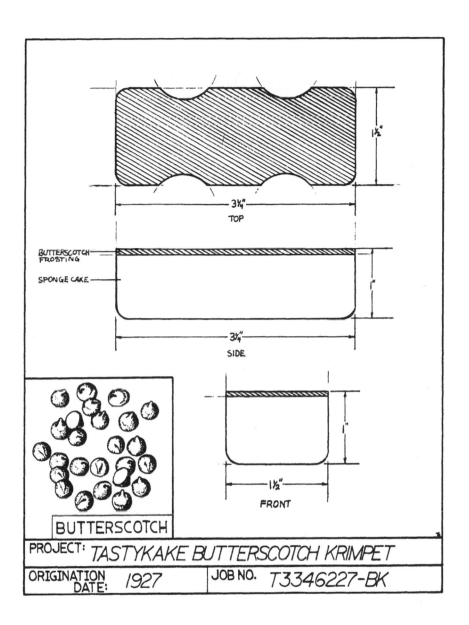

1½"

3¼"

TOP

BUTTERSCOTCH FROSTING

SPONGE CAKE

1"

3¼"

SIDE

1"

1½"

FRONT

BUTTERSCOTCH

PROJECT: TASTYKAKE BUTTERSCOTCH KRIMPET

ORIGINATION DATE: 1927

JOB NO. T3346227-BK

TASTYKAKE CHOCOLATE CUPCAKES

☆　♥　☎　✎　✈　✉　✂　☞　❀

In 1914, the founders of the Tasty Baking Company set out to create "the cake that made Mother stop baking." The idea of small, pre-wrapped cakes made fresh at the bakery and delivered to local grocery stores was especially appealing back then. Tastykake products remain popular; every day the company ships and sells millions of Tastykake products. Perhaps the success of the product over the years lies in the secret recipes that have gone remarkably unchanged since they were first created. These chocolate cupcakes in several varieties are the company's top-selling item, with more than 7 million baked weekly.

You'll need a pastry bag to make the filled variety.

CUPCAKES

One 18.25-ounce box Duncan Hines Moist Deluxe Devil's Food cake mix

3 eggs
1/2 cup vegetable oil
1 1/3 cups water

CHOCOLATE ICING

5 1/3 tablespoons (2/3 stick) butter, softened
1/2 cup semisweet chocolate chips

1 1/2 teaspoons vanilla extract
1 tablespoon milk
2 1/4 cups powdered sugar

BUTTERCREAM ICING

5 1/3 tablespoons (2/3 stick) butter, softened
1 1/2 teaspoons vanilla extract

2 1/2 tablespoons milk
1/8 teaspoon salt
3 cups powdered sugar

½ cup shortening	Pinch salt
½ teaspoon vanilla extract	1 cup powdered sugar

1. Preheat the oven to 350°F.
2. Make the cupcakes according to the directions on the box of cake mix. (Combine the ingredients, mix for 2 minutes, pour into lightly greased muffin cups, and bake for 19 to 22 minutes.)
3. While the cupcakes bake, make the chocolate and/or buttercream icings.

   Chocolate icing: In a mixing bowl, combine the butter with the chocolate chips melted in a microwave set on high for 30 to 45 seconds. Blend in the vanilla, milk, and powdered sugar and beat with an electric mixer until smooth and creamy.

   Buttercream icing: Combine all the ingredients in a mixing bowl and beat until smooth.
4. If you're making the filled cupcakes, combine the ingredients for the filling in another mixing bowl and beat until fluffy.
5. When the cupcakes are cool, complete each by following the directions below for your preference.

   • MAKES 24 CUPCAKES

Chocolate-Iced Cupcakes

First spread a layer of chocolate frosting on each cupcake. Then, using a pastry bag with a small, round tip, draw a single straight line of buttercream icing down the middle of the chocolate icing.

Buttercream-Iced Cupcakes

First spread a layer of buttercream icing evenly over the top of each cupcake. Then, using a pastry bag with a small, round tip, draw a straight line of chocolate icing down the middle of the buttercream icing.

Creme-Filled Cupcakes

If it's filled cupcakes you want, you need to fill them before you spread on the frosting. How do you do this? It's really very easy.

Use a toothpick or wooden skewer to make a hole in the top of the unfrosted cupcake. Stick the toothpick into the middle of the cupcake and then twirl it around to carve out a cavity in the middle of the cake. This is where the filling will go.

Use a pastry bag to inject a small amount (about 1 teaspoon) of filling into each cupcake, to fill the hole. When you ice your cupcakes, the icing will neatly hide the hole you made.

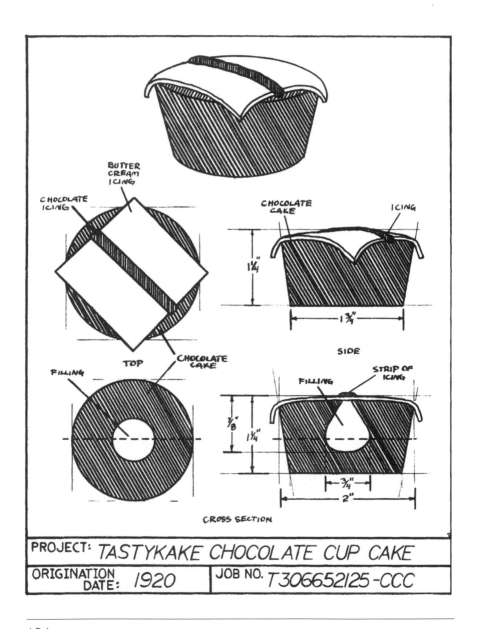

BUTTER CREAM ICING

CHOCOLATE ICING

CHOCOLATE CAKE

ICING

1¼"

1¾"

SIDE

TOP

CHOCOLATE CAKE

FILLING

FILLING

STRIP OF ICING

⅞"

1¼"

¾"

2"

CROSS SECTION

PROJECT: *TASTYKAKE CHOCOLATE CUP CAKE*

ORIGINATION DATE: *1920*   JOB NO. *T306652125-CCC*

TASTYKAKE PEANUT BUTTER KANDY KAKES

☆　♥　☎　✎　✈　✉　✂　☞　✿

Since it was founded in 1914, the Tasty Baking Company has continued to uphold its policy of controlled distribution to ensure freshness of its products. The company delivers only what it will sell promptly and removes cakes from the stores after just a few days in an effort to keep them from becoming stale.

As the years went by and delivery efficiency improved, transportation routes expanded from Philadelphia to New England, the Midwest, and the South. Mixing, baking, wrapping, and packaging of the products have changed from hand operations to sophisticated automated ones, cutting the production cycle from twelve hours to forty-five minutes, and loading time from five hours to forty-five minutes.

Peanut Butter Kandy Kakes made their debut in the early 1930s as *Tandy Takes*. The name was eventually changed, and the company claims you could make almost 8 million peanut butter sandwiches with the quantity of peanut butter used in Kandy Kakes each year.

4 egg whites
One 16-ounce box golden pound
    cake mix
⅔ cup water

1 cup peanut butter
½ cup powdered sugar
One 11.5-ounce bag Hershey milk-
    chocolate chips

1. Preheat the oven to 325°F.
2. Beat the egg whites until fluffy.
3. Blend the egg whites with the cake mix and water.
4. Pour tablespoon-size dollops of batter into each cup of a well-greased muffin tin. Bake for 10 minutes, or until a toothpick

stuck in center of cake comes out clean. Make five batches. Clean muffin tin for later use. Do not grease.

5.   Combine the peanut butter and sugar.

6.   While the pound-cake rounds cool, heat the chocolate chips in a double boiler over low heat, stirring often. You can also melt them in a microwave oven set on high for 2 minutes, stirring once halfway through the heating time.

7.   When the chocolate is soft, line the bottom half of each muffin-tin cup with shortening; then use a spoon to spread a thin layer of chocolate in each cup.

8.   With your fingers, spread a thin layer of peanut butter over the chocolate.

9.   Place a cake round on the peanut-butter layer.

10.   Spread a layer of chocolate over the top of each cake, spreading to the sides to cover the entire surface.

11.   Cool in the refrigerator for 10 minutes and turn out of the tin.

- MAKES 30 CAKES

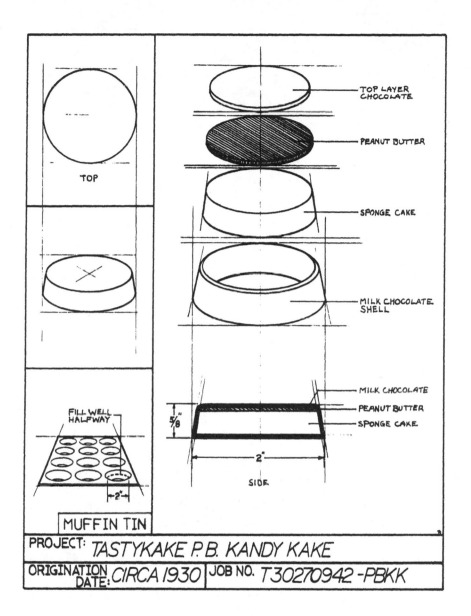

TOP

TOP LAYER
CHOCOLATE

PEANUT BUTTER

SPONGE CAKE

MILK CHOCOLATE
SHELL

MILK CHOCOLATE
PEANUT BUTTER
SPONGE CAKE

$\frac{5}{8}$"

2"

SIDE

FILL WELL
HALFWAY

2"

MUFFIN TIN

PROJECT: *TASTYKAKE P.B. KANDY KAKE*

ORIGINATION DATE: *CIRCA 1930*   JOB NO. *T30270942 -PBKK*

TWIN DRAGON
ALMOND COOKIES

☆　　❤　　☎　　✎　　✈　　✉　　✂　　☞　　✿

According to Main On Foods, the manufacturer and distributor of Twin Dragon Almond Cookies, the original recipe was brought to this country in 1951 by a Chinese baker who owned a small corner shop in downtown Los Angeles. That retail bakery is gone now, but its most popular product, the world's best-tasting almond cookie, is still selling big.

3 cups all-purpose flour
1 teaspoon baking soda
½ teaspoon salt
1 cup blanched almonds
1 cup granulated sugar

1 ½ cups lard (see Tidbits, next page)
1 teaspoon almond extract
1 egg, beaten
⅛ cup water

1. Preheat the oven to 350°F.
2. Mix the flour, baking soda, and salt.
3. In a blender, grind ½ cup blanched almonds to a fine powder. Add to the flour mixture.
4. Cream the sugar, lard, almond extract, egg, and water, and add to the dry mixture. Mix thoroughly.
5. Form into 1-inch balls and place on an ungreased cookie sheet 2 inches apart.
6. Press one of the remaining almonds into the center of each ball, while flattening it slightly with fingers.
7. Brush each cookie lightly with beaten egg.
8. Bake for 20 minutes, or until cookies are light brown around edges.

- MAKES 2 DOZEN COOKIES

TIDBITS

If your daily allowance of lard will be exceeded by this recipe, feel free to substitute vegetable shortening.

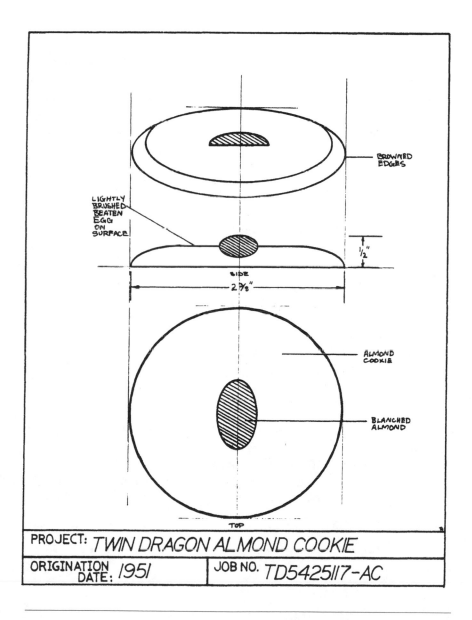

BROWNED
EDGES

LIGHTLY
BRUSHED
BEATEN
EGG
ON
SURFACE

½"

SIDE

2⅞"

ALMOND
COOKIE

BLANCHED
ALMOND

TOP

PROJECT: *TWIN DRAGON ALMOND COOKIE*

ORIGINATION DATE: *1951*

JOB NO. *TD5425117-AC*

WENDY'S CHILI

☆   ♥   ☎   ✎   ✈   ✉   ✂   ☛   ✿

In 1969, at the ripe old age of thirty-seven, R. David Thomas left a job at Arthur Treacher's Fish & Chips to open the first Wendy's at 257 E. Broad Street in downtown Columbus, Ohio. Only three years later Thomas began franchising the Wendy's concept, and by the end of its first nine years, Wendy's International had dotted the country with more than 1,000 units.

Thomas has served this chili since day one. The recipe has changed a bit over the years, but the chili you'll taste here is a clone of Wendy's current recipe. Try topping it with freshly grated cheese and chopped onion, extras that you can request at the restaurant.

2 pounds ground beef
One 29-ounce can tomato sauce
One 29-ounce can kidney beans (with liquid)
One 29-ounce can pinto beans (with liquid)
1 cup diced onion (1 medium onion)
½ cup diced green chili (2 chilies)

¼ cup diced celery (1 stalk)
3 medium tomatoes, chopped
2 teaspoons cumin powder
3 tablespoons chili powder
1½ teaspoons black pepper
2 teaspoons salt
2 cups water

1. Brown the ground beef in a skillet over medium heat; drain off the fat.
2. Using a fork, crumble the cooked beef into pea-size pieces.
3. In a large pot, combine the beef plus all the remaining ingredients, and bring to a simmer over low heat. Cook, stirring every 15 minutes, for 2 to 3 hours.

   • MAKES ABOUT 12 SERVINGS

Variations

For spicier chili, add ½ teaspoon more black pepper.

For much spicier chili, add 1 teaspoon black pepper and 1 table-spoon cayenne pepper.

And for a real stomach stinger, add 5 or 6 sliced jalapeño peppers to the pot.

Leftovers can be frozen for several months.

WENDY'S FROSTY

The founder of Wendy's International, R. David Thomas, named the restaurant he established in 1969 after his eight-year-old daughter, Melinda Lou, who was nicknamed Wendy by her brother and sisters. Wendy says, "Dad wanted a name that was easy to remember and that was an all-American mug." Wendy is grown up now, but Dave Thomas still uses her eight-year-old freckle-faced likeness on his restaurant signs. He remembers that his daughter was very embarrassed by the exposure. Thomas told *People* magazine, "I'm not sure I would do it again."

Wendy's International now operates some 3,800 restaurants in 49 states and 24 countries overseas, racking up sales of more than $3 billion a year. Wendy's restaurants have served the now-famous Frosty since 1969. In 1991 an astounding 17.5 million gallons of the frozen confection were served worldwide.

¾ cup milk
¼ cup chocolate-drink powder (Nestlé
    Quik is best)

4 cups vanilla ice cream

1. Combine all of the ingredients in a blender. Blend on medium speed until creamy. Stir if necessary.
2. If too thin, freeze the mixture in the blender or in cups until thicker.

    • MAKES 2 DRINKS

WENDY'S GRILLED CHICKEN FILLET SANDWICH

☆　♥　☎　✎　✈　✉　✂　☛　✿

In 1990, Wendy's not only added this new sandwich to its growing menu, but also added more international restaurants to the chain, including stores in Indonesia, Greece, Turkey, and Guatemala. Wendy's now claims more than 4,000 outlets around the world, with more than $3 billion in sales.

This is an excellent sandwich if you like grilled chicken, and it contains only nine grams of fat, if you're counting.

1 plain hamburger bun	1 lettuce leaf
½ skinned, boneless chicken breast	1 large tomato slice
Salt to taste	
1 tablespoon Wishbone Honey Dijon salad dressing	

1. Heat the grill or broiler to medium heat.
2. Brown the faces of the bun in a frying pan over medium heat.
3. Cook the chicken breast for 6 to 10 minutes per side, or until done. Salt each side during the cooking.
4. Spread the salad dressing on the top bun.
5. Place the cooked chicken on the bottom bun. Top with the lettuce leaf, tomato slice, and top bun, in that order.
6. Microwave on high for 15 seconds.

- MAKES 1 SANDWICH

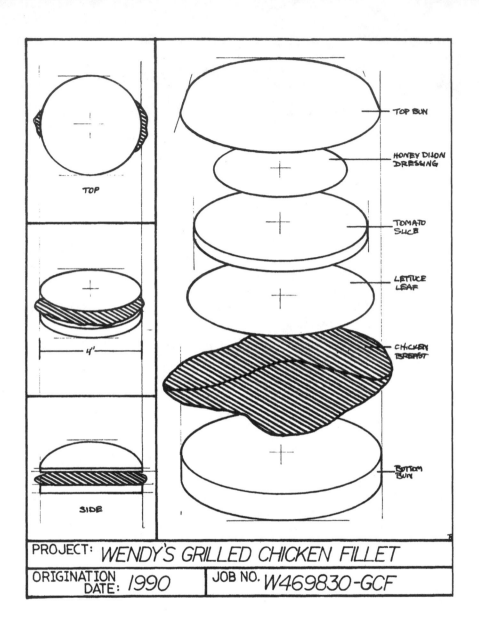

TOP

4"

SIDE

TOP BUN

HONEY DIJON DRESSING

TOMATO SLICE

LETTUCE LEAF

CHICKEN BREAST

BOTTOM BUN

PROJECT: *WENDY'S GRILLED CHICKEN FILLET*

ORIGINATION DATE: *1990*

JOB NO. *W469830-GCF*

WENDY'S JUNIOR BACON CHEESEBURGER

☆　♥　☎　✎　✈　✉　✂　☞　✿

Surely when Dave Thomas opened his first Wendy's Old Fashioned Hamburgers restaurant in 1969 and named it after his daughter, he never imagined the tremendous success and growth his hamburger chain would realize. He also could not have known that in 1989 he would begin starring in a series of television ads that would give Wendy's the biggest customer awareness level since its famous "Where's the beef?" campaign.

In that same year, Wendy's introduced the Super Value Menu, a selection of items all priced under a buck. The Junior Bacon Cheeseburger was added to the selection of inexpensive items and quickly became a hit.

1 plain hamburger bun	1 slice American cheese
1/3 pound ground beef	2 strips cooked bacon
Salt to taste	1 lettuce leaf
1 tablespoon mayonnaise	1 tomato slice

1. Brown the faces of the bun in a frying pan over medium heat. Keep the pan hot.
2. Form the ground beef into a square patty approximately 4 × 4 inches.
3. Cook the patty in the pan for 3 to 4 minutes per side, or until done. Salt each side during the cooking.
4. Spread the mayonnaise on the top bun.
5. Place the patty on the bottom bun. On top, stack the cheese, bacon (side by side), lettuce leaf and tomato slice, in that order. Top off with the top bun.

- MAKES 1 BURGER

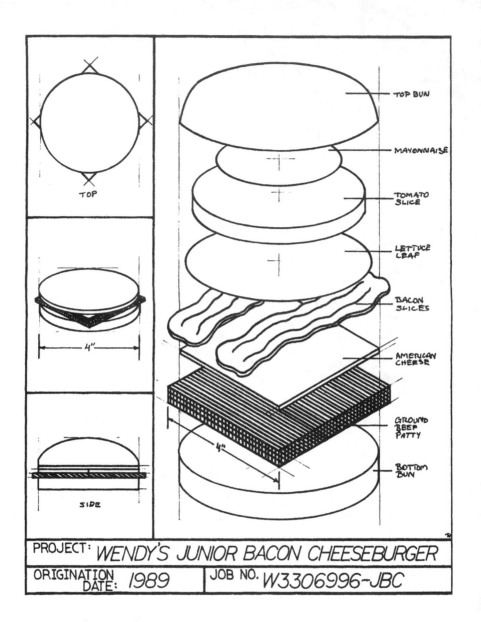

TOP

SIDE

4"

4"

TOP BUN

MAYONNAISE

TOMATO SLICE

LETTUCE LEAF

BACON SLICES

AMERICAN CHEESE

GROUND BEEF PATTY

BOTTOM BUN

PROJECT: *WENDY'S JUNIOR BACON CHEESEBURGER*
ORIGINATION DATE: *1989*   JOB NO. *W3306996-JBC*

WENDY'S SINGLE

☆   ♥   ☎   ✎   ✈   ✉   ✂   ☛   ✿

In 1984, the diminutive Clara Peller blurted out in a series of four television ads the memorable phrase that would pop up on T-shirts and in presidential campaigns: "Where's the beef?" The ad was devised by Wendy's advertising agency to attack the misconception that its Single hamburger was smaller than its competitors' "big name" hamburgers. The campaign was so original that it stole the show at the 1984 Clio Awards, winning the advertising industry's highest honors and registering the highest consumer awareness level in the industry's history.

1 plain hamburger bun	½ teaspoon prepared mustard
¼ pound ground beef	1 lettuce leaf
Salt to taste	3 raw onion rings
1 teaspoon catsup	1 large tomato slice
1 tablespoon mayonnaise	3 to 4 dill pickle slices

1. Brown the faces of the bun in a large frying pan over medium heat. Keep the pan hot.
2. On waxed paper, shape the ground beef into an approximately 4 × 4-inch square. It's best to freeze this patty ahead of time for easier cooking. Don't defrost before cooking.
3. Cook the burger in the pan for 3 minutes per side, or until done. Salt both sides during the cooking.
4. Spread the catsup and then the mayonnaise on the top bun.
5. Put the cooked patty on the bottom bun. On top of the meat, spread the mustard, then place the lettuce, onion, tomato, and pickles, in that order.
6. Top off with the top bun and microwave for 15 seconds.

• MAKES 1 BURGER

Single with Cheese

For a Single with cheese, place 1 slice of American cheese (not processed cheese food) on the beef patty when assembling the burger.

Double and Double with Cheese

Make this burger the same way as the Single, but stack another patty
on the first one so that you have a total of ½ pound ground beef.

If you want a Double with cheese, put one slice of cheese between the two beef patties.

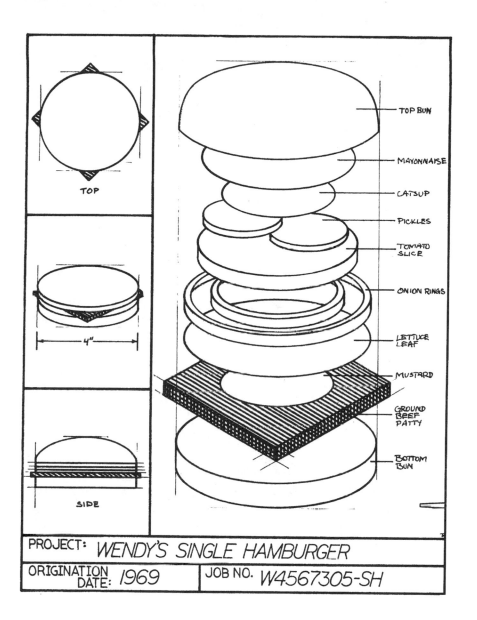

TOP

TOP BUN

MAYONNAISE

CATSUP

PICKLES

TOMATO SLICE

ONION RINGS

LETTUCE LEAF

MUSTARD

GROUND BEEF PATTY

BOTTOM BUN

4"

SIDE

PROJECT: *WENDY'S SINGLE HAMBURGER*

ORIGINATION DATE: *1969*   **JOB NO.** *W4567305-SH*

WHITE CASTLE BURGERS

☆　♥　☎　✎　✈　✉　✄　☛　✿

Nicknamed "Sliders" and "Gut Bombers," these famous tiny burgers were one of the earliest fast-food creations. It all started in 1921 when E. W. Ingram borrowed $700 to open a hamburger stand in Wichita, Kansas. He was able to pay the loan back within ninety days. Ingram chose the name White Castle because "white" signified purity and cleanliness, while "castle" represented strength, permanence, and stability. White Castle lived up to its name, maintaining permanence and stability by growing steadily over the years to a total of 275 restaurants.

Ingram's inspiration was the development of steam-grilling, a unique process that helps the burgers retain moisture. The secret is simply to grill the meat over a small pile of onions. Five holes in each burger help to ensure thorough cooking without having to flip the patties.

Today customers can still buy these burgers "by the sack" at the outlets, or pick them up in the freezer section of most grocery stores.

1 pound ground beef
8 hot-dog buns or 16 hamburger buns
½ medium onion
Salt to taste

Pepper to taste
American cheese (optional)
Pickle slices (optional)

1. Prepare the beef ahead of time by separating into sixteen 1-ounce portions and flattening each on waxed paper into very thin square patties, about 2½ inches on a side. Using a small circular object like the tip of a pen cap, make five small, evenly spaced holes in each patty. Freeze the patties (still on the waxed paper) completely and you're ready to cook.

2. If you're using hot-dog buns, cut off the ends and then cut each

bun in half to make 2 buns from each. If you're using hamburger buns, cut each down to about a 2½-inch square.

3. Slice the onion into match-size pieces.

4. Grill the faces of the buns in a large pan over medium heat.

5. In the hot pan, spread out tablespoon-size piles of onions 3 inches apart. Salt and pepper each pile of onions.

6. On each pile of onions place a frozen beef patty. You may have to spread the onions out some so that the hamburger lies flat. Salt each patty as it cooks.

7. Cook each burger for 4 to 5 minutes on the onions. If you made the burgers thin enough, the holes will ensure that each patty is cooked thoroughly without flipping them over. Covering the frying pan will help to ensure that the patties cook through.

8. Assemble by sandwiching the patty and onions between each grilled bun.

- MAKES 16 BURGERS

TIDBITS

If you want to add pickle slices to your burger, as you can at White Castle outlets, stack them on top of the grilled onions.

For a cheeseburger, you'll have to cut a slice of American cheese to the same size as your burger, and then it goes on top of the onions, under the pickles, if you use pickles. Got it?

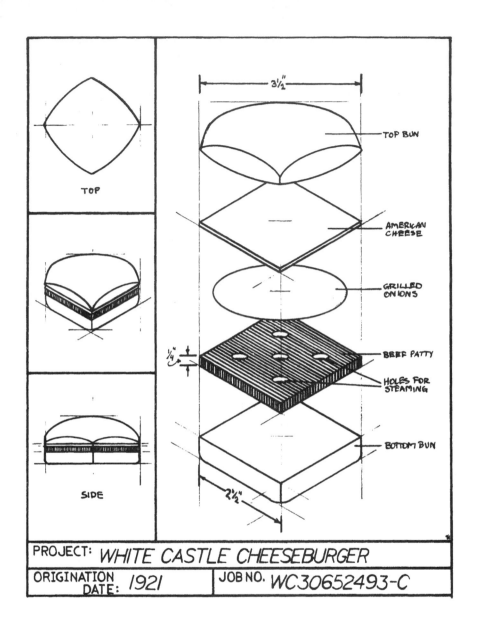

TOP

SIDE

3½"

TOP BUN

AMERICAN CHEESE

GRILLED ONIONS

¼"

BEEF PATTY

HOLES FOR STEAMING

BOTTOM BUN

2½"

PROJECT: *WHITE CASTLE CHEESEBURGER*

ORIGINATION DATE: *1921*

JOB NO. *WC30652493-C*

YOO-HOO CHOCOLATE DRINK

☆   ♥   ☎   ✎   ✈   ✉   ✂   ☛   ✿

In the early 1920s the Olivieri family had found modest success with a small company named Yoo-Hoo that produced and sold Yoo-Hoo fresh-squeezed fruit juice. But Mr. Natale Olivieri thought that adding a chocolate drink to his line would increase his sales dramatically.

A New York company named Marvis was already selling a chocolate drink, but it contained many chemicals used as preservatives. To be consistent with his policy of using only natural ingredients, Mr. Olivieri had to develop a way of bottling the chocolate drink without using additives. His solution came one day when he was helping his wife bottle her homemade tomato sauce. He noticed that she was using heat to keep the tomato sauce from spoiling, so he prepared six bottles of chocolate drink the same way. After a while, three of the six bottles spoiled, but three others remained perfect, leading him to believe he was on to something. That was Yoo-Hoo's beginning. And it didn't take long for the drink to become so successful that a major bottler began to distribute the product.

The Yoo-Hoo fresh-fruit drinks are gone now, but the high-quality chocolate-milk drink is still made from the finest cocoas available. And today it comes in two other flavors—strawberry and coconut. Sales continue to grow.

½ cup chocolate-drink powder (Nestlé Quik is best)

1 ½ cups nonfat dry milk

3 cups water

1.   Mix all of the contents in a blender for about 30 seconds.
2.   Refrigerate until cool.

• MAKES 2 DRINKS

YORK PEPPERMINT PATTIE

In York, Pennsylvania, Henry C. Kessler first concocted this confection in the late 1930s at his candy factory, the York Cone Company. The company was originally established to make ice cream cones, but by the end of World War II, the peppermint patty had become so popular that the company discontinued all other products. In 1972, the company was sold to Peter Paul, manufacturers of Almond Joy and Mounds. Cadbury USA purchased the firm in 1978, and in 1988 the York Peppermint Pattie became the property of Hershey USA.

Many chocolate-covered peppermints had been made before the York Peppermint Pattie came on the market, but Kessler's version was firm and crisp, while the competition was soft and gummy. One former employee and York resident remembered the final test the patty went through before it left the factory. "It was a snap test. If the candy didn't break clean in the middle, it was a second."

For years, seconds were sold to visitors at the plant for fifty cents a pound.

1 egg white	Cornstarch for dusting
4 cups powdered sugar	One 12-ounce bag semisweet
1/3 cup light corn syrup	chocolate chips
1/2 teaspoon peppermint oil or extract	

1. In a medium bowl, beat the egg white until frothy but not stiff. Don't use a plastic bowl for this.
2. Slowly add the powdered sugar while blending with an electric mixer set on medium speed.
3. Add the corn syrup and peppermint oil or extract and knead

the mixture with your hands until it has the smooth consistency of dough. Add more powdered sugar if necessary, until mixture is no longer sticky.

4. Using a surface and rolling pin heavily dusted with cornstarch, roll out the peppermint dough until it is about ¼ inch thick.

5. Punch out circles of peppermint dough with a biscuit cutter or a clean can with a diameter of about 2½ inches. Make approximately 20, place them on plates or cookie sheets, and let them firm up in the refrigerator, about 45 minutes.

6. Melt the chocolate chips in a microwave set on high for 2 minutes. Stir halfway through the heating time. Melt thoroughly, but do not overheat.

7. Drop each patty into the chocolate and coat completely. Using a large serving fork, or 2 dinner forks, one in each hand, lift the coated patty from the chocolate. Gently tap the forks against the bowl to knock off the excess chocolate, and place each patty on wax paper.

8. Chill the peppermint patties until firm, about 30 minutes.

• MAKES 20 PEPPERMINT PATTIES

TIDBITS

Being generous with the cornstarch will make it easier to work with the peppermint filling. Liberal dusting will ensure that your filling won't stick.

For your first batch, you'll find the dipping process smoother if you make smaller patties—about 1 inch in diameter. Try resting each pattie on a large serving fork, and tapping the fork against the side of the bowl to knock off excess chocolate after dipping.

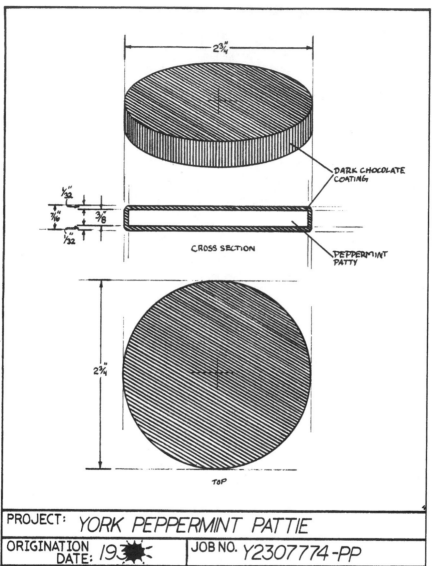

2¾"

DARK CHOCOLATE
COATING

1/32"
7/16"
3/8
1/32"

CROSS SECTION

PEPPERMINT
PATTY

2¾"

TOP

PROJECT: YORK PEPPERMINT PATTIE

ORIGINATION
DATE: 193█

JOB NO. Y2307774-PP

PART II

RESTAURANT CLONES

INTRODUCTION

Now it's time for something a little different.

It was a blast writing *Top Secret Recipes* that were inspired by convenience food—both fast food and packaged food, like Big Macs, Snickers, Oreos, and Twinkies. Sure, dissecting hamburgers, candy bars, cookies, and snack cakes is strange, sticky, tedious work; but when long-time aficionados of these goodies claim the copycat recipe was "right on," or when a blindfolded talk-show host is genuinely fooled in a taste test on live TV, I have to feel encouraged to continue the quest for clones.

So, as I was mulling over the next Top Secret mission, I noticed that in 1996 America reached a milestone in the full-service restaurant business. For the first time ever in one year, our hungry nation spent a gastronomic $100 billion, gobbling up the sit-down meals prepared by these rapidly expanding chains—casual diners and steakhouses like Big Boy, The Olive Garden, Outback, Chili's, and Applebee's. That got me thinking. In light of this landmark occasion, it seemed the perfect time for *Top Secret Recipes* to shift its focus, do a little snooping around in the full-service sector, and clone some dishes from the popular restaurant chains Americans have been frequenting in record numbers. But, wait a minute we're not just talking about cookies and burgers here. These are sit-down meals, with appetizers, entrees, side dishes, and desserts ... from chains all over the country. Would this be an impossible mission? Eagerly I chose to accept it. And I'm happy to say after more than a year of tasty field work: mission accomplished!

THE CRITERIA

The casual and fine dining restaurant chains that are referred to as "full-service" in the food biz are the sole subject of this formula-cracking section. Just for clarity's sake, "full-service" excludes "quick-service" or "fast food" restaurants. That means you won't find recipes here for Wendy's or Taco Bell or Burger King where you order your paper-wrapped food over a counter or from a drive-thru window (look for those recipes in Part I of this book).

At a full-service chain you typically order from a menu while sitting down at a private table. You are usually waited on, you can order a beer, you can pay with a credit card, and you are expected to leave a tip. A full-service restaurant can be a steakhouse, a family diner, a casual dinner house, a fancy restaurant, or extravagant theme chain.

Altogether, the selection of restaurants represented here total 19,000 single outlets grossing more than $25 billion a year. Many of the chains are at the top of the list in annual sales figures, but to maintain a bit of variety, I've picked some chains that are smaller in total size with only a regional presence. A few of the chains represented are located mostly in the South, such as Cracker Barrel, Western Sizzlin', and Shoney's; some are more likely to be found in the Northeast, such as Chi-Chi's and Perkins; and a couple of the chains come from the West, like Marie Callender's and Stuart Anderson's Black Angus. You'll also find that many of the chains are national, like the ubiquitous Pizza Hut, Red Lobster, and Denny's. A book like this wouldn't be complete without recognizing the ultra-hot theme restaurant segment, which includes Hard Rock Cafe, Planet Hollywood, and Dive!

TOP 10 FULL-SERVICE RESTAURANT CHAINS

1995 RANKING	RESTAURANT	UNITS	1995 SALES IN $ MILLIONS
1	Pizza Hut	12,140	7,900.0
2	Red Lobster	727	1,930.0
3	Denny's	1,553	1,490.0
4	Shoney's	822	1,260.4
5	The Olive Garden	494	1,260.0
6	Applebee's	666	1,250.0
7	Chili's Grill & Bar	490	1,060.0
8	T.G.I. Friday's	535	1,043.0
9	Big Boy	850	970.0
10	Outback Steakhouse	320	827.0

SOURCE: *Restaurants & Institutions*

Because the average American eats out 198 times a year or 4 times a week, chances are very good that you've noshed at one or more of these establishments in the past. You may even be familiar with several of the dishes that inspired the recipes in this book. That's good. Now you can take the *Top Secret Recipes* taste test. Compare what you make to the original menu item and you should find your version tastes just like the dish from the restaurant. To ensure that this is the case, I've tested the recipes numerous times. If my version didn't taste like the real dish, it didn't go in the book. Sure, the *Top Secret Recipes* version may not be prepared the exact same way as the original, but as long as the finished product is identical in taste, how we get to that point is inconsequential. Be aware that my intention here is not to steal the original recipe from the creators, only to duplicate the finished product as closely as possible, with ingredients you can find in any supermarket.

I've had to visit most of these restaurants several times to obtain all of the necessary information to assemble the recipes. Any information I obtained about these dishes came from talking to servers or hosts/hostesses (some more cooperative than others), just as any other customer might ask about a particular dish. Everything else I needed to know came from examining the dish itself.

You'd think that I was the only goofball out there traveling from restaurant to restaurant, quizzing waitresses and cooks, loading leftovers into Tupperware and Ziploc bags under dining room tables and into coolers stashed in car trunks. But there are many other more professional and much sneakier sleuths out there working for major restaurant companies, whose job it is to analyze the competitors' high-profit dishes and create a version for their own chain. If they succeed, they'll put those dishes on their own menu, maybe change the dish just slightly, and give it a new name.

You may not know that the double decker Big Mac, which I cloned in Part I, is not McDonald's own creation as many would believe, but rather a knock-off of the double-decker sandwich first created by the founder of the Big Boy chain 30 years before it was served under the Golden Arches (Big Boy's version is included in this section). On many menus today you'll find a common appetizer called potato skins, but you probably didn't know that it was T.G.I. Friday's that first introduced the dish to the world in 1974. And more recently, the popular fried Bloomin' Onion that was created by one of the Outback Steakhouse founders has become one of the most duplicated appetizers today, complete with the spicy dipping sauce and different names like "Awesome Blossom" and "Texas Tumbleweed."

WHY CLONE?

In the competitive arena of food service where the failure rate is a brutal 85 percent, operators are masters at inventing new and exciting dishes, creating new trends, or further exploiting existing ones and building menus around them ... even if a bit of cloning goes on. Successful restaurant operators are adept at attacking our taste buds with a flavorful frontal assault that will make us come back for more.

The recipes picked for this book should tickle your taste buds the same way as their original counterparts. Sure, making these dishes at home is not as easy as going out to the restaurant, and there's no way this book can substitute for the experience of dining out and mingling with others in a relaxing environment. That's why a book like this could never put a dent in the profit margin of these large chains. But when the time comes that you decide you want to do some cooking of your own, perhaps some entertaining, now you've got some tasty and familiar alternatives for the menu. Beyond that, I think you'll find home-cloning has additional benefits:

Because several of the restaurants are regional, there's no place in the entire country where you can get everything represented here. Making the dish at home is one way to find out how the other half dines. If you live on the West Coast you can enjoy East Coast fare like the food from Chi-Chi's or Cracker Barrel without having to take a very, very long drive. That is, until these chains expand into your neck of the woods.

Secondly, dining out regularly can get to be quite expensive. Sure, you don't want to have to cook all of the time, but why not stay in and make your favorite restaurant dishes at home once in a while to save a little cash? From this purely random selection you can see the big savings:

Planet Hollywood
    Chicken Crunch   Menu: $6.50   Home version: $2.12
Applebee's
    Quesadillas   Menu: $4.99   Home version: $1.11
Shoney's Hot
    Fudge Cake   Menu: $1.89   Home version: $0.65

Restaurants have to price their products to pay for operating overhead like servers, managers and chefs, leases and advertising. Your dish will cost less since you don't have these sorts of expenses.

Thirdly, you can alter the dishes to suit your taste. If you need your version of the Bloomin' Onion dipping sauce a little spicier, add more horseradish or cayenne pepper. If you want the sauce to be lower in calories, use a light mayonnaise that can be found in practically every market these days. Experiment and customize the dishes to suit your dietary needs and preferences.

You also have the ability now to create menus for entire meals that consist of a mix of dishes from different restaurants. You might try the clone recipe for Outback's Walkabout Soup as an appetizer, followed by the Western T-bone from Stuart Anderson's Black Angus, with a side of Texas Rice from Lone Star. Follow that up with a Strawberry Tallcake for Two from Ruby Tuesday and you've just eaten a meal that you could only get from lots of traveling around with doggie bags.

Here are some other suggestions:

For dinner:

          Shoney's Slow-Cooked Pot Roast
          Houlihan's Smashed Potatoes
          Sizzler Cheese Toast
          Cheesecake Factory Key Lime Cheesecake

Or:

          Houlihan's Houli Fruit Fizz
          T.G.I. Friday's Potato Skins
          Tony Roma's Original Baby Back Ribs
          Bennigan's Cookie Mountain Sundae

Or:

> Hooters Buffalo Shrimp
> California Pizza Kitchen Thai Chicken Pizza
> Chi-Chi's Mexican "Fried" Ice Cream

For an old-fashioned, country-style dinner:

> Marie Callender's Famous Golden Cornbread
> Shoney's Country Fried Steak
> Houlihan's Smashed Potatoes
> Marie Callender's Banana Cream Pie

For an Italian dinner:

> Cheesecake Factory Bruschetta
> Olive Garden Toscana Soup
> Planet Hollywood Pizza Bread
> Olive Garden Alfredo Pasta

For a little surf and turf:

> Salad w/Olive Garden Italian Salad Dressing
> Stuart Anderson's Black Angus Cheesy Garlic Bread
> Red Lobster Broiled Lobster
> Ruth's Chris Petite Filet
> Ruth's Chris Creamed Spinach or Potatoes Au
>   Gratin

For breakfast:

> Cracker Barrel Hash Brown Casserole
> Perkins Country Club Omelette

For lunch:

> Hooters Pasta Salad
> Dive! Sicilian Sub Rosa
> Hard Rock Cafe Orange Freeze

For the vegetarian:

> Dive! Carrot Chips
> Big Boy Cream of Broccoli Soup
> Hard Rock Cafe Grilled Vegetable Sandwich
> Shoney's Hot Fudge Cake

For munching while watching the big game:

> Hooters Buffalo Chicken Wings
> Olive Garden Hot Artichoke & Spinach Dip
> Pizza Hut Original Stuffed Crust Pizza

For a party:

> T.G.I. Friday's Nine-Layer Dip
> Applebee's Pizza Sticks
> Outback Gold Coast Coconut Shrimp
> Hard Rock Cafe Watermelon Ribs
> Ruth's Chris Potatoes Au Gratin
> Red Robin Mountain High Mudd Pie
> T.G.I. Friday's Smoothies

These are just some ideas. Surely there are many great combinations of these dishes, and I'm sure you can come up with some of your own that will include clones of creations from the restaurants that you like best.

Lastly, just for fun, you'd like to know if this smarty-pants author can really do what he says he can—create recipes that taste just like the real deal. Take the Top Secret Challenge. Get some of these dishes to go, make the clone, put on some blindfolds and give it the true taste test. If all goes well, you should have a tough time identifying the real product over the phony. My fingers are crossed.

SOME QUICK TIPS

To help ensure that all goes well, here are some quick words of advice on how to get the best results from your cloning experience:

- Read the entire recipe through before you start cooking. There's been many a time I didn't familiarize myself with a recipe first, only to discover halfway through that I wouldn't be able to finish, since I didn't have the right equipment or ingredients. You will need to know if you'll be using the barbecue, so you can refill the propane that ran out last Saturday. You will want to know that you need an 8-inch springform pan before you start the cheesecake. Read ahead and minimize the surprises.

- Read the "Tidbits" section at the end of any recipe that has one. That section may offer some helpful advice or recipe variations you might want to try.
- Know the yield before you start. I've designed several of the recipes, especially sandwiches, to yield only enough for one serving, but those recipes can be easily doubled, tripled, or quadrupled to serve more.
- Refer to the "blueprints." Each of the recipes has been written so that you shouldn't need to refer to a drawing for help. But, you'll find the drawings give you a good idea what you're shooting for. As they say, a picture is worth a thousand words. When it comes to kitchen cloning, perhaps it's worth even more than that.
- Identify parts of the recipes that can be used for other dishes. Many of the recipes include dips, dressings, and sauces which are great stand-alone recipes to use in another dish you may create. You may find that the teriyaki sauce in the Western Sizzlin' "Teriyaki" Chicken or the honey-lime dressing for Chili's Caribbean Chicken Salad can be used as delicious marinades in other recipes.

So, clone away and, most important, have fun with it. I hope you enjoy trying these recipes as much as I did creating them. Perhaps many will become permanent additions to your home menus.

I'd love to hear if you have any requests for additional recipes in future volumes of *Top Secret Recipes* as many of the recipes in this book started with a request from readers like you. For more *Top Secret Recipes* information and to contact me, come visit the *Top Secret Recipes* website at: **www.topsecretrecipes.com.**

TABLE FOR TWO:
THE RESTAURANT TALE

Somewhere around 1500 B.C. in ancient Egypt, the first full-service food establishment on the planet opened its doors. No one is sure of the name; so we'll just call it "Happy Joseph's Nile Inn." You see, Joe, the proprietor, was a bright man. His ancestors had been prospering for thousands of years, with everything they required to lead comfortable lives being provided by the rich, fertile lands surrounding the nearby Nile River. But, you know how it is—give an ancient Egyptian a millennium or two, and he's going to want more than the same old figs and geese and robes and jewelry enjoyed by his great-great-great-great-great-great-great grandparents.

Happy Joe was a thoughtful man who watched as merchants set out in large caravans on journeys to great lands hundreds of miles away. The melange of cloth, tools, fruits, vegetables, and livestock that these merchants brought back would make them wealthy and popular. Soon many more merchants seeking similar wealth would set out on such journeys in search of better weapons, more colorful dyes, and a beer that still tasted great, but was a little less filling.

Joe knew these weary travelers would require a cozy place to stop, kick off the sandals, and get some shuteye for the night; a place that could shelter them from the cold and offer them some nourishment. The trips were treacherous, filled with adventure, and plagued by robbers—this was work that made a man ravenous and weary. Happy Joseph's Nile Inn provided the men with a welcome bellyful of grub and a cozy bed of straw in exchange for precious goods off their wagons.

Though this may have been the first restaurant in the world, it bore little similarity to the restaurants we know today. When you stopped in at Happy Joe's you wouldn't have been seated at a private table by a smiling hostess, nor would you choose your meal from a colorful menu, nor would you eat your food with a fork or knife. At Joe's place there was one long wooden table where everybody sat to eat and you picked your entree from the livestock or produce you carried with you on your journey (yes, it was B.Y.O.). Joe merely prepared it for you using his own knives and pots and a great little charcoal stove that worked much like the stoves we use today. Joe grilled your antelope meat and offered you beer or wine, while his wife baked delicious bread. When the food was ready you helped yourself and sat on a bench to eat with your fingers. Then you cheerfully passed out in the corner amongst a pile of your companions.

Happy Joe's became exceedingly popular. But time eventually took its toll and Joe grew too old for the work. One day he and his wife closed up the business for good and retired to a small southern beach community.

Though he did marvelous things with gazelle butt steaks, Joe's food would hardly be missed. By then many other entrepreneurs had followed in Joe's footsteps to open their own inns along the expanding trade routes. Eventually this included the entire eastern end of the Mediterranean Sea. By now these inns were providing their own food—no longer did you have to bring it with you. If you arrived at the right time, you could help yourself to a share of whatever was cooking in the pot or baking in the stove. If you got there late in the evening, you had better like your meat very well done, cold, or both. That is, if there was any left.

These inns were soon offering more comforts and pleasures to the weary travelers. Prostitution became a popular service exchanged for money and goods in these establishments. Merchants served coffees and pastries to the customers—predecessors to today's popular coffeehouses (which generally lack the carnal offerings). The menus were improving considerably at these inns, which were now selling a variety of foods including fresh vegetables and fruits, fish, duck, goose, beef, milk, cheese, butter, fancy cakes, date and palm wine, and beer. This was a time of great growth and development in the early food-service business, for many of the same techniques of food preparation that we use today have origins in ancient Egypt. Nevertheless, historians still argue amongst themselves whether this is when the slogan "Eat at Joe's" was first used.

GREASE IN GREECE

In 1000 B.C. the center of civilization moved up the eastern end of the Mediterranean and then west to Greece. Here, it was the duty of the slaves to do all of the cooking. At first, the slaves were female—just about every household had a couple—with very basic cooking skills. Then there began a shift toward male slaves who were very skilled in all aspects of cooking. These special slaves, or *magieros*, gained much respect for their duties in the kitchen. A magiero was encouraged to develop new dishes and earned public acclaim for fancy feasts prepared by assistants under his control. These were the original chefs responsible for making the art of cooking a respectable profession.

Those ancient Greeks, what trendsetters they were. It was the Greeks who developed the custom of three meals that is familiar in much of the world today, although the types of food eaten at these meals has changed significantly. For example, shortly after getting out of bed it was customary to eat a meal called *ariston*, which included bread dipped in wine. Just try explaining that one at work. The next meal was called *diepnon* and was eaten shortly after noon. It consisted of a dish that varied from household to household, but could have included breads, cakes and porridge, vegetables and fruits, plus eggs, poultry, or fish. The main meal of the day would come shortly after sunset and was called *cena* or *derpon*. This meal, like our dinner, consisted of meat with vegetables and bread or other side dishes, and a dessert. The Greeks used olive oil in place of butter and they sweetened their food with honey.

The ancient Greeks loved to eat in groups. They would throw huge parties in dining clubs and gorge themselves with food prepared by magieros and their apprentices. This was their version of the full-service restaurant. The custom was to lie on the left side on rows of cushioned couches and eat with the right hand from baskets of food brought to them. There were no utensils to speak of except maybe a spoonlike implement used to handle gravies, sauces, and soups. The only knife in the dining room was handled by the carver, whose job it was to ensure that everyone's meat had been cut into bite-size pieces. "Oh, carve boy! Chop-chop."

In 146 B.C. the Romans conquered the Greeks, and that was the end of that party.

Although handy in a battle, the ancient Romans were pigs. On a daily basis they would eat all their meals at one sitting that would start at around one o'clock in the afternoon, after the close of business. Then they would eat and eat and eat, sometimes through the night and into the next day. The Roman emperor Nero had been known to eat continuously for thirty-six hours.

The first part of the meal was *gustaus*, which might include eggs, vegetables, and shellfish. The main course, or *mensa prima*, consisted of stews or roasted veal, fish, or fowl. For dessert, *mensa secunda*, came pastries, honey-sweetened cakes, fruits, jams, and sweetmeats. On special occasions this afternoon meal was expanded to include six courses or more. But that was nothing. It was in the commonly celebrated banquets and dinner parties that Romans demonstrated their hedonistic and gastronomic overindulgences.

You'd be challenged to find an establishment that throws a party like those the Romans enjoyed. Huge sums of money were spent and crowds of people would jam into extravagantly furnished dining halls. Sandals were removed and feet were washed by slaves. Upon cloth-covered tables was served course after course of food and wine. Guests used spoons and forks and knives and toothpicks to eat from ornate serving platters. They were required to bring their own napkins, but that was okay, since they could wrap up leftovers to take home—the first doggie bags!

Several hours into these dinner parties, when the guests could eat no more, they would force themselves to vomit, and start all over again. As this went on for seven, eight, nine hours, and as the wine was taking its toll, robes were removed and the party degenerated into a huge sexual orgy. The slaves that earlier had been serving food would now be beaten for amusement and the banquet hall would be in shambles.

Sure, this sounds more like a college frat party than a dining experience, but the Romans also had establishments that somewhat resembled our modern restaurants. They were called *taberna meritoria* or taverns of merit. Here guests would sit in dining halls at long tables and were served food while the proprietor watched from a raised platform at the front of the room. If the food was not satisfactory the cook would be flogged in the dining room. This little incentive encouraged a culinary artistry similar to that of the ancient Greeks, with care taken to present the food most elegantly.

Magieros continued to teach the Romans about cooking and many were freed by grateful masters who appreciated their skill in the kitchen. The kitchen was now separated from other rooms and departmentalized, and the first cookbook was written during this era, by Apicus, in A.D. 25. The title, crudely translated: "Please Don't Flog Before You Try My Grilled Hog."

THE MIDDLE AGES SUCKED

The Middle or Dark Ages added virtually nothing to our cuisine or dining customs. When the Greek and Roman empires vanished, records of their culinary achievements were left undiscovered until after the demise of this medieval era.

For the next 1400 years, civilization in Europe seemed to move backward into a dark time where kings ruled from cold stone castles and the lower classes lived in small mud or thatch huts. While poor farmers were living on tiny meals of turnips, cabbage, and salt pork, feudal rulers were stuffing themselves on as many as thirty meals a day. Still, the food was bland and stuck together with thick sauces and gravies so that it could be eaten with only the hands. Utensils and plates were not used. The food was cut into bite-size portions and poured into hollowed-out loaves of bread called "trenchers." A spoon-like implement had been developed, but it was so difficult to use, everyone preferred to use their fingers.

In the castles, meals were served in huge dining halls filled with hundreds of people who just stood around talking until they could take their turn at the grub. The room was usually filled with smoke from a huge fire blazing in the center of the room. Knights would bring their horses into the hall, so that they would be ready for battle, and dogs were rummaging through the straw for bones and scraps of food. This loud, smelly occasion was more like a dirt-cheap, Podunk wedding reception from hell, than a time to enjoy a decent meal. Let's set that clock forward, quick.

NOW WE'RE GETTING THERE

The 1500s saw a noticeable improvement in food and culinary artistry, at last. Spices were coming in from the Orient to put some zing into the bland, nearly tasteless food of the Middle Ages. The kingdoms were dissolving and people were beginning to rediscover food.

In the seventeenth century, the table fork was reintroduced to the world. This was significant for the changes the implement would bring to the consistency and form of food. The sticky goo that had become an important ingredient in finger food of the Dark Ages was no longer a necessity. Shortly thereafter the dinner plate that had been missing from food service since Roman times was back, and the culinary arts flourished.

Chefs designed creative and tasty dishes, and brought a new era of professionalism to the industry. The highly talented chefs gained a great deal of respect and wealth, and dressed as noblemen.

The eighteenth century saw rapid growth throughout Europe. Because of this, meat, bread, and other foods were in scarce supply. So the King of France established a system that gave exclusive rights to a group of cooks to sell specific prepared meals. This small group of cooks offered these high-quality, expensive meals to only those who could afford them. Other, less wealthy customers had to settle for the lower-quality, meatless food prepared by soup vendors.

One of these merchants was Boulanger, a man who, in 1765, saw a need for more substance in his dishes. He had no license to sell meat, but had created a soup consisting of sheep's feet in cream sauce (Mmm, mmm good). To sell his soup he couldn't mention meat, or risk arrest, so he put a sign over his shop which said, "Boulanger sells magical restoratives." The dish was a big hit and his shop became very popular. Soon the word "restorative" evolved into "restaurant," now the accepted term for an establishment committed solely to the business of providing meals to the public.

It didn't take long for restaurants to start popping up all over the place throughout France. The French Revolution forced many of the wealthy aristocrats to lose valuable property, so they had to let go of their private chefs. With nothing else to do, these talented artisans opened their own restaurants, and soon there was a surge of fancy eateries. By 1804, Paris boasted more than 400 restaurants, many of them responsible for creating scores of now-famous dishes—a redeeming factor for a nation that 150 years later would consider Jerry Lewis a genius.

FIRST ON THE BLOCK IN AMERICA

In Boston, a man named Samuel Cole saw the opportunity to pocket some serious coin from the increasing number of travelers along a major roadway, much like his Egyptian predecessor, Happy Joe. So, in 1734, he opened up a joint called "Cole's" to service the constant flow of stagecoaches full of hungry travelers. Sammy referred to his new place as an "ordinary," or "tavern," which was just another name for an "inn" in New England. But, unlike everyone else in the inn business, Sammy didn't take overnight guests (and he didn't take American Express). This set Cole's apart from the rest as the first establishment to concentrate on preparing and serving food to guests who would not be spending the night. Cole's became America's first restaurant.

Through the 1700s, taverns dotted the roadsides as settlers migrated across America. The food served in these establishments remained unexciting, ordinary fare, served from a kettle which hung over a flame in the fireplace. But in 1827, that would begin to change. This was the year that John Delmonico, a Swiss immigrant, opened the world-renowned restaurant Delmonico's in New York City.

Delmonico's brought a touch of class to the food-service industry. The restaurant served food with great attention to every aspect of its preparation and presentation. Its extensive menu was printed in both French and English, and every waiter was bilingual. At Delmonico's you dined at cloth-covered tables, you chose your wine from an extensive list, and enjoyed a wide selection of European entrees never before served in the United States. All of this while surrounded by a clientele from the upper crust, including businessmen and statesmen, presidents and dignitaries.

Delmonico's attention to detail set the pace for fancy restaurants that would come in future years, many of them directly influenced by John Delmonico's concept. Delmonico would even copy himself, by opening up branches of his own restaurant in other locations—a trend very popular today. Delmonico's was the first documented restaurant in the U.S. to serve "Hamburg Steak," a broiled chopped steak dish that would evolve into America's most popular food: the hamburger.

The original Delmonico's survived for 96 years, finally closing its doors in 1923, but not before making the full-service fine dining experience a popular institution.

MODERN DEVELOPMENTS AT LAST

As the world's first cafeteria was being created in San Francisco during the gold rush of 1849, significant developments were being made in kitchen equipment. In 1850 the cast iron stove was invented. It gave way to the gas stove in the 1870s as lines were built to pump gas into the growing cities. By 1889, the hot water heater was created, which helped dishwashers to clean dishes without tying up the stove with pots of boiling water. Food that had been stored in simple iceboxes (metal boxes with ice in them) was now being stored in mechanical, ammonia-driven refrigerators. These creations would help to improve the quality of food served in restaurants into the twentieth century and beyond.

As the 1900s rolled around, several new inventions were being put to the test in the company restaurant at the Sears and Roebuck mail-order firm in Chicago. The company had just opened the largest food-service operation in the world to feed its employees at lunchtime. And, oh, what a lunchtime it was! One hundred employees operated five restaurants with two thousand seats; they served 12,500 meals a day. A machine made ice around the clock and dishes were washed by an automatic dishwashing machine. Automation was leading to more efficiency in the kitchen, so that restaurants could serve customers faster, and be prepared for the next arrivals instantaneously.

Food service was getting better and faster. With the popularity of cars on the rise, Roy Allen devised the first drive-in refreshment stand with carhop service in Lodi, California. When Allen later teamed up with Frank Wright, signs would be raised with the initials "A&W," marking a growing number of root beer outlets that all became part of the world's first franchise.

Two years later Royce Hailey would open the first of many Pig

Stands in Dallas, Texas, serving sandwiches hot off the grill to customers who drove up in their cars. By 1930 there were thirty Pig Stands across the country, and carhop service evolved into a drive-up window, much like those we're used to today. Fast food had arrived.

TABLE FOR TWO

When alcohol was put on a nationwide ban in 1919, soda fountains got a boost in popularity as people looked for a refreshing recreational replacement. Prior to prohibition the pharmacist would be the one to supply the alcohol, so naturally the drugstores became host to the many soda fountains, serving ice cream, root beer, and tonics. Pharmacists were eager to replace their lost alcohol sales.

One day while working as a concessionaire at a soda fountain in the Franklin Institute exhibit in Philadelphia, Robert Green ran out of the cream that was used in one of the popular refreshments. He substituted a large scoop of ice cream and at that moment created the first ice cream soda. He liked what he tasted and immediately added the cool beverage to the menu. By the end of the exhibition, word had spread of the ice-cream soda and the excitement put about $600 a day into Robert's pocket.

As word got out about this new creation, the phenomenon of the ice-cream soda soon spread across the country. Fountains were serving the drink regularly to customers, and in consequence more fountains were opening in drugstores, in markets, and on street corners.

One of the drugstores that had been losing money was purchased in 1925 by a guy named Howard Johnson. He served his homemade ice cream and ice-cream sodas at the soda fountain inside the drugstore, but soon added hot dogs and hamburgers to the menu. When he began to turn a profit, Howard turned the drugstore into a restaurant and expanded into other regions. Howard Johnson became the first person to establish a mass-market menu for a full-service restaurant chain.

In 1936, Bob Wian was set on buying a ten-stool hamburger stand in Glendale, California, from a couple of elderly ladies. Since he couldn't pony up the cash, he sold his prized 1933 DeSoto roadster for $350 and secured the deal. He called his new restaurant "Bob's Pantry," a name that would only last a short while.

When Bob created his now-famous double-decker hamburger dubbed "the Big Boy," Bob quickly changed the name of his restaurant chain and franchised like crazy. Big Boy restaurants dotted the nation, and by the time he was thinking about retirement in 1960, Bob's Big Boy was the second largest restaurant chain in the world, raking in $200 million a year—Howard Johnson's was first on the list, while McDonald's sat down at number three. Bob Wian built his last Big Boy in 1964, and today many of the original restaurants have been sold and converted to other restaurants.

As the fifties rolled around, popularity of the drive-in restaurant was at an all-time high. Customers seeking speed and convenience with their meals could just pull their cars into a stall and the food would be brought out to them, usually on a tray that hooked over the rolled-down window. The McDonald brothers had a drive-in in 1948 in San Bernardino. That was the first McDonald's, and it was racking up annual receipts of $200,000. There were many others too: Sonic, Blackies, Porky's, and a place called Mel's, made famous in the movie "American Graffiti."

But, as America entered the sixties, problems plagued the drive-in. Loud, rock-and-roll playing teenagers, looking for some action and a place to hang out, began overwhelming the parking lots. The cars that had pulled into the stalls would stay there as the youngsters socialized, keeping the paying customers away. The drive-ins had become tiny traffic jams of hormonally overwhelmed teens cruising for a date. The families looking to go out for a quick, quiet bite to eat could no longer enjoy the experience. Soon, under government pressure, practically all of the 2000 or so drive-ins in the country were shut down.

Meanwhile, the restaurant boom was shifting into fifth gear. Shoney's emerged in 1947 as a franchise of the Big Boy chain, then later would spin off on its own. In 1953, Danny's Donuts opened and eventually evolved into Denny's. The first International House of Pancakes opened its doors in 1958, around the same time a fresh new concept called Sizzler came onto the scene. Sizzler was an affordable steakhouse that combined sit-down dining with fast-food service. You'd order your steak at the front counter and then wait for your number to be called to pick it up. When you had your meal you'd find a seat in the dining room and eat as you would in a full-service restaurant.

In 1965, the face of casual dining would change significantly with the opening of the first T.G.I. Friday's in New York City. The restaurant was initially designed as a place for singles to meet, and was so popular that police had to build barricades around the restaurant to control the crowds. Soon this concept of the upbeat, entertaining atmosphere would be imitated the country over, and casual dining would get a huge shot in the tush.

TOP 10 RESTAURANT COMPANIES

1995 RANKING	COMPANY	FISCAL 1995 SALES IN $ MILLIONS
1	**PepsiCo, Inc.** (Pizza Hut, Taco Bell, KFC, Hot 'N Now, Chevy's, Eastside Mario's)	9,202.0
2	**McDonald's Corp.** (McDonald's)	4,474.0
3	**Darden Restaurants, Inc.** (Red Lobster, Olive Garden, Bahama Breeze)	3,200.0
4	**Flagstar Cos. Inc.** (Denny's, Hardees, Quincy's, El Pollo Loco)	2,381.0
5	**Wendy's International** (Wendy's Old-Fashioned Hamburgers)	1,416.3
6	**Imasco Ltd.** (Hardees, Roy Rogers)	1,300.0
7	**Brinker International** (Chili's, Romano's, Macaroni Grill, On the Border)	1,160.0
8	**Family Restaurants** (Chi-Chi's, El Torito, Coco's, Carrows, Reuben's, Jojos)	1,134.0
9	**Little Caesar's** (Little Caesar's Pizza)	1,000.0
10	**Metromedia** (Bennigan's, Ponderosa, Steak & Ale, Bonanza Family Grill)	986.0

SOURCE: *Nation's Restaurant News*

When the first Hard Rock Cafe opened in London in 1971, a new trend emerged. With donated sequined jackets, gold records, and guitars hanging from the walls, this restaurant incorporated rock-and-roll nostalgia into its design. It wasn't enough to go to a restaurant just for food anymore, now people looked to be entertained. Surprisingly, it took twenty years for the trend to really mushroom. In 1991, the first Planet Hollywood opened in New York just down the street from the New York Hard Rock Cafe. Planet Hollywood was essentially the Hard Rock concept, with a Hollywood twist. Instead of displaying music memorabilia, Planet Hollywood is decorated with props and costumes from movies and television.

The smashing success of these "theme restaurants" created a surge of openings in the nineties. Today, in addition to the Hard Rock Cafe and Planet Hollywood, we have the Official All-Star Cafe, The Harley Davidson Cafe, The Motown Cafe, The Fashion Cafe, Dive!, House of Blues, and the NASCAR cafe, with several other new concepts in the pipeline.

THE CRYSTAL BALL

Restaurants have come a long way since the days of Happy Joseph's Nile Inn. Since the number of restaurants opening their doors is increasing every day at a phenomenal rate, so is the competition. To keep up, these full-service chains are having to overhaul menus on a regular basis. Gone are the days when owners could only change their menus once a year. Today menu items are added and dropped as often as every two months, and new concepts for food must constantly be explored. Many of these chains find they need to remodel their restaurants every five to seven years to stay fresh and interesting, and to hold onto their loyal customer base.

We're likely to see more restaurants developed with a heavy dose of fun and entertainment as a main component. In a recent survey, 44 percent of those polled said they want an upbeat entertaining atmosphere in the restaurants they frequent. That's probably why we're seeing numerous new concepts for theme restaurants similar to House of Blues, Dive!, or Planet Hollywood, and successful restaurants with a friendly, party-like atmosphere such as Applebee's, T.G.I. Friday's, and Red Robin.

With the recent dietary concerns regarding calories and fat intake, most of these chains have included special choices on their menus under headings like "Guiltless Grill," "Low-Fat and Fabulous," and "Lightside." The dishes usually include grilled chicken, pastas, and salads. It's a sure bet that we'll see more of this trend as restaurant chains unveil new dishes developed with health-conscious eaters in mind.

As long as we have to sustain our biological need for food, and because we are part of a society constantly craving speed, convenience, and entertainment, restaurants in America will flourish. Just exactly what new trends might develop in the future as restaurants continue to duke it out for our dining dollars is anyone's guess. The battlefield is littered with failures of one of the country's most competitive and cutthroat industries. If Happy Joe were in the business today, he might not be so happy.

But, who knows, he might have made millions sparking a trend in gazelle butt sandwiches. Think about it—drive-thru outlets dotting the globe, all with big neon signs off the highways bearing his infamous slogan: "Eat at Joe's. Get Your Butt Over Here, Now!"

Hmmm ...

APPLEBEE'S QUESADILLAS

☆　♥　☎　✎　✈　✉　✂　☞　✿

Menu Description: "Two cheeses, bacon, tomatoes, onions & jalapenos grilled between tortillas with guacamole, sour cream & salsa."

When Bill and T. J. Palmer opened their first restaurant in Atlanta, Georgia, in 1980, they realized their dream of building a full-service, reasonably-priced restaurant in a neighborhood setting. They called their first place T.J. Applebee's Edibles & Elixirs, and soon began franchising the concept. In 1988 some franchisees bought the rights to the name and changed it to Applebee's Neighborhood Grill & Bar. By that time, there were 54 restaurants in the organization. Today there are over 650, making Applebee's one of the fastest-growing restaurant chains in the world.

According to waiters at the restaurant, the easy-to-make and slightly spicy quesadillas are one of the most popular appetizers on the Applebee's menu. The recipe calls for 10-inch or "burrito-size" flour tortillas, which can be found in most supermarkets, but any size can be used in a pinch. Look for the jalapeño "nacho slices" in the ethnic or Mexican food section of the supermarket. You'll find these in jars or cans. Cilantro, which is growing immensely in popularity, can be found in the produce section near the parsley, and is also called fresh coriander or Chinese parsley.

Two 10-inch ("burrito-size") flour tortillas
2 tablespoons butter, softened
1/3 cup shredded Monterey Jack cheese
1/3 cup shredded Cheddar cheese
1/2 medium tomato, chopped
2 teaspoons diced onion

1 teaspoon diced canned jalapeño ("nacho slices")
1 slice bacon, cooked
1/4 teaspoon finely chopped fresh cilantro
Dash salt

Sour cream   *Salsa*
Guacamole

1. Heat a large frying pan over medium heat.
2. Spread half of the butter on one side of each tortilla. Put one tortilla, butter side down, in the hot pan.
3. Spread the cheeses evenly onto the center of the tortilla in the pan. You don't have to spread the cheese all the way to the edge. Leave a margin of an inch or so all the way around.
4. Sprinkle the tomato, onion, and jalapeño over the cheese.
5. Crumble the slice of cooked bacon and sprinkle it over the other ingredients.
6. Sprinkle the cilantro and a dash of salt over the other ingredients.
7. Top off the quesadilla with the remaining tortilla, being sure that the buttered side is facing up.
8. When the bottom tortilla has browned, after 45 to 90 seconds, flip the quesadilla over and grill the other side for the same length of time.
9. Remove the quesadilla from the pan, and, using a sharp knife or pizza cutter, cut the quesadilla three times through the middle like a pizza, creating 6 equal slices. Serve hot with sour cream, guacamole, and salsa on the side.

- SERVES 1 OR 2 AS AN APPETIZER

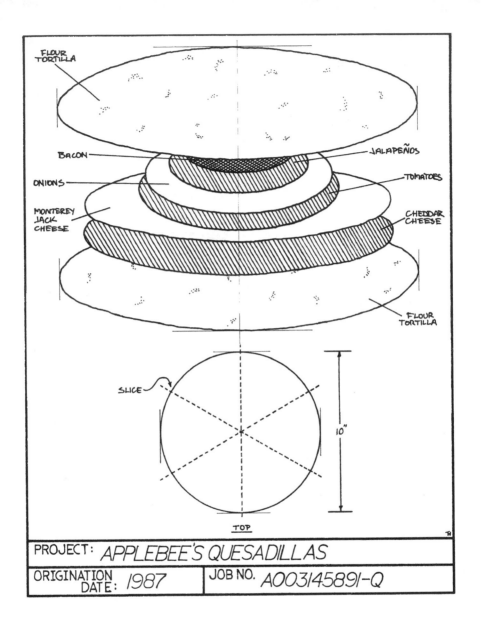

FLOUR
TORTILLA

BACON

JALAPEÑOS

ONIONS

TOMATOES

MONTEREY
JACK
CHEESE

CHEDDAR
CHEESE

FLOUR
TORTILLA

SLICE

10"

TOP

PROJECT: *APPLEBEE'S QUESADILLAS*

ORIGINATION
DATE: *1987*

JOB NO. *A003145891-Q*

APPLEBEE'S PIZZA STICKS

☆ ♥ ☎ ✎ ✈ ⊠ ✂ ☞ ✿

Menu Description: "Parmesan: Thin crusty strips of pizza dough topped with herbs & melted Italian cheese, served with marinara sauce.
Loaded: Add Italian sausage & pepperoni."

Each Applebee's makes an effort to decorate the inside of the restaurant with pictures and memorabilia from the neighborhood in which it is located. You'll see photographs of local heroes and students, license plates, banners, old souvenirs, trinkets, and antiques— all representing area history. Take a look around the walls of the next Applebee's you visit. Maybe you can find something you lost several years ago.

Meanwhile, here's a find: pizza sticks that are made from dough that is proofed, fried, and then broiled. The frying adds a unique flavor and texture to the dough that you won't get with traditional pizza. I've designed this recipe to use the premade dough that comes in tubes (you know, like the stuff from that dough boy). But you can make this with any dough recipe you might like, or with one from this book (which I know you'll like, see page 437). Just roll the dough into a 10 × 15-inch rectangle before slicing.

These appetizers can be made either in the Parmesan version without meat, or "loaded" with sausage and pepperoni. This recipe yields a lot, so it makes good party food.

MARINARA DIPPING SAUCE

One 8-ounce can tomato sauce
1 tomato, chopped
1 tablespoon diced onion
1 teaspoon sugar

½ teaspoon dried oregano
⅛ teaspoon salt
⅛ teaspoon dried basil

PARMESAN PIZZA STICKS

One 10-ounce tube instant pizza
  dough (Pillsbury is good)
2 to 4 cups vegetable oil for frying
1¾ cups grated mozzarella cheese
¼ cup grated fresh Parmesan cheese

½ teaspoon dried oregano
¼ teaspoon dried basil
¼ teaspoon caraway seeds
¼ teaspoon garlic salt

OPTIONAL (FOR THE "LOADED")

3 ounces pepperoni, diced
3 ounces Italian sausage, cooked and
  crumbled

1. Preheat the oven to 425°F.
2. Prepare the dipping sauce by combining all of the marinara ingredients in a small, uncovered saucepan and bringing the mixture to a boil. Reduce the heat, cover, and simmer the sauce for
   ½ hour. (The sauce can be made ahead and kept, refrigerated,
   for several days.)
3. Prepare the pizza sticks by first proofing the dough. Unroll the
   dough onto a cutting board and straighten the edges. It should
   form a rectangle that is longer from left to right than top to bottom. With a sharp knife or pizza cutter, slice through the middle
   of the dough lengthwise. This will divide the rectangle into two
   thinner rectangles that will measure 4 to 5 inches from top to
   bottom.
4. Slice the dough from top to bottom into 1½-inch-wide pieces.
   You should have somewhere between 20 and 24 dough slices.
5. Place the slices onto a greased cookie sheet about ½ inch apart
   and bake for 3 minutes. You may have to use more than one
   cookie sheet. This will proof the dough so that it becomes stiff.
6. Heat vegetable oil in a frying pan or deep fryer to 350°F. Oil
   should be at least ½ inch deep if using a stovetop pan. You will
   want to use more oil with a deep fryer.
7. Fry pizza sticks 5 to 6 at a time for about 1 minute per side or
   until they are a dark golden brown. Remove them from the oil
   onto a cloth or paper towel to drain.

8. When all the pizza dough sticks are fried, arrange them once again on the cookie sheet(s). You may want to line the cookie sheets with foil to make cleanup easier. Preheat the broiler.
9. Sprinkle the mozzarella cheese evenly over the dough.
10. Sprinkle the Parmesan cheese evenly over the mozzarella.
11. Combine the oregano, basil, caraway seeds, and garlic salt in a small bowl. If your oregano and basil are fairly coarse you can use your thumb and first finger to crunch the spice up a little, making it a finer blend.
12. Sprinkle the spice mixture over the cheese.
13. If you want to make the "loaded" variety, sprinkle the pepperoni and sausage over the top of the pizza sticks.
14. Broil the pizza sticks for 2 minutes or until the cheese is melted. Serve hot with dipping sauce on the side.

- SERVES 6 TO 8 AS AN APPETIZER

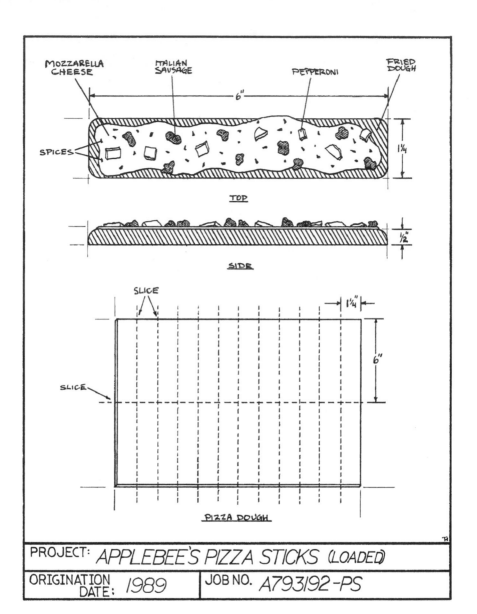

MOZZARELLA CHEESE   ITALIAN SAUSAGE   PEPPERONI   FRIED DOUGH

SPICES

6"

1¼

TOP

SIDE

½

SLICE

SLICE

1¼"

6"

PIZZA DOUGH

PROJECT: *APPLEBEE'S PIZZA STICKS (LOADED)*

ORIGINATION DATE: *1989*

JOB NO. *A793192-PS*

APPLEBEE'S ORIENTAL CHICKEN SALAD

☆　♥　☎　✎　✈　✉　✂　☞　✿

Menu Description: "Crisp Oriental greens topped with chunks of crunchy Chicken Fingers, toasted almonds & crispy rice noodles tossed in a light Oriental vinaigrette."

Applebee's 60-item menu is revised at least twice a year. That means about 40 percent of the entire menu changes on a regular basis, with those selections varying from location to location. The other 60 percent are items found on menus in all of the Applebee's restaurants, and they seldom change. This practice of constant menu retooling is becoming more frequent in all of the large restaurant chains these days. As competition grows, the chains find they must alter their menus regularly to keep discriminating customers interested.

Even though the Oriental Chicken Salad, which is considered one of the restaurant's signature items, has been on the menu for some time now, it's possible that by the time you are reading this book it has been replaced by another salad selection. If that happens, here's the only way you can still enjoy this salad creation—by making your own. You'll love the Oriental dressing with the unique, nutty flavor of roasted sesame oil. This type of oil is becoming quite popular today and can be found in the supermarket near the other oils or where the Asian food is displayed.

ORIENTAL DRESSING

3 tablespoons honey
1 ½ tablespoons white vinegar
4 teaspoons mayonnaise

1 tablespoon Grey Poupon Dijon
　mustard
⅛ teaspoon sesame oil

SALAD

2 to 4 cups vegetable oil for frying	*3 cups chopped romaine lettuce*
I egg	*I cup chopped red cabbage*
½ cup milk	*I cup chopped napa cabbage*
½ cup all-purpose flour	*½ carrot, julienned or shredded*
½ cup cornflake crumbs	*I green onion, sliced*
I teaspoon salt	*I tablespoon sliced almonds*
¼ teaspoon pepper	*⅓ cup chow mein noodles*
I boneless, skinless chicken breast half	

1. Using an electric mixer, blend together all the ingredients for the dressing in a small bowl. Put the dressing in the refrigerator to chill while you prepare the salad.
2. Preheat the oil in a deep fryer or frying pan over medium heat. You want the temperature of the oil to be around 350°F. If using a frying pan, the oil should be around ½ inch deep. More oil can be used in a deep fryer so that the chicken is immersed.
3. In a small, shallow bowl beat the egg, add the milk, and mix well.
4. In another bowl, combine the flour with the cornflake crumbs, salt, and pepper.
5. Cut the chicken breast into 4 or 5 long strips. Dip each strip of chicken first into the egg mixture then into the flour mixture, coating each piece completely.
6. Fry each chicken finger for 5 minutes or until the coating has darkened to brown.
7. Prepare the salad by tossing the romaine with the red cabbage, napa cabbage, and carrot.
8. Sprinkle the green onion on top of the lettuce mixture.
9. Sprinkle the almonds over the salad, then the chow mein noodles.
10. Cut the chicken into bite-size chunks. Place the chicken on the salad, forming a pile in the middle. Serve with the salad dressing on the side.

• SERVES I AS AN ENTREE (CAN BE DOUBLED)

APPLEBEE'S CLUB HOUSE GRILL

☆　♥　☎　✎　✈　✉　✂　☛　✿

Menu Description: "Applebee's signature hot club sandwich with warm sliced ham & turkey, Cheddar, tomatoes, mayonnaise & Bar-B-Que sauce on thick-sliced grilled French bread. Served with a side of coleslaw."

Here's a sandwich which Applebee's claims is a signature item for the chain. I can see why—it's creative, yet simple. And pretty tasty. It's a cross between a club sandwich and a grilled cheese. So, if you like both of those, you'll love this. And it helps that the sandwich is easy to make when you're as lazy as I am.

For the sliced turkey and ham, go to your deli service counter in the supermarket and get the stuff they machine-slice real thin for sandwiches. This usually tastes the best. If you don't have a service counter, you can find the thin-sliced meats prepackaged near the hot dogs and bologna.

2 thick slices French bread
1 tablespoon butter, softened
2 teaspoons mayonnaise
1/3 cup shredded Cheddar cheese
2 slices deli-sliced turkey breast

2 slices deli-sliced ham
2 slices tomato
2 teaspoons barbecue sauce (Bullseye
　is best)

1. Spread the butter evenly over one side of each slice of bread.
2. Put one slice of bread, butter side down, into a preheated frying pan over medium heat.
3. Spread the mayonnaise over the unbuttered side of the grilling bread.
4. Sprinkle half of the Cheddar cheese over the mayonnaise.

5. Lay the turkey and ham in the pan next to the bread for about 30 seconds to heat it up.
6. When it's warm, lay the turkey on the cheese.
7. Place the tomato slices on the turkey.
8. Spread the barbecue sauce over the tomato slices.
9. Lay the ham on the tomatoes.
10. Sprinkle the remainder of the cheese over the ham.
11. Top off the sandwich with the other slice of bread, being sure that the buttered side is facing up.
12. By now the first side of bread should be golden brown. Flip the sandwich over and grill the other side for 2 to 3 minutes or until golden brown as well.
13. Remove the sandwich from the pan and cut in half diagonally. Serve with additional barbecue sauce on the side.

- SERVES 1 AS AN ENTREE (CAN BE DOUBLED)

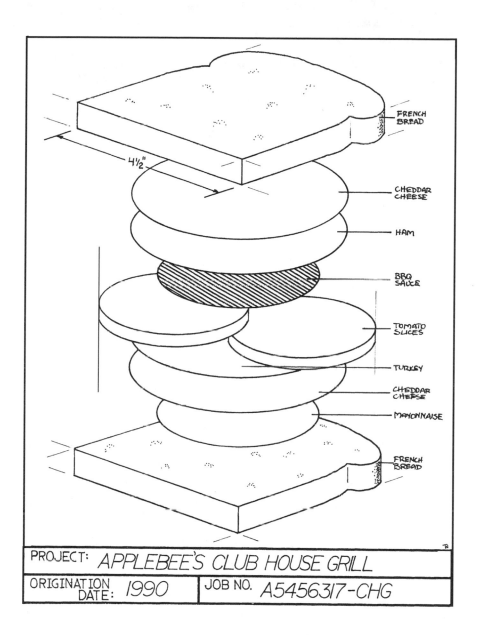

FRENCH BREAD

4½"

CHEDDAR CHEESE

HAM

BBQ SAUCE

TOMATO SLICES

TURKEY

CHEDDAR CHEESE

MAYONNAISE

FRENCH BREAD

PROJECT: *APPLEBEE'S CLUB HOUSE GRILL*

ORIGINATION DATE: *1990*

JOB NO. *A5456317-CHG*

APPLEBEE'S TIJUANA "PHILLY" STEAK SANDWICH

☆　♥　☎　✎　✈　✉　✄　☞　✿

Menu Description: "Lean shaved 'Philly' steak folded into a grilled tortilla roll with Monterey Jack & Cheddar, sautéed mushrooms, onions, tomatoes, bacon & jalapeños."

With the acquisition of 13 Rio Bravo Cantinas in 1994, Applebee's made its move into the competitive "Mexican casual dining sector." Perhaps it's the company's interest in Mexican food that inspired this Philadelphia-Tijuana hybrid sandwich. The steak, cheese, mushrooms, and onions give the sandwich a Philly taste, while the tomatoes, bacon, jalapeños, and the tortilla take you across the border.

I really like this newer addition to the menu, probably because I'm a big cheese-steak fan who also loves Mexican food. As you can see from this dish and the one before it, Applebee's has a knack for breathing new life into old sandwich concepts. I hope you'll find this one worth a try.

You shouldn't have any trouble locating the ingredients, except maybe the cilantro. It's becoming very popular so hopefully it will be easy to find. Just look in the produce section near the parsley, where it might also be called fresh coriander or Chinese parsley (not to be confused with Italian parsley). *¡Muy bien!*

1 mushroom, diced
1 tablespoon plus ½ teaspoon butter, softened
Salt
Pepper

3 ounces chipped beef or 1 ½ slices Steak-Umm frozen sandwich steaks
¼ cup shredded Cheddar cheese

¼ cup shredded Monterey Jack cheese
One 10-inch ("burrito-size") flour tortilla
1 heaping tablespoon diced tomato
1 teaspoon diced red onion
¼ teaspoon finely chopped fresh
  cilantro
1 slice bacon, cooked

ON THE SIDE

Shredded lettuce
Sour cream

Salsa

1. Sauté the mushroom in a small pan with ½ teaspoon butter and a dash of salt and pepper. The mushroom pieces should start to turn brown when they are done.
2. Break or cut the beef into bite-size pieces and grill it in another pan over medium heat until brown. Add a dash of salt and pepper. Drain off the fat.
3. Build your sandwich by first sprinkling both cheeses into the center of the tortilla. Keep in mind when adding the cheese that you will be folding in the sides like a burrito, so leave some room on each side.
4. Sprinkle the tomato, onion, sautéed mushroom, and cilantro over the cheese.
5. Crumble the bacon and sprinkle it over the cheese as well.
6. Sprinkle the cooked beef over the other ingredients, then add a bit more salt and pepper, if desired.
7. Fold the sides in, then use the 1 tablespoon butter to butter the top and bottom of the "sandwich" and grill it in a hot pan over medium heat for 2 minutes per side, or until the tortilla becomes golden brown and the cheese is melted.
8. Slice the "sandwich" in half diagonally and serve hot on a plate with shredded lettuce, sour cream, and salsa on the side.

• SERVES 1 AS AN ENTREE (CAN BE DOUBLED)

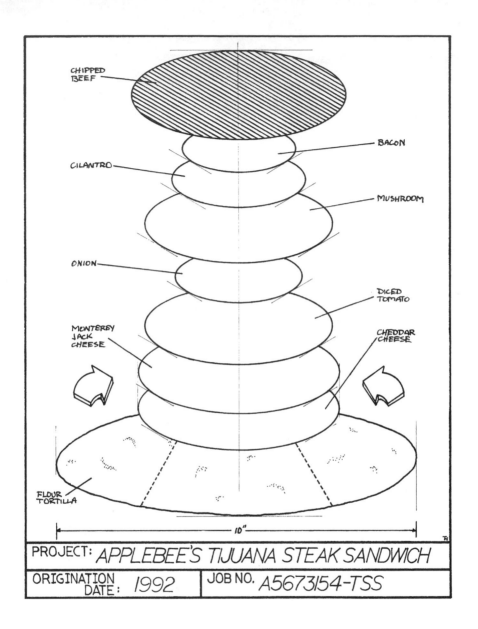

CHIPPED BEEF

BACON

CILANTRO

MUSHROOM

ONION

DICED TOMATO

MONTEREY JACK CHEESE

CHEDDAR CHEESE

FLOUR TORTILLA

10"

PROJECT: *APPLEBEE'S TIJUANA STEAK SANDWICH*

ORIGINATION DATE: *1992*

JOB NO. *A5673154-TSS*

BENIHANA HIBACHI CHICKEN AND HIBACHI STEAK

☆　♥　☎　✎　✈　✉　✂　☞　✿

When 20-year-old Rocky Aoki came to New York City from Japan with his wrestling team in 1959 he was convinced it was the land of opportunity. Just five years later he used $10,000 he had saved plus another $20,000 that he borrowed to open a Benihana steakhouse on the West Side of Manhattan. His concept of bringing the chefs out from the back kitchen to prepare the food in front of customers on a specially designed hibachi grill was groundbreaking. The restaurant was such a smashing success that it paid for itself within six months.

The most popular items at the restaurant are the Hibachi Chicken and Hibachi Steak, which are prepared at your table on an open hibachi grill. But, since most home kitchens are not fitted with a hibachi grill, you'll have to improvise. You will likely have to use two pans; one for the meat and mushrooms, and the other for the remaining vegetables. And since many of today's cooking surfaces are coated with scratchable, nonstick coatings, we won't be slicing the meat and vegetables while they are sizzling on the hot cooking surface as the Benihana chefs do. Nor will you be required to flip a mushroom into your hat.

*4 boneless, skinless chicken breast
　halves
1 large onion
2 medium zucchini
2 cups sliced mushrooms
2 tablespoons vegetable oil
6 tablespoons soy sauce*

*4 tablespoons butter
Salt
Pepper
2 teaspoons lemon juice
3 teaspoons sesame seeds
6 cups bean sprouts*

Mustard Sauce (page 258)   *Ginger Sauce (page 259)*

1. Before you begin cooking be sure that the chicken, onion, zucchini, and mushrooms have been sliced into bite-size pieces. For the onion, slice it as if you were making onion rings, then quarter those slices. For the zucchini, first slice them into long, thin strips, then cut across those strips four or five times to make bite-size pieces that are 1 to 1½ inches long.
2. Spread 1 tablespoon of oil in a large frying pan over medium/high heat. Spread another tablespoon of oil in another pan over medium/high heat.
3. Begin by sautéing the sliced chicken in one of the pans. Add 1 tablespoon of soy sauce, 1 tablespoon of butter, and a dash of salt and pepper to the chicken.
4. Add the onion and zucchini to the other pan. Add 2 tablespoons soy sauce, 1 tablespoon butter, and a dash of salt and pepper. Sauté the vegetables as long as the chicken is cooking, being sure to stir both pans often.
5. When the chicken has sautéed for about 2 minutes or when it appears white on all sides, slide the meat to one side of the pan, pour lemon juice on it, then add the mushrooms to the other side of the pan. Pour 1 tablespoon of the soy sauce over the mushrooms, then add 1 tablespoon of butter plus a dash of salt and pepper. Continue to stir both pans.
6. After 6 to 8 minutes, or when the chicken is done, sprinkle 1 teaspoon of sesame seeds over the chicken, then mix the chicken with the mushrooms. Spoon the chicken mixture in four even portions on four plates next to four even portions of the vegetables from the other pan.
7. Pour the bean sprouts into the same pan in which you cooked the vegetables, and cook over high heat. Add 2 tablespoons soy sauce, 1 tablespoon butter, and a dash of salt and pepper.
8. Cook the sprouts for only a minute or two, or until they have tenderized. Just before you serve the sprouts, sprinkle 2 teaspoons of sesame seeds on them. Serve the sprouts next to the

chicken and vegetables with mustard sauce and ginger sauce on the side.

- SERVES 3 TO 4 AS AN ENTREE

Hibachi Steak

You can also make a Hibachi Steak like you would find at the restaurant. Just follow the chicken recipe, substituting a 16-ounce sirloin steak for the chicken. Also eliminate the lemon juice and sesame seeds from the recipe.

Keep in mind that your sliced beef will likely cook in half the time of the chicken, depending on how rare you like it.

BENIHANA
DIPPING SAUCES

☆　♥　☎　✎　✈　✉　✂　☞　✿

The origin of the name of this chain of Japanese steakhouses dates back to 1935. That's when founder Rocky Aoki's father, Yunosuke Aoki, opened a small coffee shop in Japan and named it "Benihana" after a wild red flower that grew near the front door of his shop. Next time you're at Benihana, look carefully and you'll notice that bright red flower has been incorporated into the restaurant's logo.

With most of the cooking performed before your eyes on an open hibachi grill, Benihana maintains a much smaller kitchen than most restaurants, allowing practically the entire restaurant to become productive, money-generating dining space. The limited space behind the scenes is for storage, office and dressing rooms, and a small preparation area for noncooked items like these sauces. Use them to dip food in—like the Hibachi Steak or Chicken (pages 255 to 257). These sauces will go well with a variety of Asian dishes and can be frozen in sealed containers for weeks at a time.

MUSTARD SAUCE (FOR CHICKEN AND BEEF)

¼ cup soy sauce
¼ cup water
2 teaspoons Oriental mustard*

2 teaspoons heavy cream
½ teaspoon garlic powder

Combine all of the ingredients in a small bowl and mix until well combined. Chill before serving.

*Can be found in the international or Asian food section of your supermarket.

GINGER SAUCE (FOR VEGETABLES AND SEAFOOD)

¼ cup chopped onion
¼ cup soy sauce
1 clove garlic, minced
½ ounce gingerroot (a nickel-size
    slice), peeled and chopped

Juice of ½ lemon (2 tablespoons)
½ teaspoon sugar
¼ teaspoon white vinegar

Combine all of the ingredients in a blender and blend on low speed for 30 seconds or until the gingerroot and garlic have been puréed. Chill before serving.

- MAKES ⅔ CUP OF EACH SAUCE

BENIHANA
JAPANESE FRIED RICE

☆　♥　☎　✎　✈　✉　✂　☛　✿

The talented chefs at Benihana cook food on hibachi grills with flair and charisma, treating the preparation like a tiny stage show. They juggle salt and pepper shakers, trim food with lightning speed, and flip shrimp and mushrooms perfectly onto serving plates or into their tall chef's hat.

One of the side dishes that everyone seems to love is the fried rice. At Benihana this dish is prepared by chefs with precooked rice on open hibachi grills, and is ordered à la carte to complement any Benihana entree, including Hibachi Steak and Chicken. I like when the rice is thrown onto the hot hibachi grill and seems to come alive as it sizzles and dances around like a bunch of little jumping beans. Okay, so I'm easily amused.

This version of that popular side dish will go well with just about any Japanese entree and can be partially prepared ahead of time, and kept in the refrigerator until the rest of the meal is close to done (check out the "Tidbits").

1 cup uncooked long grain converted or parboiled rice (not instant or quick white rice)	½ cup diced onion (½ small onion)
	1½ tablespoons butter
	2 tablespoons soy sauce
2 eggs, beaten	Salt
1 cup frozen peas, thawed	Pepper
2 tablespoons finely grated carrot	

1. Cook the rice following the instructions on the package. This should take about 20 minutes. Pour the rice into a large bowl to let it cool.
2. Scramble the eggs in a small pan over medium heat. Chop

scrambled chunks of egg into small pea-size bits with your spatula while cooking.

3. When the rice has cooled, add the peas, carrot, eggs, and onion to the bowl. Carefully toss all of the ingredients together.
4. Melt the butter in a large frying pan over medium/high heat.
5. When the butter has completely melted, dump the rice mixture into the pan and add the soy sauce plus a dash of salt and pepper. Cook the rice mixture for 6 to 8 minutes, stirring often.

- SERVES 4 AS A SIDE DISH

TIDBITS

This fried rice can be prepared ahead of time by cooking the rice, then adding the peas, carrot, and scrambled egg plus half of the soy sauce. Keep this refrigerated until you are ready to fry it in the butter. That's when you add the salt, pepper, and remaining soy sauce.

BENNIGAN'S BUFFALO CHICKEN SANDWICH

☆　♥　☎　✎　✈　✉　✂　☛　✿

Menu Description: "Our spicy sauce tops a tender, fried, marinated chicken breast. Served with a tangy bleu cheese dressing."

When the first Bennigan's opened in Atlanta, Georgia, in 1976, it resembled an Irish pub. The green decor with brass accents, the Irish-style memorabilia hanging on the walls, and the upbeat friendly atmosphere made the establishment extremely popular, especially during St. Patrick's Day celebrations. Originally, the restaurant was best known for the bar, which served tasty appetizers and creative drinks, but that has since changed. As the restaurant chain expanded across the country, its menu grew to more than 50 items, making 220-outlet Bennigan's a popular casual dining stop.

If you're a big buffalo wings fan, as I am, you'll really dig this sandwich that puts the zesty flavor of hot wings between two buns. This recent addition to the Bennigan's menu has become a popular pick for the lunch or dinner crowd that likes its food on the spicy side. Feel free to double the recipe, but fry the chicken breasts one at a time.

Oil for deep-frying
½ cup all-purpose flour
½ teaspoon salt
½ cup whole milk
1 boneless, skinless chicken breast half
1 hamburger bun

1 leaf green leaf lettuce
2 slices tomato
1 slice red onion
2 tablespoons Louisiana Hot Sauce or
　Frank's Red Hot

ON THE SIDE

Bleu cheese dressing

1. Preheat the oil to 350°F in a deep fryer or a large frying pan over medium heat. Use just enough oil to cover the chicken breast.

2. Stir together the flour and salt in a medium bowl. Pour the milk into another medium bowl.

3. Trim the chicken of any fat. Cut the thin, pointed end off the breast. Pound on the chicken with a meat-tenderizing mallet to flatten the breast and shape it to fit better on the bun.

4. Dip the chicken in milk, then in the flour, being sure to coat the entire surface of the chicken. Take the coated chicken breast and repeat the process. Let the chicken sit in the refrigerator for 10 to 15 minutes.

5. Drop the chicken breast into the hot oil and fry for 10 minutes or until the outside becomes golden brown. Drain on paper towels.

6. As the chicken is frying, toast or grill the face of the hamburger bun until light brown.

7. The sandwich is served open face, so place the bun face up on the plate. On the face of the top bun place the leaf of lettuce.

8. On the lettuce stack two slices of tomato.

9. Separate the slice of red onion and place 2 to 3 rings of onion on the tomato slices.

10. When the chicken breast has cooked and drained, place it in a plastic container that has a lid. Pour the hot sauce into the container, put the lid on top, and shake gently to coat the chicken with hot sauce. Be sure to shake only enough to coat the chicken. If you shake too hard, the crispy coating will fall off the chicken.

11. Stack the chicken breast on the bottom half of the hamburger bun and place it on the plate beside the top half of the sandwich. Serve open face, with bleu cheese dressing on the side.

- SERVES 1 AS AN ENTREE (CAN BE DOUBLED)

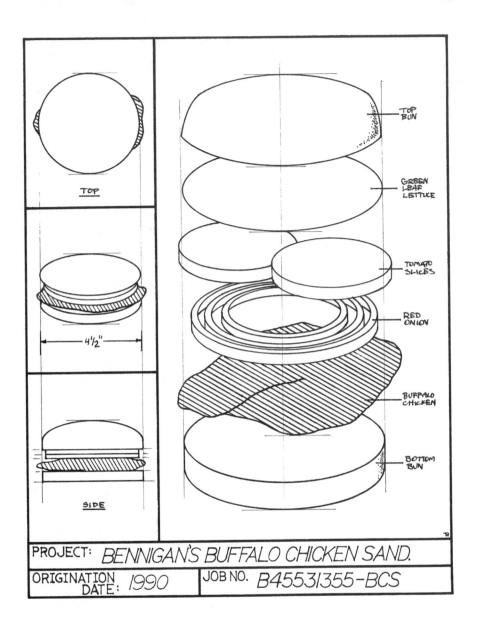

TOP

SIDE

4½"

TOP BUN

GREEN LEAF LETTUCE

TOMATO SLICES

RED ONION

BUFFALO CHICKEN

BOTTOM BUN

PROJECT: *BENNIGAN'S BUFFALO CHICKEN SAND.*

ORIGINATION DATE: *1990*

JOB NO. *B45531355-BCS*

BENNIGAN'S CALIFORNIA TURKEY SANDWICH

☆　♥　☎　✎　✈　✉　✂　☞　✿

Menu Description: "Sliced turkey, avocado, tomato, sprouts, and lettuce with mayonnaise on wheat bread."

The successful chain of Bennigan's restaurants is owned by Metromedia, one of the largest privately held partnerships in the country. Metromedia ranks second on the list of the country's largest casual dining restaurant companies, just behind Little Caesar's Pizza. Other restaurant chains controlled by Metromedia include Steak and Ale, Montana Steak Company, Ponderosa Steakhouse, and Bonanza Steakhouse chains. Altogether Metromedia owns more than 1500 restaurants that ring up nearly half a billion dollars in revenue each year.

It's funny how any sandwich with avocados, sprouts, tomatoes, and lettuce in it winds up with "California" somewhere in the name. This recipe is not exactly a healthier alternative with all the mayonnaise and avocado in there, but if it's low-fat you're looking for, simply substitute a "light" mayonnaise for the regular stuff, ditch the avocado, and you're on your way to the beach.

2 slices wheat bread	½ cup alfalfa sprouts
1 tablespoon mayonnaise	1 leaf green leaf lettuce
¼ pound deli-sliced turkey breast	½ small avocado
2 slices tomato	Salt

1. Spread ½ tablespoon of mayonnaise on one face of each slice of bread.
2. Assemble the sandwich by stacking the turkey on the mayonnaise side of one slice of bread.

3. Place the tomato slices on the turkey.
4. Arrange the sprouts on top of the tomato slices.
5. Place the lettuce leaf on the sprouts.
6. Slice the avocado into thin slices and arrange the slices on the lettuce.
7. Top off the sandwich by placing a slice of bread, mayo side down, on the avocado.
8. Cut the sandwich twice, diagonally from corner to corner, making four triangular pieces.
9. Stick a toothpick straight down through the middle of each sandwich piece to hold it together.

- SERVES 1 AS AN ENTREE (CAN BE DOUBLED)

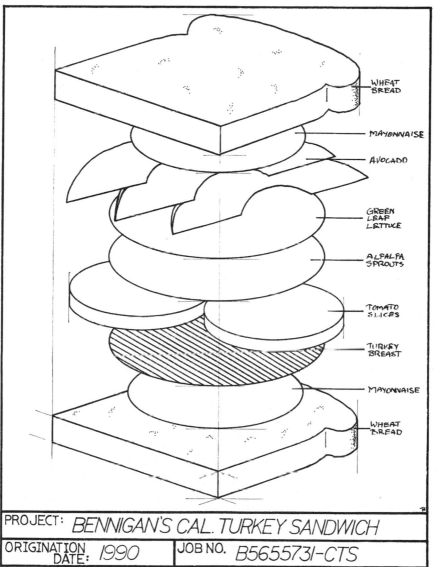

WHEAT
BREAD

MAYONNAISE

AVOCADO

GREEN
LEAF
LETTUCE

ALFALFA
SPROUTS

TOMATO
SLICES

TURKEY
BREAST

MAYONNAISE

WHEAT
BREAD

PROJECT: *BENNIGAN'S CAL. TURKEY SANDWICH*

ORIGINATION
DATE: *1990*

JOB NO. *B565573I-CTS*

BENNIGAN'S COOKIE MOUNTAIN SUNDAE

☆　♥　☎　✎　✈　✉　✂　☞　✿

Menu Description: "Four scoops of vanilla ice cream between two giant chocolate chip cookies. Drizzled with hot fudge and sprinkled with powdered sugar."

Bennigan's puts a twist on the traditional sundae with this sweet treat. Although this dessert was created for the Bennigan's menu, the original sundae has been with us since the turn of the century. Here's some cool history for you: This was a time when alternatives to alcohol were in high demand, so soda fountain proprietors began inventing new drinks. Ice cream sodas—scoops of ice cream combined with soda water and a squirt of flavored syrup—became so popular that Americans were enjoying them to the point of gluttony, especially on the Sabbath day. The treat was soon referred to as the "Sunday Soda Menace," and after Evanston, Illinois, became the first city to enact laws against selling ice cream sodas (shame!), the new prohibition was spreading nationwide. First alcohol, then sodas … you can bet a substitute was in order.

One day a soda fountain clerk, prohibited from selling sodas, served up a bowl of ice cream to a customer who requested a dribbling of chocolate syrup on the top. The fountain clerk, upon tasting the dish himself, found that he had discovered a new taste sensation, and soon the dessert was offered to everyone on Sundays only. Eventually that day of the week would be adopted as the name of the delicious ice-cream dish, with a bit of a spelling change to satisfy the scrutinizing clergy. The "soda-less soda" that we now call a sundae was born.

This recipe makes enough giant chocolate cookies for six or seven sundaes, but you don't have to serve them all at once. Store the cookies in an airtight container and assemble the sundaes as you need them ... on any day of the week.

CHOCOLATE CHIP COOKIES

½ cup softened butter
¼ cup granulated sugar
¾ cup packed brown sugar
I egg
I teaspoon vanilla
I ¼ cups all-purpose flour

½ teaspoon salt
½ teaspoon baking powder
½ teaspoon baking soda
I cup semisweet chocolate chips
  (6 ounces)

½ gallon vanilla ice cream
One 16-ounce jar hot fudge topping

Powdered sugar

1. Preheat the oven to 350°F.
2. Make the cookies by creaming together the butter, sugars, egg, and vanilla in a medium-size bowl.
3. In a separate bowl, sift together the flour, salt, baking powder, and baking soda. Combine the dry ingredients with the butter mixture and mix well.
4. Add the chocolate chips and mix once more.
5. Roll the dough into golfball-size portions and place them 4 inches apart on an ungreased cookie sheet. With your hand, press down on the dough to flatten it to about ½ inch thick. You will likely have to use two cookie sheets for the 12 to 14 cookies the recipe will make. If you use the same cookie sheet for the second batch, be sure to let it cool before placing the dough on it.
6. Bake the cookies for 12 to 14 minutes or until they become a light shade of brown.
7. The cookies served with this dessert have a hole in the center so that when you pour on the hot fudge it flows down through the hole onto the ice cream in the middle. When you take the cookies out of the oven, use the opening of an empty glass soda or beer bottle like a cookie cutter to cut a 1-inch hole in the center of each cookie. Turn the bottle upside down and press the opening into the center of each cookie, rotating the bottle back and forth until the center of the cookie is cut out. Because

the cookie centers will push into the bottle as you go, you'll have to rinse the bottle out before recycling. (If you prefer, you can punch holes in just half of the cookies; these will be the cookies that are stacked on top of the ice cream.)

8. When the cookies have cooled, take four small scoops (about ¼ cup each) of ice cream and arrange them on the top of one cookie that has been placed in the center of the serving plate.

9. Place another cookie on top of the ice cream.

10. Heat up the fudge in a microwave or in the top of a double boiler just long enough to soften the topping so that it is easy to pour. Pour 3 to 4 tablespoons of hot fudge over the top cookie. Let the fudge drizzle down the sides of the ice cream and through the hole that has been cut in the center of the top cookie.

11. Use a sifter or fine strainer to spread a dusting of powdered sugar onto the sundae and around the surface of the serving plate. Repeat with the remaining ingredients for the desired number of servings. The leftover ingredients (if any) can be saved for additional servings later.

- SERVES 6 TO 7

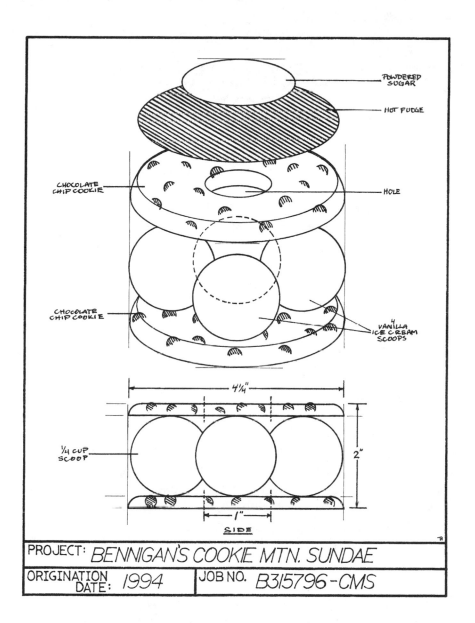

POWDERED SUGAR

HOT FUDGE

CHOCOLATE CHIP COOKIE

HOLE

CHOCOLATE CHIP COOKIE

4 VANILLA ICE CREAM SCOOPS

4¼"

2"

1"

¼ CUP SCOOP

SIDE

PROJECT: *BENNIGAN'S COOKIE MTN. SUNDAE*

ORIGINATION DATE: *1994*

JOB NO. *B315796-CMS*

BIG BOY CREAM OF BROCCOLI SOUP

☆   ♥   ☎   ✎   ✈   ✉   ✂   ☞   ✿

Menu Description: "Our famous Big Boy soups and chili are made fresh daily from fresh vegetables, pure cream and only the finest ingredients."

In 1936, Bob Wian had to make the painful decision to sell his cherished 1933 DeSoto roadster to buy a ten-stool lunch counter from a pair of elderly ladies in Glendale, California. He named his new restaurant Bob's Pantry, and went to work behind the counter himself. Receipts from his first day totaled only twelve dollars. But with the creation of a new hamburger just the next year, and a name change to Bob's Big Boy, business took off. Within three years Bob had expanded his first store and built another location in Los Angeles. In 1948 Bob Wian was voted mayor of Glendale.

A cup of the broccoli soup makes a great first course or a nice partner to a sandwich. I first designed this recipe using frozen broccoli, but the frozen stuff just isn't as tasty as a big bunch of firm, fresh broccoli. So go shopping, and get chopping.

Served in a large bowl, this soup can be a small meal in itself, or it serves four as an appetizer. Try it with a pinch of shredded Cheddar cheese on top.

4 cups chicken broth
1 large bunch broccoli, chopped
    (3 cups)
1/2 cup diced onion
1 bay leaf

1/4 teaspoon salt
Dash ground pepper
1/4 cup all-purpose flour
2 ounces ham (1/3 cup diced)
1/2 cup heavy cream

1. Combine the chicken broth, broccoli, onion, bay leaf, salt, and pepper in a large saucepan over high heat. When the broth

comes to a boil, turn down the heat and simmer, covered, for 30 minutes. The vegetables will become tender.

2. Remove the bay leaf and discard. Transfer a little more than half of the broth and vegetable mixture to a blender or food processor. Mix on low speed for 20 to 30 seconds. This will finely chop the vegetables to nearly a purée. (Be careful blending hot liquids. You may want to let the mixture cool a bit before transferring and blending it.)

3. Pour the blended mixture back into the saucepan over medium/low heat. Add the flour and whisk until all lumps have dissolved.

4. Add the diced ham and the cream to the other ingredients and continue to simmer for 10 to 15 minutes or until the soup is as thick as you like it.

- SERVES 4 AS AN APPETIZER OR 2 AS AN ENTREE

TIDBITS

Because some ham is much saltier than others, I was conservative on the amount of salt in this recipe. You may find that you need more.

BIG BOY ORIGINAL
DOUBLE-DECKER
HAMBURGER CLASSIC

☆　♥　☎　✎　✈　✉　✂　☞　✿

Menu Description: "¼ pound of 100% pure beef in two patties with American cheese, crisp lettuce and our special sauce on a sesame seed bun."

Bob Wian's little ten-stool diner, Bob's Pantry, was in business only a short time in Glendale, California, before establishing a following of regular customers—among them the band members from Chuck Foster's Orchestra. One February night in 1937, the band came by after a gig as they often did to order a round of burgers. In a playful mood, bass player Stewie Strange sat down on a stool and uttered, "How about something different for a change, Bob?" Bob thought it might be funny to play along and serve up Stewie a burger he could barely get his mouth around. So Bob cut a bun into three slices, rather than the usual two, and stacked on two hamburger patties along with lettuce, cheese, and his special sauce. When Stewie tasted the huge sandwich and loved it, every band member wanted his own!

Just a few days later, a plump little six-year-old named Richard Woodruff came into the diner and charmed Bob into letting him do odd jobs in exchange for a burger or two. He often wore baggy overalls and had an appetite that forced the affectionate nickname "Fat Boy."* Bob thought it was the perfect name for his new burger, except the name was already being used as a trademark for another product. So the name of the new burger, along with Bob's booming chain of

---

*Please understand that these are not my choice of words to describe young Richard Woodruff. I prefer the more socially sensitive terms: "Weight-blessed Adolescent," or "Young Adult with a Thinness Deficit." However, I do realize that neither of these descriptions would be a good name for a hamburger.

restaurants, was changed to "Big Boy." The company's tradename Big Boy character is from a cartoonist's napkin sketch of "fat boy," little Richard Woodruff.

The Big Boy hamburger was the first of the double-decker hamburgers. McDonald's Big Mac, the world's best-known burger that came more than 30 years later, was inspired by Bob Wian's original creation. See if you can get your mouth around it.

1/4 pound ground beef
1 1/2 tablespoons mayonnaise
1 teaspoon relish
1 teaspoon tomato sauce
1 sesame seed hamburger bun

Top half of additional hamburger bun
Salt
1/4 cup shredded lettuce
1 slice American cheese

1. Prepare the hamburger patties by dividing the beef in half and pressing each 1/8 pound of beef into a round patty that measures approximately 4 inches across. Because these patties are so thin, you may find them easier to cook if you press them out on waxed paper, and freeze them first. You may want to make several of these patties at once when you first purchase the ground beef, then cook them as you need them.

2. Combine the mayonnaise, relish, and tomato sauce in a small cup or bowl. This is the "secret sauce."

3. Use a serrated knife to cut the top off of the extra bun. You want to leave about a 1/2-inch, double-faced slice.

4. Toast the faces of the buns on a griddle or in a frying pan over medium heat.

5. When the buns are toasted, use the same pan to cook the beef patties. Cook the patties for about 2 minutes per side or until done, being sure to lightly salt each patty.

6. Build the burger by spreading half of the sauce on a face of the middle bun, and the other half on the face of the bottom bun.

7. Stack the lettuce on the sauce on the bottom bun.

8. Stack the cheese on the lettuce.

9. Place one beef patty on the cheese.

10. The middle bun goes next with the sauce-coated side facing up.

11. Stack the other beef patty on the middle bun.

12. Finish the burger off with the top bun. You can microwave the burger for 10 to 15 seconds if you want to warm up the buns.

   • SERVES 1 AS AN ENTRÉE (CAN BE DOUBLED)

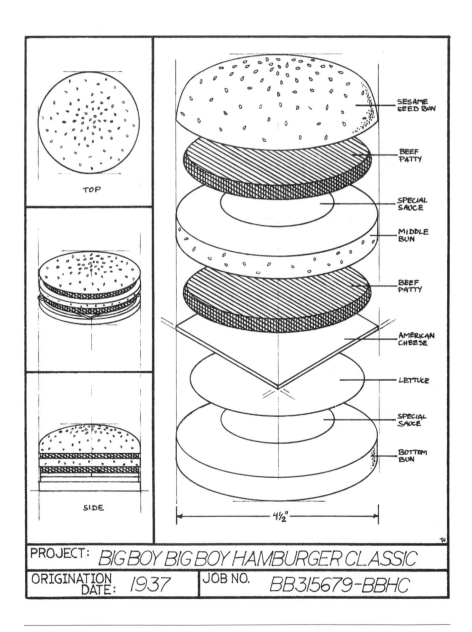

TOP

SIDE

SESAME SEED BUN

BEEF PATTY

SPECIAL SAUCE

MIDDLE BUN

BEEF PATTY

AMERICAN CHEESE

LETTUCE

SPECIAL SAUCE

BOTTOM BUN

4½"

PROJECT: *BIG BOY BIG BOY HAMBURGER CLASSIC*

ORIGINATION DATE: *1937*   JOB NO. *BB315679-BBHC*

BIG BOY CLUB SANDWICH

☆　♥　☎　✑　✈　⊠　✂　☞　✿

Menu Description: "Slices of turkey breast with bacon, tomato, lettuce and mayonnaise, stacked on toasted bread. Served with coleslaw."

When Bob Wian invented the first Big Boy double-decker hamburger in 1937, his restaurant business went through the roof. Soon a slew of imitators hit the market with their own giant-sized burgers: Bun Boy, Brawny Boy, Super Boy, Yumi Boy, Country Boy, Husky Boy, Hi-Boy, Beefy Boy, Lucky Boy, and many other "Boys" across the burger-crazed country.

By 1985 the Big Boy statues had become a common sight in front of hundreds of Bob's restaurants around the country. This was also the year the Marriott Corporation, which had purchased Bob's from a retiring Bob Wian in 1967, created a national ballot to decide whether the Big Boy character would stay or go. Thousands of voters elected to keep the tubby little tike, but his days were numbered. In 1992, Marriott chose to sell all of the Bob's Big Boys to an investment group. Those mostly West Coast Big Boys were later converted to Coco's or Carrow's restaurants, and there the Big Boy went bye-bye. The Elias Brothers, a Michigan-area franchiser for many years, purchased the Big Boy name from Marriott in 1987, and today is the sole Big Boy franchiser worldwide.

The Club Sandwich is one of Big Boy's signature sandwiches, and remains one of the most popular items on the menu since it was introduced in the mid-70s.

3 slices white or wheat bread
1½ tablespoons mayonnaise
1 lettuce leaf
1 slice Swiss cheese (optional)

2 ounces deli-sliced turkey breast
2 slices tomato
3 slices bacon, cooked

1. Toast the slices of bread.
2. Spread the mayonnaise evenly on one face of each slice of toast.
3. Build the sandwich by first stacking the lettuce leaf on the mayonnaise on one slice of toast. You will most likely have to cut or fold the lettuce so that it fits.
4. The Swiss cheese goes on next. This is an optional step since I've been served the original sandwich with the cheese, but the description of the sandwich and the photograph in the menu exclude it.
5. On the Swiss cheese, if you use it, stack the slices of turkey. Fold over the slices and arrange them neatly.
6. Stack a piece of toast, mayo side down, onto the turkey.
7. On top of the toast, arrange the tomato slices.
8. Lay the bacon, side by side, onto the tomatoes.
9. Top off the sandwich with the last piece of toast, mayo side down.
10. Slice the sandwich with two diagonal cuts from corner to corner, in an "x."
11. Push a toothpick down through the center of each triangular sandwich quarter. Spin each slice around 180° so that the center of the sandwich is now pointed out. Serve with French fries or with coleslaw arranged in the center of the plate of sandwich pieces.

- SERVES 1 AS AN ENTREE (CAN BE DOUBLED)

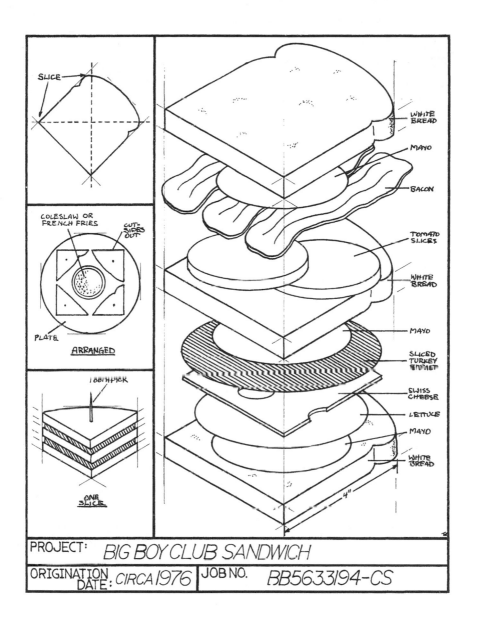

SLICE

COLESLAW OR
FRENCH FRIES

CUT-
SIDES
OUT

PLATE

ARRANGED

TOOTHPICK

ONE
SLICE

WHITE
BREAD

MAYO

BACON

TOMATO
SLICES

WHITE
BREAD

MAYO

SLICED
TURKEY
BREAST

SWISS
CHEESE

LETTUCE

MAYO

WHITE
BREAD

4"

PROJECT: *BIG BOY CLUB SANDWICH*

ORIGINATION
DATE: *CIRCA 1976*

JOB NO. *BB5633194-CS*

CALIFORNIA PIZZA KITCHEN ORIGINAL BBQ CHICKEN PIZZA

☆　♥　☎　✎　✈　✉　✂　☞　✿

Menu Description: "Introduced in our first restaurant in 1985. With barbecued chicken, sliced red onion, cilantro, and smoked Gouda cheese."

In 1985, attorneys Larry Flax and Rick Rosenfield traded in their private practice, which included defending mob bosses and union officials, for a specialty pizza chain. These two "amateur chefs" say they were influenced by Wolfgang Puck, whose Spago restaurant in Los Angeles was the first to create pizza with unusual toppings. Now they have developed a niche somewhere between gourmet food and traditional Italian-style pizzas, creating what one magazine described as "designer pizza at off-the-rack prices." In addition to the pastas, soups, and salads on its nothing-over-ten-dollars menu, California Pizza Kitchen offers 25 unique pizza creations that reflect the current trends in dining. When Cajun food was in style, the Cajun chicken pizza was a top seller; today that item has been replaced with Southwestern pizza varieties.

As the menu explains, the Barbecued Chicken Pizza was one of the first pizzas served at California Pizza Kitchen. Ten years later it remained the top-selling pizza creation.

You can use this recipe to make your pizza with premade or packaged dough, but I highly recommend taking the time to make the dough yourself. You'll find that it's worth the extra work. This recipe took a lot of time to perfect, and if you prepare the dough one day ahead of time, the result should convince you never to use packaged dough again.

THE CRUST

⅓ cup plus I tablespoon warm water
    (105° to 115°F)
¾ teaspoon yeast
I teaspoon sugar

I cup bread flour
½ teaspoon salt
½ tablespoon olive oil

or

Commercial pizza dough or dough mix or One 10-inch unbaked commercial
    crust

THE TOPPING

I boneless, skinless chicken breast half
½ cup Bullseye Original barbecue
    sauce
I½ teaspoons olive oil
I cup shredded mozzarella

½ cup grated Gouda cheese (smoked,
    if you can find it)
½ cup sliced red onion
2 teaspoons finely chopped fresh
    cilantro*

1. If you are making a homemade crust, start the dough one day before you plan to serve the pizza. In a small bowl or measuring cup dissolve the yeast and sugar in the warm water. Let it sit for 5 minutes until the surface of the mixture turns foamy. (If it doesn't foam, either the yeast was too old— i.e., dead—or the water was too hot—i.e., you killed it. Try again.) Sift together the flour and salt in a medium bowl. Make a depression in the flour and pour in the olive oil and yeast mixture. Use a fork to stir the liquid, gradually drawing in more flour as you stir, until all the ingredients are combined. When you can no longer stir with a fork, use your hands to form the dough into a ball. Knead the dough with the heels of your hands on a lightly floured surface for 10 minutes, or until the texture of the dough is smooth. Form the dough back into a ball, coat it lightly with oil, and place it into a clean bowl covered with plastic wrap. Keep the bowl in a warm place for about 2 hours to allow the dough to double in size. Punch down the dough and put it back into the covered bowl and into your refrigerator overnight. Take the dough from the refrigerator 1 to 2 hours before you plan to build the pizza so that the dough can warm up to room temperature.

*Found in the produce section near the parsley. Also known as fresh coriander or Chinese parsley.

If you are using a commercial dough or dough mix, follow the instructions on the package to prepare it. You may have to set some of the dough aside to make a smaller, 10-inch crust.

2. Cut the chicken breast into bite-size cubes and marinate it in ¼ cup of the barbecue sauce in the refrigerator for at least 2 hours.

3. When the chicken has marinated, preheat the oven to 500°F. Heat a small frying pan on your stove with about 1½ teaspoons of olive oil in it. Sauté the chicken in the pan for about 3 to 4 minutes or until done.

4. Form the dough into a ball and roll out on a floured surface until very thin and 10 inches in diameter. Put your pizza crust onto a baking sheet or pizza pan, and spread the remaining ¼ cup of barbecue sauce evenly over the pizza crust.

5. Sprinkle ½ cup of the mozzarella and all of the Gouda cheese over the sauce.

6. Add the chicken next.

7. The red onion goes next.

8. Sprinkle the remaining ½ cup mozzarella around the center of the pizza.

9. Cilantro goes on top of the mozzarella.

10. Bake the pizza for 10 to 12 minutes or until the crust is light brown.

11. When the pizza is done, remove it from the oven and make 4 even cuts across the pie. This will give you 8 slices.

- SERVES 2 AS AN ENTREE

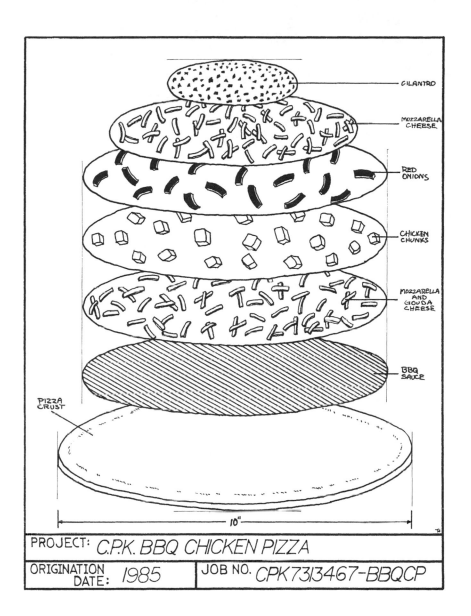

CILANTRO

MOZZARELLA
CHEESE

RED
ONIONS

CHICKEN
CHUNKS

MOZZARELLA
AND
GOUDA
CHEESE

BBQ
SAUCE

PIZZA
CRUST

10"

PROJECT: *C.P.K. BBQ CHICKEN PIZZA*

ORIGINATION
DATE: *1985*

JOB NO. *CPK7313467-BBQCP*

CALIFORNIA PIZZA KITCHEN THAI CHICKEN PIZZA

Menu Description: "With pieces of chicken marinated in a spicy peanut-ginger and sesame sauce, green onions, bean sprouts, julienne carrots, cilantro and roasted peanuts."

After the first California Pizza Kitchen opened in Beverly Hills in 1985 success came quickly: there are currently 78 restaurants in 18 states. In 1992, huge food conglomerate PepsiCo paid over $70 million for a 70 percent share of the company—just eight years after Larry and Rick started the company. As for those two, well, they pocketed $18 million apiece, or around 70 times their initial investment in 1985.

Thai Chicken Pizza is one of the oldest varieties of pizza still on the menu, and remains a favorite. If you prefer, you can make this pizza with a store-bought package dough or dough mix, but I recommend making the crust yourself. If you decide to do that, make it one day ahead of time so that it can rise slowly in the refrigerator.

THE CRUST

⅓ cup plus 1 tablespoon warm water
    (105° to 115°F)
¾ teaspoon yeast
1 teaspoon granulated sugar
1 cup bread flour
½ teaspoon salt

½ tablespoon olive oil
or
Commercial pizza dough or dough mix
or
One 10-inch unbaked commercial
    crust

PEANUT SAUCE

1/4 cup creamy peanut butter
2 tablespoons teriyaki sauce (or
    marinade)
2 tablespoons hoisin
1 clove garlic, minced
1/2 teaspoon crushed red pepper flakes
1 tablespoon granulated sugar

1 tablespoon brown sugar
2 tablespoons water
2 teaspoons sesame oil
1 teaspoon soy sauce
1 1/2 teaspoons minced onion
1 teaspoon minced gingerroot

TOPPINGS

1 boneless, skinless chicken breast half
1 1/2 teaspoons olive oil
1 1/4 cups grated mozzarella
1 to 2 green onions

1/2 cup bean sprouts
1/2 carrot, julienned or grated (1/4 cup)
2 teaspoons minced cilantro*
1 tablespoon chopped peanuts

1. Prepare the crust following the directions from step 1 on page 281.

2. Mix together the ingredients for the peanut sauce in a small bowl. Pour this mixture into a food processor or blender and blend for about 15 seconds or until the garlic, onion, and ginger are reduced to small particles. Pour this mixture into a small pan over medium heat and bring it to a boil. Cook for 1 minute. Don't cook too long or the sauce will become lumpy. (You may, instead, use a microwave for this step. Pour the mixture into a small microwavable bowl and heat for 1 to 2 minutes.) The peanut sauce should be darker now.

3. Slice the chicken into bite-size chunks.

4. Pour one-third of the peanut sauce over the chicken. Place in a sealed container in the refrigerator and marinate for at least 2 hours. I like to use a small resealable plastic bag for this. The chicken gets very well coated this way.

5. Heat 1 teaspoon of oil in a small pan over medium/high heat.

6. Cook the marinated chicken for 3 to 4 minutes in the pan.

7. Roll out your pizza crust and place on the baking sheet or pizza pan as in step 4, page 283. Preheat the oven to 475°F.

8. Spread a thin coating of the remaining peanut sauce (the stuff

*Cilantro is found in the produce section of your supermarket, usually near the parsley.

you *didn't* marinate the chicken in) on the pizza crust. You may have sauce left over.

9. Sprinkle I cup of the grated mozzarella over the peanut sauce.

10. Slice the green onion lengthwise into thin strips (julienne), then cut across the strips, slicing the onion into 2-inch matchstick strips. Spread the onions over the cheese.

11. Arrange the chicken on the pizza.

12. Next go the sprouts and the julienned carrots.

13. Sprinkle what's left of the mozzarella (¼ cup) just over the center area of the pizza.

14. Sprinkle the cilantro over the mozzarella, then the chopped nuts on top.

15. Bake the pizza for 10 to 12 minutes or until the crust turns light brown.

16. After removing the pizza from the oven, cut across it 4 times to make 8 slices.

• SERVES 2 AS AN ENTREE

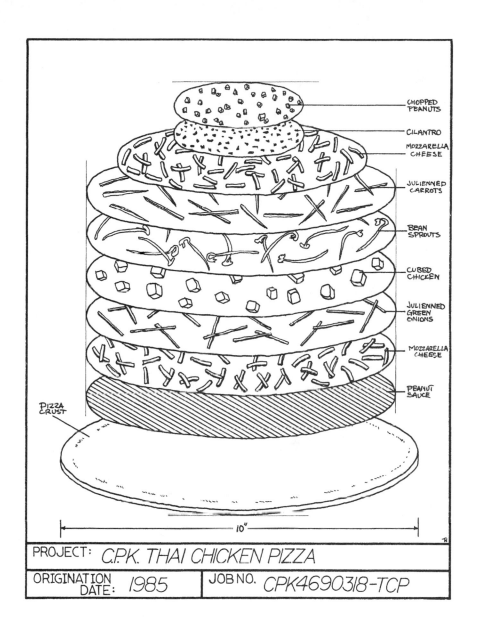

CHOPPED PEANUTS

CILANTRO

MOZZARELLA CHEESE

JULIENNED CARROTS

BEAN SPROUTS

CUBED CHICKEN

JULIENNED GREEN ONIONS

MOZZARELLA CHEESE

PEANUT SAUCE

PIZZA CRUST

10"

PROJECT:	*C.P.K. THAI CHICKEN PIZZA*	
ORIGINATION DATE:	*1985*	JOB NO. *CPK4690318-TCP*

CALIFORNIA PIZZA KITCHEN SOUTHWESTERN BURRITO PIZZA

☆　♥　☎　✐　✈　⌧　✄　☛　✿

Menu Description: "With grilled chicken breast marinated in lime and herbs, Southwestern black beans, fire-roasted mild chilies, sweet white onions and Cheddar cheese. Served with green tomatillo salsa and sour cream."

California Pizza Kitchen uses imported Italian wood-fired ovens to bake the specialty pizzas. These ovens reach temperatures over 800°F, allowing the pizzas to cook in just three minutes. This technique keeps ingredients from drying out so that the pizzas don't require as much cheese as in traditional recipes.

Unfortunately, most of us don't have wood-burning pizza ovens in our kitchens so I have designed these recipes to work in a conventional oven with a minimum of cheese. If you have a pizza stone, use it. If you have a hard time finding tomatillos (they look like small green tomatoes with a thin papery skin and are found in the produce section), you can use canned green salsa. Look for fresh cilantro in the produce section.

You have the option of using a store-bought crust or instant pizza dough, but I can't say enough about making the dough yourself from the recipe here. You just have to plan ahead, making the dough one day before you plan to bake the pizza. This way the dough will get to rest and will rise slowly in the refrigerator—a great technique the pros use.

THE CRUST

1/3 cup plus 1 tablespoon warm water
    (105° to 115°F)
3/4 teaspoon yeast
1 teaspoon sugar
1 cup bread flour
1/2 teaspoon salt

1/2 tablespoon olive oil
or
One 10-inch unbaked commercial
    crust
or
Commercial pizza dough or dough mix

MARINATED CHICKEN

1 tablespoon fresh lime juice
1 tablespoon plus 1 teaspoon olive oil
1 tablespoon soy sauce
2 cloves garlic, pressed
2 teaspoons chopped fresh cilantro
1 teaspoon salt
1/2 teaspoon crushed red pepper flakes
1 skinless, boneless chicken breast half

3/4 cup canned refried black beans
1 tablespoon water
1/4 teaspoon cayenne pepper
1/4 cup sliced white onion
1 whole canned mild green chili
1/2 cup shredded Monterey Jack cheese
1 cup shredded Cheddar cheese

TOMATILLO SALSA (OPTIONAL)

3/4 cup chopped tomatillos (about 4)
3 whole canned mild green chilies
    (4-ounce can)

1/4 fresh jalapeño
2 tablespoons chopped onion
Dash salt

ON THE SIDE

Sour cream

1. Prepare the crust following directions from step 1 on page 281.
2. Make the marinade by combining the lime juice, 1 tablespoon olive oil, soy sauce, garlic, cilantro, salt, and pepper flakes in a blender or in a small bowl with an electric mixer for only 5 seconds or so, just until the ingredients are well combined.
3. Cut the chicken into bite-size cubes, then marinate the chicken breast in the lime mixture for at least 2 hours.
4. When the chicken has marinated, heat up a small skillet with the remaining 1 teaspoon of olive oil over high heat. Cook the chicken in the pan for 2 to 4 minutes or until it is cooked through.

5. Mix the black beans with the water and cayenne pepper.
6. Roll out the pizza crust and place it on the baking sheet or pizza pan as in step 4, page 283. Preheat the oven to 475°F.
7. Spread the black bean mixture evenly over the crust.
8. Now arrange the chicken evenly over the black beans.
9. Spread the onions over the chicken.
10. Take the chili pepper and carefully slice it in half, crossways. Then slice the two halves into very thin strips. Sprinkle the chili over the onions.
11. Spread the Monterey Jack over the pizza.
12. Top it off with the Cheddar.
13. Cook the pizza for 12 to 15 minutes or until the crust begins to turn brown.
14. While the pizza cooks, combine all the ingredients for the tomatillo salsa in a food processor or blender. Run on low speed for about 15 seconds.
15. When the pizza is done, remove it from the oven and immediately make 4 even cuts through the middle, creating 8 slices of pizza. Serve with tomatillo salsa and sour cream on the side.

• SERVES 2 AS AN ENTREE

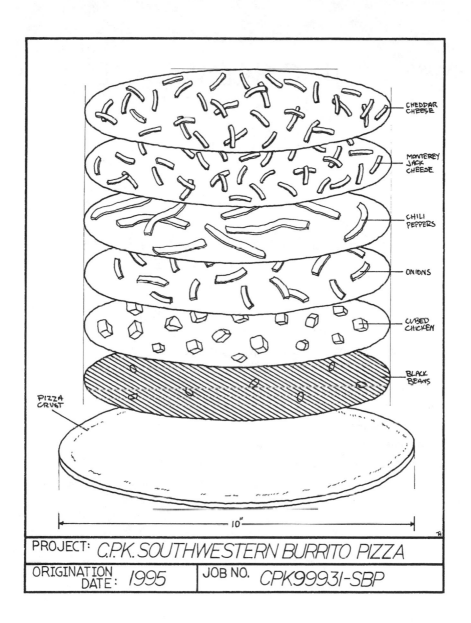

CHEDDAR CHEESE

MONTEREY JACK CHEESE

CHILI PEPPERS

ONIONS

CUBED CHICKEN

BLACK BEANS

PIZZA CRUST

10"

PROJECT: *C.P.K. SOUTHWESTERN BURRITO PIZZA*

ORIGINATION DATE: *1995* JOB NO. *CPK99931-SBP*

THE CHEESECAKE FACTORY BRUSCHETTA

☆ ♥ ☎ ✎ ✈ ✉ ✄ ☞ ✿

Menu Description: "Grilled Bread Topped with Fresh Chopped Tomato, Red Onion, Garlic, Basil and Olive Oil."

In 1972, Oscar and Evelyn Overton moved from Detroit to Los Angeles to build a wholesale bakery that would sell cheesecakes and other high-quality desserts to local restaurants. Business was a booming success, but some restaurants balked at the high prices the bakery was charging for its desserts. So in 1978 the couple's son David decided to open a restaurant of his own—the first Cheesecake Factory restaurant— in posh Beverly Hills. The restaurant was an immediate success and soon David started a moderate expansion of the concept. Sure, the current total of 20 restaurants doesn't seem like a lot, but this handful of stores earns the chain more than $100 million in business each year. That's more than some chains with four times the number of outlets rake in.

Bruschetta is one of the top-selling appetizers at the restaurant chain. Bruschetta is toasted bread flavored with garlic and olive oil, broiled until crispy, and then arranged around a pile of tomato-basil salad in vinaigrette. This salad is scooped onto the bruschetta, like a dip, and then you open wide. This version makes five slices just like the dish served at the restaurant, but the recipe can be easily doubled.

1 ½ cups chopped Roma plum
    tomatoes (6 to 8 tomatoes)
2 tablespoons diced red onion
1 large clove garlic, minced

2 tablespoons chopped fresh basil
    (4 to 6 small leaves)
2 tablespoons olive oil
½ teaspoon red wine vinegar

¼ teaspoon salt
Dash ground black pepper
½ loaf French baguette or crusty
    Italian bread (5 to 7 slices)

¼ teaspoon garlic salt
2 to 3 sprigs Italian parsley

1. Combine the tomatoes, red onion, garlic, and basil in a medium bowl.
2. Add ½ tablespoon of oil, vinegar, salt, and pepper and mix well. Cover the bowl and let it sit in the refrigerator for at least 1 hour.
3. When you are ready to serve the dish, preheat your broiler and slice the baguette in 1-inch slices on a 45-degree angle to make 5 slices of bread.
4. Combine the remaining 1½ tablespoons of oil with the garlic salt.
5. Brush the entire surface of each slice of bread (both sides) with the olive oil mixture. Broil the slices of bread in the oven for 1½ to 2 minutes per side or until the surface of the bread starts to turn brown.
6. Arrange the bread like a star or spokes of a wheel on a serving plate. Pour the chilled tomato mixture in a neat pile onto the bread slices where they meet at the center of the plate. Garnish with Italian parsley.

• SERVES 2 AS AN APPETIZER

TIDBITS

There is a variation on this recipe if your bread has a hard crust. The more traditional method of rubbing the bread with the garlic clove is done as follows:

After you slice the bread, slice a clove of garlic in half and rub it around the edge of the crust on both sides of the bread. Rub the olive oil on the bread and lightly salt each slice, if you like. Grill the bread the same way as above in step 5.

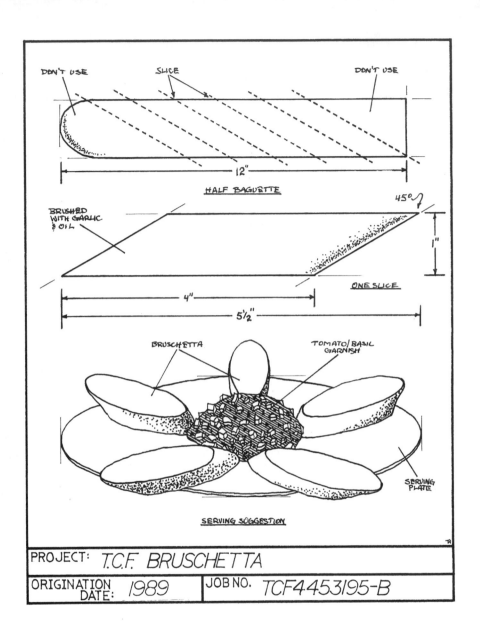

DON'T USE · SLICE · DON'T USE

12"

HALF BAGUETTE

BRUSHED WITH GARLIC & OIL

45°

1"

ONE SLICE

4"

5½"

BRUSCHETTA · TOMATO/BASIL GARNISH

SERVING PLATE

SERVING SUGGESTION

PROJECT:	*T.C.F. BRUSCHETTA*

ORIGINATION DATE:	*1989*	JOB NO.	*TCF4453195-B*

THE CHEESECAKE FACTORY AVOCADO EGGROLLS

☆ ♥ ☎ ✎ ✈ ✉ ✂ ☞ ✿

Menu Description: "Chunks of Fresh Avocado, Sun-Dried Tomato, Red Onion and Cilantro Deep Fried in a Crisp Chinese Wrapper."

In 1995, Forbes Magazine named the Cheesecake Factory in its list of the 200 best small companies in America. At 20 stores now, the Cheesecake Factory plans to grow at a modest rate of about 5 new restaurants per year, and still does not franchise.

Here's something different that I think you'll really like. The Avo-cado Eggrolls are one of the most popular appetizers on the menu at the Cheesecake Factory, and it's not hard to see why. The combination of hot avocado, sun-dried tomatoes, and the cilantro-tamarind sauce is one of the most unique and tasty flavors I've enjoyed at any of the restaurant chains. The trickiest part might be finding the tamarind pulp at your market. It's a brown, sticky pulp that looks sort of like puréed prunes, and can be found in the spice section or near the ethnic foods—or try a Middle Eastern market. The pulp often contains the large seeds of the fruit, so be sure to remove them before measuring. If you can't find the tamarind, you can get by substituting smashed raisins or prunes.

EGGROLLS

1 large avocado	*Pinch salt*
2 tablespoons chopped sun-dried tomatoes (bottled in oil)	*3 eggroll wrappers*
1 tablespoon minced red onion	*1 egg, beaten*
½ teaspoon chopped fresh cilantro	*Vegetable oil for frying*

¼ cup chopped cashews

⅔ cup chopped fresh cilantro

2 cloves garlic, quartered

2 green onions, chopped

1 tablespoon sugar

1 teaspoon ground black pepper

1 teaspoon cumin

4 teaspoons white vinegar

1 teaspoon balsamic vinegar

½ cup honey

½ teaspoon tamarind pulp

Pinch ground saffron

¼ cup olive oil

1. After you peel the avocado and remove the pit, dice it into bite-size pieces.

2. In a small bowl, gently combine the avocado with the tomatoes, red onion, ½ teaspoon cilantro, and a pinch of salt. Be careful not to smash the avocado.

3. Prepare the eggrolls by spooning ⅓ of the filling into an eggroll wrapper. With the wrapper positioned so that one corner is pointing toward you, place the filling about 1 inch from the bottom corner and 1 inch from each side. Roll the bottom corner up over the filling, then roll the filling up to about the middle of the wrapper. Brush the remaining corners and edges of the wrapper with the beaten egg. Fold the left and right corners over the filling and "glue" the corners to the wrapper. Finish by rolling the wrapper and filling up over the top corner. Press on the wrapper to ensure it is sealed. Repeat these steps with the remaining two eggrolls and keep them covered in the refrigerator while you make the dipping sauce.

4. Prepare the sauce by combining the cashews, cilantro, garlic, green onions, sugar, black pepper, and cumin in a food processor or blender. Blend with short bursts until the mixture is well blended, and the cashews and garlic have been chopped into pieces about half the size of a grain of rice.

5. Combine the vinegars, honey, tamarind, and saffron in a small bowl. Heat the mixture for about 1 minute in a microwave, then stir until the tamarind pulp dissolves completely.

6. Pour the tamarind mixture into the blender or food processor with the cashew mixture and mix with short bursts until well combined (about 20 seconds).

7. Pour the blended sauce into a small bowl. Add the oil and stir by hand. Cover and refrigerate the sauce for at least 30 minutes before serving.

8. Heat oil in a deep fryer or a deep pan over medium heat. You want the oil to be deep enough to cover the eggrolls.

9. When the oil is hot, fry the eggrolls for 3 to 4 minutes or until golden brown. Drain on paper towels.

10. When the eggrolls can be safely touched, slice once diagonally across the middle of each one and serve them arranged around a sauce dish filled with the dipping sauce.

- SERVES 1 OR 2 AS AN APPETIZER

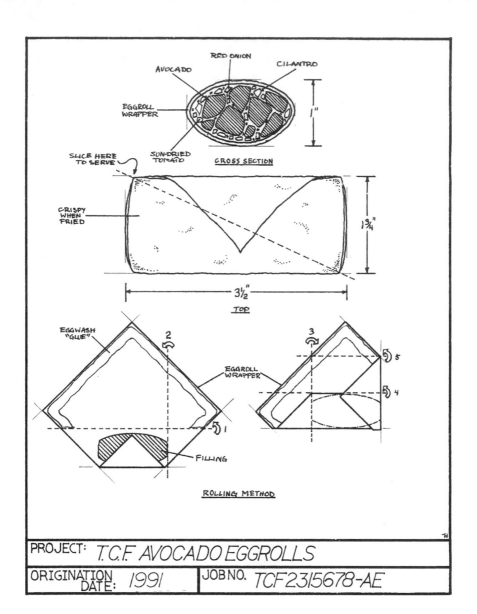

RED ONION

AVOCADO

CILANTRO

EGGROLL
WRAPPER

1"

SUN-DRIED
TOMATO

CROSS SECTION

SLICE HERE
TO SERVE

CRISPY
WHEN
FRIED

1¾"

3½"

TOP

EGGWASH
"GLUE"

2

3

EGGROLL
WRAPPER

5

4

1

FILLING

ROLLING METHOD

PROJECT: T.C.F. AVOCADO EGGROLLS

ORIGINATION DATE: 1991

JOB NO. TCF2315678-AE

THE CHEESECAKE FACTORY CAJUN JAMBALAYA PASTA

☆ ♥ ☎ ✎ ✈ ✉ ✂ ☛ ✿

Menu Description: "Our most popular dish! Shrimp and Chicken Sautéed with Onions, Peppers and Tomatoes in a Very Spicy Cajun Sauce. All on top of Fresh Fettuccine."

The Cheesecake Factory's founder, David Overton, says it was his unfamiliarity with the restaurant business that contributed to the company's success. In an interview with *Nation's Restaurant News* David says, "We did not know anything about running restaurants. We just knew that people valued fresh foods. In some ways our naiveté helped us because we didn't know what you are not supposed to do."

I think we all know it helps to serve good food and that's an area in which the Cheesecake Factory excels. The pastas and salads top the list of big sellers, but it's the Cajun Jambalaya Pasta that holds the pole position, according to the menu description of this dish. Jambalaya is a spicy Creole dish that usually combines a variety of ingredients including tomatoes, onions, peppers, and some type of meat with rice. Rather than the traditional rice, the Cheesecake Factory has designed its version to include two types of fettuccine—an attractive mix of standard white noodles and green spinach-flavored noodles.

This recipe makes 2 huge portions, like those served in the restaurant. It's actually enough food for a family of four.

½ teaspoon white pepper
½ teaspoon cayenne pepper
1 ½ teaspoons salt
½ teaspoon paprika
¼ teaspoon garlic powder

¼ teaspoon onion powder
2 skinless, boneless chicken breast
   halves
½ pound large shrimp, peeled and
   deveined

5 quarts water
6 ounces plain fettuccine
6 ounces spinach fettuccine
2 tablespoons olive oil
2 medium tomatoes, chopped
1 small green bell pepper, sliced
1 small red bell pepper, sliced

1 small yellow bell pepper, sliced
1 small white onion, sliced
1½ cups chicken stock
1 tablespoon arrowroot or cornstarch
2 tablespoons white wine
2 teaspoons chopped fresh parsley

1. Make a Cajun seasoning blend by combining the white pepper, cayenne pepper, salt, paprika, garlic powder, and onion powder in a small bowl.

2. Cut the chicken breasts into bite-size pieces. Use about one-third of the seasoning blend to coat the chicken pieces.

3. In another bowl, sprinkle another one-third of the spice blend over the shrimp.

4. Start your pasta cooking by bringing 5 quarts of water to a boil over high heat. Add both fettuccines to the hot water, reduce the heat to medium, and simmer for 12 to 14 minutes or until the pasta is tender.

5. While the fettuccine cooks, heat 1 tablespoon of the olive oil in a large frying pan or skillet over high heat. When the oil is hot, sauté the chicken in the pan for about 2 minutes per side or until the surface of the chicken starts to turn brown.

6. Add the shrimp to the pan with the chicken and cook for another 2 minutes, stirring occasionally to keep the shrimp from sticking. When the chicken and shrimp have been seared, pour the contents of the pan onto a plate or into a bowl. Do not rinse the pan!

7. Put the pan back over the high heat and add the remaining tablespoon of oil to the pan. Add the tomatoes, peppers, and onion to the oil. Sprinkle the veggies with the remaining spice blend and sauté for about 10 minutes or until the vegetables begin to turn dark brown or black.

8. Add the chicken and shrimp to the vegetables and pour ¾ cup of the chicken stock in the pan. Cook over high heat until the stock has been reduced to just about nothing. Add the remaining ¾ cup of the stock to the pan. The liquid should become dark as it deglazes the pan of the dark film left by the spices and

cooking food. Stir constantly, scraping the blackened stuff on the bottom of the pan. Reduce the broth a bit more, then turn the heat down to low.

9. Combine the arrowroot with the wine in a small bowl. Stir until it is dissolved. Add this to the pan and simmer over low heat until the sauce thickens slightly.

10. When the fettuccine is done, drain it and spoon half onto a plate. Spoon half of the jambalaya over the fettuccine. Sprinkle half of the parsley over the top. Repeat for the second serving.

- SERVES 2 AS A LARGE ENTREE

TIDBITS

You may also be able to find fettuccine that comes in a 12-ounce box with a combination of plain and spinach noodles. One brand is Ronzoni. This variety is perfect for this recipe, and you won't have any leftover noodles in opened boxes.

THE CHEESECAKE FACTORY PUMPKIN CHEESECAKE

☆　♥　☎　✎　✈　✉　✂　☞　❀

While most restaurant chains attempt to keep their menus simple so as to not tax the kitchen, the Cheesecake Factory's menu contains more than 200 items. Perhaps it's the time spent reading the 17-page menu that leads to the one- and two-hour waits for a table that customers not only expect, but cheerfully endure for lunch or dinner, or just for a taste of the delicious Pumpkin Cheesecake or any of the other 40 cheesecake selections.

Use an 8-inch springform pan for this recipe. If you don't have one, you should get one. They're indispensable for thick, gourmet cheesecake and several other scrumptious desserts. If you don't want to use a springform pan, this recipe will also work with two 9-inch pie plates. You'll just end up with two smaller cheesecakes.

1 ½ cups graham cracker crumbs
5 tablespoons butter, melted
1 cup plus 1 tablespoon sugar
Three 8-ounce packages cream
　　cheese, softened
1 teaspoon vanilla

1 cup canned pumpkin
3 eggs
½ teaspoon cinnamon
¼ teaspoon nutmeg
¼ teaspoon allspice
Whipped cream

1.　Preheat the oven to 350°F.
2.　Make the crust by combining the graham cracker crumbs with the melted butter and 1 tablespoon sugar in a medium bowl. Stir well enough to coat all of the crumbs with the butter, but not so much as to turn the mixture into paste. Keep it crumbly.
3.　Press the crumbs onto the bottom and about two-thirds of the way up the sides of the springform pan. You don't want the

crust to form all of the way up the back of each slice of cheesecake. Bake the crust for 5 minutes, then set it aside until you are
ready to fill it.

4. In a large mixing bowl combine the cream cheese, 1 cup sugar,
and vanilla. Mix with an electric mixer until smooth.

5. Add the pumpkin, eggs, cinnamon, nutmeg, and allspice and continue to beat until smooth and creamy.

6. Pour the filling into the pan. Bake for 60 to 70 minutes. The top
will turn a bit darker at this point. Remove from the oven and allow the cheesecake to cool.

7. When the cheesecake has come to room temperature, put it
into the refrigerator. When the cheesecake has chilled, remove
the pan sides and cut the cake into 8 equal pieces. Serve with a
generous portion of whipped cream on top.

• SERVES 8

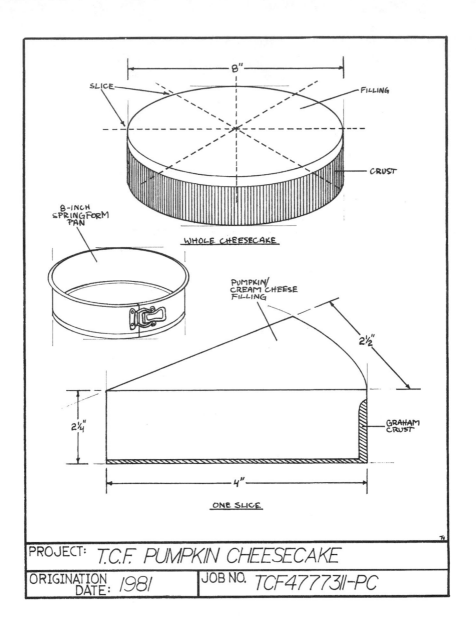

8"

SLICE

FILLING

CRUST

WHOLE CHEESECAKE

8-INCH
SPRINGFORM
PAN

PUMPKIN/
CREAM CHEESE
FILLING

2½"

2¼"

GRAHAM
CRUST

4"

ONE SLICE

PROJECT: *T.C.F. PUMPKIN CHEESECAKE*

ORIGINATION DATE: *1981*

JOB NO. *TCF4777311-PC*

THE CHEESECAKE FACTORY
KEY LIME CHEESECAKE

☆　♥　☎　✎　✈　✉　✂　☞　✿

Just 15 minutes after the very first Cheesecake Factory opened in Beverly Hills back in 1978, the lines began forming. Here's their cheesecake twist on the delicious Key lime pie. Since Key limes and Key lime juice can be hard to find, this recipe uses standard lime juice, which can be purchased bottled or squeezed fresh. If you can find Key lime juice, bear in mind that Key limes are more tart, and use only half as much juice. This recipe also requires a springform pan. If you don't have one, you can use two 9 inch pie pans and make two smaller cheesecakes.

1¾ cups graham cracker crumbs
5 tablespoons butter, melted
1 cup plus 1 tablespoon sugar
Three 8-ounce packages cream
　　cheese, softened

1 teaspoon vanilla
½ cup fresh lime juice (about 5 limes)
3 eggs
Whipped cream

1.　Preheat the oven to 350°F. Make the crust by combining the graham cracker crumbs with the butter and 1 tablespoon sugar in a medium bowl. Stir well enough to coat all of the crumbs with the butter. Keep it crumbly.

2.　Press the crumbs onto the bottom and about one half of the way up the sides of an 8-inch springform pan. You don't want the crust to form all the way up the back of each slice of cheesecake. Bake the crust for 5 minutes, then set it aside until you are ready to fill it.

3.　In a large mixing bowl combine the cream cheese, 1 cup sugar, and vanilla. Mix with an electric mixer until smooth.

4. Add the lime juice and eggs and continue to beat until smooth and creamy.
5. Pour the filling into the pan. Bake for 60 to 70 minutes. If the top of the cheesecake is turning light brown, it's done. Remove from the oven and allow it to cool.
6. When the cheesecake has come to room temperature, put it into the refrigerator. When the cheesecake has chilled, remove the pan sides and cut the cake into 3 equal pieces. Serve with a generous dollop of whipped cream on top.

- SERVES 8

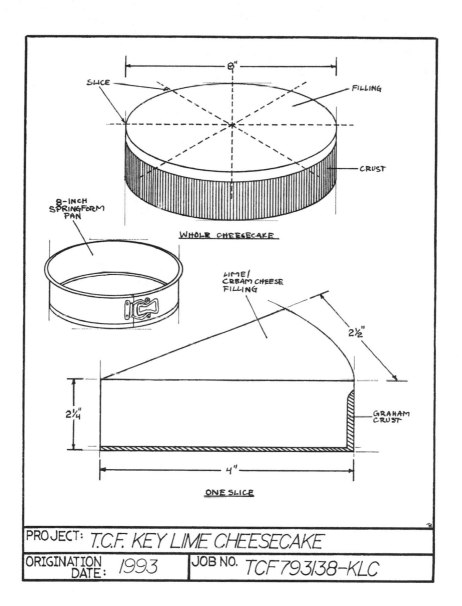

SLICE

FILLING

8"

CRUST

8-INCH
SPRINGFORM
PAN

WHOLE CHEESECAKE

LIME/
CREAM CHEESE
FILLING

2½"

2¼"

GRAHAM
CRUST

4"

ONE SLICE

PROJECT: *T.C.F. KEY LIME CHEESECAKE*

ORIGINATION
DATE: *1993*

JOB NO. *TCF 793138-KLC*

CHI-CHI'S
NACHOS GRANDE

☆　♥　☎　✎　✈　✉　✂　☛　✿

Menu Description: "Seasoned beef, refried beans and cheese."

Marno McDermott was a successful Minneapolis restaurateur, opening a chain of Mexican restaurants in the seventies called Zapata's against the advice of skeptics who said he would never be able to sell Mexican food to the large population of Scandinavians in the area. Marno proved them wrong then, and once again in 1976, when he partnered with Max McGee, a former Green Bay Packer football player, to open the first Chi-Chi's in Richfield, Minnesota. The restaurant was built inside a deserted Kroger grocery store and became instantly famous for the intensely flavored and larger-than-usual portions of food. To keep volume high, Chi-Chi's designed a custom computer-driven system that clocks every aspect of service from the time each server enters an order to when the order is placed in front of customers. Special attention was given to the design of the menu's items as well, with each dish taking no more than nine minutes to prepare, even during the rush hours.

Since you're starting from scratch, this appetizer will probably take longer than nine minutes to make, but not by much. At the restaurant you can order the Nachos Grande with beef, chicken, seafood, or a combination; here I've described methods to recreate the beef and chicken versions. You can choose to make the nachos from store-bought tortilla chips or make them yourself with the recipe in "Tidbits." Personally I think the fresh, home-fried type tastes the best. If you're up for the task, amigos, I say give it a go.

Beef Nachos Grande

½ pound ground beef
1 teaspoon chili powder (Spanish blend)
½ teaspoon salt
½ teaspoon dried minced onion
⅛ teaspoon paprika
2 tablespoons water

8 "restaurant-style" corn tortilla chips
½ cup refried beans
1½ cups shredded Cheddar cheese
½ cup shredded Monterey Jack cheese
¼ cup diced onion
1 large red jalapeño (or green)

ON THE SIDE

Sour cream
Guacamole

Salsa

1. Preheat the oven to 375°F.
2. Brown the ground beef in a skillet over medium heat. Use a spatula or fork to crumble the beef into small pieces as it cooks. When you no longer see pink in the meat, drain off the fat.
3. To the meat, add the chili powder, salt, dried onion, paprika, and water. Simmer over medium/low heat for 10 minutes.
4. If you are going to prepare your own tortilla chips, do that following the instructions in "Tidbits" while the meat is simmering.
5. Heat the refried beans in a small saucepan over low heat or in the microwave for about 2 minutes.
6. Mix the two cheeses together in a small bowl.
7. Arrange the tortilla chips on a baking sheet or an oven-safe ceramic plate. Spread about a tablespoon of refried beans on each chip.
8. Sprinkle a couple of tablespoons of spiced beef onto the beans on each chip. Press down on the beef to make a flat surface for the cheese.
9. Carefully pile a small handful of cheese on each chip.
10. Sprinkle a pinch of the diced onion over the cheese.
11. Place a slice of jalapeño on top of the onion.
12. Bake the chips for 8 to 10 minutes or until the cheese has melted. Serve with your choice of sour cream, guacamole, and salsa on the side.

Chicken Nachos Grande

2 tablespoons lime juice	1 boneless, skinless chicken breast
1/4 cup water	8 "restaurant style" corn tortilla chips
1 tablespoon vegetable oil	1 cup salsa
1/4 teaspoon liquid smoke	1 1/2 cups shredded Cheddar cheese
2 teaspoons vinegar	1/2 cup shredded Monterey Jack cheese
1 clove garlic, pressed	1/4 cup diced onion
Salt	1 large red jalapeño pepper (or green)
Pepper	

1. Combine the lime juice, water, oil, liquid smoke, vinegar, and garlic. Add a little salt and pepper and marinate the chicken in the mixture for at least 2 hours.
2. Grill the chicken on your preheated barbecue or stovetop grill or griddle for 4 to 5 minutes per side or until done. Dice the chicken. Preheat the oven to 375°F.
3. Instead of refried beans as in the previous recipe, spread 1 tablespoon of salsa on each of the eight chips. Sprinkle some chicken over the top and build the rest of the nacho the same way as the beef version: Cheeses, onion, then a jalapeño slice.
4. Bake for 8 to 10 minutes. Serve with sour cream, guacamole, and additional salsa on the side.

- SERVES 2 TO 4 AS AN APPETIZER

TIDBITS

If you want to make your own tasty tortilla chips, buy some 6-inch corn tortillas and cut two of them twice—like a small pizza—into 4 equal triangular pieces (making a total of 8 slices). Drop the tortilla slices 4 at a time into a frying pan filled with about 1/2 inch of oil that has preheated over medium heat. Chips should bubble rapidly and will only need to fry 30 to 45 seconds per side. They should become a bit more golden in color, and very crispy. Drain the chips on a rack or on some paper towels. Salt to taste.

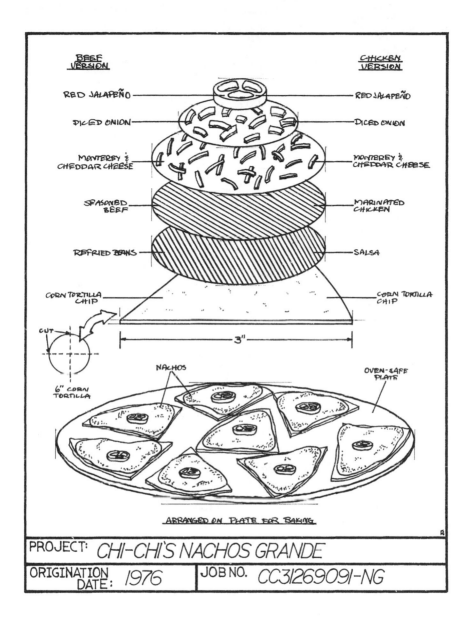

BEEF VERSION

CHICKEN VERSION

RED JALAPEÑO — — RED JALAPEÑO

DICED ONION — — DICED ONION

MONTEREY & CHEDDAR CHEESE — — MONTEREY & CHEDDAR CHEESE

SEASONED BEEF — MARINATED CHICKEN

REFRIED BEANS — SALSA

CORN TORTILLA CHIP — CORN TORTILLA CHIP

3"

CUT

6" CORN TORTILLA

NACHOS

OVEN-SAFE PLATE

ARRANGED ON PLATE FOR BAKING

PROJECT: *CHI-CHI'S NACHOS GRANDE*

ORIGINATION DATE: *1976*

JOB NO. *CC3I269091-NG*

CHI-CHI'S SWEET CORN CAKE

☆　♥　☎　✎　✈　✉　✄　☞　✿

Chi-Chi's cofounder Marno McDermott named his restaurant chain after his wife Chi Chi. He claims the name is quite memorable as it translates in Spanish into something a lot like "hooters" in English. The Minneapolis Star quoted McDermott in 1977 shortly after the first Chi-Chi's opened in Richfield, Minnesota, "English-speaking patrons remember it because it's catchy. And the Spanish-speaking customers are amused. Either way it doesn't hurt business."

One of the side dishes included with several of the entrees at Chi-Chi's is the Sweet Corn Cake. It's sort of like cornbread but much softer and sweeter, almost like corn pudding. You'll find it goes well with just about any Mexican dish. The recipe incorporates a *bain marie* or water bath—a technique of baking used commonly for custards and mousses to keep them from cracking or curdling. This is done by simply placing the covered baking pan of batter into another larger pan filled with a little hot water before baking.

½ cup (1 stick) butter, softened	⅓ cup sugar
⅓ cup masa harina*	2 tablespoons heavy cream
¼ cup water	¼ teaspoon salt
1 ½ cups frozen corn, thawed	½ teaspoon baking powder
¼ cup cornmeal	

1. Preheat the oven to 375°F.
2. Blend the butter in a medium bowl with an electric mixer until creamy. Add the masa harina and water to the butter and beat until well combined.

*A Mexican corn flour used to make tortillas. It is usually found in Latin-American groceries and in the supermarket next to the flour.

3. Put the defrosted corn into a blender or food processor and, with short pulses, coarsely chop the corn on low speed. You want to leave several whole kernels of corn. Stir the chopped corn into the butter and masa harina mixture. Add the corn-meal to the mixture. Combine.

4. In another medium bowl, mix together the sugar, cream, salt, and baking powder. When the ingredients are well blended, pour the mixture into the other bowl and stir everything together by hand.

5. Pour the corn batter into an ungreased 8 × 8-inch baking pan. Smooth the surface of the batter with a spatula. Cover the pan with aluminum foil. Place this pan into a 13 × 9-inch pan filled one-third of the way up with hot water. Bake for 50 to 60 minutes or until the corn cake is cooked through.

6. When the corn cake is done, remove the small pan from the larger pan and let it sit for at least 10 minutes. To serve, scoop out each portion with an ice cream scoop or rounded spoon.

- SERVES 8 TO 10 AS A SIDE DISH

CHI-CHI'S TWICE GRILLED BARBECUE BURRITO

☆ ♥ ☎ ✎ ✈ ✉ ✂ ☛ ❀

Menu Description: "Grilled steak or chicken wrapped in a flour tortilla with cheese and sautéed vegetables. Then the burrito is basted with spicy barbecue sauce and grilled again. Served with Spanish rice and sweet corn cake."

This dish bursts with the Southwestern flavors that have become so popular lately. Southwestern dishes like fajitas and specialty burritos are the latest rage in the restaurant industry, and now more chains than ever are creating their own spicy, Southwestern-style goodies.

I think you'll really enjoy this one. Chi-Chi's has taken fajita-style grilled beef, rolled it up like a burrito, grilled it again, and then smothered it with smoky barbecue sauce. The dish has quickly become a favorite menu item at Chi-Chi's and a favorite for people tiring of the same old Mexican food. Fire up the grill and give this zesty recipe a try.

MARINADE

1/3 cup water
1/4 cup lime juice
1 large clove garlic, pressed or grated
2 tablespoons vegetable oil
2 teaspoons vinegar
2 teaspoons soy sauce

1/2 teaspoon liquid smoke
1/2 teaspoon chili powder
1/2 teaspoon cayenne pepper
1 teaspoon salt
1/4 teaspoon pepper
Dash of onion powder

1 pound sirloin steak
1 red bell pepper, sliced
1 green bell pepper, sliced
1 Spanish onion, sliced

2 tablespoons vegetable oil
Two 10-inch flour tortillas
3 tablespoons Bullseye original
    barbecue sauce

1. Combine all of the ingredients for the marinade in a small bowl. Set aside ¼ cup of the marinade. Store it in a sealed container in the fridge until you need it. Marinate the steak in the refrigerator with the remaining marinade for several hours. Overnight is best. Be sure the steak isn't too thick. If it's more than ½ inch thick, slice it thinner.

2. Grill the steak on a hot barbecue or preheated stovetop grill for 4 to 5 minutes per side or until done. Cook less for a rarer steak, longer if you want it well done.

3. While the steak grills, sauté the peppers and onion in 1 tablespoon of vegetable oil over high heat. When the vegetables are tender, add the ¼ cup of marinade you set aside. Continue sautéing the vegetables until they brown.

4. When the steak is done, slice it into long strips that are no more than ½ inch thick and ½ inch wide. Keep the grill on.

5. Lay the tortillas in a hot pan over low heat to make them warm and pliable. Turn them as they heat up. It should only take a few seconds to get the tortillas warm enough to bend without cracking. Lay each warm tortilla on a clean surface and fill each one with equal portions of grilled steak. Position the steak near the bottom edge of the burrito with about a 1-inch "margin."

6. Take half of the sautéed peppers and onions and split it between the two burritos, laying it on the steak.

7. Roll the burrito by folding the bottom up and over the filling. Fold in the sides, and then roll the filling up over twice, being careful to make a neat little package.

8. Rub 1 teaspoon of vegetable oil over the entire surface of each burrito.

9. Put the burritos, seam side down, back on your barbecue grill set on medium heat for 1 to 2 minutes. When the bottom of the burrito begins to char, turn the burritos over. By now the tortilla should be stiff and crunchy making it easy to roll the burrito over without the filling falling out. Grill the tops of the burritos for 1 to 2 minutes more, or until the surface begins to char.

10. Transfer the burritos from the grill to two serving plates with the seam side down. Coat the top of each burrito with 1 to 1½ tablespoons of barbecue sauce.

11. Split the remaining peppers and onions and spread them over the top of the two burritos.

   • SERVES 2 AS AN ENTREE

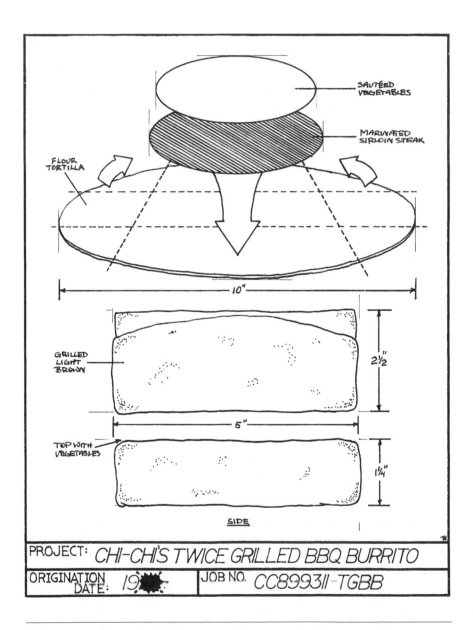

CHI-CHI'S MEXICAN "FRIED" ICE CREAM

☆ ♥ ☎ ✎ ✈ ▣ ✂ ☛ ✿

Menu Description: "Our specialty! French Vanilla ice cream with a crunchy, crispy cinnamon coating. Served with your choice of honey, chocolate or strawberry topping."

Cooks at Chi-Chi's chain of Mexican restaurants are instructed to *not* memorize recipes for the dishes they make. Management says each chef is required to consult the company cookbooks every time they whip up a meal, so that each dish tastes exactly the same in every Chi-Chi's any time of the day. Perhaps it's that practice that has made Chi-Chi's the largest Mexican restaurant chain in the country.

This crispy-coated ice cream sundae is not exactly fried as you may expect by the name. The scoop of vanilla ice cream is actually rolled in cornflake crumbs that have been flavored with sugar and cinnamon, giving it the appearance and texture of being fried. It's a simple idea that tastes just great, and is well worth a try. Chi-Chi's calls this their "specialty" and claims it's the most requested dessert item on the menu.

½ cup vegetable oil
Two 6-inch flour tortillas
½ teaspoon ground cinnamon
2 tablespoons sugar

¼ cup cornflake crumbs
2 large scoops vanilla ice cream
1 can whipped cream
2 maraschino cherries with stems

TOPPING (OPTIONAL)

Honey
Chocolate syrup

Strawberry topping

1. Prepare each tortilla by frying it in the hot oil in a frying pan over medium/high heat. Fry each side of the tortilla for about 1 minute until crispy. Drain the tortillas on paper towels.
2. Combine the cinnamon and sugar in a small bowl.
3. Sprinkle half of the cinnamon mixture over both sides of the fried tortillas, coating evenly. Not all of the sugar mixture will stick to the tortillas, and that's okay.
4. Combine the other half of the cinnamon mixture with the cornflake crumbs in another small bowl. Pour the cornflake mixture into a wide, shallow bowl or onto a plate.
5. Place a large scoop of ice cream in the cornflake crumbs, and with your hands roll the ice cream around until the entire surface is evenly coated with cornflake crumbs. You should not be able to see the ice cream.
6. Place the ice cream scoop on the center of a cinnamon/sugar-coated tortilla.
7. Spray whipped cream around the base of the ice cream. Spray an additional pile of cream on top of the ice cream.
8. Put a cherry in the top pile of whipped cream. Repeat for the remaining scoop of ice cream. Serve with a side dish of honey, chocolate syrup, or strawberry topping, if desired.

• SERVES 2

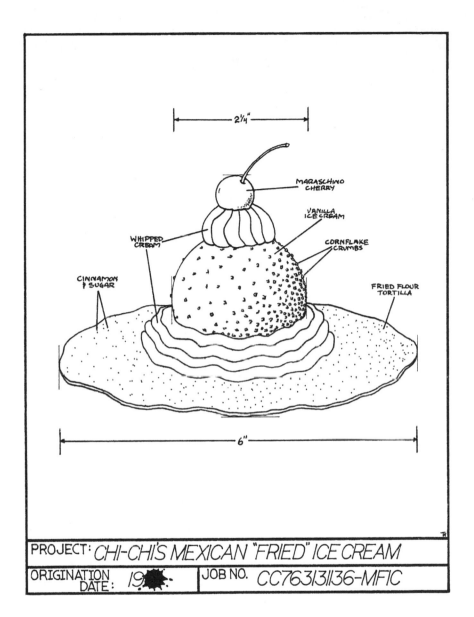

2¼"

MARASCHINO CHERRY

VANILLA ICE CREAM

WHIPPED CREAM

CORNFLAKE CRUMBS

CINNAMON & SUGAR

FRIED FLOUR TORTILLA

6"

PROJECT: *CHI-CHI'S MEXICAN "FRIED" ICE CREAM*

ORIGINATION DATE: *19*⬛

JOB NO. *CC76.31.31.136-MFIC*

CHILI'S GRILLED CARIBBEAN SALAD

☆　♥　☎　✎　✈　✉　✂　☞　✿

Menu Description: "Grilled, marinated chicken breast, mixed greens, pico de gallo, pineapple chunks, tortilla strips & honey-lime dressing."

Larry Levine started building his chain of Chili's restaurants in Dallas in 1975. At that time Chili's was basically a hamburger joint with a gourmet touch, dining room service and booze. Even though the menu then offered only eleven items, the restaurant was so popular that throngs of hungry customers waited patiently in lines extending into the parking lots. This caught the eye of the persuasive restaurateur Norman Brinker, who, in 1983, convinced Larry to sell his chain of Chili's restaurants, which by then had grown to a total of thirty.

　　Before Norman had stepped into the picture, more than 80 percent of Chili's business was in hamburgers. Today a much larger menu reflects the current trends in food, and salads are some of the best-selling items. These days the Grilled Caribbean Salad with the tasty honey-lime dressing is the salad of choice.

HONEY-LIME DRESSING

¼ cup Grey Poupon Dijon mustard	1 tablespoon sesame oil
¼ cup honey	1½ tablespoons apple cider vinegar
1½ tablespoons sugar	1½ teaspoons lime juice

　　Blend all the ingredients in a small bowl with an electric mixer. Cover and chill.

PICO DE GALLO

2 medium tomatoes, diced
½ cup diced Spanish onion
2 teaspoons chopped fresh jalapeño
    pepper, seeded and de-ribbed

2 teaspoons finely minced fresh
    cilantro*
Pinch of salt

Combine all the ingredients in a small bowl. Cover and chill.

SALAD

4 boneless, skinless chicken breast
    halves
½ cup teriyaki marinade, store bought
    or your own (page 539)
4 cups chopped iceberg lettuce

4 cups chopped green leaf lettuce
1 cup chopped red cabbage
1 5.5-ounce can pineapple chunks in
    juice, drained
10 tortilla chips

1. Marinate the chicken in the teriyaki for at least 2 hours. You can use a resealable plastic bag for this. Put the chicken into the bag and pour in the marinade, then toss it into the fridge.
2. Prepare the barbecue or preheat a stovetop grill. Grill the chicken for 4 to 5 minutes per side or until done.
3. Toss the lettuce and cabbage together, then divide the greens into two large individual-serving salad bowls.
4. Divide the pico de gallo and pour it in two even portions over the greens.
5. Divide the pineapple and sprinkle it on the salads.
6. Break the tortilla chips into large chunks and sprinkle half on each salad.
7. Slice the grilled chicken breasts into thin strips, and spread half the strips onto each salad.
8. Pour the dressing into two small bowls and serve with the salads.

- SERVES 2 AS AN ENTREE

*Found in the produce section; also known as fresh coriander and Chinese parsley.

CHILI'S FAJITAS FOR TWO

☆　♥　☎　✎　✈　✉　✄　☛　✿

Menu Description: "A pound of steak, chicken or combination on a sizzling skillet. Peppers available w/Fajitas upon request."

Chili's is perhaps the restaurant most responsible for introducing the famous finger food known as fajitas to the mass market. Company CEO Norman Brinker discovered the dish at a small restaurant on a visit to San Antonio, Texas. When Chili's put the item on its menu in the early eighties, sales immediately jumped a whopping 25 percent. One company spokesperson told *Spirit* magazine, "I remember walking into one of the restaurants after we added them to the menu and all I could see were wisps of steam coming up from the tables. That revolutionized Chili's."

Today Chili's serves more than 2 million pounds of fajitas a year. If all of the flour tortillas served with those fajitas were laid end-to-end, they'd stretch from New York to New Zealand, on the other side of the earth!

Today just about every American knows what fajitas are—the Southwestern-style grilled chicken, beef, or seafood, served sizzling on a cast iron skillet. And everyone has their own method of arranging the meat and onions and peppers in a soft tortilla with globs of pico de gallo, cheese, guacamole, lettuce, sour cream, and salsa. The tough part is trying to roll the thing up and take a bite ever so gracefully without squeezing half of the filling out the backside of the tortilla onto the plate, splattering your clean clothes, while goo goes dripping down your chin. This recipe is guaranteed to be as delicious and messy as the original.

1/4 cup fresh lime juice
1/3 cup water
2 tablespoons vegetable oil
1 large clove garlic, pressed
3 teaspoons vinegar
2 teaspoons soy sauce

1/2 teaspoon liquid smoke
1 teaspoon salt
1/2 teaspoon chili powder
1/2 teaspoon cayenne pepper
1/4 teaspoon ground black pepper
Dash onion powder

2 boneless, skinless chicken breast
    halves or 1 pound top sirloin or a
    combination of 1 chicken breast
    half and 1/2 pound sirloin
1 Spanish onion, sliced
1 tablespoon vegetable oil

1 teaspoon soy sauce
2 tablespoons water
1/2 teaspoon lime juice
Dash ground black pepper
Dash salt

ON THE SIDE

1/2 cup pico de gallo (page 321)
1/2 cup grated Cheddar cheese
1/2 cup guacamole
1/2 cup sour cream

1 cup shredded lettuce
6 to 8 six-inch flour tortillas
Salsa

1. Combine all of the ingredients for the marinade in a small bowl. Soak your choice of meat in the marinade for at least 2 hours. If you are just using the sirloin, let it marinate overnight, if possible.

2. When the meat has marinated, preheat your barbecue or stove-top grill to high.

3. Preheat a skillet over medium/high heat. Sauté the onion slices in the oil for 5 minutes. Combine the soy sauce, water, and lime juice in a small bowl and pour it over the onions. Add the black pepper and continue to sauté until the onions are translucent and dark on the edges (4 to 5 more minutes). Salt to taste.

4. While the onions are sautéing, grill the meat for 4 to 5 minutes per side or until done.

5. While the meat and onions are cooking, heat up another skillet (cast iron if you have one) over high heat. This will be your sizzling serving pan.

6. When the meat is done remove it from the grill and slice it into thin strips.

7. Remove the extra pan from the heat and dump the onions and

any liquid into it. If you've made it hot enough the onions should sizzle. Add the meat to the pan and serve immediately with pico de gallo, Cheddar cheese, guacamole, and sour cream arranged on a separate plate on a bed of shredded lettuce. Steam the tortillas in a moist towel in the microwave for 30 seconds and serve on the side. Serve salsa also, if desired.

Assemble fajitas by putting the meat into a tortilla along with your choice of condiments. Roll up the tortilla and scarf out.

- SERVES 2 AS AN ENTREE

TIDBITS

At Chili's, bell peppers are optional with this dish. If you like peppers, combine a small sliced green or red bell pepper with the onion, and sauté the vegetables together. Follow the rest of the steps as described.

CHILI'S PEANUT BUTTERCUP CHEESECAKE

☆　♥　☎　✎　✈　⊠　✂　☛　✿

Menu Description: "Chocolate & vanilla marbled cheesecake on a chocolate cookie crust, topped w/fudge & Reese's Peanut Butter Cup pieces."

If I had to pick one person in the restaurant business with the most respected and distinguished career, it would have to be Norman Brinker. The 65-year-old CEO of Brinker International is still building on a success story that spans four decades, and recently detailed his life in an autobiography, *On the Brink*. Back in the fifties, Norman took a job with Robert Peterson, who had just a few years earlier opened the first Jack-in-the-Box in San Diego, California. By the age of 34, Norman owned 20 percent of Jack-in-the-Box, giving him enough capital to set out on his own venture. In 1964 he opened a fifties-style coffee shop in downtown Dallas called Brinks. He sold that eatery a year later for $6,000 and sank that cash into a new chain that would become one of his most successful ventures. Norman opened the first Steak and Ale in 1966, took the chain public in 1971, then 10 years later sold the whole kit-and-caboodle for $100 million to the Pillsbury Company (that's some serious dough, boy). Pillsbury kept him on to run the operation, but Norman needed new action. In 1983, he purchased Chili's from founder Larry Levine and within 12 years built the chain into a billion-dollar company. Today Norman continues to watch Brinker International grow as new concepts like Cozymel's and Romano's Macaroni Grill are added to his long list of restaurant chain successes.

Speaking of rich, here's a tasty dessert for anyone who digs cheesecake and peanut butter cups. Use an 8-inch springform pan for this recipe if you have one. If not, you can also use two 9-inch pie pans and make two smaller cheesecakes. For the Oreo cookie crumbs, you can crumble three Oreo cookies, after removing the filling, or you can find packaged Oreo crumbs in the baking section of your supermarket near the graham cracker crumbs.

1 cup graham cracker crumbs
¼ cup Oreo chocolate cookie crumbs
    (3 cookies with filling removed)
⅓ cup butter, melted
¼ cup smooth peanut butter (not
    chunky)
Three 8-ounce packages cream
    cheese, softened

3 eggs
1 cup sour cream
1 cup sugar
1½ teaspoons vanilla
¼ cup chocolate syrup
1 cup fudge topping
4 chilled regular-size Reese's peanut
    butter cups (not bite-size)

1.   Preheat the oven to 375°F.
2.   In a medium bowl combine the graham cracker crumbs, chocolate cookie crumbs, and melted butter.
3.   Press the crumbs firmly over just the bottom of an 8-inch springform pan. Bake for 6 to 8 minutes.
4.   When the crust is cool, spread the peanut butter in a circle in the center of the crust. (You may soften the peanut butter for 30 seconds in the microwave to make it easier to spread.) You don't need to spread the peanut butter to the edge—leave about an inch margin all around.
5.   You'll need two separate bowls for the two fillings, one larger than the other. In the larger bowl, with an electric mixer, beat together the cream cheese, eggs, sour cream, sugar, and vanilla until smooth.
6.   Remove 1 cup of the cream cheese mixture and pour it into the smaller bowl. Add the chocolate syrup to this mixture and combine.
7.   Pour the large bowl of filling into the pan and spread it evenly over the crust.
8.   Pour the chocolate filling onto the other filling and spread it out. Using the tip of a knife, swirl the chocolate into the white filling beneath it. A couple of passes should be enough.
9.   Lower the oven temperature to 350°F. Bake the cheesecake for 70 to 80 minutes or until it becomes firm in the center. Remove from the oven and allow it to cool.
10.   When the cheesecake is completely cool, soften the fudge top-

ping in a double boiler or the microwave for about 45 seconds, then spread it out evenly over the cheesecake. Be sure to cover the entire surface of the filling.

11. Unwrap the peanut butter cups and chop them into small chunks.

12. Sprinkle the peanut butter cup pieces and any crumbs over the top of the cheesecake. Chill.

13. Slice the cake 5 times through the middle to make 10 slices.

• SERVES 10

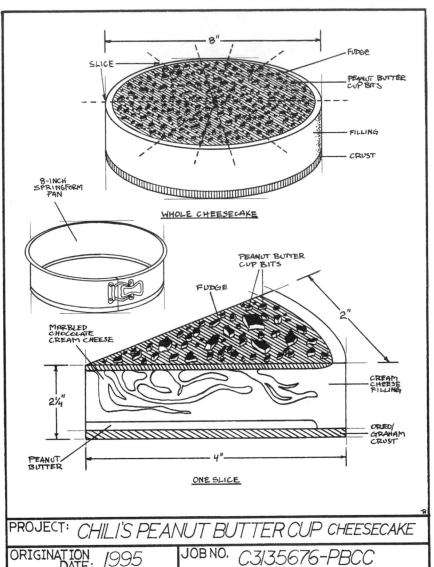

8"

SLICE

FUDGE

PEANUT BUTTER CUP BITS

FILLING

CRUST

WHOLE CHEESECAKE

8-INCH SPRINGFORM PAN

PEANUT BUTTER CUP BITS

FUDGE

MARBLED CHOCOLATE CREAM CHEESE

2"

CREAM CHEESE FILLING

2¼"

OREO/ GRAHAM CRUST

PEANUT BUTTER

4"

ONE SLICE

PROJECT: *CHILI'S PEANUT BUTTER CUP CHEESECAKE*

ORIGINATION DATE: 1995

JOB NO. C3135676-PBCC

CRACKER BARREL HASH BROWN CASSEROLE

☆　♥　☎　✎　✈　✉　✂　☞　❀

Menu Description: "Made from scratch in our kitchens using fresh Grade A Fancy Russet potatoes, fresh chopped onion, natural Colby cheese and spices. Baked fresh all day long."

In the late sixties Dan Evins was a Shell Oil "jobber" looking for a new way to market gasoline. He wanted to create a special place that would arouse curiosity, and would pull travelers off the highways. In 1969 he opened the first Cracker Barrel just off Interstate 40 in Lebanon, Tennessee, offering gas, country-style food, and a selection of antiques for sale. Today there are over 260 stores in 22 states, with each restaurant still designed as a country reststop and gift store. In fact, those stores (which carry an average of 4,500 different items apiece) have made Cracker Barrel the largest retailer of American-made finished crafts in the United States.

Those who know Cracker Barrel well love the restaurant for its delicious home-style breakfasts. This casserole, made with hash browns, Colby cheese, milk, beef stock, and spices is served with many of the classic breakfast dishes at the restaurant. The recipe here is designed for a skillet that is also safe to put in the oven. If you don't have one of those, you can easily transfer the casserole to a baking dish after it is done cooking on the stove.

One 26-ounce bag frozen country-style
　　hash browns
2 cups shredded Colby cheese
1/4 cup minced onion
1 cup milk

1/2 cup beef stock or canned broth
2 tablespoons butter, melted
Dash garlic powder
1 teaspoon salt
1/4 teaspoon ground black pepper

1. Preheat the oven to 425°F.
2. Combine the frozen hash browns, cheese, and onion in a large bowl.
3. Combine the milk, beef stock, half the melted butter, the garlic powder, salt, and black pepper in another bowl. Mix until well blended, then pour the mixture over the hash browns and mix well.
4. Heat the remaining butter in a large, ovenproof skillet over high heat.
5. When the skillet is hot, spoon in the hash brown mixture. Cook the hash browns, stirring occasionally, until hot and all of the cheese has melted (about 7 minutes).
6. Put the skillet into the oven and bake for 45 to 60 minutes or until the surface of the hash browns is dark brown.

- SERVES 4 TO 6 AS A SIDE DISH

TIDBITS

If your skillet isn't ovenproof (because it has a plastic handle, for example), you can also spoon the potatoes into a glass 9 × 9-inch baking dish and microwave the potatoes until they are hot and the cheese has melted. Then put that baking dish into the 425°F oven until the surface of the hash browns has browned.

If you can't find Colby cheese, you can also use Cheddar cheese for this recipe. Colby, however, is preferred.

CRACKER BARREL EGGS-IN-THE-BASKET

☆　♥　☎　✎　✈　⊠　✄　☛　❀

Menu Description: "Two slices of sourdough bread grilled with an egg in the middle, served with thick sliced bacon or smoked sausage patties and fried apples or hash brown casserole."

Breakfast is a popular meal at Cracker Barrel restaurants. Just to prove it, the restaurant has some amazing statistics printed on the back of their breakfast menus:

"Each Spring 607,142 Sugar Maple Trees must be tapped to produce enough pure maple syrup for our guests.

"It takes 5,615,000,000 (THAT'S BILLION!) coffee beans each year to satisfy our guests' needs for coffee. Each tree produces only 1 pound of coffee per year ... that's 1,560,000 trees."

And if you've ever wondered who the man is on the restaurant's logo:

"Uncle Herschel, the country gentleman on our logo, really is the uncle of Cracker Barrel president, Dan Evins."

This recipe is from an old-fashioned egg-in-the-hole meal that I used to make all the time as a kid. Heck, I thought my family had invented it! I was surprised to see this offered on the Cracker Barrel menu, and then I was thrilled to find it tasted just like the homemade version we used to make years ago. This version of the Cracker Barrel classic goes great with the Hash Brown Casserole recipe (page 329). If you're making this for more than just one person, the recipe is easily doubled or quadrupled.

2 thick slices sourdough bread
2 tablespoons butter, softened

2 eggs
Salt to taste

Sausage   *Thick-sliced bacon*

1.   Heat a large frying pan or griddle over medium heat.
2.   Spread the butter evenly over one face of each slice of bread.
3.   Use a biscuit cutter or any jar or container you can find with a diameter of about 2¼ inches to cut a circle out of the center of each slice of bread.
4.   Grill the bread and the hole you cut out, butter side down, in the hot pan for 2 minutes or until it just starts to turn brown.
5.   Drop a little butter in the hole of each slice of bread, then carefully crack an egg into each hole. Be sure not to break the yolks. Salt lightly.
6.   When the eggs have cooked for 1 to 2 minutes, carefully flip each one over without breaking the yolks or flinging raw egg goo all over the stovetop. Also, flip the cut-out "holes."
7.   Cook for another minute or so until the eggs are cooked the way you like them. Serve the eggs, grilled bread, and "holes" with hash browns or Hash Brown Casserole, and bacon or sausage.

   • SERVES 1 (CAN BE DOUBLED)

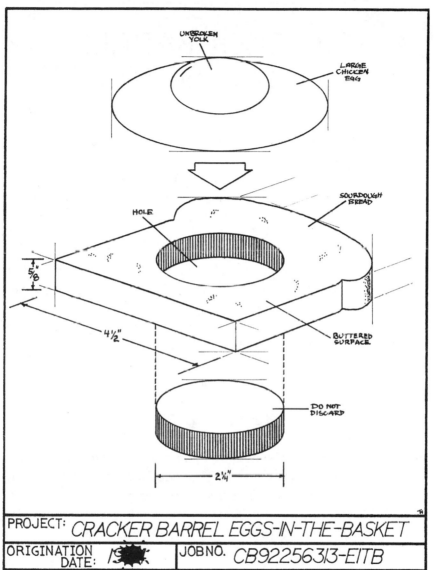

UNBROKEN YOLK

LARGE CHICKEN EGG

HOLE

SOURDOUGH BREAD

5/8"

4½"

BUTTERED SURFACE

DO NOT DISCARD

2¼"

PROJECT: *CRACKER BARREL EGGS-IN-THE-BASKET*

ORIGINATION DATE:

JOBNO. *CB92256313-EITB*

CRACKER BARREL CHICKEN & DUMPLINS

☆　♥　☎　✎　✈　✉　✂　☛　✿

Menu Description: "We use only the 'best of the breast' chicken tenderloin in our recipe. Our dumplins are made from scratch, then hand rolled and cut into strips before simmering to perfection in chicken stock."

By 1977 there were thirteen Cracker Barrel stores located in Georgia and Tennessee, with all of them based on founder Dan Evins' original concept of a restaurant and store built around gasoline pumps. But with the oil embargo and energy crisis of the mid-seventies, Cracker Barrel started building stores that did not offer gas. Soon all of the original thirteen stores were converted so that today not one Cracker Barrel lets you "filler-up" while you fill yourself up.

Another old-time favorite at Cracker Barrel is the Chicken & Dumplins on the lunch and dinner menu. The nice thing about this version of the popular classic dish is that it creates its own tasty gravy. As the "dumplins" dissolve some, the flour thickens the stock into a creamy sauce. Just remember to let your dough rest a bit before rolling it to cut out the dumplins. This will allow the gluten in the flour to work much better. Use extra flour on your cutting board and rolling pin if the dough is too tacky, and try not to roll the dough too thin.

CHICKEN AND BROTH

3 quarts water
One 3- to 4-pound chicken, cut up
1 ½ teaspoons salt
1 small onion, sliced
2 stalks celery, chopped
1 clove garlic, peeled and quartered

1 bay leaf
4 to 6 whole parsley leaves
1 teaspoon coarsely ground black pepper
1 tablespoon lemon juice

"DUMPLINS"

2 cups all-purpose flour

1 tablespoon baking powder

1 1/4 teaspoons salt

1 cup plus 2 tablespoons milk

1. Bring the water to a boil in a large pot. Add the chicken, 1 tea-spoon of salt, onion, celery, garlic, bay leaf, and parsley to the pot. Reduce the heat to simmer and cook the chicken, uncovered, for 2 hours. The liquid will reduce by about one third.

2. When the chicken has cooked, remove it from the pot and set it aside. Strain the stock to remove all the vegetables and floating scum. You only want the stock and the chicken, so toss every-thing else out.

3. Pour 1 1/2 quarts (6 cups) of the stock back into the pot (keep the leftover stock, if any, for another recipe—it can be frozen). You may also want to use a smaller pot or a large saucepan for this. Add coarsely ground pepper, the remaining 1/2 teaspoon salt, and the lemon juice, then reheat the stock over medium heat while preparing the dumplins.

4. For dumplins, combine the flour, baking powder, 1 1/4 teaspoons salt, and milk in a medium bowl. Stir well until smooth, then let the dough rest for to 5 to 10 minutes. Roll the dough out onto a floured surface to about a 1/2-inch thickness.

5. Cut the dough into 1/2-inch squares and drop each square into the simmering stock. Use all of the dough. The dumplins will first swell and then slowly shrink as they partially dissolve to thicken the stock into a white gravy. Simmer for 20 to 30 minutes until thick. Stir often.

6. While the stock is thickening, the chicken will have become cool enough to handle. Tear all the meat from the bones and remove the skin. Cut the chicken meat into bite-size or a little bigger than bite-size pieces and drop them into the pot. Discard the skin and bones. Continue to simmer the chicken and dumplins for another 5 to 10 minutes, but don't stir too vigorously or the chicken will shred and fall apart. You want big chunks of chicken in the end.

7. When the gravy has reached the desired consistency, ladle four portions onto plates and serve hot. Serve with your choice of steamed vegetables, if desired.

    • SERVES 4 AS AN ENTREE

DENNY'S
SCRAM SLAM

Menu Description: "Three eggs scrambled with Cheddar cheese, mushrooms, green peppers and onions, then topped with diced tomatoes. Served with hashed browns, sausage, bacon and choice of toast, Homestyle buttermilk biscuit or English muffin."

In 1953, Harold Butler realized his dream of opening a donut shop. The little shop in Lakewood, California was called Danny's Donuts, and Harold's philosophy was simple: "We're going to serve the best cup of coffee; make the best donuts; give the best service; keep everything spotless; offer the best value; and stay open 24 hours a day."

That little donut store made $120,000 in its first year—a good bit of change for any restaurant in 1953. When customers requested more than fried dough with a hole in the middle, Harold began offering sandwiches, breakfasts, and other meals, and in 1954 changed the name to Danny's Coffee Shops. The name of the chain would eventually change again, this time to Denny's—now the nation's largest full-service restaurant chain.

In 1977, Denny's introduced the Grand Slam Breakfast—a value-priced breakfast that included eggs, sausage, bacon, and pancakes. Later, the successful Grand Slam Breakfast specials expanded to include other variations including the French Slam, Southern Slam, and the Scram Slam, the last a popular vegetable-and-scrambled-egg creation you can now make for yourself.

1 slice white onion, diced (¼ cup)	6 eggs, beaten
¼ green bell pepper, diced (¼ cup)	1 cup shredded Cheddar cheese
4 mushrooms, sliced (1 cup)	Salt
1½ tablespoons butter	½ tomato, chopped

Bacon   *Hash browns*
Sausage

1. In a small skillet, sauté the onion, green pepper, and mushrooms in 1 tablespoon of the butter over medium heat for about 5 minutes or until the mushrooms are tender.
2. In another larger skillet over medium heat, melt the remaining ½ tablespoon butter. Add the beaten eggs. Stir the eggs as they cook to scramble them.
3. When the eggs have cooked for 5 to 7 minutes and are no longer runny, add the cheese and stir. Add the sautéed onions, green pepper, and mushrooms along with a dash of salt and cook the eggs until done.
4. Divide the eggs onto two plates and sprinkle chopped tomatoes over each helping. Serve with bacon, sausage, and hash browns on the side.

    • SERVES 2

DENNY'S MOONS OVER MY HAMMY

☆　♥　☎　✎　✈　▣　✂　☛　✿

Menu Description: "The supreme ham and egg sandwich, made with Swiss and American cheese on grilled sourdough. Served with choice of hashed browns or French fries."

With its goofy-yet-memorable name, Moons Over My Hammy is a delicious and versatile scrambled egg sandwich that can be eaten for breakfast with hash browns on the side, or for lunch with a side of French fries. When you get the sourdough bread for this recipe, try to find a good-quality loaf with large slices.

Butter, softened
2 eggs, beaten
Salt
2 ounces deli-sliced ham
2 slices sourdough bread

1 to 2 slices processed Swiss cheese
　(Kraft Singles)
1 to 2 slices American cheese (Kraft
　Singles)

ON THE SIDE

Hash browns　　　　　　　　　French fries

1.　Put two medium-size skillets over medium heat. In one skillet, add a little butter and scramble the two eggs. Salt the eggs to taste. In the other skillet, brown the stack of sliced ham without separating the slices.
2.　When the stack of ham slices has browned a bit on both sides, remove it from the pan. Butter one side of each slice of sourdough bread and put one slice into the pan, buttered side down, to grill.

3. Immediately put the slice(s) of Swiss cheese onto the face-up, unbuttered side of the bread that is grilling.
4. Stack the heated ham slices on the Swiss cheese.
5. Scoop the scrambled eggs out of the other pan with a large spatula and place them on the ham.
6. Place the slice(s) of American cheese on the eggs.
7. Top off the sandwich with the remaining slice of sourdough bread. Make sure the unbuttered side faces the cheese.
8. By this time the bread touching the pan should be grilled to a golden brown. Carefully flip the sandwich over and grill the other side for about 2 minutes or until brown.
9. Slice the sandwich diagonally through the middle and serve with hash browns or French fries on the side.

• SERVES 1 (CAN BE DOUBLED)

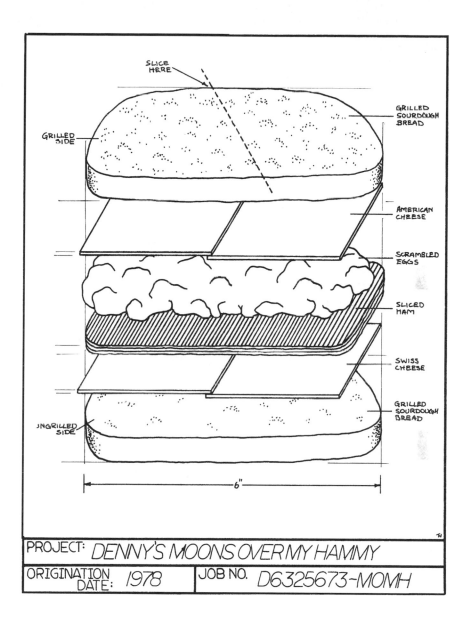

SLICE HERE

GRILLED SOURDOUGH BREAD

GRILLED SIDE

AMERICAN CHEESE

SCRAMBLED EGGS

SLICED HAM

SWISS CHEESE

GRILLED SOURDOUGH BREAD

UNGRILLED SIDE

6"

| PROJECT: *DENNY'S MOONS OVER MY HAMMY* |
| ORIGINATION DATE: *1978* | JOB NO. *D6325673-MOMH* |

DENNY'S
THE SUPER BIRD

Menu Description: "A Denny's original. Sliced turkey breast with Swiss cheese, bacon and tomato on grilled sourdough. Served with French fries and pickle chips."

Now you can munch down your own clone of this popular palate pleaser, The Super Bird, a cross between a grilled cheese and a club, and Denny's top-selling sandwich. When shopping for sourdough bread, try to find a high-quality loaf with large slices. The thin-sliced turkey breast is best purchased at your market's deli service counter where they cut it while you wait. If you don't have a service counter like this near you, you can use the prepackaged thin-sliced meats located in the cold deli section. Or you can move.

3 ounces deli-sliced turkey breast	*Salt*
2 large slices sourdough bread	*2 slices bacon, cooked*
Butter, softened	*2 slices tomato*
2 slices processed Swiss cheese (Kraft Singles)	

ON THE SIDE

French fries	*Pickles*

1. Heat a skillet or frying pan over medium heat. Grill the stack of turkey breast in the pan without separating the stack until the meat is golden brown on both sides.
2. While the turkey is browning, butter one side of each slice of sourdough bread. Place one slice of bread in the pan, buttered side down.

3. Place two slices of Swiss cheese on the unbuttered side of the bread grilling in the pan.
4. Put the stack of turkey breast slices on the Swiss cheese. Sprinkle with a bit of salt.
5. Place the cooked bacon on the turkey breast.
6. Stack the tomato slices on the bacon next.
7. Top off the sandwich with the remaining slice of sourdough bread. Be sure to place the bread with the unbuttered side facing the tomato slices.
8. When the slice of bread on the bottom has grilled until golden brown, carefully flip the sandwich over to grill the other slice.
9. After about 2 minutes, when the bread has grilled to a golden brown, remove the sandwich from the pan and slice the sandwich twice with a sharp knife, creating 3 equal-size pieces. Serve with French fries and pickles, if desired.

- SERVES 1 (CAN BE DOUBLED)

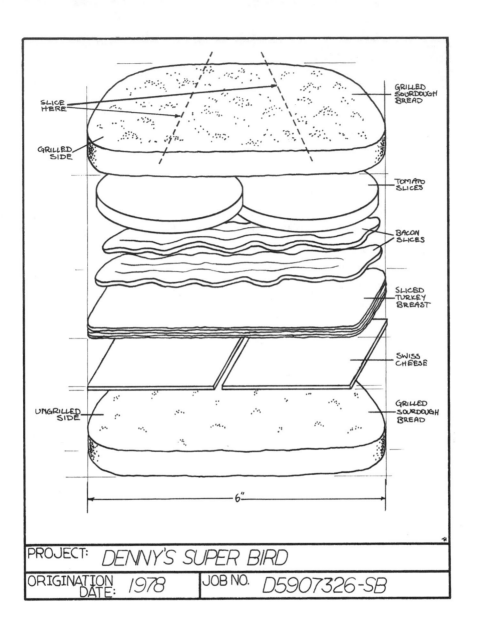

SLICE HERE

GRILLED SOURDOUGH BREAD

GRILLED SIDE

TOMATO SLICES

BACON SLICES

SLICED TURKEY BREAST

SWISS CHEESE

UNGRILLED SIDE

GRILLED SOURDOUGH BREAD

6"

PROJECT:	DENNY'S SUPER BIRD	
ORIGINATION DATE: 1978	JOB NO.	D5907326-SB

DIVE!
CARROT CHIPS

☆ ♥ ☎ ✎ ✈ ✉ ✂ ☞ ✿

Menu Description: "Crisp, lightly fried carrots, choice of two dips."

In 1992, Steven Spielberg organized a search for a hoagie like those he remembered from his childhood in Phoenix, Arizona. The famed director sent his assistants out to search L.A. for the perfect submarine sandwich, and from the 20 sandwiches brought back to him, not one passed the test. Former chairman of Walt Disney Studios and close friend Jeffrey Katzenberg was in on the taste test that day and agreed that most of the sandwiches were either too soggy or too leathery. The two began tossing the idea around of opening their own restaurant to reinvent the submarine sandwich with fresh baked bread and unique combinations of ingredients—like what Spago's and California Pizza Kitchen were doing with pizza. Partnered with Mark and Larry Levy of Levy Restaurants, the two movie moguls tasted over 100 sandwich recipes before finding two dozen they liked. A year of planning went by to build a deep-sea theme around the recipes, and in 1994, the first Dive! restaurant opened in L.A.

In addition to the gourmet sandwiches on the menu, Dive! features pastas, salads, burgers, and delicious appetizers like carrot chips complete with your choice of dipping sauces. Because the carrots need to be sliced no thicker than 1/16 inch, you'll probably have to use a thin-slicing machine such as a mandoline for this recipe. I tried doing it by hand, and it's practically impossible to get the carrots a uniform thickness without using a gadget.

6 carrots   *4 to 6 cups canola oil*

ON THE SIDE

Barbecue sauce (commercial brand, or White Cheddar Dipping Sauce
    see page 537)   (follows)
Cajun Mayonnaise Dipping Sauce
    (follows)

1. Peel the carrots, then slice them crosswise in half. Use a slicer to make lengthwise, thin slices of carrot, no more than 1/16 inch thick.
2. Heat the oil in a deep pot or deep fryer to 350°F.
3. Drop a handful of carrot slices at a time into the hot oil. Fry the carrots for 10 to 15 seconds or until they turn a dark brown. Remove the carrots from the oil; drain and cool the carrots on paper towels, then put them in a large, shallow bowl. Serve with ketchup, a store-bought dip (such as barbecue sauce), or your choice of dipping sauces from the recipes here.

- SERVES 4 AS AN APPETIZER OR SNACK

CAJUN MAYONNAISE DIPPING SAUCE

1/2 cup mayonnaise   1/8 teaspoon ground black pepper
1 teaspoon lemon juice   1/8 teaspoon paprika
1/4 teaspoon cayenne pepper   1/8 teaspoon dried thyme
1/8 teaspoon garlic powder   Dash salt
1/8 teaspoon onion powder   Pinch dried oregano

1. Combine all of the ingredients in a small bowl.
2. Cover and refrigerate for several hours or overnight before serving.

WHITE CHEDDAR DIPPING SAUCE

1/2 cup heavy cream   1 tablespoon butter
1 to 2 ounces white Cheddar cheese,
    grated or chopped

1. Combine all of the ingredients in a small saucepan over medium heat.
2. Bring the mixture to a boil, then reduce the heat and simmer for 10 minutes. By then the sauce should have thickened. Serve hot.

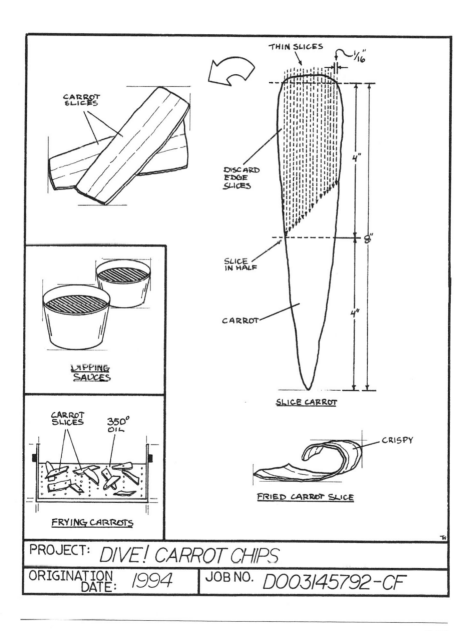

PROJECT: *DIVE! CARROT CHIPS*

ORIGINATION DATE: *1994*   JOB NO. *D003145792-CF*

DIVE!
SICILIAN SUB ROSA

☆　♥　☎　✎　✈　✉　✂　☛　❀

Menu Description: "Our traditional sub with capocollo, mortadella, Genoa salami, prosciutto ham, provolone cheese, roasted red peppers, fresh basil, lettuce, sliced tomato, onions and vinaigrette. Served hot or cold."

Casino magnate Steve Wynn teamed up with Steven Spielberg, Jeffrey Katzenberg, and the Levy Brothers for the second Dive! restaurant, which opened in Las Vegas in March of 1995. Like the first restaurant, which opened the year before in Los Angeles, the Vegas Dive! features Spielbergian special effects designed by Hollywood set builders, such as bubbling portholes, spinning gauges, working periscopes, steaming pipes, and a simulated dive run by a computer every hour. Driving down the Vegas "strip" you can't miss the giant nose of a submarine crashing through a 30-foot wall of water, which pumps 100 gallons of water per foot per minute down thick glass window panes. A pool below explodes with synchronized depth charges that splash passersby at random intervals. Back inside, if you look carefully, you can see the partners' initials stenciled on torpedoes hanging high over the heads of diners.

The Dive! concept was built around submarine sandwiches and the Sicilian Sub Rosa is its signature traditional Italian submarine sandwich. It's said to be cofounder Steven Spielberg's favorite and now you can make a version all your own. Try to get all of the meat sliced fresh at a full-service deli counter, if you have one at your supermarket.

VINAIGRETTE

¼ cup light olive oil	Dash ground black pepper
1 tablespoon red wine vinegar	Dash salt
½ teaspoon lemon juice	Dash garlic powder

1 handful of thinly sliced and separated red onion rings (about ⅛ onion)	1 ounce deli-sliced mortadella
	1 ounce deli-sliced Genoa salami
	1 ounce deli-sliced provolone cheese
One 7-inch baguette	1 ounce roasted red peppers (canned or homemade, see "Tidbits")
1 leaf green leaf lettuce	4 to 5 small fresh basil leaves
1 ounce deli-sliced prosciutto	3 tomato slices
1 ounce deli-sliced capocollo	

1. Mix the vinaigrette ingredients together in a small bowl and add the sliced and separated red onion rings to the bowl. Let the onions marinate for at least a couple hours. Overnight is even better.

2. When the onions are ready, slice open the baguette, without cutting all of the way through. Brush a generous amount of the vinaigrette on the faces of the baguette.

3. Spread the leaf of lettuce on the baguette.

4. Arrange the prosciutto over the lettuce.

5. Next, stack the capocollo.

6. On the capocollo goes the mortadella.

7. Then the Genoa salami.

8. Next is the provolone.

9. Arrange the roasted red peppers on the provolone cheese.

10. Spread the fresh basil leaves on the sandwich next.

11. Arrange the sliced tomatoes on the basil leaves.

12. Remove the red onions from the vinaigrette and spread them on top of the tomatoes.

13. Close the sandwich and use toothpicks to keep it that way to serve. If you want the sandwich hot, before you close it, put it in a preheated 450 degree F oven for 4 minutes and then broil it for 2 minutes. The cheese should melt slightly and the bread will become slightly browned. Slice the sandwich in half before serving.

• SERVES 1 (CAN BE DOUBLED)

TIDBITS

Canned roasted peppers are usually pretty good, but if you want to make great roasted peppers yourself, put a whole red bell pepper directly on the burner of a gas stove set to medium heat or on a pan in an oven set to broil. Turn the pepper often with tongs until most of the skin of the pepper is charred black. Immediately drop the pepper into a bowl of ice water and carefully peel the skin away. Remove the seeds, chop the remaining pepper into slices for your sandwich and store the leftovers in a sealed container in the refrigerator.

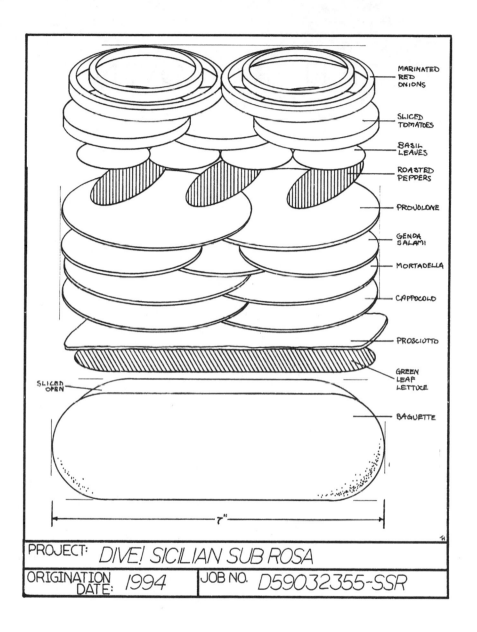

MARINATED
RED
ONIONS

SLICED
TOMATOES

BASIL
LEAVES

ROASTED
PEPPERS

PROVOLONE

GENOA
SALAMI

MORTADELLA

CAPPOCOLO

PROSCIUTTO

GREEN
LEAF
LETTUCE

BAGUETTE

SLICED
OPEN

7"

PROJECT: *DIVE! SICILIAN SUB ROSA*

ORIGINATION
DATE: *1994*

JOB NO. *D59032355-SSR*

DIVE! BRICK OVEN MUSHROOM AND TURKEY CHEESE SUB

☆ ♥ ☎ ✎ ✈ ✉ ✄ ☞ ✿

Menu Description: "Our fresh roasted turkey, brick oven roasted seasonal mushrooms with white cheddar cheese and melted Swiss cheese. Served hot."

Although not intended to be a restaurant where sightseers are encouraged to catch a glimpse of celebrities, many stars have been spotted at the L.A. location of this trendy new theme eatery. Through the "hatch" have walked the likes of Candice Bergen, Warren Beatty, Michael Keaton, Tom Hanks, Michael Douglas, and Rob Reiner. Pierce Brosnan and Henry Winkler have become regulars, and for some time cofounder Steven Spielberg could be seen eating there weekly. At least ten new Dive! locations are being planned for additional U.S. and international markets including New York, Chicago, Mexico, and Japan.

For this sandwich, inspired by Dive!'s popular Brick Oven Mushroom and Turkey Cheese Sub, you will likely not have the luxury of a brick oven to roast the mushrooms, but I've found the recipe is just as tasty as the real thing with sautéed mushrooms. It's important that you find the freshest bread your market has available, and if possible, get the turkey sliced for you at a full-service deli counter. A sandwich is only as good and as fresh as its ingredients, so try to find the best your market has to offer.

4 mushrooms, sliced (½ to ¾ cup)
1 tablespoon butter
Salt
Pepper
6 ounces deli-sliced, roasted turkey breast

¼ cup White Cheddar Dipping Sauce (page 346)
One 7-inch baguette, sliced open
2 ounces Swiss cheese, sliced

1. Preheat the oven to 450°F.
2. Sauté the mushroom slices in the butter. Season with salt and pepper.
3. Heat the roasted turkey breast in a microwave oven or in another pan until warm.
4. Heat the White Cheddar Dipping Sauce until it is hot, if it's not hot already.
5. Split the baguette without cutting all of the way through. Hinge the bread open and spread some of the cheese sauce on the faces of the bread.
6. Load the turkey breast into the sliced baguette. Salt and pepper it.
7. Pour the remaining cheese sauce over the turkey.
8. Spread the mushrooms over the cheese sauce.
9. Bake the open sandwich for 4 minutes. Put the Swiss cheese on top of the other ingredients and bake for 2 minutes more, or just until the cheese is melted. Slice the sandwich in half before serving.

• SERVES 1 (CAN BE DOUBLED)

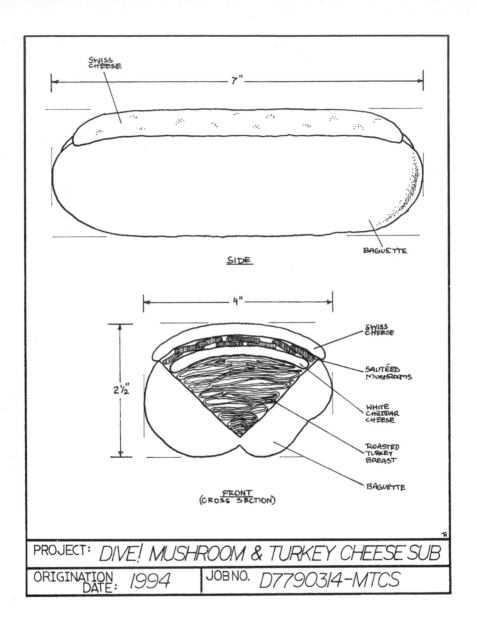

SWISS
CHEESE

7"

SIDE

BAGUETTE

4"

2½"

SWISS
CHEESE

SAUTÉED
MUSHROOMS

WHITE
CHEDDAR
CHEESE

ROASTED
TURKEY
BREAST

BAGUETTE

FRONT
(CROSS SECTION)

PROJECT: *DIVE! MUSHROOM & TURKEY CHEESE SUB*

ORIGINATION
DATE: *1994*

JOB NO. *D7790314-MTCS*

DIVE! S'MORES

☆　♥　☎　✎　✈　✉　✂　☛　✿

Menu Description: "Graham crackers, milk chocolate and toasted marshmallows, streaked with chocolate sauce."

Large screens inside each Dive! display videos of underwater scenes filmed in the waters of Micronesia, Bermuda, San Salvador, and Florida. Diners eat gourmet submarine sandwiches as giant sea turtles and sharks swim by coral reefs and underwater caves. When the alarm sounds and lights flash, it's time for the restaurant to take its simulated hourly dive. Video in the portholes and on the giant projection screens changes to comedy footage from vintage movies and clips of unlikely locales for a huge submarine such as a backyard swimming pool.

Along with the two dozen or so gourmet sandwiches and other tasty entrees, Dive! features a delectable selection of desserts. One of them is Dive! S'mores, a creation inspired by the traditional treat that's prepared around campfires with marshmallows toasted on sticks. This version assembled with graham crackers, chocolate bars, and marshmallows is broiled in a hot oven just long enough to brown the tops of the marshmallows. If you've got a craving for S'mores and are nowhere near a campfire and/or don't have sticks, here's your quick fix.

2 whole graham crackers (4 sections, not separated)
Two 1½-ounce Hershey milk chocolate bars

16 large marshmallows
2 tablespoons Hershey's chocolate syrup, in squirt bottle

1.　Preheat the broiler. Arrange the graham crackers side by side on an oven-safe plate (such as ceramic). You can also use a baking sheet.
2.　Stack the milk chocolate bars side by side on top of the graham crackers.

3. Arrange the marshmallows on the chocolate in 4 rows—4 across, 4 down.
4. Broil the dessert on the middle rack for 1 to 3 minutes or until the marshmallows turn light brown on top.
5. Remove the dessert from the oven. If you used a baking sheet, carefully slide the dessert onto a serving plate. With the squirt bottle, immediately drizzle the chocolate syrup over the marshmallows in a sweeping back-and-forth motion. Drizzle the chocolate diagonally across the dessert one way, and then the other, creating a cross-hatch pattern. Allow the chocolate to overshoot the dessert so that it creates a decorative pattern on the serving plate as well.

- SERVES 2 TO 4

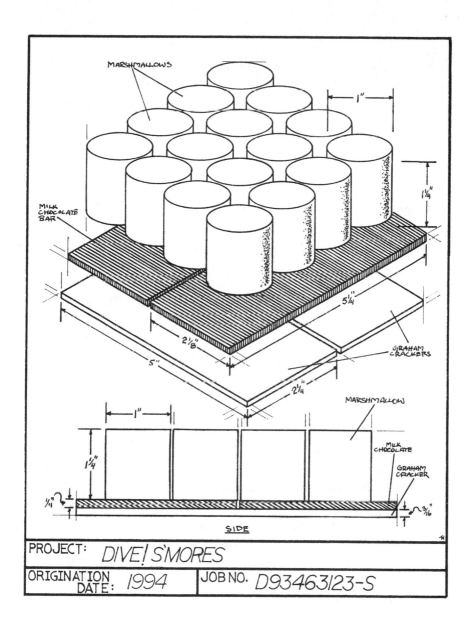

MARSHMALLOWS

MILK
CHOCOLATE
BAR

1"

1¼"

5¼"

GRAHAM
CRACKERS

2⅛"

5"

2¼"

MARSHMALLOW

MILK
CHOCOLATE

GRAHAM
CRACKER

1"

1¼"

¼"

³⁄₁₆"

SIDE

PROJECT: *DIVE! S'MORES*

ORIGINATION DATE: *1994*

JOB NO. *D93463123-S*

HARD ROCK CAFE
FILET STEAK SANDWICH

☆　♥　☎　✎　✈　⊠　✂　☞　✿

Menu Description: "Filet mignon grilled to perfection, sliced thin, with shredded lettuce, tomato and spicy mustard. Served on a sourdough French roll with fries and a salad."

When the first Hard Rock Cafe opened in 1971 on Old Park Lane in London, England, not one guitar or gold record decorated the walls. The burger joint was the inspiration of two Americans, Peter Morton and Isaac Tigrett, who couldn't find a decent American-style hamburger anywhere in London and decided to do something about it. The restaurant soon became famous only for its food, until along came Eric Clapton, who donated his guitar as a joke. Up on the wall it went. Not wanting to be outdone, Pete Townsend of The Who soon offered up a guitar of his own to be hung on the wall next to Clapton's with a note: "Mine's as good as his." That started a wave of donations from rock and rollers through the decades; and thus was born the world's first theme restaurant. Soon more Hard Rock Cafes were opening around the world, with the first one in America opening in Los Angeles in 1982. After that came New York City, San Francisco, Chicago, Houston, New Orleans, Maui, Las Vegas, Aspen, Newport Beach, and many more—a total of 58 so far. The success of the Hard Rock Cafe spawned a trend which now includes other restaurants built around themes ranging from movies to fashion to motorcycles to blues.

Here is an easy-to-make sandwich that features a tender, sliced filet mignon. It's a clone of one of the Hard Rock's more popular recent additions to the menu. This recipe suggests another way you can serve those filet mignons you've been saving in the freezer.

Two 6- to 8-ounce filet mignon steaks
Salt and pepper
2 sourdough French rolls
3 tablespoons mayonnaise

3 tablespoons spicy mustard
6 slices tomato
1 cup shredded iceberg lettuce

1. Preheat the barbecue or stovetop grill.
2. Since most filets are usually cut pretty thick (1 inch or more) you will want to slice your filets through the middle before grilling, making four thinner filets that are around ½ inch each.
3. Cook your filets over a hot grill for 2 to 4 minutes per side or until cooked to your preference. Be sure to salt and pepper both sides of each filet.
4. As the meat cooks, prepare your rolls by slicing them into top and bottom halves.
5. Spread the mayonnaise on the face of each top half.
6. Spread the mustard onto the face of each bottom half.
7. When the filets are done, slice them into ½-inch-thick strips.
8. Arrange the sliced filets evenly over the mustard on each bottom roll.
9. Place the tomato slices over the filets.
10. Put the shredded lettuce on top of the tomatoes.
11. Place the top buns on the lettuce and slice the sandwiches diagonally into two even halves. Hold each sandwich half together with toothpicks to serve.

• SERVES 2 AS AN ENTRÉE

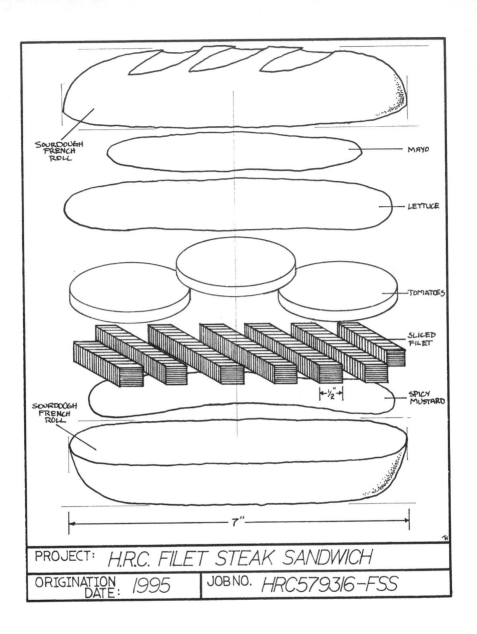

SOURDOUGH
FRENCH
ROLL

MAYO

LETTUCE

TOMATOES

SLICED
FILET

SPICY
MUSTARD

SOURDOUGH
FRENCH
ROLL

½"

7"

PROJECT: H.R.C. FILET STEAK SANDWICH

ORIGINATION DATE: 1995

JOB NO. HRC579316-FSS

HARD ROCK CAFE GRILLED VEGETABLE SANDWICH

☆ ♥ ☎ ✎ ✈ ✉ ✂ ☛ ✿

Menu Description: "Grilled eggplant, zucchini, summer squash, and roasted red peppers. Served on a sourdough French roll with your choice of fries or watermelon."

Pop artist Andy Warhol called Hard Rock Cafe the "Smithsonian of Rock and Roll." In fact, the Hard Rock Cafe chain owns more artifacts of rock history than anyone in the world—somewhere around 30,000 in all. The chain has been collecting the artifacts, which decorate each of the 58 Hard Rock Cafes, for more than two decades. Because of this, some of the memorabilia you see in the restaurants, especially the older ones, were donated from artists even before they were famous.

As the chain grew larger over the years, cofounders Peter Morton and Isaac Tigrett grew tired of their business relationship. The company was eventually divided, with Isaac operating foreign Hard Rocks, and Peter taking over the stateside cafes. In 1988, Isaac sold his shares to Britain's Rank Organization and then partnered with actor Dan Aykroyd to open the House of Blues chain. In 1996, just a week before the Hard Rock celebrated its 25th anniversary, Peter sold his shares to Rank as well (for $410 million in cash!), consolidating the chain once again.

If you don't eat meat, or even if you do, you'll find this grilled vegetable sandwich makes a great meal in itself for lunch or dinner. I'm not usually one to go for strictly vegetarian sandwiches, but when I first tried this one I was surprised at how good it was. Now I veg out with this sandwich regularly. Hopefully you will too.

6 tablespoons mayonnaise
1/2 teaspoon chopped fresh parsley
Pinch dried oregano
Salt
1 red bell pepper
1 small zucchini
1 yellow summer squash
1/4 eggplant

1/4 cup olive oil
2 sourdough French rolls
1 tablespoon freshly grated Parmesan
    cheese
6 to 8 separated onion ring slices
    (2 whole slices)
3 to 4 slices tomato (1 medium tomato)
2 leaves red leaf lettuce

1. Preheat the barbecue or stovetop grill.
2. To prepare a spread, put 3 tablespoons of the mayo into a small bowl and add the parsley, oregano and a pinch of salt. Set this and the remaining mayonnaise aside until you're ready to make the sandwich.
3. Prepare the bell pepper by cutting it into quarters and seeding it. Brush the entire surface of the pepper with olive oil.
4. Slice the zucchini, squash, and eggplant into lengthwise slices no more than 1/8 to 1/4 inch thick. Brush these slices with oil as well.
5. Cook the red pepper on a hot grill for 2 or 3 minutes. At that point add the remaining vegetables to the grill and cook everything for 4 to 5 more minutes or until all the vegetables are tender. Be sure to salt the vegetables and, of course, turn them halfway through the cooking time.
6. When the veggies are tender and begin to char, remove them from the grill and prepare each sandwich by first cutting the French rolls in half lengthwise through the middle.
7. Spread the parsley-mayonnaise over the face of the bottom halves.
8. Arrange the zucchini onto the rolls.
9. Stack the yellow squash next.
10. Eggplant goes on top of that.
11. Peel the skin off the red peppers, then stack the peppers on the eggplant.
12. Divide the Parmesan cheese and sprinkle it over the peppers.
13. Arrange the onions on the peppers.
14. Tomato slices go on the onions.
15. Tear the red lettuce leaves so that they fit on the tomatoes.
16. Divide the remaining 3 tablespoons of mayonnaise and spread it

on the face of the top rolls and stack the rolls on the lettuce to finish off your sandwiches.

17. Cut the sandwiches diagonally through the middle and pierce each half with a toothpick before serving.

• SERVES 2 AS AN ENTREE

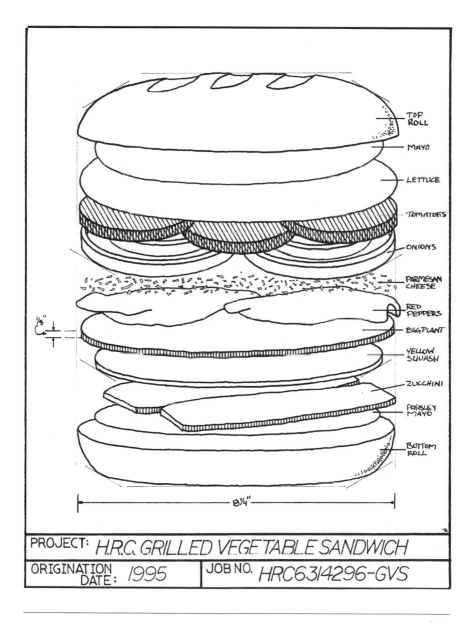

TOP ROLL
MAYO
LETTUCE
TOMATOES
ONIONS
PARMESAN CHEESE
RED PEPPERS
EGGPLANT
YELLOW SQUASH
ZUCCHINI
PARSLEY MAYO
BOTTOM ROLL

1/8"

8¼"

PROJECT: *H.R.C. GRILLED VEGETABLE SANDWICH*

ORIGINATION DATE: *1995*   JOB NO. *HRC6314296-GVS*

HARD ROCK CAFE FAMOUS BABY ROCK WATERMELON RIBS

☆   ♥   ☎   ✎   ✈   ✉   ✂   ☛   ✿

Menu Description: "Texas style ribs basted in our special water-melon B.B.Q. sauce, grilled and served with fries and a green salad."

The collection of rock and roll memorabilia is different in each Hard Rock Cafe. You may find artifacts that come from recording stars of the fifties, like Elvis Presley and Fats Domino, to more contemporary artists such as Prince, Pearl Jam, and Nirvana. Usually there are several gold and platinum records donated from artists, sequined stage costumes, and famous guitars, some even left in a smashed condition as they were donated straight from a performance. The Hard Rock also collects movie memorabilia, such as Tom Cruise's pilot helmet from the movie *Top Gun* and the Indiana Jones jacket from *Raiders of the Lost Ark.*

In 1995, Hard rock cofounder Peter Morton opened the world's first rock-and-roll hotel, The Hard Rock Hotel and Casino, in Las Vegas. Peter now operates the hotel and his swank restaurant Morton's in Hollywood, California—the famous location of many a celebrity power meal over the years.

I thought these ribs with a barbecue sauce made from water-melon rind had a unique and memorable flavor begging to be duplicated at your next power meal. The sauce is sweet and slightly tangy, and the ribs are so tender they melt in your mouth. It's the slow-cooking process that makes them that way. Throwing them on the grill at the last minute is not meant to cook them so much as it is to add the smoky flavor and slight charring that good ribs require. If possible, make the watermelon barbecue sauce a day ahead so the ribs can marinate in it overnight. If you don't have time for that, at least marinate the ribs for a couple of hours.

Watermelon rind from about ½ of a
    small watermelon
I cup dark corn syrup
½ cup water
¼ cup tomato ketchup

¼ cup distilled vinegar
¾ teaspoon crushed red pepper flakes
½ teaspoon liquid smoke
¼ teaspoon black pepper
4 pounds baby back ribs

1. For the puréed watermelon rind, you want to cut off the green skin and about half an inch of the hard white part, keeping the part of the watermelon that is lighter red to white. This is the tender part of the rind. Try to stay away from the harder, white rind just inside the green skin. Put the rind into a food processor and purée for only about 10 seconds. Strain the liquid from the pulp and use I cup of pulp, measured after straining.

2. Combine the watermelon pulp with the remaining ingredients for the sauce in a medium saucepan over high heat. Bring the mixture to a boil, then reduce the heat and simmer, covered, for about I hour or until it's as thick as you like it.

3. Cut racks of ribs into plate-size portions of about 6 or 7 rib bones each. Brush the ribs with the barbecue sauce and wrap each rack individually in aluminum foil. Be sure to save some sauce for later. Let the ribs marinate in the refrigerator for a couple of hours at least. (Overnight is best.)

4. Preheat the oven to 300°F. To cook the ribs, set them with the seam of the foil facing up, into the oven. Bake for 2 to 2½ hours or until the rib meat has pulled back from the cut end of the bones by about ½ inch. They should be very tender.

5. Remove the ribs from the foil and brush on some additional sauce. Grill the ribs on a hot barbecue for 2 to 4 minutes per side or until you see several spots of charred sauce. Be sure to watch the ribs so that they do not burn. Serve with leftover sauce on the side.

- SERVES 2 TO 4 AS AN ENTREE

HARD ROCK CAFE ORANGE FREEZE

☆ ♥ ☎ ✎ ✈ ⊠ ✂ ☞ ✿

Menu Description: "Fresh squeezed O.J. and orange sherbet."

The Hard Rock Cafe chain has been committed to a "Save the Planet" campaign for some time now. The chain recycles all of the glass bottles, paper, and cardboard boxes, and uses no polystyrene. Water in the restaurant is only served on request. At the restaurants in Los Angeles and Newport Beach electronic tote boards have been erected to "tick away by the second the acres of remaining rainforest on the planet while also displaying the world's population count as it continues to explode, reminding us all to be conscious of our decreasing natural resources." In addition, any leftover food is donated to local charities that feed the homeless. That's cool, eh?

You'll find the Orange Freeze is pretty cool also, especially on a hot summer day. This refreshing dessert item at the Hard Rock is easy to duplicate at home with just a few ingredients and a couple minutes in front of a blender.

2 cups orange sherbet or sorbet
1 cup fresh squeezed orange juice

¼ cup milk
1 sprig of fresh spearmint

1. Put the sherbet, juice, and milk in a blender and blend for 15 seconds or just until all the sherbet is smooth. You may have to stop the blender and stir the sherbet up a bit to help it combine.
2. Pour the orange freeze into a tall, chilled glass. Place a sprig of fresh spearmint in the top and serve immediately.

• SERVES 1 AS DESSERT OR BEVERAGE

TIDBITS

This is also good with a little whipped cream on top.

HOOTERS
BUFFALO CHICKEN
WINGS

☆　♥　☎　✎　✈　✉　✄　☞　✿

Menu Description: "Nearly world famous. Often imitated, hardly ever duplicated."

Hooters is to chicken wings what McDonald's is to hamburgers," claims promotional material from the company. True, the six fun-loving midwestern businessmen who started Hooters in Clearwater, Florida, on April Fool's Day in 1983 chose a classic recipe for chicken wings as their feature item. But while some might say it's the Buffalo Wings that are their favorite feature of Hooters, others say it's the restaurant chain's trademark Hooters girls—waitresses casually attired in bright orange short-shorts and skin-tight T-shirts. Apparently it's a combination that works.

Today there are nearly 200 Hooters across the United States serving more than 150 tons of chicken wings every week. I've tasted lots of chicken wings, and I think these are some of the best wings served in any restaurant chain today. The original dish can be ordered in 10-, 20- or 50-piece servings; or if you want to splurge, there's the "Gourmet Chicken Wing Dinner" featuring 20 wings and a bottle of Dom Perignon champagne, for only $125. To further enhance the Hooters experience when you serve these messy wings, throw a whole roll of paper towels on the table, rather than napkins, as they do in the restaurants.

Vegetable oil for frying
¼ cup butter
¼ cup Crystal Louisiana Hot Sauce or
　Frank's Red Hot Cayenne Sauce

Dash ground pepper
Dash garlic powder
½ cup all-purpose flour
¼ teaspoon paprika

¼ teaspoon cayenne pepper   *10 chicken wing pieces*
¼ teaspoon salt

ON THE SIDE

Bleu cheese dressing   *Celery sticks*

1. Heat oil in a deep fryer to 375°F. You want just enough oil to cover the wings entirely—an inch or so deep at least.
2. Combine the butter, hot sauce, ground pepper, and garlic powder in a small saucepan over low heat. Heat until the butter is melted and the ingredients are well-blended.
3. Combine the flour, paprika, cayenne pepper, and salt in a small bowl.
4. If the wings are frozen, be sure to defrost and dry them. Put the wings into a large bowl and sprinkle the flour mixture over them, coating each wing evenly. Put the wings in the refrigerator for 60 to 90 minutes. (This will help the breading to stick to the wings when fried.)
5. Put all the wings into the hot oil and fry them for 10 to 15 minutes or until some parts of the wings begin to turn dark brown.
6. Remove the wings from the oil to a paper towel to drain. But don't let them sit too long, because you want to serve the wings hot.
7. Quickly put the wings into a large bowl. Add the hot sauce and stir, coating all of the wings evenly. You could also use a large plastic container (such as Tupperware) with a lid for this. Put all the wings inside the container, add the sauce, put on the lid, then shake. Serve with bleu cheese dressing and celery sticks on the side.

   • SERVES 3 TO 5 AS AN APPETIZER

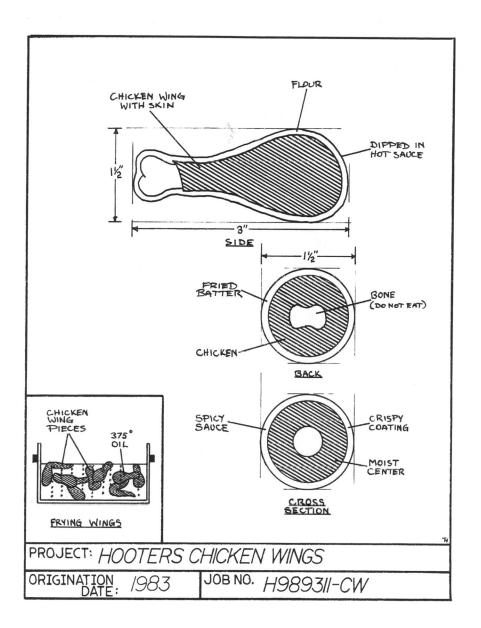

CHICKEN WING
WITH SKIN

FLOUR

DIPPED IN
HOT SAUCE

1½"

3"

SIDE

1½"

FRIED
BATTER

BONE
(DO NOT EAT)

CHICKEN

BACK

CHICKEN
WING
PIECES

375°
OIL

FRYING WINGS

SPICY
SAUCE

CRISPY
COATING

MOIST
CENTER

CROSS
SECTION

PROJECT: *HOOTERS CHICKEN WINGS*

ORIGINATION DATE: *1983*   **JOB NO.** *H989311-CW*

HOOTERS BUFFALO SHRIMP

☆ ♥ ☎ ✎ ✈ ✉ ✂ ☛ ✿

Menu Description: "It don't get no batter than this."

With the double-entendre name and female servers (many of whom, off-duty, are models), Hooters has become a company with critics. Several years ago a group of Hooters Girls in Minneapolis sued the company on grounds of sexual harassment, saying that the uniforms featuring shorts and tight T-shirts or tank tops were demeaning. Ultimately, the women dropped the suit. But more recently, the Equal Employment Opportunity Commission ordered the company to hire men on the foodservice staff. Hooters countered with a sarcastic million-dollar advertising campaign featuring a mustachioed man named "Vince" dressed in Hooters Girl getup. Once again, that suit was dropped.

Vice president of marketing Mike McNeil told *Nation's Restaurant News*, "Hooters Girls are actually wearing more clothing than what most women wear at the gym or the beach. It's part of the concept. I don't think the world would be a better place if we had guys be Hooters Girls." You may agree or disagree, but the fact is that Hooters is currently the country's thirteenth largest dinner house chain and one of the fastest growing, with an increasing number of diners discovering Buffalo Shrimp, a delicious spin-off of Buffalo Chicken Wings.

Vegetable oil for frying
1/4 cup butter
1/4 cup Crystal Louisiana Hot Sauce or
    Frank's Red Hot Cayenne Sauce
Dash ground pepper
Dash garlic powder

1/8 teaspoon paprika
12 uncooked large shrimp
1 egg, beaten
1/2 cup milk
1 cup all-purpose flour

Lemon wedges

1. Heat oil in a deep fryer to 375°F. You want the oil deep enough to cover the shrimp completely.

2. Combine the butter, hot sauce, ground pepper, garlic powder, and paprika in a small saucepan over low heat. Heat until the butter is melted and the ingredients are well blended.

3. Prepare the shrimp by cutting off the entire shell, leaving only the last segment of the shell and the tailfins. Remove the vein from the back and clean the shrimp. Then, with a paring knife, cut a deeper slice where you removed the vein (down to the tail), so that you can fan the meat out. Be careful not to cut too deep. This will butterfly the shrimp.

4. Combine the egg with the milk in a small bowl. Put the flour into another bowl.

5. Dredge each shrimp in the milk mixture, then coat it with the flour. Make sure each shrimp is evenly coated. When you have coated all of the shrimp with flour, let them sit for about 10 minutes in the refrigerator before frying.

6. Fry the shrimp in the hot oil for 7 to 10 minutes or until the tip of each tail begins to turn dark brown. Remove the shrimp from the oil to paper towels briefly, to drain.

7. Quickly put the shrimp into a large bowl, add the hot sauce and stir, coating each shrimp evenly. You could also use a large plastic container with a lid for this. Put all the shrimp inside, add the sauce, put on the lid, then gently turn the container over a few times to coat all of the shrimp. Serve with wedges of lemon on the side.

- SERVES 3 TO 4 AS AN APPETIZER

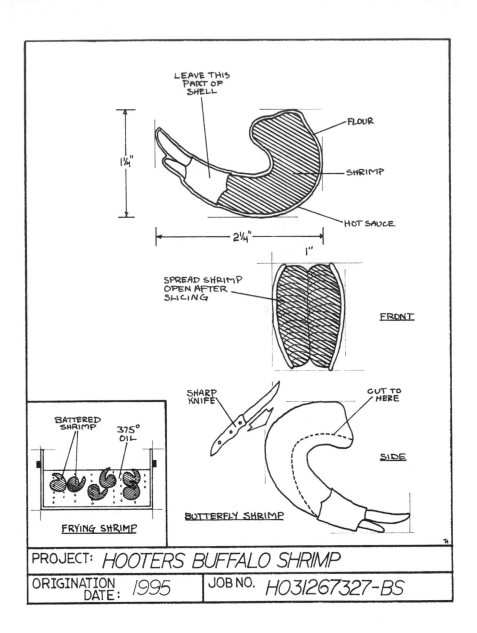

LEAVE THIS PART OF SHELL

FLOUR

SHRIMP

HOT SAUCE

1¼"

2¼"

1"

SPREAD SHRIMP OPEN AFTER SLICING

FRONT

SHARP KNIFE

CUT TO HERE

SIDE

BUTTERFLY SHRIMP

BATTERED SHRIMP

375° OIL

FRYING SHRIMP

PROJECT: *HOOTERS BUFFALO SHRIMP*

ORIGINATION DATE: *1995*

JOB NO. *H031267327-BS*

HOOTERS PASTA SALAD

☆　♥　☎　✎　✈　▣　✂　☞　✿

Menu Description: "Rotini, cukes, tomatoes, scallions and vinaigrette dressing on the side."

On the back of each menu at this popular dinner house chain is the "Hooters Saga"—a tongue-in-cheek tale of the restaurant's origin. The story claims that the chain's founders, referred to as "the Hooters Six," were arrested shortly after opening the first Hooters restaurant "for impersonating restauranteurs (sic). There were no indictments," the story explains. "But the stigma lingers on."

Even though the "saga" claims the building for the first Hooters restaurant was originally going to be used as a "giant walk-in dumpster," each Hooters outlet is designed to look like a Florida beachhouse. And whether it's December or July, day or night, you'll notice the trademark multicolored Christmas lights are always on.

Since Hooters is more than just Buffalo wings and shrimp, I thought I'd include a clone for a newer item on the menu. You'll love the tasty tri-color pasta salad tossed with tomatoes, cucumbers, and green onion, and a delicious vinaigrette. Use this Top Secret version of the pink vinaigrette dressing on a variety of salads or sub sandwiches, or even as a marinade.

VINAIGRETTE DRESSING

⅔ cup vegetable oil
⅓ cup red wine vinegar
1 ½ tablespoons sugar
1 tablespoon Grey Poupon Dijon mustard
2 teaspoons minced shallot
1 teaspoon lemon juice
½ teaspoon dried thyme

¼ teaspoon dried parsley flakes
¼ teaspoon garlic powder
⅛ teaspoon salt
⅛ teaspoon coarsely ground black pepper
⅛ teaspoon dried basil
⅛ teaspoon dried oregano
Dash onion powder

4 quarts water	1 large or 2 medium tomatoes
1 pound rainbow rotini or tri-color radiatore (red, green, and white colors)	1 green onion
	¼ cup minced cucumber
	Salt
1 to 2 teaspoons vegetable oil	Green leaf lettuce (optional, for garnish)

1. Make the dressing: Use an electric mixer to combine all of the dressing ingredients in a bowl. Mix on high speed for about a minute or so until the dressing becomes thick and creamy. Put the dressing in a sealed container and store it in the refrigerator until ready to toss with the chilled pasta.

2. Bring 4 quarts of water to a boil over high heat and add the pasta. Cook for 12 to 14 minutes, until tender, then drain it.

3. Spray the pasta with a gentle stream of cold water to help cool it off. Drizzle the oil over the cooling pasta to keep it from sticking together. Gently toss the pasta, then put it into a covered container and let it cool in the refrigerator for 30 minutes or so.

4. While the pasta is cooling down, prepare the vegetables: remove the seeds and soft pulp from the tomato(es) before dicing; use only the green part of the green onion (or scallions); and be sure to mince the cucumber into very small pieces.

5. When the pasta is no longer warm, add the diced tomato, green onion, and cucumber. Sprinkle salt over the pasta salad to taste and put it back in the refrigerator until well chilled.

6. When the pasta has chilled, spoon it onto plates and place the vinaigrette dressing on the side. For a cool garnish like that served in the restaurant, spread some leaves of green leaf lettuce onto each plate, then spoon the pasta onto the lettuce. You may also toss the salad with the dressing ahead of time rather than serving it on the side. But don't do this too far in advance or the pasta tends to soak up the dressing.

• SERVES 4 AS A LUNCH OR LIGHT DINNER

TIDBITS

Although I didn't detect it in the original vinaigrette dressing for this pasta salad, for best flavor I recommend substituting ½ clove of minced or grated garlic into the blend, for the ¼ teaspoon of garlic powder.

HOULIHAN'S
HOULI FRUIT FIZZ

☆ ♥ ☎ ✎ ✈ ✉ ✂ ☛ ✿

Menu Description: "Houlihan's own blend of Ocean Spray Cranberry Juice Cocktail, orange juice, pineapple juice and Sprite."

Restaurateurs Joseph Gilbert and John Robinson needed a name for the new restaurant they planned to open in the Country Club Plaza of Kansas City, Missouri. To make the job easy, they kept the name of the location's previous tenant—a clothing store called Houlihan's Men's Wear—and opened Houlihan's Old Place in 1972. This was at the time when T.G.I. Friday's was popularizing casual dining, so the concept was an instant hit. That early success led to more Houlihan's opening in other states, and another multi-million dollar chain was born.

The Houli Fruit Fizz is a simple blend of fruit juices and Sprite that can be served with a meal or enjoyed on its own. This drink is one of Houlihan's own classic, signature recipes.

One 12-ounce can cold Sprite   *¼ cup cold orange juice*
½ cup cold pineapple juice   *1 cup cold cranberry juice*

Combine all of the ingredients in a pitcher and pour into two glasses over ice. Be sure all of the ingredients are cold when combined.

• SERVES 2

HOULIHAN'S 'SHROOMS

Menu Description: "Jumbo mushroom caps filled with herb and garlic cheese, lightly battered and fried. Served with zesty horse-radish and mustard dip made with Grey Poupon."

In a March 1986 story which ran in the *Kansas City Times*, a feud erupted between Gilbert/Robinson, the parent company of Houlihan's restaurant at the time, and two guys building their own chain of bars called Mike Houlihan's. The president of the Houlihan's chain, Fred Hipp, said that at first Houlihan's didn't mind so much, asking kindly that the name not be used. But when Mike Heyer and John Houlihan opened a Mike Houlihan's in St. Louis only a few blocks away from an original Houlihan's restaurant, Fred saw no choice but to sue. Soon, residents with the surname Houlihan were writing to Fred urging him to drop the lawsuit. "You'll feel better, thirteen hundred Houlihans will feel better, and two stubborn Irishmen will have $50,000 to buy more Irish whiskey," said one letter.

Here's another Houlihan's classic recipe called 'Shrooms: cheese-filled, batter-fried mushrooms served piping hot. You have the choice of making the herb-flavored cheese filling from the recipe here, or if you're feeling especially lazy, you can buy a similar premade filling (check out the "Tidbits"). Be careful when you first bite into these puppies. Straight out of the fryer, the hot cheese filling can squirt from the center and inflict burning pain on your tongue and lips similar to that of molten lava. Believe me, I know.

HERB CHEESE FILLING

⅛ teaspoon dried summer savory
⅛ teaspoon garlic powder

⅛ teaspoon salt
Dash dried parsley flakes

Dash dried tarragon
Dash ground pepper

1/3 cup whipped cream cheese

6 to 8 large button mushrooms
1 cup unbleached flour
1 1/2 teaspoons salt

1/2 teaspoon cayenne pepper
1/2 cup milk
Vegetable oil for frying

DIPPING SAUCE

1/2 cup mayonnaise
2 teaspoons Grey Poupon Dijon
    mustard

1 teaspoon white vinegar
2 teaspoons prepared horseradish
1/2 teaspoon sugar

1. Combine the savory, garlic powder, 1/8 teaspoon salt, parsley, tar-
    ragon, and pepper in a small bowl and use your fingers or the
    back of a spoon to crush the spices into much smaller pieces. If
    you have a mortar and pestle, use that. Just be sure you don't
    pulverize the spices into dust.
2. Combine the spice mixture with the cream cheese and let it sit
    for 10 to 15 minutes or longer so that the flavors integrate.
3. Clean the mushrooms and remove the stems, leaving only
    the caps.
4. When the cheese has rested, use a teaspoon to fill the mush-
    room caps with the herb cheese.
5. Combine the flour with 1 1/2 teaspoons salt and the cayenne
    pepper in a small bowl.
6. Pour the milk into another small bowl.
7. Dip each mushroom first in the milk then into the flour mixture.
    Do this twice for each mushroom so that each one has been
    double-coated with flour.
8. Put the coated mushrooms into the freezer for at least 3 hours.
    This will keep the coating from falling off, and it will keep the
    cheese inside from expanding too fast and leaking out of the
    mushroom when frying.
9. Meanwhile, make the dipping sauce by combining all of the in-
    gredients in a small bowl. Keep the sauce covered and chilled
    until you are ready to serve it.
10. When the mushrooms are frozen, heat the oil in a deep fryer or
    deep pot to 350°F. Use enough oil to completely cover the

mushrooms (at least a couple inches deep). Fry the mushrooms for 8 to 10 minutes or until the outside turns golden brown. Drain the mushrooms on a rack or paper towels. Let the mushrooms sit for a couple minutes before serving—they will be very hot inside. Serve with dipping sauce on the side.

• SERVES 2 TO 3 AS AN APPETIZER

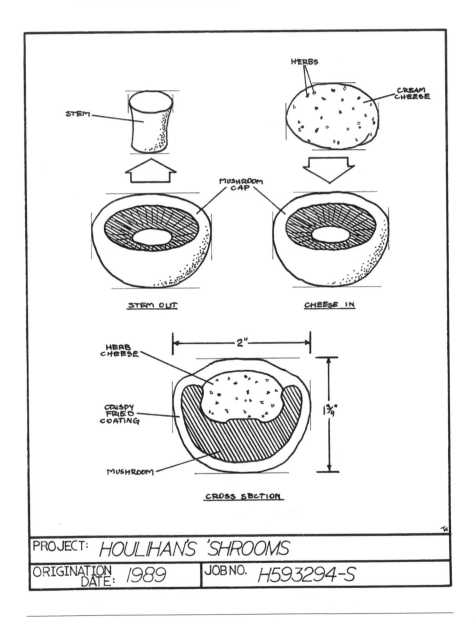

STEM

HERBS

CREAM CHEESE

MUSHROOM CAP

STEM OUT

CHEESE IN

HERB CHEESE

CRISPY FRIED COATING

MUSHROOM

2"

1¾"

CROSS SECTION

PROJECT: *HOULIHAN'S 'SHROOMS*

ORIGINATION DATE: *1989*

JOB NO. *H593294-S*

TIDBITS

If you're feeling lazy, rather than make your own cheese filling you can purchase one of the 4-ounce preblended herb cheeses made by Rondele or Alouette. They're usually found near the cream cheese in the supermarket.

You can also make a lighter version of this recipe by substituting a lower fat cream cheese. The preblended cheeses come in light versions as well.

HOULIHAN'S SMASHED POTATOES

☆　♥　☎　✎　✈　✉　✂　☞　✿

Here's a great way to make mashed potatoes, Houlihan's style. The Smashed Potatoes at the restaurant chain are considered one of Houlihan's specialty signature dishes. This à la carte dish is unique because of the added fresh onion, spices, and sour cream; and especially because of the finishing touch—some onion straws sprinkled on top. It's important when making your own version that you not entirely mash the potatoes, but instead leave a few small potato chunks for texture. Once you make homemade mashed potatoes this way, you'll never want to make them any other way.

4 medium or 2 large russet potatoes, peeled
½ cup milk
½ teaspoon salt
¼ teaspoon coarsely ground black pepper

1 tablespoon fresh minced onion
2 tablespoons sour cream
Dash garlic powder
¼ cup French's French Fried Onions (onion straws)

1. Slice the potatoes into 1-inch cubes and boil in 6 cups of salted water for 15 to 20 minutes or until soft and tender.

2. Drain off the water and use a fork or potato masher to mash the potatoes. Stop mashing when there are still some small chunks of potato left. It's the chunky consistency that makes these potatoes unique.

3. Immediately add the remaining ingredients, excluding the fried onions, to the pan and put it back over low heat. Reheat the potatoes for 5 minutes, stirring to mix in the other ingredients.

4. Serve the potatoes with a sprinkling of about 1 tablespoon of fried onions on top of each serving.

• SERVES 4 AS A SIDE DISH

If you wish, you can make the onion straws yourself following the recipe on page 472.

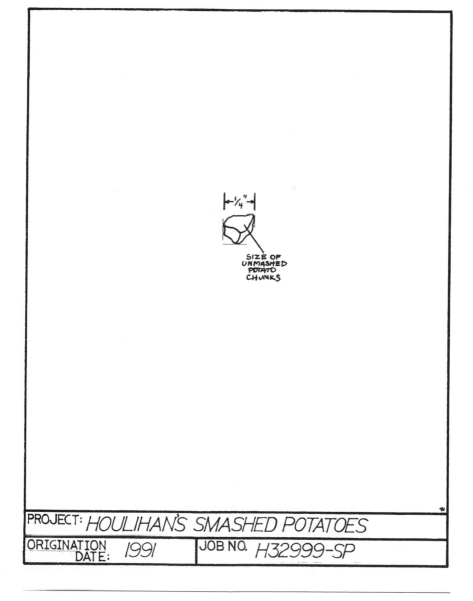

INTERNATIONAL HOUSE OF PANCAKES FRENCH TOAST

☆　♥　☎　✎　✈　✉　✄　☞　✿

Menu Description: "Six triangular slices with powdered sugar."

Now in its 38th year, IHOP has become one of the recognized leaders for breakfast dining, serving up thousands of omelettes, waffles, blintzes, and pancakes each and every day.

Among the popular morning meals is IHOP's classic French toast. You'll notice the addition of a little bit of flour to the batter to make this version of French toast more like the dish you get at the restaurant. The flour helps to create a thicker coating on the bread, almost like a tender crepe on the surface, keeping the bread from becoming too soggy.

2 eggs	⅛ teaspoon salt
½ cup milk	3 teaspoons butter
1 teaspoon vanilla	6 slices thick-sliced French bread
3 tablespoons all-purpose flour	1 tablespoon powdered sugar

ON THE SIDE

Butter	Pancake syrup

1.   Beat the eggs in a large shallow bowl.
2.   Add the milk, vanilla, flour, and salt to the eggs. Beat the mixture with an electric mixer. Be sure all the flour is well combined.
3.   Heat a large skillet over medium heat. When the surface is hot, add about a teaspoon of butter.
4.   Dip the bread, a slice at a time, into the batter, being sure to

coat each side well. Drop the bread into the hot pan (as many as will fit at one time) and cook for 2 to 3 minutes per side or until the surface is golden brown. Repeat with the remaining pieces of bread.

5. Cut each piece of toast in half diagonally. Arrange six halves of the toast on two plates by neatly overlapping the slices. Sprinkle about ½ tablespoon of powdered sugar over the tops of the toast slices on each plate. Serve with butter and syrup on the side.

- SERVES 2 (CAN BE DOUBLED)

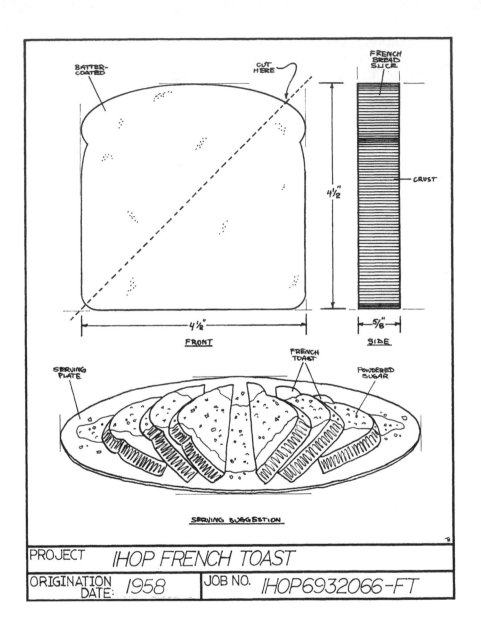

BATTER-COATED

CUT HERE

FRENCH BREAD SLICE

CRUST

4½"

4½"

⅝"

FRONT

SIDE

SERVING PLATE

FRENCH TOAST

POWDERED SUGAR

SERVING SUGGESTION

PROJECT	*IHOP FRENCH TOAST*	
ORIGINATION DATE: *1958*	JOB NO.	*IHOP6932066-FT*

INTERNATIONAL HOUSE OF PANCAKES CHEESE BLINTZ

☆ ♥ ☎ ✎ ✈ ✉ ✂ ☞ ✿

Menu Description: "Crepe-style pancakes filled with a blend of cheeses with strawberry preserves and sour cream."

Detroit's mayoral candidate Sharon McPhail and Detroit schools superintendent David Snead often dined in the city's hottest spot for power breakfasts—the local IHOP. Perhaps it was that first little something in common that eventually led to the two exchanging vows in front of 1,800 guests in a 1995 wedding ceremony. It was dubbed Detroit's "wedding of the year." That particular IHOP, which just happens to be owned by singer Anita Baker's husband, Walter Bridgforth, has seen a 200 percent jump in business.

You'll enjoy this simple recipe for crepes, which, when filled with cheese, become delicious blintzes. The restaurant uses a type of cheese that is similar to soft farmer's cheese, but you can make this with cream cheese, or even with yogurt that has been strained to make it thicker. Any way you decide to go, you're in for a treat.

CREPES

1 ½ cups all-purpose flour
2 cups milk
3 tablespoons butter, melted
2 tablespoons granulated sugar
2 eggs

½ teaspoon vanilla
½ teaspoon baking powder
½ teaspoon salt

Butter (for pan)

FILLING

I cup cottage cheese	¼ cup powdered sugar
I cup soft farmer cheese or softened cream cheese (see Tidbits)	¼ teaspoon vanilla

ON THE SIDE

Sour cream	Powdered sugar
Strawberry preserves	

1. Use an electric mixer to blend together all the crepe ingredients except the butter for the pan in a large bowl. Blend just until smooth. The batter will be very thin.
2. Combine the filling ingredients in a medium bowl and mix by hand. Keep the filling nearby.
3. Preheat a 10-inch frying pan over medium heat. (This size pan tapers to about 8 inches at the bottom.) When the pan is hot, add about ½ teaspoon of butter.
4. When the butter has melted, pour ⅓ cup of batter into the pan. Swirl the batter so that it entirely coats the bottom of the pan. Cook for 1½ to 2 minutes or until golden brown on one side.
5. Use a spatula to lift an edge of the crepe. Grab it with your finger, slip the spatula underneath, and quickly flip it over. Cook for another 1½ minutes or until a bit lighter shade of brown than the first side, then slide it out of the pan. Repeat with the rest of the batter and stack the finished crepes on top of each other to keep them warm.
6. Heat the cheese filling in the microwave for 1 to 2 minutes or until it is hot.
7. When ready to fill the crepes, place each crepe, dark side down, on a plate. Pour 2 to 3 tablespoons of cheese filling across the center of the crepe. Fold the sides in and turn the entire blintz over (to hide the seam) onto a serving plate. You can use a knife to cut the rounded ends off the blintzes if you like. Repeat with the remaining blintzes.
8. Serve 2 to 3 blintzes on a plate with a dollop of sour cream and 2 dollops of strawberry preserves carefully arranged on the

plate next to the blintzes. Sprinkle the blintzes with powdered sugar.

• SERVES 3 TO 4 (10 TO 12 BLINTZES)

TIDBITS

If you would like to make this recipe with a lowfat or nonfat filling, re-place the cream cheese or farmer's cheese with strained yogurt—a yo-gurt solid that is thick like cheese. To make it, pour a cup of lowfat or nonfat yogurt into a coffee filter placed inside a strainer. Put the strainer over a bowl and into the refrigerator for 4 to 5 hours so that all of the liquid whey strains out of the yogurt. What you have left in the strainer is a thick, nutritious yogurt cheese that can be used in place of cream cheese or sour cream in this recipe and many others.

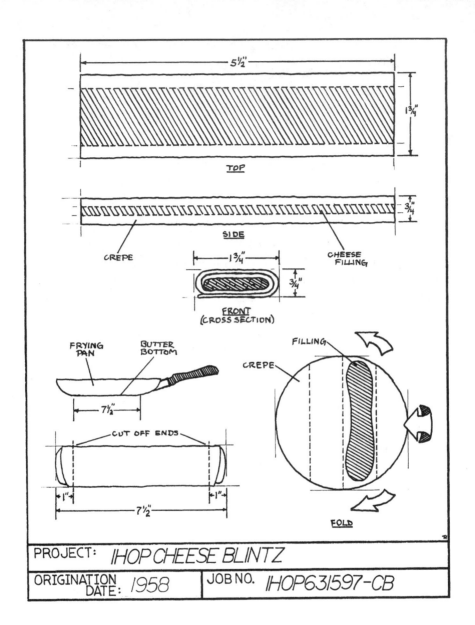

TOP

5½"

1¾"

SIDE

¾"

CREPE

CHEESE
FILLING

1¾"

¾"

FRONT
(CROSS SECTION)

FRYING
PAN

BUTTER
BOTTOM

7½"

FILLING

CREPE

CUT OFF ENDS

1"

1"

7½"

FOLD

PROJECT: IHOP CHEESE BLINTZ

ORIGINATION
DATE: 1958

JOB NO. IHOP631597-CB

INTERNATIONAL HOUSE OF PANCAKES BANANA NUT PANCAKES

☆　♥　☎　✎　✈　✉　✄　☞　✿

Menu Description: "Four banana-flavored pancakes garnished with fresh banana and chopped pecans. Served with banana-flavored syrup."

You'll find sixteen varieties of pancakes on the IHOP menu, including one of the newest flavors: pumpkin pancakes. IHOP claims to sell over 400,000 pancakes each day. That's a lot of pancakes. So many, in fact, that if all of those flapjacks were served up on one plate, it would make a giant stack taller than the Sears Tower in Chicago. And probably much tastier.

　　According to servers, of all the pancake flavors and varieties, the Banana Nut Pancakes are one of the most often requested. I've included a recipe for the banana-flavored syrup here, but you can use any flavor syrup, including maple, on these babies.

BANANA SYRUP

1/2 cup corn syrup
1/2 cup sugar
1/2 cup water

1/4 teaspoon banana extract or
　flavoring

PANCAKES

1 1/4 cups all-purpose flour
1 1/2 cups buttermilk
1 egg
1/4 cup vegetable oil
2 tablespoons sugar
1 teaspoon baking powder

1 teaspoon baking soda
1/2 tablespoon banana extract or
　flavoring
1/4 teaspoon salt
2/3 cup chopped pecans
1 banana

1. Make the banana syrup first by combining all the syrup ingredi-ents—except for the banana extract—in a small saucepan over high heat, stirring occasionally. When the mixture begins to boil, remove it from the heat and stir in the banana extract.
2. In a large bowl, combine all the ingredients for the pancakes ex-cept the pecans and the banana. Use an electric mixer to blend until smooth.
3. Heat a large frying pan or griddle over medium heat, and coat it with butter or nonstick cooking spray when hot.
4. Pour ¼-cup dollops of batter into the pan. Realize the batter will spread out to about 4 inches across, so leave enough room if you are cooking more than one at a time. Granted, some pans may only hold one or two at a time. Sprinkle about ½ table-spoon pecans into the center of each pancake immediately after you pour the batter so that the nuts are "cooked in."
5. Cook the pancakes for 1 to 2 minutes per side or until golden brown.
6. Slice the banana, divide it up, and serve it on top of a stack of 3 to 4 pancakes with the remaining chopped pecans divided and sprinkled on top of each stack.

    • SERVES 3 TO 4

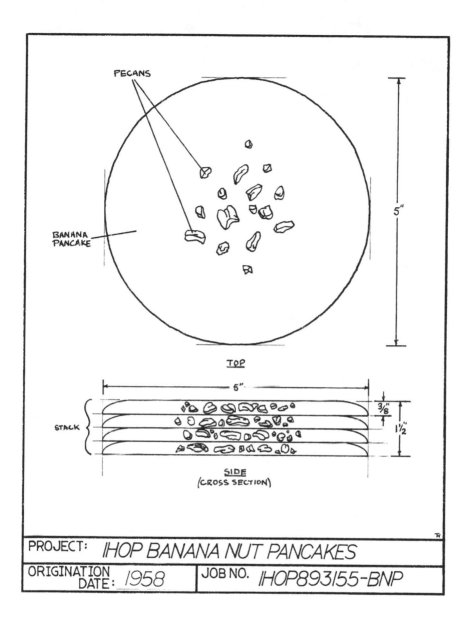

PECANS

BANANA
PANCAKE

5"

TOP

5"

STACK

3/8"

1½"

SIDE
(CROSS SECTION)

PROJECT: *IHOP BANANA NUT PANCAKES*

ORIGINATION DATE: *1958*   JOB NO. *IHOP893155-BNP*

INTERNATIONAL HOUSE OF PANCAKES FAJITA OMELETTE

☆　♥　☎　✎　✈　✉　✂　☛　✿

Menu Description: "Seasoned chicken or beef with onions, diced green peppers, cheese, and chile salsa."

Pancakes are obviously the signature entree, but IHOP serves a variety of breakfast selections—more than 65 items! Along with a cup of coffee from the trademarked "Never Empty Coffee Pot," diners can choose from about a dozen different omelette selections including the Santa Fe Omelette, International Omelette, Chorizo and Cheese Omelette, and the delicious Fajita Omelette.

In my version of the original favorite, you can use either chicken or beef.

1 boneless, skinless chicken breast half
　　or 6-ounce flank steak
½ teaspoon vegetable oil
½ teaspoon lime juice
¼ teaspoon chili powder
⅛ teaspoon salt
⅛ teaspoon cumin
Dash garlic powder
Dash black pepper
½ green bell pepper, diced (about
　　½ cup)

¼ medium Spanish onion, diced
　　(about ½ cup)
1 small tomato, diced (about ½ cup)
2 teaspoons butter
5 large eggs, beaten
1 cup shredded Cheddar cheese
⅓ cup salsa
2 tablespoons sour cream

1.　Pound the chicken breast or flank steak between sheets of plastic wrap until about ¼ inch thick, then cut the meat into bite-size pieces.

2. Pour the oil into a medium skillet over high heat. Add the meat and sauté it for a couple of minutes until it starts to brown.

3. Add the lime juice to the meat. Blend the spices together in a small bowl, then add this mixture to the meat. Mix well until blended in.

4. Add the pepper and onion to the meat and simmer for 5 to 10 minutes over medium heat or until the veggies begin to turn brown. Add the tomato and cook another 2 minutes.

5. Set a large skillet over medium heat. Add 1 teaspoon of butter to the pan.

6. When the butter has melted, add half of the beaten eggs to the pan and swirl to coat the entire bottom of the pan.

7. Cook the eggs for a minute or so or until the top surface is beginning to get firm. Be sure the bottom is not getting too brown before the top cooks. If you notice this happening, turn down the heat.

8. Sprinkle about ¼ cup of cheese down the center of the eggs.

9. Spoon a heaping tablespoon of salsa over the cheese.

10. Spoon one-fourth of the meat and vegetables onto the salsa.

11. Fold the edges over the center of the omelette and let it cook for another minute or so.

12. Carefully flip the omelette over in the pan with the seam side down. Let it cook for another minute or two, then slide it out onto a serving plate. Keep this omelette hot in a slow oven while you prepare the other one.

13. When both omelettes are done, spoon the remaining meat and vegetables over each of the omelettes.

14. Sprinkle a couple tablespoons of cheese over the other topping.

15. Add 2 tablespoons of salsa.

16. Then add a 1-tablespoon dollop of sour cream to the salsa on the middle of the omelette.

- SERVES 2

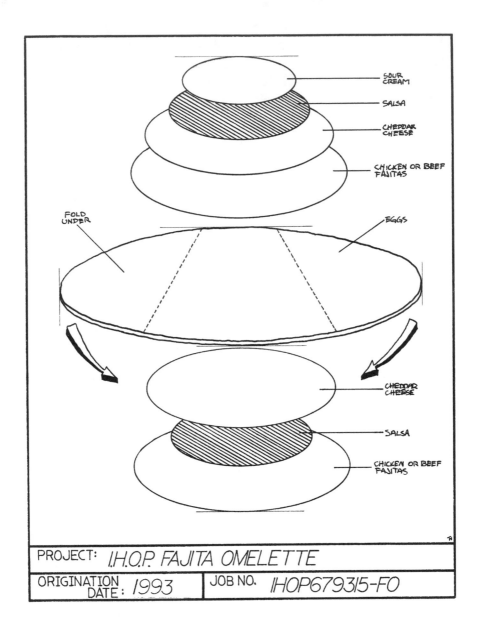

SOUR CREAM

SALSA

CHEDDAR CHEESE

CHICKEN OR BEEF FAJITAS

FOLD UNDER

EGGS

CHEDDAR CHEESE

SALSA

CHICKEN OR BEEF FAJITAS

PROJECT: *I.H.O.P. FAJITA OMELETTE*

ORIGINATION DATE: *1993*

JOB NO. *IHOP679315-FO*

LONE STAR STEAKHOUSE & SALOON AMARILLO CHEESE FRIES

☆ ♥ ☎ ✎ ✈ ⊠ ✄ ☛ ✿

Menu Description: "Lone Star fries smothered in Monterey Jack and Cheddar cheese, topped with bacon and served with ranch dressing."

Growth by this newcomer to the steakhouse segment has been phenomenal. So far, there are over 160 Lone Stars across the country, most of them in the East and Midwest. There are even four in Australia. The company is the fastest growing steakhouse chain in the country, and if you don't have one near you yet, you probably will soon.

Amarillo Cheese Fries are made with thick-sliced unpeeled potatoes. The recipe here is created from scratch, using freshly sliced potatoes. But, if this is one of those days when you just don't feel up to slicing and frying some russets, you can also use a bag of frozen steak fries. Just be aware that those will likely be made from peeled potatoes, unlike the real thing that is served at the restaurant. I've also included a cool recipe for homemade ranch dressing to dip the fries in, if you decide you'd like to make yours from scratch.

3 unpeeled russet potatoes	1 cup shredded Monterey Jack cheese
4 to 6 cups vegetable oil for frying	3 slices bacon, cooked
1 cup shredded Cheddar cheese	1/3 cup ranch dressing

1. Slice the potatoes into wide rectangular slices. They should be about ¼ inch thick and ¾ inch wide. You should end up with around 12 to 15 slices per potato. Keep the potato slices immersed in water until they are ready to fry so that they don't turn brown.

2. Heat the oil in a deep fryer or deep pan to 350°F. Dry the potato slices on paper towels and fry them for 1 minute in the hot oil. This is the blanching stage. Remove the potatoes from the oil and drain until they cool, about 10 minutes.
3. When the potato slices are cool, fry them for 5 more minutes or until they are a light golden brown. Drain.
4. Preheat your oven to 375°F, then arrange the fries on an oven-safe plate.
5. Sprinkle the Cheddar cheese over the fries.
6. Sprinkle the Monterey Jack cheese over the Cheddar.
7. Crumble the cooked bacon and sprinkle it over the cheese.
8. Bake the fries in the oven for 5 minutes or until the cheese has melted. Serve hot with bottled ranch dressing or make your own with the recipe offered here.

- SERVES 4 TO 6 AS AN APPETIZER OR SNACK

TIDBITS

You can also make this recipe using a 32-ounce bag of store-bought frozen steak fries. Just cook them following the directions on the bag, adding the toppings in the last 5 minutes of baking.

If you want to make your own ranch dressing for dipping instead of buying it at the store, here is a good recipe that I came up with:

RANCH DRESSING

¼ cup mayonnaise
1 tablespoon buttermilk
½ teaspoon sugar
¼ teaspoon vinegar
¼ teaspoon garlic powder
¼ teaspoon finely chopped fresh dill

¼ teaspoon finely chopped fresh parsley
⅛ teaspoon onion powder
Dash salt
Dash paprika

Combine all of the ingredients in a small bowl and let them chill for an hour or two.

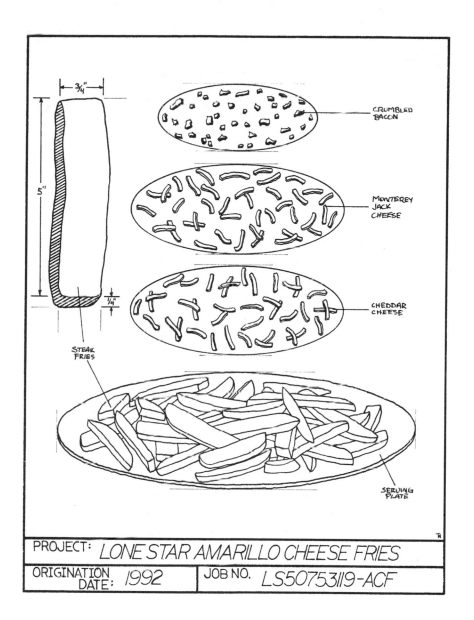

¾"

5"

¼"

CRUMBLED
BACON

MONTEREY
JACK
CHEESE

CHEDDAR
CHEESE

STEAK
FRIES

SERVING
PLATE

PROJECT: *LONE STAR AMARILLO CHEESE FRIES*

ORIGINATION
DATE: *1992*

JOB NO. *LS50753119-ACF*

LONE STAR STEAKHOUSE & SALOON BLACK BEAN SOUP

☆   ♥   ☎   ✎   ✈   ✉   ✂   ☛   ✿

This restaurant boasts a unique "Texas roadhouse" ambiance. When you walk into any Lone Star restaurant, the first thing you'll notice is the crackling of peanut shells beneath your feet. When you're seated you get your own free bucket of peanuts to munch on, and you just flip the shells onto the wood plank floors. Western music plays over the speakers, and every hour or so the wait staff breaks into a funky little honky tonk line dance next to your table while the crunching peanut shells add a unique percussion element.

The spicy black bean soup is a popular item on the Lone Star menu. Here's a way to make a version of your own that can be served as an appetizer or as a meal in itself. It's great with a garnish of freshly diced red onion, jalapeños, and sour cream on top.

Two 15-ounce cans black beans
¼ cup diced red onion
2 teaspoons chopped pickled jalapeño
    slices ("nacho slices")
1 teaspoon sugar

1 teaspoon cider or wine vinegar
2 cloves garlic, minced
¼ teaspoon salt
¼ teaspoon cayenne pepper
½ teaspoon chili powder

GARNISH

4 teaspoons chopped red onion
6 to 8 jalapeño slices

1 tablespoon sour cream

1. Pour the canned beans along with the liquid into a medium saucepan. Add the remaining soup ingredients and mix.
2. Bring the soup to a boil, then reduce the heat to low and sim-

mer, covered, for about 1 hour, adding water if necessary or until it's as thick as you like.

3.   Serve each bowl of soup with a garnish of red onion, jala-
      peño slices, and sour cream arranged carefully in the center of
      the soup.

   • SERVES 4 AS AN APPETIZER, 2 AS AN ENTREE

TIDBITS

This soup is also very good with a bit of chopped fresh cilantro added
to it while simmering and/or as a garnish. You may want to try some
shredded Cheddar or Monterey Jack cheese on top as well.

LONE STAR STEAKHOUSE & SALOON TEXAS RICE

☆　♥　☎　✎　✈　✉　✂　☛　✿

The best selling menu items at the Lone Star Steakhouse & Saloon are the mesquite grilled steaks. The USDA choice-graded steaks are hand-cut fresh daily and displayed in a glass meat counter that is visible from the dining area of each restaurant. Customers are encouraged to view the meat for themselves and personally select the steak they wish to eat.

Even though much of the beef, chicken, and fish served at the restaurant is mesquite grilled, you may not have the equipment to cook your meat that way. Never fear, you can still have this popular and tasty side dish alongside another entree or steak cooked up any way you like. Rice this good goes with just about anything.

2 cups beef stock or canned beef
　　broth
1 cup uncooked long grain parboiled or
　　converted (not instant or quick)
　　white rice
1 tablespoon vegetable oil

⅓ cup diced white onion
3 to 4 mushrooms, sliced
½ cup frozen peas
¼ teaspoon chili powder
¼ teaspoon salt

1.　Bring the beef stock to a boil over high heat in a medium saucepan.
2.　Add the rice to the stock, cover the pan, reduce heat to low, and simmer for 20 minutes.
3.　When the rice has cooked for about 10 minutes, heat the oil in a skillet over medium heat.
4.　When the oil is hot, add the onion and mushrooms to the pan and sauté for 5 minutes.

5. When the rice is done, pour it into the skillet with the mushrooms and onion. Turn the heat to medium/low and add the frozen peas, chili powder, and salt to the rice. Heat the mixture, stirring often, for 3 to 4 minutes or until the peas are tender.

    • SERVES 2 AS A SIDE DISH

TIDBITS

It's important that you use converted or parboiled rice for this recipe, and others that call for white rice. Sure, this type of rice may take longer to cook than instant rice, but all its nutrients and taste haven't been stripped out—which is exactly what happens in the process that creates the popular quick-cooking, 5-minute stuff. You don't need that junk. Converted rice is one of the best rices to use in cooking because it doesn't get too mushy or sticky, and the grains don't easily split open.

LONE STAR STEAKHOUSE & SALOON SWEET BOURBON SALMON

☆　♥　☎　✎　✈　✉　✂　☞　❀

Menu Description: "Fresh salmon filet, marinated and mesquite grilled."

It is said that Americans eat an estimated 63 pounds of beef per capita, and we get a lot of it in chain restaurants. But for those of you who want something other than beef, Lone Star has additional selections including the Sweet Bourbon Salmon.

　　Don't worry if you can't mesquite grill your salmon, it's the sweet bourbon marinade that makes this dish so tasty. Not only is this marinade good on salmon, but on other fish and chicken as well. If you do happen to use a charcoal grill and have some mesquite smoking chips on hand, soak a handful of chips in water for a couple hours and then arrange them on the red-hot coals. This will give your salmon a taste even closer to the original.

SWEET BOURBON MARINADE

¼ cup pineapple juice
2 tablespoons soy sauce
2 tablespoons brown sugar
1 teaspoon Kentucky bourbon

¼ teaspoon cracked black pepper
⅛ teaspoon garlic powder
½ cup vegetable oil

Two 8-ounce salmon fillets

2 teaspoons snipped fresh chives

1. Combine the pineapple juice, soy sauce, brown sugar, bourbon, pepper and garlic powder in a medium bowl. Stir to dissolve the sugar. Add the oil.
2. Be sure all of the skin is removed from the salmon. Place the fillets in a shallow dish and pour the bourbon marinade over them, saving a little to brush on the fish as it cooks. Put a lid over the fish and refrigerate for at least an hour. A few hours is even better.
3. Preheat your barbecue or stovetop grill over medium/high heat.
4. Cook the fish for 5 to 7 minutes per side or until each fillet is cooked all the way through. Regularly brush the fillets with the marinade.
5. Arrange the fillets on each plate with the chives sprinkled over the top.

• SERVES 2 AS AN ENTREE

MARIE CALLENDER'S FAMOUS GOLDEN CORNBREAD

☆　♥　☎　✎　✈　✉　✂　☞　❀

The American restaurant business has been shaped by many young entrepreneurs, so determined to realize their dreams of owning a hot dog cart or starting a restaurant that they sell everything they own to raise cash. Food lore is littered with these stories, and this one is no exception. This time the family car was sold to pay for one month's rent on a converted World War II army tent, an oven, refrigerator, rolling pin, and some hand tools. It was 1948, and that's all that Marie Callender and her family needed to make enough pies to start delivering to restaurants in Long Beach, California.

It was pies that started the company, but soon the bakeries became restaurants and they started serving meals. One of my favorites is the Famous Golden Cornbread and whipped honey butter that comes with many of the entrees. What makes this cornbread so scrumptious is its cake-like quality. The recipe here requires more flour than traditional cornbread recipes, making the finished product soft and spongy just like Marie's.

1 1/4 cups all-purpose flour
3/4 cup cornmeal
2 teaspoons baking powder
1/3 cup sugar

3/4 teaspoon salt
1 1/4 cups whole milk
1/4 cup shortening
1 egg

HONEY BUTTER

1/2 cup (1 stick) butter, softened

1/3 cup honey

1. Preheat the oven to 400°F.
2. Combine the flour, cornmeal, baking powder, sugar, and salt in a medium bowl.
3. Add the milk, shortening, and egg and mix only until all the ingredients are well combined.
4. Pour the batter into a greased 8 X 8-inch pan.
5. Bake for 25 to 30 minutes or until the top is golden brown. Let the cornbread cool slightly before slicing it with a sharp knife into 9 pieces.
6. For the honey butter, use a mixer on high speed to whip the butter and honey together until smooth and fluffy.

    • MAKES 9 PIECES

MARIE CALLENDER'S CHICKEN POT PIE

☆ ♥ ☎ ✎ ✈ ✉ ✂ ☞ ✿

Menu Description: "Tender chunks of chicken with seasonings and vegetables."

All the Marie Callender's restaurants try to maintain a homestyle ambiance, kind of like being at Grandma's house for dinner. The wall-coverings reflect styles of the thirties and forties and are complemented by dark mahogany-stained, wood-paneled walls and brass fixtures. You'll also find old-fashioned furnishings, many of them throwbacks to the forties, the time of this restaurant chain's founding fifty years ago.

The menu, which features meatloaf, pot roast, and country fried steak, reflects a satisfying homestyle cuisine that today is all too rare. If you wondered whether a company that is known for its great dessert pies could make a great pot pie ... it can.

For this recipe, try to use small 16-ounce casserole dishes that measure 4 or 5 inches across at the top. Any casserole dishes that come close to this size will probably work; the yield will vary depending on what size dishes you decide to use.

CRUST

1 ½ cups all-purpose flour	3 tablespoons ice water
¾ teaspoon salt	⅔ cup cold butter
2 egg yolks	

FILLING

1 cup sliced carrots (3 carrots)	4 boneless, skinless chicken breast
1 cup sliced celery (1 stalk)	halves
2 cups frozen peas	4 tablespoons butter
1 cup chopped white onion	5 tablespoons all-purpose flour

2½ cups chicken broth   Dash pepper
⅔ cup milk   1 egg, beaten
½ teaspoon salt

1. Prepare the crust by sifting together the flour and salt in a medium bowl. Make a depression in the center of the flour with your hand.
2. Put the yolks and ice water into the depression. Slice the butter into tablespoon-size portions and add it into the flour depression as well.
3. Using a fork, cut the wet ingredients into the dry ingredients. When all of the flour is moistened, use your hands to finish combining the ingredients. This will ensure that the chunks of butter are well blended into the dough. Roll the dough into a ball, cover it with plastic wrap and put it into the refrigerator for 1 to 2 hours. This will make the dough easier to work with.
4. When the dough has chilled, preheat the oven to 425°F and start on the filling by steaming the vegetables. Steam the carrots and celery for 5 minutes in a steamer or a saucepan with a small amount of water in the bottom. Add the frozen peas and onions and continue to steam for an additional 10 to 12 minutes or until the carrots are tender.
5. Prepare the chicken by poaching the breasts in lightly salted boiling water for 8 to 10 minutes.
6. In a separate large saucepan, melt the butter over medium heat, remove from the heat, then add the flour and whisk together until smooth. Add the chicken broth and milk and continue stirring over high heat until the mixture comes to a boil. Cook for an additional minute or so until thick, then reduce the heat to low.
7. Cut the poached chicken into large bite-size chunks and add them to the sauce. Add the salt and a dash of pepper.
8. Add the steamed vegetables to the sauce and simmer the mixture over medium/low heat for 4 to 5 minutes.
9. As the filling simmers, roll out the dough on a floured surface. Use one of the casserole dishes you plan to bake the pies in as a guide for cutting the dough. The filling will fit four 16-ounce casserole dishes perfectly, but you can use just about any size

single-serving casserole dishes or oven-safe bowls for this recipe. Invert one of the dishes onto the dough and use a knife to cut around the rim. Make the cut about a half-inch larger all of the way around to give the dough a small "lip," which you will fold over when you cover the pie. Make four of these.

10. Spoon the chicken and vegetable filling into each casserole dish and carefully cover each dish with the cut dough. Fold the edge of the dough over the edge of each dish and press firmly so that the dough sticks to the outer rim. Brush some beaten egg on the dough on each pie.

11. Bake the pies on a cookie sheet for 30 to 45 minutes or until the top crust is light brown.

- SERVES 4

MARIE CALLENDER'S
BANANA CREAM PIE

☆ ♥ ☎ ✎ ✈ ✉ ✂ ☞ ✿

Menu Description: "Fresh ripe bananas in our rich vanilla cream, topped with fresh whipped cream or fluffy meringue."

Bakers get to work by 5 A.M. at Marie Callender's to begin baking over 30 varieties of pies. Huge pies. Pies that weigh nearly three pounds apiece. The fresh, creamy, flaky, delicious pies that have made Marie Callender's famous in the food biz. On those mornings about 250 pies will be made at each of the 147 restaurants. Modest, I suppose, when compared with Thanksgiving Day when the stores can make up to 3,500 pies each.

For now though, we'll start with just one—banana cream pie with flaky crust, whipped cream, and slivered almonds on top. This recipe requires that you bake the crust unfilled, so you will have to use a pie weight or other oven-safe object to keep the crust from puffing up. Large pie weights are sold in many stores, or you can use small metal or ceramic weights (sold in packages) or dried beans on the crust which has first been lined with aluminum foil or parchment paper.

1/4 cup butter
1/4 cup shortening
1 1/4 cups all-purpose flour
1 tablespoon sugar

1/4 teaspoon salt
1 egg yolk
2 tablespoons ice water
1/2 teaspoon vinegar

FILLING

2/3 cup sugar
1/4 cup cornstarch
1/2 teaspoon salt
2 3/4 cups whole milk

4 egg yolks, beaten
1 tablespoon butter
2 teaspoons vanilla
2 ripe bananas, sliced

I can whipped cream	¼ cup slivered almonds

1. Beat together the butter and shortening until smooth and creamy and chill until firm.
2. Sift together the flour, sugar, and salt in a medium bowl.
3. Using a fork, cut the butter and shortening into the dry ingredients, until the mixture has a consistent texture. Mix egg yolk, ice water, and vinegar into the dough, then form it into a ball and refrigerate it for I hour so that it will be easier to work with.
4. Preheat the oven to 450°F. When the dough has chilled, roll it out and press it into a 9-inch pie plate.
5. Press parchment paper or aluminum foil into the crust and weight the crust down with a ceramic pie weight or another pie pan filled with dried beans. This will prevent the crust from puffing up and distorting. Bake for 15 minutes, then remove the weight or pan filled with beans and prick the crust with a fork to allow steam to escape. Bake for another 5 to 10 minutes, or until the crust is golden brown. Let the crust cool.
6. Make the filling by sifting together the sugar, cornstarch, and salt into a medium saucepan.
7. Blend the milk, eggs, and butter in a medium bowl, then add the mixture to the dry ingredients and cook over medium heat stirring constantly for 6 to 8 minutes or until the mixture boils and thickens, then cook for I minute more.
8. Remove the filling from the heat, and mix in the vanilla.
9. Put plastic wrap on the surface of the filling and let it cool to about room temperature. The plastic wrap will prevent the top of the filling from becoming gummy.
10. When the filling has cooled, remove the plastic wrap and add the sliced bananas. Stir.
11. Pour the filling into the pie shell and chill for a couple of hours before serving. Slice across the pie 3 times to make 6 large slices. Serve each slice topped with fresh whipped cream and slivered almonds.

- SERVES 6

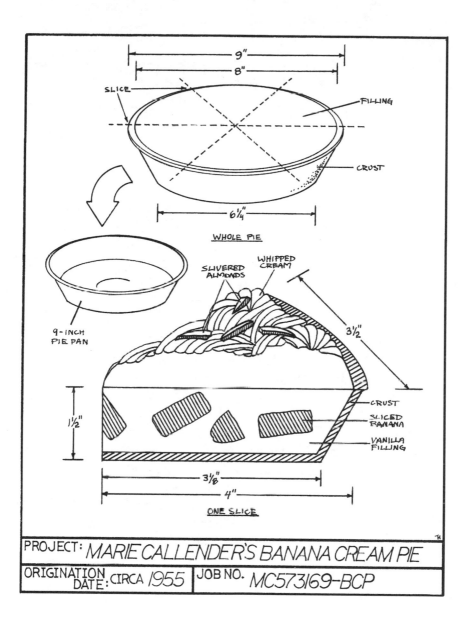

9"

8"

SLICE

FILLING

CRUST

6¼"

WHOLE PIE

9-INCH
PIE PAN

SLIVERED
ALMONDS

WHIPPED
CREAM

3½"

CRUST

SLICED
BANANA

VANILLA
FILLING

1½"

3⅛"

4"

ONE SLICE

PROJECT: *MARIE CALLENDER'S BANANA CREAM PIE*

ORIGINATION DATE: CIRCA *1955*   JOB NO. *MC573169-BCP*

OLIVE GARDEN ITALIAN SALAD DRESSING

☆   ♥   ☎   ✏   ✈   ✉   ✄   ☛   ✿

In the 1970s, food conglomerate General Mills set out to expand its growing restaurant business. A research team was organized to study the market, and to conduct interviews with potential customers on what they would want in a restaurant. Seven years later, in 1982, the first Olive Garden restaurant opened its doors in Orlando, Florida. Today it is the number one Italian restaurant chain in the country with over 470 stores.

One of the favorites at the Olive Garden is an item that isn't even mentioned in the menu: the Italian salad dressing served on the house salad that comes with every meal. The dressing became so popular that the chain now sells it by the bottle "to go" in each restaurant. Now you can make a version of the dressing for yourself that tastes just like the original, but will cost much less. The secret to thickening this dressing is to use dry pectin, a natural ingredient often used to thicken jams and jellies. Pectin can be found in most stores in the aisle with baking and cooking supplies or near the canning items.

½ cup white vinegar
⅓ cup water
⅓ cup vegetable oil
¼ cup corn syrup
2½ tablespoons grated Romano cheese
2 tablespoons dry pectin
2 tablespoons beaten egg or egg
    substitute

1¼ teaspoons salt
1 teaspoon lemon juice
½ teaspoon minced garlic
¼ teaspoon dried parsley flakes
Pinch of dried oregano
Pinch of crushed red pepper flakes

Combine all of the ingredients with a mixer on medium speed or in a blender on low speed for 30 seconds. Chill at least 1 hour. Serve over mixed greens or use as a marinade.

• MAKES 1½ CUPS

OLIVE GARDEN HOT ARTICHOKE-SPINACH DIP

☆　♥　☎　✎　✈　✉　✂　☞　❁

Menu Description: "A creamy hot dip of artichokes, spinach and parmesan with pasta chips."

It's interesting to note that just about every aspect of the Olive Garden restaurants was developed from consumer research conducted in a corporate think tank by the General Mills corporation. Restaurant-goers were questioned about preferences such as the type of food to be served, the appearance and atmosphere of the restaurant, even the color of the candle holders on each table. The large tables and the comfy chairs on rollers that you see today at the Olive Garden restaurants came out of these vigorous research sessions.

　　I'm not sure if this dish came from those sessions, but according to servers at the Olive Garden, the Hot Artichoke-Spinach Dip is one of the most requested appetizers on the menu. The restaurant serves the dip with chips made from fried pasta, but you can serve this version of the popular appetizer with just about any type of crackers, chips, or toasted Italian bread, like bruschetta.

½ cup frozen chopped spinach,
　　thawed
1 cup chopped artichoke hearts
　　(canned or frozen and thawed)
8 ounces cream cheese

½ cup grated Parmesan cheese
½ teaspoon crushed red pepper flakes
¼ teaspoon salt
⅛ teaspoon garlic powder
Dash ground pepper

ON THE SIDE

Crackers
Chips

Sliced, toasted bread

1. Boil the spinach and artichoke hearts in a cup of water in a small saucepan over medium heat until tender, about 10 minutes. Drain in a colander when done.
2. Heat the cream cheese in a small bowl in the microwave set on high for 1 minute. Or, use a saucepan to heat the cheese over medium heat just until hot.
3. Add the spinach and artichoke hearts to the cream cheese and stir well.
4. Add the remaining ingredients to the cream cheese and combine. Serve hot with crackers, chips, or toasted bread for dipping.

- SERVES 4 AS AN APPETIZER

TIDBITS

It's easy to make a lighter version of this dip by using a reduced fat cream cheese in the same measurement.

OLIVE GARDEN TOSCANA SOUP

☆　♥　☎　✎　✈　✉　✂　☞　✿

Menu Description: "Spicy sausage, russet potatoes, and cavolo greens in a light creamy broth."

For two years after the first Olive Garden restaurant opened in 1982, operators were still tweaking the restaurant's physical appearance and the food that was served. Even the tomato sauce was changed as many as 25 times.

This soup blends the flavors of potatoes, kale, and Italian sausage in a slightly spicy chicken and cream broth. When I first tried the soup at the restaurant I was surprised at how good it was. I'd never had any soup with the leafy, healthy, spinach-like kale in it (found in most produce sections), and the combination of flavors was addicting. When you try this version for yourself I think you'll agree.

2¾ cups chicken stock or broth
¼ cup heavy cream
1 medium russet potato
2 cups chopped kale

½ pound spicy Italian sausage
¼ teaspoon salt
¼ teaspoon crushed red pepper flakes

1. Grill or sauté the sausage. When cooked and cooled, cut the sausage at an angle into slices about ½ inch thick. Add the sausage to the soup.
2. Combine the stock and cream in a saucepan over medium heat.
3. Slice the unpeeled potato into ¼-inch slices, then quarter the slices and add them to the soup.
4. Add the kale.
5. Add the spices and let the soup simmer for about 1 hour. Stir occasionally.

• SERVES 4 AS AN APPETIZER, 2 AS AN ENTREE

OLIVE GARDEN ALFREDO PASTA

☆　♥　☎　✎　✈　✉　✂　☞　✿

Menu Description: "Our classically rich blend of cream, butter and parmesan cheese with a hint of garlic."

The Alfredo Pasta served at the Olive Garden is a tasty, classic recipe. Although rich and creamy, the simplicity of this recipe made it hard for me to resist. This is one of those fail-safe recipes that can be made quickly and easily with just a few ingredients.

Serve this dish with a Toscana soup appetizer and some garlic bread and you've got a tasty meal just like one you might get at the restaurant chain—except this version will cost less, you can enjoy it in the comfort of home, and you won't have to tip.

½ cup (1 stick) butter
2 cups heavy cream
⅛ teaspoon garlic powder
⅛ teaspoon ground black pepper

One 12-ounce box fettuccine pasta (or your choice of pasta)
¼ cup grated Parmesan cheese

1.　Melt the butter in a medium saucepan over medium heat.
2.　Add the cream, garlic powder, and pepper and simmer for 10 to 12 minutes or until thick.
3.　At the same time, bring 4 to 6 quarts of water to a boil and add the pasta.
4.　When the Alfredo sauce has reached your desired consistency, stir in the Parmesan cheese.
5.　When the pasta is cooked, drain it. Serve the pasta on plates with Alfredo sauce poured over the top.

• SERVES 2 TO 3 AS AN ENTREE

OUTBACK
STEAKHOUSE
BLOOMIN' ONION

☆ ♥ ☎ ✎ ✈ ✉ ✂ ☛ ✿

Menu Description: "An Outback Ab-original from Russell's Marina Bay."

If you go to an Outback Steakhouse expecting exotic Aussie prairie food that someone like Crocodile Dundee would have enjoyed, you're gonna be a bit disappointed, mate. Except for a little Australia-themed paraphernalia on the walls, like boomerangs and pictures of kangaroos, the restaurant chain is about as "down under" as McDonald's is Irish. The three founders, Tim Gannon, Chris Sullivan, and Bob Basham, are all U.S. boys. And the menu, which is about 60 percent beef, contains mainly American fare with cute Australian names like The Melbourne, Jackeroo Chops, and Chicken on the Barbie.

The founders say they chose the Aussie theme because "Most Australians are fun-loving and gregarious people and very casual people. We thought that's exactly the kind of friendliness and atmosphere we want to have in our restaurants."

In only six years, Outback Steakhouse has become our number one steakhouse chain—in part because of the Bloomin' Onion: a large, deep-fried onion sliced to look like a flower in bloom that was created by one of the restaurant's founders. What makes this appetizer so appealing besides its flowery appearance is the onion's crispy spiced coating, along with the delicious dipping sauce, cleverly presented in the center of the onion.

Although the restaurant uses a special device to make the slicing process easier, you can make the incisions with a sharp knife. It just takes a steady hand and a bit of care.

½ cup mayonnaise

2 teaspoons ketchup

2 tablespoons cream-style horseradish

¼ teaspoon paprika

¼ teaspoon salt

⅛ teaspoon dried oregano

Dash ground black pepper

Dash cayenne pepper

THE ONION

I egg

I cup milk

I cup all-purpose flour

I ½ teaspoons salt

I ½ teaspoons cayenne pepper

½ teaspoon ground black pepper

I teaspoon paprika

¼ teaspoon dried oregano

⅛ teaspoon dried thyme

⅛ teaspoon cumin

I jumbo sweet yellow or white onion
    (¾ pound or more)

Vegetable oil for frying

1. Prepare the dipping sauce by combining all of the ingredients in a small bowl. Keep the sauce covered in your refrigerator until needed.

2. Beat the egg and combine it with the milk in a medium bowl big enough to hold the onion.

3. In a separate bowl, combine the flour, salt, peppers, paprika, oregano, thyme, and cumin.

4. Now it's time to slice the onion—this is the trickiest step. First slice ¾ inch to I inch off the top and bottom of the onion. Remove the papery skin. Use a thin knife to cut a 1-inch diameter core out of the middle of the onion. Now use a very sharp, large knife to slice the onion several times down the center to create the "petals" of the completed onion. First slice through the center of the onion to about three-fourths of the way down. Turn the onion 90° and slice it again in an "x" across the first slice. Keep slicing the sections in half, very carefully, until you've cut the onion 16 times. Do not cut down to the bottom. The last 8 slices are a little hairy, just use a steady hand and don't worry if your onion doesn't look like a perfect flower. It'll still taste good.

5. Spread the "petals" of the onion apart. The onion sections tend to stick together, so you'll want to separate them to make coat-

ing easier. To help separate the "petals," plunge the onion into boiling water for 1 minute, and then into cold water.

6. Dip the onion in the milk mixture, and then coat it liberally with the dry ingredients. Again separate the "petals" and sprinkle the dry coating between them. Once you're sure the onion is well-coated, dip it back into the wet mixture and into the dry coating again. This double dipping makes sure you have a well-coated onion because some of the coating tends to wash off when you fry. Let the onion rest in the refrigerator for at least 15 minutes while you get the oil ready.

7. Heat oil in a deep fryer or deep pot to 350°F. Make sure you use enough oil to completely cover the onion when it fries.

8. Fry the onion right side up in the oil for 10 minutes or until it turns brown.

9. When the onion has browned, remove it from the oil and let it drain on a rack or paper towels.

10. Open the onion wider from the center so that you can put a small dish of the dipping sauce in the center. You may also use plain ketchup.

• SERVES 2 TO 4 AS AN APPETIZER OR SNACK

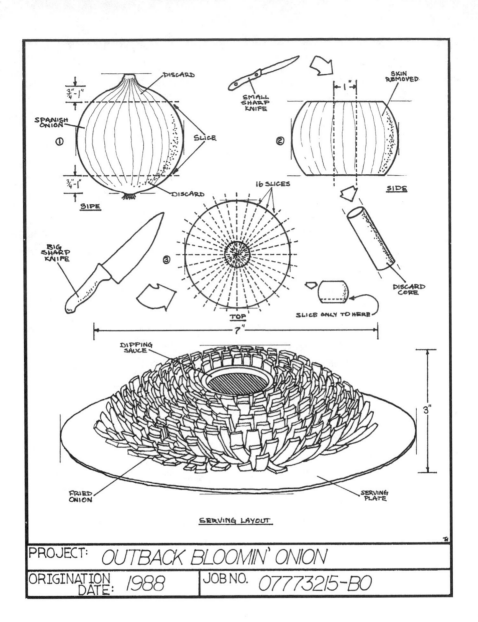

SPANISH ONION ①
DISCARD
SLICE
DISCARD
$\frac{3}{4}" - 1"$
$\frac{3}{4}" - 1"$
SIDE

SMALL SHARP KNIFE
SKIN REMOVED
1"
SIDE ②

BIG SHARP KNIFE
16 SLICES
③ TOP
7"

DISCARD CORE
SLICE ONLY TO HERE

DIPPING SAUCE
FRIED ONION
SERVING PLATE
3"

SERVING LAYOUT

PROJECT:	*OUTBACK BLOOMIN' ONION*	
ORIGINATION DATE: *1988*	JOB NO.	*07773215-BO*

OUTBACK STEAKHOUSE GOLD COAST COCONUT SHRIMP

☆　♥　☎　✎　✈　✉　✂　☞　✿

Menu Description: "Six colossal shrimp dipped in beer batter, rolled in coconut, deep-fried to a golden brown and served with marmalade sauce."

The three founders of Outback Steakhouse are an experienced lot of restaurateurs. Tim Gannon, Chris Sullivan, and Bob Basham had each worked for the Steak & Ale chain of restaurants at one time or another, as well as other large casual dining chains. When the three got together and decided they wanted to open a few restaurants in the Tampa, Florida, area, they had modest ambitions.

Basham told *Food & Beverage* magazine, "We figured if we divided up the profits with what we thought we could make out of five or six restaurants, we could have a very nice lifestyle and play a lot of golf." The first six restaurants opened within 13 months. Eight years later the chain had grown to over 300 restaurants, and the three men now have a very, very nice lifestyle indeed.

Coconut Shrimp is a sweet and crispy fried appetizer not found on most other menus, especially with the delicious marmalade sauce. Outback servers claim it's a top seller.

At the restaurant chain, you get six of these shrimp to serve two as an appetizer, but since we're taking the time to make the batter and use all of that oil, I thought I'd up the yield to a dozen shrimp to serve four as an appetizer. If you don't want to make that many, you can use the same recipe with fewer shrimp and save the leftover batter to make more later or just toss it out.

1 cup flat beer
1 cup self-rising flour
2 cups sweetened coconut flakes
    (1 7-ounce package)
2 tablespoons sugar

½ teaspoon salt
12 jumbo shrimp
Vegetable oil for frying
Paprika

MARMALADE SAUCE (FOR DIPPING)

½ cup orange marmalade
2 teaspoons stone-ground mustard
    (with whole-grain mustard seed)

1 teaspoon prepared horseradish
Dash salt

1.   For the batter, use an electric mixer to combine the beer, flour, ½ cup coconut flakes, sugar, and salt in a medium-size bowl. Mix well, then cover and refrigerate at least 1 hour.

2.   Prepare your marmalade sauce by combining all four ingredients in a small bowl. Cover and refrigerate this for at least 1 hour as well.

3.   Prepare the shrimp by deveining and peeling off the shell back to the tail. Leave the last segment of the shell plus the tailfins as a handle.

4.   When the batter is ready, preheat oil in a deep pot or deep fryer to about 350°F. Use enough oil to completely cover the shrimp. Pour the remainder of the coconut into a shallow bowl.

5.   Be sure the shrimp are dry before battering. Sprinkle each shrimp lightly with paprika before the next step.

6.   Dip one shrimp at a time into the batter, coating generously. Drop the battered shrimp into the coconut and roll it around so that it is well coated.

7.   Fry four shrimp at a time for 2 to 3 minutes or until the shrimp become golden brown. You may have to flip the shrimp over halfway through cooking time. Drain on paper towels briefly before serving with marmalade sauce on the side.

- SERVES 4 AS AN APPETIZER

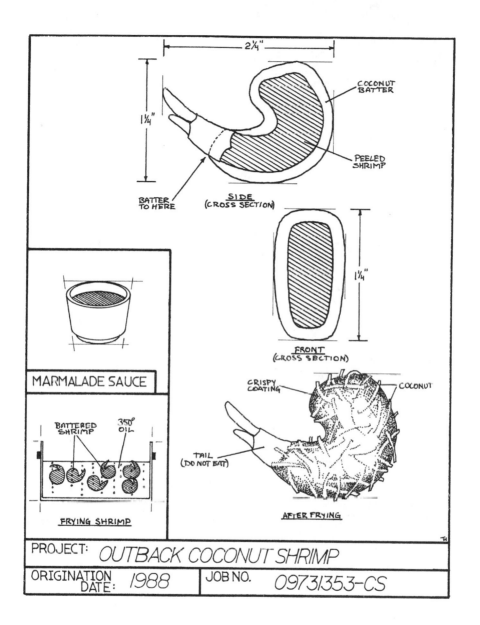

2¼"

1¼"

COCONUT
BATTER

PEELED
SHRIMP

BATTER
TO HERE

SIDE
(CROSS SECTION)

1¼"

FRONT
(CROSS SECTION)

MARMALADE SAUCE

BATTERED
SHRIMP

350°
OIL

FRYING SHRIMP

CRISPY
COATING

COCONUT

TAIL
(DO NOT EAT)

AFTER FRYING

PROJECT: OUTBACK COCONUT SHRIMP

ORIGINATION
DATE: 1988

JOB NO. 0973135.3-CS

OUTBACK STEAKHOUSE WALKABOUT SOUP

☆ ♥ ☎ ✎ ✈ ✉ ✄ ☞ ✿

Menu Description: "A unique presentation of an Australian favorite. Reckon!"

Here's a great way to start off dinner. The menu claims the Walkabout Soup is an Australian favorite. While that may or may not be true, this creamy onion soup with two types of cheese on top is at least a favorite of mine. If you can boil water and slice onions, you'll have no problem with this easy-to-make version of the chain's top secret formula.

8 cups water
8 beef bouillon cubes
3 medium white onions
1 teaspoon salt
1 teaspoon black pepper

¾ cup all-purpose flour
1 cup heavy cream
1¼ cups shredded Cheddar cheese
¼ cup shredded Monterey Jack cheese

1. Heat the water to boiling in a large pan. Add the bouillon cubes and dissolve.
2. Cut the onions into thin slices, then quarter the slices. Add to the broth.
3. Add salt and pepper.
4. Bring the mixture back to boiling, then turn the heat down and simmer, uncovered, for 1 hour.
5. While stirring, sift the flour into the soup. Continue to stir if any large lumps of flour develop. Be careful when you stir; aggressive agitation or using a whisk may tear the onions apart. As the soup continues to cook, any lumps should dissolve.

6. After 30 minutes of additional simmering, add the cream and 1 cup Cheddar cheese. Continue to simmer the soup for another 5 to 10 minutes.

7. Serve the soup hot after sprinkling a tablespoon each of shredded Monterey Jack and Cheddar on top.

- SERVES 4 AS AN APPETIZER

OUTBACK STEAKHOUSE ALICE SPRINGS CHICKEN

☆   ♥   ☎   ✎   ✈   ✉   ✂   ☛   ✿

Menu Description: "Grilled chicken breast and bacon smothered in mushrooms, melted Monterey Jack and Cheddar cheeses, with honey mustard sauce."

In the late eighties, as the public's concern about eating beef was growing, the restaurant industry saw a big shift toward chicken meals. In the midst of a poultry-crazy country, the last thing you'd expect anyone to do is open a steakhouse. But that's exactly what the boys who founded Outback Steakhouse did. And by the time their restaurant had become the sixth largest dinnerhouse chain in the country, they had proven that what many people still want is a big honkin' slab of beef.

With a menu dominated by beef items, it's nice to find that the restaurant can do great things with chicken meals as well, such as the Alice Springs Chicken. You'll love the mushrooms, bacon, cheese, and honey mustard piled on a chicken breast that's been grilled on the "barbie."

HONEY MUSTARD MARINADE

½ cup Grey Poupon Dijon mustard
½ cup honey

1 ½ teaspoons vegetable oil
½ teaspoon lemon juice

4 skinless, boneless chicken breast
*   halves*
1 tablespoon vegetable oil
2 cups sliced mushrooms (10 to
*   12 mushrooms)*

2 tablespoons butter
Salt
Pepper
Paprika
8 slices bacon, cooked

1 cup shredded Monterey Jack cheese
1 cup shredded Cheddar cheese

2 teaspoons finely chopped fresh
parsley

1. Use an electric mixer to combine the Dijon mustard, honey, 1½ teaspoons oil, and lemon juice in a small bowl. Whip the mixture for about 30 seconds.
2. Pour about two-thirds of the marinade over the chicken breasts and marinate them, covered, in the refrigerator for about 2 hours. Chill the remaining marinade until later.
3. After the chicken has marinated, preheat the oven to 375°F and heat up an ovenproof frying pan large enough to hold all four breasts and 1 tablespoon of oil over medium heat. (If you don't have an ovenproof skillet, transfer the chicken to a baking dish for baking.) Sear the chicken in the pan for 3 to 4 minutes per side or until golden brown. Remove the pan from the heat, but keep the chicken in the pan.
4. As the chicken is cooking, in a small frying pan sauté the sliced mushrooms in the butter.
5. Brush each seared chicken breast with a little of the reserved honey mustard marinade (not the portion that the chicken soaked in), being sure to save a little extra that you can serve on the side later with the dish.
6. Season the chicken with salt, pepper, and a dash of paprika.
7. Stack two pieces of cooked bacon, crosswise, on each chicken breast.
8. Spoon the sautéed mushrooms onto the bacon, being sure to coat each breast evenly.
9. Spread ¼ cup of Monterey Jack cheese onto each breast followed by ¼ cup of Cheddar.
10. Bake the pan of prepared chicken breasts for 7 to 10 minutes or until the cheese is thoroughly melted and starting to bubble.
11. Sprinkle each chicken breast with ½ teaspoon parsley before serving. Put extra honey mustard marinade into a small bowl to serve on the side.

- SERVES 4 AS AN ENTREE

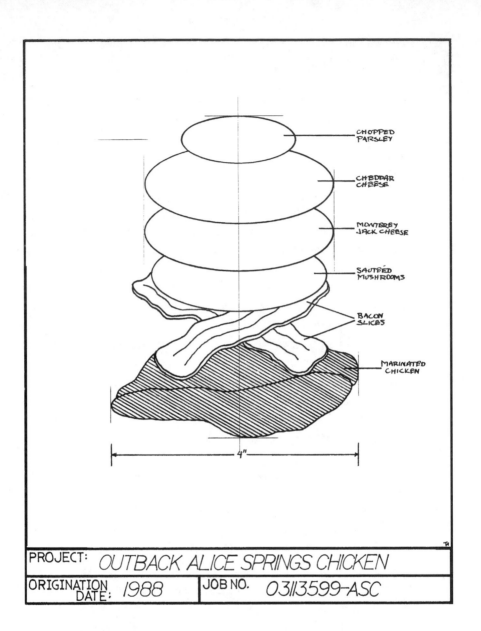

CHOPPED
PARSLEY

CHEDDAR
CHEESE

MONTEREY
JACK CHEESE

SAUTÉED
MUSHROOMS

BACON
SLICES

MARINATED
CHICKEN

4"

PROJECT:	*OUTBACK ALICE SPRINGS CHICKEN*	
ORIGINATION DATE: *1988*	JOB NO.	*03113599-ASC*

PERKINS FAMILY RESTAURANTS POTATO PANCAKES

☆   ♥   ☎   ✎   ✈   ⊠   ✂   ☛   ✿

Menu Description: "Hearty pancakes made with grated potatoes, onions and parsley."

When Matt and Ivan Perkins tasted the food at Smitty's Pancake House in Seattle, they were smitten. Soon they had purchased the rights to William Smith's recipes, which had been perfected at his renowned restaurant since it opened just after World War II. In 1958, the brothers realized their dream and opened a Smitty's restaurant of their own in Cincinnati, Ohio. When the brothers decided to give the chain an identity all its own, all of the Smitty's were changed to Perkins, and business continued to thrive through the years.

If you've never tried potato pancakes from Perkins or any restaurant, now's the time. This is a tasty, classic breakfast recipe that doesn't necessarily have to be for breakfast. I've given you the option to make the pancakes with frozen hash brown potatoes or with fresh potatoes you shred by hand. The fresh potatoes obviously taste better, but if you're in a rush, go with frozen. It may sound strange if you haven't tried it, but maple or maple-flavored syrup goes great on these hotcakes. At least I think so. You may just want some butter and powdered sugar on top.

1 cup all-purpose flour
1 cup whole milk
4 eggs
3 tablespoons butter, melted
3 tablespoons sugar
1/4 teaspoon baking powder

1/2 teaspoon salt
1 tablespoon chopped fresh parsley
1 tablespoon minced onion
2 1/2 cups frozen hash browns
    (defrosted) or shredded fresh
    potatoes (3 to 4)

Butter   *Syrup*

1. Combine all of the ingredients, except the potatoes, in a large mixing bowl. Beat by hand or with an electric mixer until smooth.

2. Add the potatoes to the batter and mix by hand until the potatoes are well combined.

3. Let the batter rest while you preheat a skillet or griddle to about medium heat. Grease the pan with a little butter. You may also use nonstick spray.

4. Ladle ¼-cup dollops of batter into the pan. Cook as many at a time as will fit comfortably in your pan. Cook each pancake for 1½ to 2 minutes per side until brown. Serve in a fanned-out stack with a pat of butter on top. Serve syrup on the side, if desired.

- SERVES 3 TO 4 AS A BREAKFAST OR SIDE DISH

TIDBITS

Because fresh shredded potatoes have more moisture than frozen, you may need to add a couple tablespoons more flour to the batter if you decide to shred your own spuds.

PERKINS FAMILY RESTAURANT GRANNY'S COUNTRY OMELETTE

☆ ♥ ☎ ✎ ✈ ✉ ✂ ☞ ✿

Menu Description: "Brimming with a blend of diced ham, onions, crisp celery and green peppers folded into a rich, luscious cheese sauce. With hashed browns tucked inside."

The same year that Matt and Ivan Perkins opened their first diner, they started selling franchise rights to other entrepreneurs. Back then, the name for the chain west of the Mississippi was still Smitty's, and to the east it became Perkins Pancake House. Soon, the name was changed to Perkins Cake & Steak. But that wouldn't last either. In the seventies the western chain of Smitty's and the eastern Perkins consolidated, and Perkins Family Restaurants, as we know it today, was born.

Secret breakfast recipes are what originally made Perkins famous. The trademarked Granny's Country Omelette is a popular menu selection from the "Premium Omelettes" column. It's a clever design for an omelette with the hash browns hidden away inside the folded eggs in a compartment separate from the other filling ingredients. The trick here is getting the folding right. I've tried to describe it as clearly as possible in the preparation steps, but if that confuses you, consult the illustration—as they say, "a picture is worth a thousand words."

I cup frozen hash browns, uncooked
2 tablespoons butter
½ green bell pepper, diced (½ cup)
½ red bell pepper, diced (½ cup)

2 slices white onion, diced (½ cup)
2 tablespoons minced celery
5 ounces ham, diced (½ cup)
½ pound Velveeta cheese spread

3 tablespoons milk   *Salt*
6 large eggs

1. Cook the hash browns following the directions on the package.
2. Sauté the vegetables in 1 tablespoon of butter over medium/high heat. Cut the ham into very small cubes and toss it in with the vegetables. After 3 to 5 minutes, when the ham starts to brown, it's ready.
3. Prepare the cheese sauce while the ham and vegetables are cooking. In a small saucepan, combine the cheese spread with the milk over low heat. Stir occasionally until melted. Be careful not to burn it.
4. Use a 12-inch frying pan or omelette pan for making the omelette. While the pan is preheating over medium heat, beat the eggs in a mixing bowl until smooth and creamy, but not foamy. Put ½ tablespoon of butter into the middle of the pan and swirl it around. Pour half of the beaten eggs into the buttered pan and swirl the pan around to coat the entire bottom with eggs. You want only a thin layer of eggs in the pan. This may require that you use a bit less than half of the eggs, so you may have some beaten egg left over in the end. Salt the eggs.
5. When the eggs have cooked for a minute or so, pour a quarter of the sautéed filling onto the eggs in a vertical line to the left of the middle, leaving enough room so that you will be able to fold over the top and bottom. Spoon half of the hash browns parallel to the filling just to the right of the middle. Fold the top and bottom of the omelette in, then fold the omelette from the left, over the top of the vegetable and ham filling. Fold the omelette once again, this time from the right, over the hash browns, then fold it one more time in the same direction, into a neat little package. Let it cook for another minute or so.
6. Carefully slide the omelette out of the pan, seam-side down, onto a plate. Put this omelette into a 250°F oven to keep warm until the second omelette is done. Cook the other omelette.
7. When both omelettes are done, pour a generous helping of cheese sauce over each one and sprinkle the remaining veggies and ham over the cheese sauce.

   • SERVES 2

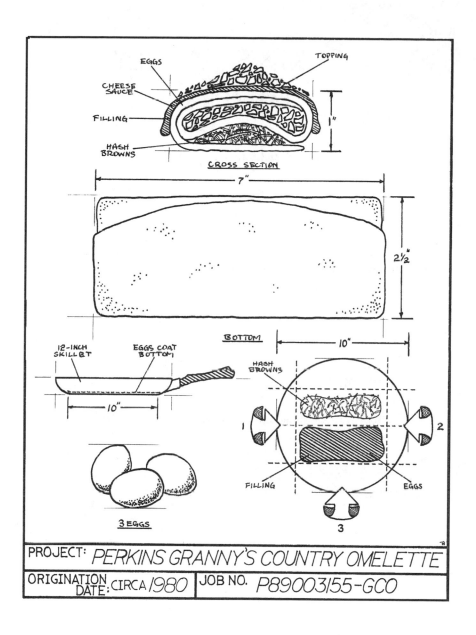

EGGS

TOPPING

CHEESE
SAUCE

FILLING

HASH
BROWNS

CROSS SECTION

7"

2½"

BOTTOM

10"

12-INCH
SKILLET

EGGS COAT
BOTTOM

10"

HASH
BROWNS

1

2

FILLING

EGGS

3

3 EGGS

PROJECT: *PERKINS GRANNY'S COUNTRY OMELETTE*

ORIGINATION
DATE: CIRCA *1980*

JOB NO. *P89003155-GCO*

433

PERKINS FAMILY RESTAURANTS COUNTRY CLUB OMELETTE

☆ ♥ ☎ ✎ ✈ ✉ ✂ ☛ ✿

Menu Description: "Oven-roasted turkey breast, real bacon pieces, green onions and fresh tomatoes. In a delicate hollandaise sauce."

This restaurant chain gained a large following early on for its home-style breakfast menu. Today, even though you can eat from the breakfast menu whenever you like, customers are picking from the lunch and dinner selections just about as often.

Since it was originally the breakfast selection that made this chain famous, I'm offering another great omelette recipe. The Country Club Omelette answers the question "What do you get when you cross a club sandwich with three eggs?" Now you can have your own version of this delicious omelette for breakfast, lunch, or dinner.

HOLLANDAISE SAUCE

½ cup butter, softened
3 egg yolks
1 tablespoon lemon juice
½ teaspoon sugar
⅛ teaspoon onion powder

⅛ teaspoon salt
Dash paprika
Dash white pepper
½ cup boiling water

8 ounces deli-sliced roasted turkey breast
4 slices bacon, cooked
1 tomato

6 large eggs
1 tablespoon butter
Salt
2 tablespoons chopped green onion

1. For the hollandaise sauce, you'll need a double boiler. Cream the butter in a small bowl, then add the egg yolks one at a time and beat with an electric mixer. Add the remaining ingredients, except for the boiling water, and mix. Add the boiling water, slowly, a little bit at a time, and stir until creamy; then pour the sauce into the top of a double boiler over boiling water. Stir continuously until thick, then turn off the heat and let the sauce keep warm over the hot water until the omelettes are done.

2. Cut the turkey breast into nickel-size pieces, crumble the bacon, and dice the tomato. Combine the three ingredients in a small skillet over low heat. You just want these ingredients to heat up while the eggs are being prepared.

3. Crack the eggs into a mixing bowl and beat by hand or with an electric mixer until smooth and creamy, but not foamy.

4. Heat a 12-inch skillet over medium heat. Add ½ tablespoon butter to the pan and swirl it around. Pour half of the eggs into the pan and swirl to cover the entire bottom surface of the pan and up the edge a bit. Salt the eggs.

5. After a minute or so add the green onions into the pan with the bacon, turkey, and tomato. Then pour one-third of the mixture into the omelette, just to the left or right of the center. Arrange the filling in a vertical line, leaving room so that you can fold in the top and bottom, and then roll the omelette over three times. After folding the omelette, cook it for another couple of minutes or until done. Slide the omelette out, seam side down, on a serving plate.

6. Repeat the process for the remaining omelette. Keep the first one warm in a 250°F oven while preparing the second.

7. When both omelettes are done, spoon a generous helping of hollandaise sauce over each one. Divide the remaining filling and spoon it over the hollandaise on each omelette.

- SERVES 2

TIDBITS

If you like, you can simplify the recipe by using a packaged dry mix for the hollandaise sauce. I've found that Knorr and McCormick make great products that taste similar to Perkins' sauce.

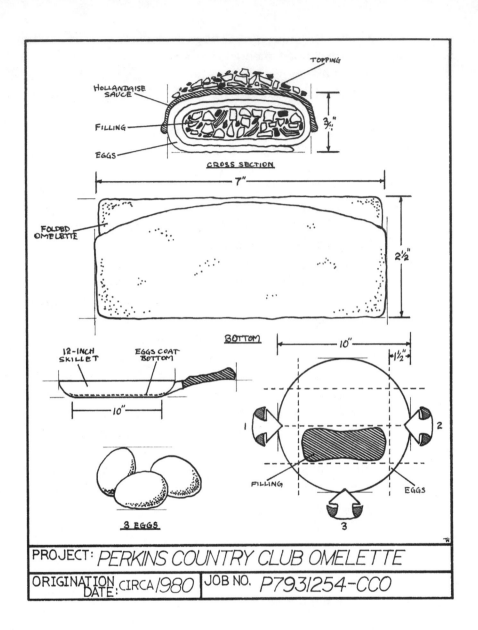

TOPPING

HOLLANDAISE
SAUCE

FILLING

EGGS

3¾"

CROSS SECTION

7"

FOLDED
OMELETTE

2½"

BOTTOM

12-INCH
SKILLET

EGGS COAT
BOTTOM

10"

10"

1½"

1

2

FILLING

EGGS

3

3 EGGS

PROJECT: *PERKINS COUNTRY CLUB OMELETTE*

ORIGINATION
DATE: CIRCA *1980*

JOB NO. *P7931254-CCO*

PIZZA HUT ORIGINAL STUFFED CRUST PIZZA

☆　♥　☎　✎　✈　✉　✂　☞　❀

Menu Description: "This unique thinner crust has a ring of cheese baked into the edge so you get cheese in the very last bite of every slice."

Brothers Dan and Frank Carney have dear old Mom to thank for helping them to become founders of the world's largest pizza chain. It was in 1958 that a family friend approached the two brothers with the idea of opening a pizza parlor, and it was the brothers' mother who lent them the $600 it took to purchase some second-hand equipment and to rent a small building. There, in the Carneys' hometown of Wichita, Kansas, the first Pizza Hut opened its doors. By 1966, there were 145 Pizza Hut restaurants doing a booming business around the country with the help of the promotional musical jingle "Putt-Putt to Pizza Hut." Today the chain is made up of more than 10,000 restaurants, delivery–carry out units, and kiosks in all 50 states and 82 foreign countries.

Introduced in 1995, the Stuffed Crust Pizza, which includes sticks of mozzarella string cheese loaded into the crust before cooking, increased business at Pizza Hut by 37 percent. Because the outer crust is filled with cheese, the chain designed a special dough formula that does not rise as high as the original. It's best to prepare your Top Secret Recipe version of this delicious crust a day before you plan to cook the pizza so that the dough can rest while the gluten in the flour forms a texture just like the original.

CRUST

¾ cup warm water (105° to 115°F)   2¼ cups bread flour
1 tablespoon sugar   1½ teaspoons salt
1¼ teaspoons yeast   1½ tablespoons olive oil

SAUCE

1 15-ounce can tomato sauce   ¼ teaspoon garlic powder
¼ cup water   ¼ teaspoon salt
1 teaspoon sugar   ⅛ teaspoon ground black pepper
¼ teaspoon dried oregano   1 bay leaf
¼ teaspoon dried basil leaves   Dash onion powder
¼ teaspoon dried thyme   ½ teaspoon lemon juice

Eight 1-ounce mozzarella string   1½ cups shredded mozzarella
    cheese sticks

TOPPINGS (YOUR CHOICE OF . . .)

pepperoni slices, chopped onions, sliced mushrooms, sliced black olives, sliced
    jalapeños (nacho slices), sliced green peppers, pineapple chunks, Italian
    sausage, sliced tomatoes, sliced ham, anchovies

1. First prepare the dough for the crust. I suggest you prepare the
    crust one day prior to baking the pizza. To get the best dough
    you need to allow it to rise in your refrigerator overnight. This
    procedure will produce a great commercial-style crust.
        Combine the warm water, sugar, and yeast in a small bowl or
    measuring cup and stir until the yeast and sugar have dissolved.
    Let the mixture sit for about 5 minutes. Foam should begin
    building up on the surface. If it doesn't, either the water was too
    hot or the yeast was dead. Throw it out and start again.
2. In a large bowl, sift together the flour and salt. Make a depres-
    sion in the center of the flour and pour in the yeast mixture.
    Add the oil.
3. Use a fork to stir the liquid in the center of the flour. Slowly
    draw in more flour, a little bit at a time, until you have to use
    your hands to completely combine all of the ingredients into
    a ball.

4. Dust a clean, flat surface with flour, and with the heel of your hands, knead the dough on this surface until it seems to have a smooth, consistent texture. This should take around 10 minutes. Rub a light coating of oil on the dough, then put it into a tightly covered container and in a warm place to rise for 2 hours or until it has doubled in size. When it has doubled in size, punch the dough down, put it back into the covered container and into the refrigerator overnight. If you don't have time for that, you can use the crust at this point. But without the long rest it just won't have the same texture as the original.

5. You can prepare the pizza sauce ahead of time as well, storing it in the refrigerator until you are ready to make the pizza. Simply combine the tomato sauce, water, and sugar with the spices and lemon juice in a small saucepan over medium heat. Heat the sauce until it starts to bubble, then turn the heat down and simmer, covered, for 30 to 60 minutes until it reaches the thickness you like. When the sauce has cooled, store it in the refrigerator in a tightly sealed container.

6. About an hour or so before you are ready to make your pizza, take the dough out of the refrigerator so that it will warm up to room temperature.

   Preheat the oven to 475°F.

   Roll the dough out on a floured surface until it is 18 inches across. Put the dough on a pizza pan that has either been greased or has a sprinkling of cornmeal on it. This will prevent your pizza from sticking. Score the pizza dough several times with a fork so that it doesn't bubble up when baked.

7. Place a ring of the string cheese sticks, end to end, around the edge of the dough, an inch in from the edge.

8. Use water on your fingertips or on a brush to moisten the outer edge of the dough, all of the way around so that it will stick when folded over. Fold the dough up and over the cheese and press it down onto itself, sealing it tightly. Form a nice, round crust as you seal the cheese inside. Lightly brush the top of the folded dough with olive oil all of the way around the edge.

9. Now spread about a cup of the pizza sauce on the crust (you will likely have enough sauce left over for another pie later). As you spread the sauce onto the crust, be sure to spread sauce all

of the way to the folded edge, enough to hide that seam you made when folding the crust over the cheese.

10. Spread the toppings other than pepperoni, sausage, ham, and olives on the pizza sauce. Sprinkle the shredded mozzarella onto the sauce and any olives or meat toppings you wish on top of the cheese.

11. Bake the pizza for 12 to 16 minutes or until the crust begins to turn dark brown and the cheese develops dark spots.

12. Slice the pizza 4 times through the center, making 8 slices.

- SERVES 3 TO 4

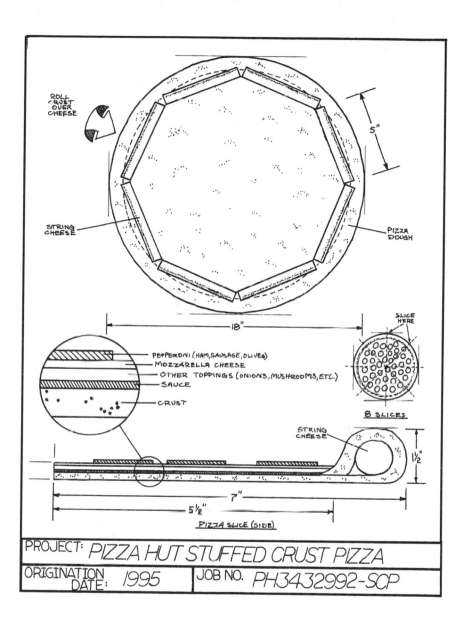

ROLL
CRUST
OVER
CHEESE

5"

STRING
CHEESE

PIZZA
DOUGH

18"

PEPPERONI (HAM, SAUSAGE, OLIVES)
MOZZARELLA CHEESE
OTHER TOPPINGS (ONIONS, MUSHROOMS, ETC.)
SAUCE
CRUST

SLICE
HERE

8 SLICES

STRING
CHEESE

1½"

7"

5½"

PIZZA SLICE (SIDE)

PROJECT:	*PIZZA HUT STUFFED CRUST PIZZA*	
ORIGINATION DATE:	1995	JOB NO. PH3432992-SCP

PEPPERONI & CHEESE STUFFED CRUST PIZZA

☆ ♥ ☎ ✎ ✈ ✉ ✂ ☛ ✿

After the sales success of the Original Stuffed Crust Pizza, Pizza Hut developed a variation which includes slices of pepperoni along with the gooey cheese in the crust of each pizza slice. The technique is very simple. Just place a slice of pepperoni every inch or so around the edge onto the dough where you will place the string cheese sticks. Each string cheese stick should be placed on top of the pepperoni slices and then the dough is folded over the cheese the same way as in the original recipe. The pepperoni slices will curl over the cheese sticks as you fold the dough over. Top and bake your pizza as described in the previous recipe. *Voilà!*

- SERVES 3 TO 4

TIDBITS

The kneading process is easy with a bread machine if you have one. Prepare the yeast, water, and sugar mixture, then add the flour, salt, and oil to the bread machine baking pan. When the yeast mixture becomes foamy on top, pour it into the baking pan and put the machine on the "dough" setting. When the dough is done, seal it up in a container and place it in the fridge overnight.

PIZZA HUT
TRIPLE DECKER PIZZA

☆　♥　☎　✎　✈　⌧　✂　☛　✿

Menu Description: "We start with a thin layer of crust, then we lay down a luscious layer of our six-cheese blend and seal it in with another thin layer of crust. We pile on your favorite Pizza Hut toppings, more cheese and bake it to gooey perfection."

You might be as surprised as I was to learn that Pizza Hut uses 2.5 percent of all the milk produced in the U.S. every year for the cheese used on the pizzas. We're talking about a lot of pizzas here—1.3 million served every day. The cheese production alone requires a herd of 250,000 dairy cows producing at full capacity 365 days a year!

Certainly even more overworked cows had to be recruited to produce the additional cheese needed for this gooey new creation. This special pizza is made with two crispy cracker-like crusts that have a hidden layer of six cheeses cooked between them. Because this pizza requires two crusts, Pizza Hut created a dough that does not rise as much as the dough used in their other pizzas. This version has been adapted from a classic recipe for soda crackers. The finished product is surely the perfect pizza for people who think they just don't get enough cheese in their diet.

CRUST

¾ teaspoon yeast
1 cup warm water (105 to 115°F)
3¾ cups all-purpose flour

2 teaspoons salt
½ teaspoon baking soda
3 tablespoons shortening
¼ cup milk

SAUCE

One 15-ounce can tomato sauce
1/4 teaspoon dried oregano
1/4 teaspoon dried basil leaves
1/4 teaspoon dried thyme
1/4 teaspoon garlic powder

1/4 teaspoon salt
1/8 teaspoon ground black pepper
1 bay leaf
1/2 teaspoon lemon juice
Dash onion powder

SIX-CHEESE BLEND

1/3 cup shredded Cheddar cheese
1/3 cup shredded Monterey Jack cheese
1/2 cup shredded mozzarella cheese

2 tablespoons shredded provolone
1 tablespoon grated Parmesan cheese
1 tablespoon grated Romano cheese

1 1/2 cups shredded mozzarella cheese

TOPPINGS (YOUR CHOICE OF . . .)

pepperoni slices, chopped onions, sliced mushrooms, sliced black olives, sliced
jalapeños ("nacho slices"), sliced green peppers, pineapple chunks, Italian
sausage, sliced tomatoes, sliced ham, anchovies

1. To prepare the crust, dissolve the yeast with the warm water in a small bowl or measuring cup and let it sit for 5 minutes.
2. Sift the flour, salt, and baking soda together in a large bowl.
3. Cut the shortening into the flour and mix the ingredients together with your hands until the shortening is reduced to tiny pea-size pieces.
4. Make an indentation in the flour and pour in the milk and yeast mixture. Using a fork, stir the liquid around in the center, slowly drawing in more flour as you stir. When all of the flour is moistened and you can no longer stir with a fork, use your hands to combine the ingredients into a ball.
5. On a lightly floured surface, knead the dough with the heel of your hands. Continue kneading until the dough is smooth and silky, about 10 minutes.
6. Form the dough into a ball and put it into a large bowl covered with plastic wrap. Let the dough rise in a warm place for about 2 hours. After 2 hours, place the covered container into the refrigerator to rise overnight. Take the dough out of the refrig-

erator 2 hours before you plan to cook the pizza so that the dough can warm up to room temperature.

7. You may want to make the pizza sauce a day ahead as well, at the same time as you prepare the dough. Combine all of the ingredients in a small saucepan over medium heat until it bubbles. Reduce the heat and simmer for about 1 hour. When the sauce is cool, store it in the refrigerator.

8. Preheat the oven to 475°. Divide the dough in half, and form the two halves into balls. On a floured surface roll out each of the dough balls until they form thin 15-inch circles. Use a fork to poke the dough several times on the surface. This will keep the crust from bubbling. Place one of the crusts on a pizza pan that has been well-greased or sprinkled with cornmeal.

9. Combine the six cheeses to make the blend for the second layer. Sprinkle the cheese blend evenly over the pizza crust in the pan. Leave about a half-inch margin around the outside edge of the dough. Moisten the dough by brushing some water around the outside edge in that margin.

10. While the top pizza dough sits on a hard, floured surface, use an inverted bowl with a 4-inch diameter as a guide to cut a 4-inch circle out of the center of the dough. This is to keep the crusts from separating at the tip of each pizza slice when cut. Carefully place the dough on top of the cheese layer and crimp the edges together. Bend the crust up to form a lip. Brush some olive oil just on that lip all of the way around the pizza.

11. Spread the pizza sauce over the surface of the top pizza dough layer to the lip around the edge.

12. Sprinkle any vegetable toppings (or pineapple) on the pizza sauce. Sprinkle the 1½ cups mozzarella cheese over the pizza to the lip around the edge. Place any meat toppings or the olives on top of the cheese.

13. Bake the pizza for 12 to 15 minutes.

14. Slice the pizza 4 times through the center, making 8 slices.

• SERVES 3 TO 4

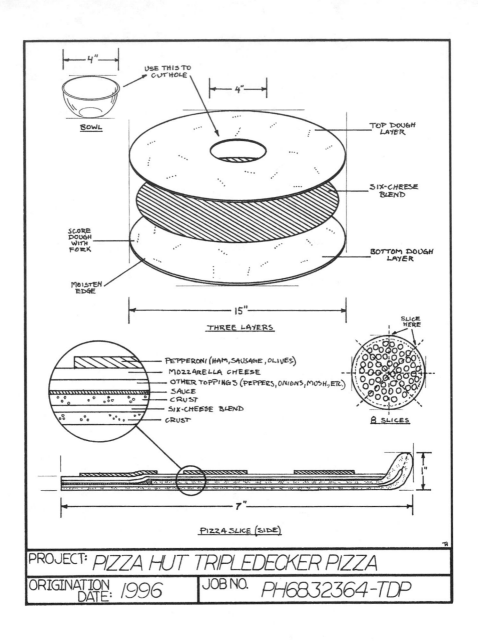

4"

BOWL

USE THIS TO
CUTHOLE

4"

TOP DOUGH
LAYER

SIX-CHEESE
BLEND

SCORE
DOUGH
WITH
FORK

BOTTOM DOUGH
LAYER

MOISTEN
EDGE

15"

THREE LAYERS

PEPPERONI (HAM, SAUSAGE, OLIVES)
MOZZARELLA CHEESE
OTHER TOPPINGS (PEPPERS, ONIONS, MUSH., ETC.)
SAUCE
CRUST
SIX-CHEESE BLEND
CRUST

SLICE
HERE

8 SLICES

1"

7"

PIZZA SLICE (SIDE)

PROJECT: PIZZA HUT TRIPLEDECKER PIZZA

ORIGINATION
DATE: 1996

JOB NO. PH6832364-TDP

PLANET HOLLYWOOD PIZZA BREAD

☆　♥　☎　✎　✈　✉　✂　☞　✿

Menu Description: "Fresh baked on premises, sliced into eight pieces, brushed with garlic butter, Parmesan cheese, mozzarella and basil, topped with chopped plum tomatoes and herbed olive oil."

In 1988, London-born restaurant mogul Robert Ian Earl joined with movie producer Keith Barrish and a gaggle of celebrities including Arnold Schwarzenegger, Sylvester Stallone, Bruce Willis, and Demi Moore to start a Hollywood-themed restaurant that is on its way to becoming his most successful venture yet. In 1991, a gala star-studded affair in New York City celebrated the opening of the world's first Planet Hollywood.

But even the coolest theme restaurant won't fly if the food doesn't please. Earl told *Nation's Restaurant News*, "People don't eat themes—no concept in the world can succeed for long unless it also delivers great food at the right price." So Planet Hollywood has created a menu of delicious dishes rivaling food from national chains that don't have a theme to lean on.

The Pizza Bread appetizer comes highly recommended by Planet Hollywood servers. The "bread" is actually just pizza dough, rolled thin, with a light layer of cheese, basil, and tomato on top; then it's baked in a special pizza oven at the restaurant. Since most of us don't have these ovens at home, this recipe has been designed for a conventional gas or electric oven.

One 12-inch thin-crust uncooked pizza
    dough (see Tidbits)
½ teaspoon garlic salt
1½ tablespoons butter, melted
1 cup shredded mozzarella cheese

2 tablespoons coarsely chopped fresh
    basil
1 small tomato, chopped (use a Roma
    or plum tomato if available)
2 tablespoons grated Parmesan cheese

1. Preheat the oven to 475°F.
2. If you are making your own crust, roll out the dough to a 12-inch diameter.
3. Mix the garlic salt with the butter.
4. Use a brush to coat the entire crust with garlic butter.
5. Spread half of the mozzarella cheese over the crust.
6. Spread the basil over the cheese.
7. Spread the remaining mozzarella over the basil.
8. Sprinkle the tomato over the cheese.
9. Bake for 8 to 10 minutes or until the surface begins to turn brown.
10. Remove the pizza bread from the oven and sprinkle the fresh Parmesan over it.
11. Slice into 8 pieces through the middle, like a pizza, and serve hot.

- SERVES 2 TO 4 AS AN APPETIZER

TIDBITS

For the dough you can use the recipe for pizza dough from page 281, or a canned tube of pizza dough (such as Pillsbury), or an instant dough mix. You will need only about 1 cup of dough after rising, which is about half a tube of the Pillsbury-type dough. Of course, I highly recommend making the dough from scratch if you have time. There's nothing in a box or can that tastes as good as the homemade stuff.

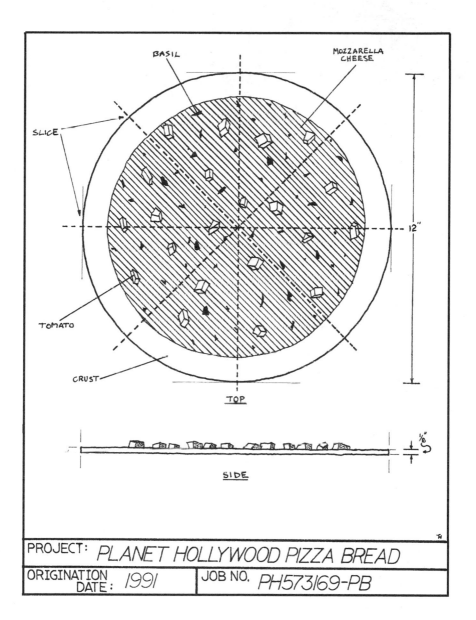

BASIL

MOZZARELLA
CHEESE

SLICE

A

12"

TOMATO

CRUST

TOP

SIDE

1/8"

PROJECT: *PLANET HOLLYWOOD PIZZA BREAD*

ORIGINATION
DATE: *1991*

JOB NO. *PH573169-PB*

PLANET HOLLYWOOD CHICKEN CRUNCH

Menu Description: "A basket of tender chicken breaded with Cap'n Crunch and seasonings, served with Creole mustard sauce."

The Orlando, Florida Planet Hollywood, which had its big opening in 1994, pulls in yearly sales receipts totaling around $50 million, making it the highest volume restaurant in America. If you've never tried the Chicken Crunch at Planet Hollywood, you're missing a treat. Sliced chicken breast fingers are coated with a crunchy, slightly sweet breading combination of Cap'n Crunch cereal and cornflake crumbs. The chicken is then deep-fried to a golden brown and served with a tasty dipping sauce made from mayonnaise, horseradish, and Dijon mustard. You've probably tasted nothing like it.

CREOLE MUSTARD SAUCE

2 tablespoons Grey Poupon Country
   Dijon mustard
3 tablespoons mayonnaise

1 teaspoon yellow mustard
1 teaspoon cream-style horseradish
1 teaspoon honey

Vegetable oil for frying
2 boneless, skinless chicken breast halves
2 cups Cap'n Crunch cereal
1/2 cup cornflake crumbs
1/2 teaspoon onion powder

1/2 teaspoon garlic powder
1/2 teaspoon salt
1/4 teaspoon white pepper
1 egg, beaten
1 cup milk

1. Preheat oil in a deep pan or deep fryer to 375°F. You want to use enough oil to completely cover the chicken 1 to 2 inches deep.

2. Combine all of the ingredients for the Creole mustard sauce in a small bowl and chill the sauce while the chicken is prepared.

3. Cut each chicken breast, lengthwise, into 5 long slices (chicken fingers).

4. Smash the Cap'n Crunch into crumbs using a food processor, or put the cereal into a plastic bag and start pounding.

5. Combine the cereals, onion powder, garlic powder, salt, and pepper in a medium bowl.

6. Combine the egg with the milk in a separate bowl.

7. Dredge each piece of chicken in the milk mixture, then completely coat it with the dry mixture. Do this for all the chicken before frying.

8. When the oil is hot, fry the chicken for 4 to 6 minutes or until golden to dark brown and crispy. Remove to paper towels or a rack to drain. Serve hot with Creole mustard sauce on the side for dipping.

- SERVES 2 TO 4 AS AN APPETIZER OR SNACK

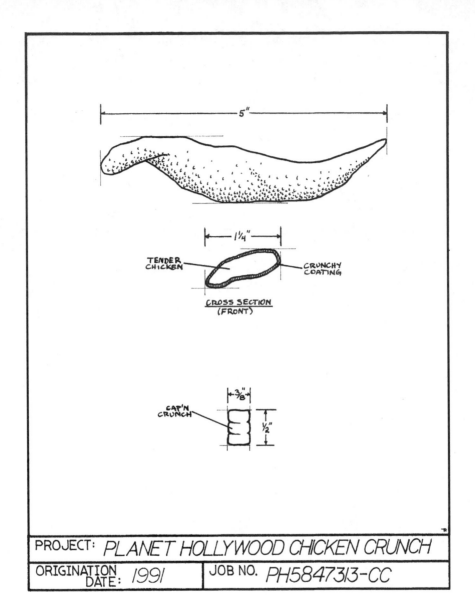

5"

TENDER
CHICKEN

CRUNCHY
COATING

1¼"

CROSS SECTION
(FRONT)

CAP'N
CRUNCH

⅜"

½"

PROJECT: PLANET HOLLYWOOD CHICKEN CRUNCH

ORIGINATION
DATE: 1991

JOB NO. PH5847313-CC

PLANET HOLLYWOOD POT STICKERS

☆　♥　☎　✎　✈　✉　✄　／　☛　✿

Menu Description: "Six pot stickers filled with fresh ground turkey meat seasoned with ginger, water chestnuts, red pepper and green onions. They are fried and served in a basket with spicy hoisin."

Planet Hollywood is known for the film and television memorabilia displayed throughout the restaurants. Some of the items on display behind thick Plexiglas include the genie bottle from *I Dream of Jeannie*, Val Kilmer's bat suit from *Batman Forever*, Tom Hanks' costume from *Forrest Gump*, Judy Garland's dress from *The Wizard of Oz*, and the painting from the set of the television show *Friends*. In addition to the memorabilia is a wall at the entrance to each restaurant that displays handprints in plaster from the likes of Mel Gibson, Jimmy Stewart, Harrison Ford, Demi Moore, Samuel L. Jackson, Paul Newman, Goldie Hawn, Patrick Swayze, and many others.

Pot stickers are a popular Asian dumpling that can be fried, steamed, or simmered in a broth. Planet Hollywood has customized its version to make them crunchier than the traditional dish, and it's a tasty twist. Since hoisin sauce would be very difficult to make from scratch, you can use a commercial brand found in most stores.

¼ pound ground turkey
½ teaspoon minced fresh ginger
1 teaspoon minced green onion
1 teaspoon minced water
　　chestnuts
½ teaspoon soy sauce
½ teaspoon ground black pepper

¼ teaspoon crushed red pepper flakes
　　(no seeds)
¼ teaspoon salt
⅛ teaspoon garlic powder
1 egg, beaten
Vegetable oil for frying
12 wonton wrapper (3 × 3-inch size)

Hoisin sauce

1. In a small bowl, combine all the ingredients except the egg, wrappers, and oil. Add 1 tablespoon of the beaten egg. Save the rest of the egg for later. Preheat oil in a deep fryer or a deep saucepan to 375°F. Use enough oil to cover the pot stickers—1 to 2 inches should be enough.

2. Invert a small bowl or glass with a 3-inch diameter on the center of a wonton wrapper and cut around it to make a circle. Repeat for the remaining wrappers.

3. Spoon ½ tablespoon of the turkey filling into the center of one wrapper. Brush a little beaten egg around half of the edge of the wrapper and fold the wrapper over the filling. Gather the wrapper as you seal it, so that it is crinkled around the edge. Repeat with the remaining ingredients.

4. Deep-fry the pot stickers, six at a time, in the hot oil for 3 to 6 minutes or until they are brown. Drain on a rack or paper towels. Serve with the hoisin sauce for dipping. If you want a spicier sauce, add some more crushed red pepper or cayenne pepper to the sauce.

- SERVES 3 TO 6 AS AN APPETIZER OR SNACK

TIDBITS

If you can't find wonton wrappers, you can also use eggroll wrappers for this recipe. Eggroll wrappers are much bigger, so you will be wasting more of the dough when you trim the wrappers to 3-inch-diameter circles. But in a pinch, this is a quick solution.

Pot sticker wrappers can also be found in some supermarkets, but I've found the wonton wrappers and eggroll wrappers, when fried, taste more like the restaurant version.

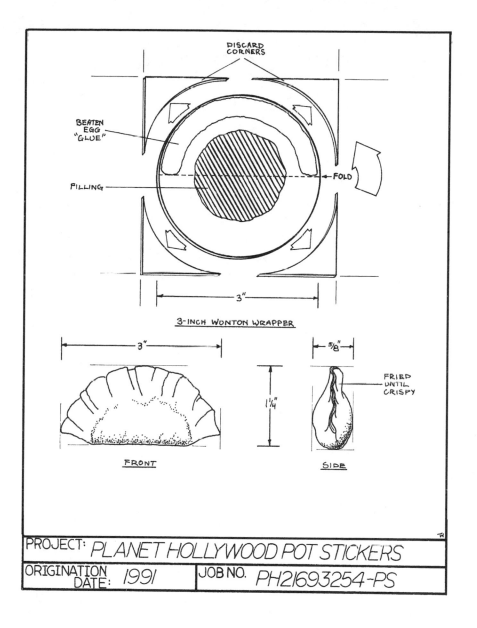

DISCARD CORNERS

BEATEN EGG "GLUE"

FILLING

FOLD

3"

3-INCH WONTON WRAPPER

3"

FRONT

1¼"

⅝"

FRIED UNTIL CRISPY

SIDE

PROJECT: *PLANET HOLLYWOOD POT STICKERS*

ORIGINATION DATE: *1991*

JOB NO. *PH21693254-PS*

RED LOBSTER
BROILED LOBSTER

☆ ♥ ☎ ✎ ✈ ✉ ✄ ☛ ✿

The namesake of the Red Lobster chain is the delicious broiled lobster, lightly seasoned, served with lemon and melted butter. Two varieties are most often available at the restaurant: Maine lobster and rock lobster. The Maine lobsters are purchased live, while rock lobster tails come frozen; and both are available in stores across the country. Rock lobsters, also known as spiny lobsters, are found in warmer waters. They have no claws, which is why you only get rock lobster tails. Each Red Lobster restaurant has a special device that bakes and broils the lobsters without burning them. Since these special broilers don't come with most homes, I've created a cooking method using a conventional oven that produces broiled lobster just like that which you can enjoy at the restaurant.

Two 6-ounce rock lobster or Maine
    lobster tails
Melted butter
¼ teaspoon salt
¼ teaspoon paprika

Dash ground black pepper
Dash cayenne pepper
Dash allspice
Lemon wedges

1. Thaw lobster tails if frozen, then preheat the oven to 425°F.
2. Each tail is prepared differently for cooking. The meat from the rock lobster is fully exposed on top of the shell for broiling, while the meat of the Maine Lobster is left in the shell.

    To prepare the rock lobster, use a kitchen scissors to cut along the top of the shell down to the tail. Crack the ribs of the shell underneath so that you can spread the shell open on top and pull the meat out down to the tail. You may have to use a spoon to pull the meat away from inside of the shell so that it will come free. Leave the end of the meat attached to the shell when you pull it out, then close the shell underneath it. Now you should be able to rest the meat back down on top of the shell. Cut about ¼ inch deep down the center of the meat so that you can pull the colored part of the meat over, exposing the white center. This may have already happened when you cut the shell open.

For the Maine lobster, slice down the top of the shell to the tail. Crack the ribs in the center along the bottom of the tail so that you can hinge the shell open from the top. Use a spoon to pull the meat away from the inside of the shell so that it is easy to eat when cooked, but leave the meat inside the shell. Slice down the middle of the meat so that you can spread open the colored part. This may have already happened when you cut the top of the shell open.

3. Brush the lobster meat with melted butter.
4. Combine the salt, paprika, peppers, and allspice in a small bowl. Sprinkle a dash of this spice combination on the top of each lobster.
5. Bake in the oven on a broiling pan for 15 minutes.
6. Turn the oven to broil and broil for an additional 6 to 8 minutes or until the meat or shell just begins to turn a light brown on top. Be careful not to burn the lobster meat. Remove from the broiler and serve with melted butter and a lemon wedge.

• SERVES 2 AS AN ENTREE

TIDBITS

If you like, you can take the Maine lobster meat out of the shell as explained in the method for the rock lobster. That's not the way Red Lobster does it, but, hey, you're not eating at Red Lobster.

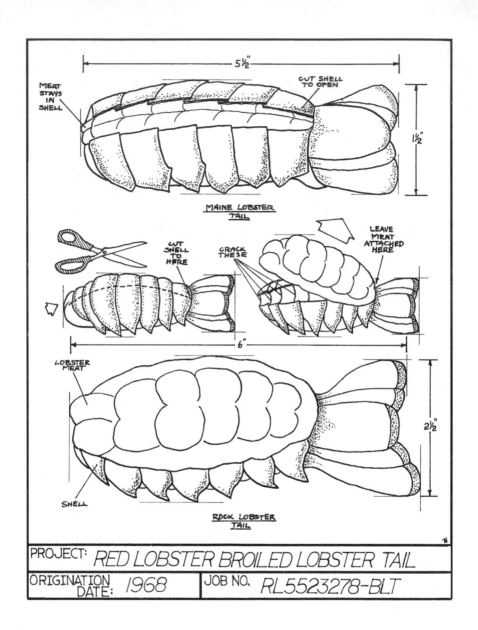

MEAT STAYS IN SHELL

CUT SHELL TO OPEN

5½"

1½"

MAINE LOBSTER TAIL

CUT SHELL TO HERE

CRACK THESE

LEAVE MEAT ATTACHED HERE

6"

LOBSTER MEAT

2½"

SHELL

ROCK LOBSTER TAIL

PROJECT: RED LOBSTER BROILED LOBSTER TAIL

ORIGINATION DATE: 1968

JOB NO. RL5523278-BLT

RED LOBSTER SCALLOPS AND BACON

☆　♥　☎　✎　✈　✉　✂　☞　✿

At the time I was researching this book there were two ways you could have your bacon and scallops at Red Lobster: wrapped and broiled, or grilled on a skewer. The former is a smaller portion to be served as an appetizer, while the skewers may be served as a main entree or part of one. I've included recipes to clone both versions.

BROILED BACON-WRAPPED SCALLOPS

4 medium sea scallops	Paprika
2 slices bacon	Ground pepper
Melted butter	1 tablespoon warm bottled clam Juice
Salt	4 toothpicks

1. Preheat the broiler to high.
2. Boil 2 to 3 cups of water in a small pan over high heat. Salt the water.
3. Boil the scallops in the water for 3 to 4 minutes, or until they firm up. Drain the scallops when they're done.
4. Cook the bacon slices for a couple minutes per side. Don't cook until crispy or you won't be able to fold the bacon around the scallops.
5. When the scallops are cool enough to touch, cut or tear a piece of partially cooked bacon in half and wrap one half over the top

of the scallop so that it meets itself underneath. Put a toothpick through the bacon to stick it in place. If you have a problem wrapping your bacon (story of my life) because it is too crispy, dip the bacon into hot or boiling water to make it more flexible. Repeat this with the remaining scallops.

6. Put the scallops on their side in an oven-safe dish and brush with melted butter.

7. Lightly season the scallops with salt, paprika, and a dash of ground pepper.

8. Broil the scallops for 5 to 6 minutes, or just until the edges begin to brown.

9. Remove the scallops from the oven and add warm clam juice to the bottom of the baking dish. Serve in the same dish.

- SERVES 2 AS AN APPETIZER

GRILLED SCALLOP AND BACON SKEWERS

1 teaspoon salt
16 sea scallops
4 round zucchini slices, ½ inch thick
2 slices bacon, cooked soft
1 tablespoon melted butter

Four 8-inch skewers
Dash of salt
Dash of paprika
Dash of ground black peppers

ON THE SIDE

Brown rice

1. Preheat the barbecue grill to medium/high heat.
2. In a large saucepan, heat 3 to 4 cups of water until boiling. Add a teaspoon or so of salt to the water.
3. Boil the scallops for 4 minutes or until they firm up.
4. Remove the scallops from the water and drain.
5. When the scallops have cooled enough to handle, begin building your 4 skewers.

6. Cut a zucchini slice in half and pierce it, round edge first, onto the skewer.
7. Slide the zucchini to the end until there's about 1 inch left on the end of the skewer.
8. Slide one scallop on next, piercing through the rounded edges.
9. Break the bacon into quarters and slide one piece of bacon on next.
10. Add two more scallops, one more piece of bacon, another scallop, and the other half of the zucchini slice (this one goes cut side first).
11. Make three more skewers exactly the same way.
12. Generously brush the skewers with melted butter.
13. Lightly season with salt, paprika, and a dash of black pepper.
14. Grill the skewers for 4 to 5 minutes per side or until the zucchini has softened. Serve the skewers over a bed of brown rice.

- SERVES 2 AS AN ENTREE

TIDBITS

For a healthier alternative, try turkey bacon with either of these recipes as a substitute for the pork bacon.

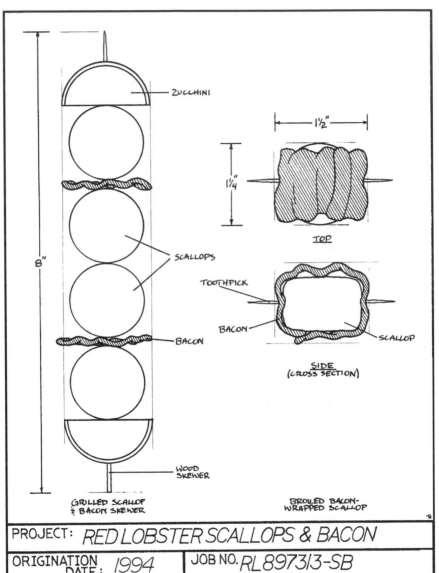

ZUCCHINI

1½"

1¼"

TOP

SCALLOPS

TOOTHPICK

BACON

BACON

SCALLOP

SIDE
(CROSS SECTION)

8"

WOOD
SKEWER

GRILLED SCALLOP
& BACON SKEWER

BROILED BACON-
WRAPPED SCALLOP

PROJECT: *RED LOBSTER SCALLOPS & BACON*

ORIGINATION
DATE: *1994*

JOB NO. *RL 897313-SB*

RED LOBSTER STUFFED SHRIMP AND STUFFED MUSHROOMS

☆　♥　☎　✎　✈　✉　✂　☞　✿

Bill Darden was only 19 when he started his restaurant career in 1939 by opening a 25-seat lunch counter called The Green Frog in Waycross, Georgia. From the start Bill's business was a hopping success. That success helped Bill to springboard into other restaurant acquisitions throughout the years including 20 Howard Johnson's restaurants. Then, in 1968, as he reached his mid-fifties, Bill took another gamble and opened a seafood restaurant in Lakeland, Florida. When deciding on a name for the new restaurant, someone suggested that since he had great luck with the name "Green Frog" in the past, why not name this one "Red Lobster." And so it was.

Here are a couple of great dishes to serve as appetizers or on the side with an entree such as broiled lobster or fish. These recipes include a stuffing that varies in the restaurants only in the type of seafood used—the stuffed shrimp contains crabmeat and the stuffed mushrooms contain lobster meat. If you like, you can use the stuffings interchangeably in the mushroom caps and shrimp.

STUFFED SHRIMP

½ cup water
3 tablespoons butter
1 tablespoon minced celery
1 tablespoon minced onion
1 tablespoon finely chopped red chili pepper

1 tablespoon finely chopped green chili pepper
¼ teaspoon dried parsley
½ teaspoon salt
Dash pepper
½ tablespoon sugar

¾ cup cornbread crumbs (Pepperidge
    Farm cornbread stuffing mix
    is good)
1 cup lump crab meat (fresh, frozen,
    or one 6-ounce can)

1 egg, beaten
20 large shrimp
¼ to ½ pound Cheddar cheese, thinly
    sliced
Paprika

1. Preheat the oven to 375°F.
2. Boil the water and 2 tablespoons butter in a medium saucepan.
3. Add the celery, onion, peppers, parsley, salt, pepper, and sugar.
4. Reduce the heat to low and let it simmer for 5 minutes.
5. Add the bread crumbs and remove from the heat.
6. Mix the crab meat with the beaten egg. Add to the breadcrumb mixture, cover, and let it sit for 5 minutes.
7. In the meantime, prepare each shrimp by cutting along the back to remove the vein and removing all of the shell except the last joint and the tip of the tail. Cut deep into the shrimp where the vein was, but not all of the way through, and spread the meat open (butterfly slice) so that each shrimp will sit in a roasting pan, cut side up, with its tail sticking up. Repeat for all of the shrimp and arrange in a baking dish.
8. Scoop about 1 tablespoon of stuffing onto the top of the spread-out portion of each shrimp.
9. Melt the remaining tablespoon of butter and brush it over the surface of each stuffed shrimp. Scoot all the shrimp close together after you do this.
10. Spread thin slices of cheddar cheese evenly over the entire surface of all of the shrimp. Sprinkle on a dash of paprika.
11. Bake the shrimp for 15 to 20 minutes or until the shrimp are completely cooked. Broil for an additional 1 to 2 minutes to brown the cheese just slightly.

STUFFED MUSHROOMS

1. Follow the above directions for the stuffing, but substitute 1 cup cooked lobster meat for the crab meat. If you broil the tail from a live lobster for another recipe, such as the one on page 456, you can use the meat from the legs and claws for this recipe. Simply cook the remaining lobster in the shell for 15 to 20 minutes in rapidly boiling salted water. Use a nut cracker to remove the meat. You may also use canned lobster meat for this recipe, although fresh lobster meat tastes much better.

2. Instead of shrimp, use 20 to 24 (about 1 pound) mushrooms with stems removed.

3. Fill the mushroom caps with 2 to 3 teaspoons of stuffing, brush with melted butter, and top with slices of Monterey Jack cheese rather than Cheddar.

4. Season lightly with paprika, then bake the mushrooms in a roasting pan or baking dish in a preheated oven set on 375°F for about 12 minutes, or until the cheese is melted. Broil for 1 to 2 minutes to slightly brown the cheese.

- SERVES 4 TO 6 AS AN APPETIZER

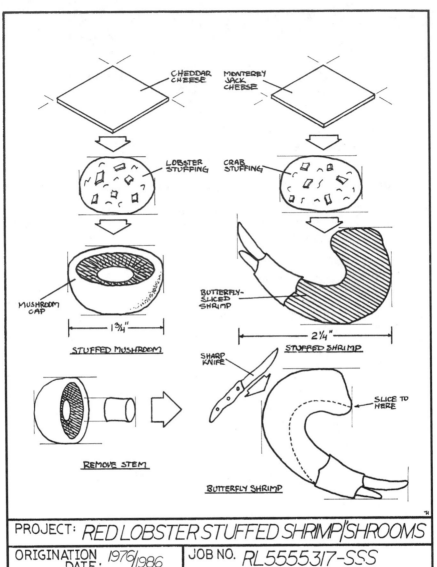

CHEDDAR CHEESE

MONTEREY JACK CHEESE

LOBSTER STUFFING

CRAB STUFFING

MUSHROOM CAP

BUTTERFLY-SLICED SHRIMP

1 3/4"

2 1/4"

STUFFED MUSHROOM

STUFFED SHRIMP

SHARP KNIFE

SLICE TO HERE

REMOVE STEM

BUTTERFLY SHRIMP

PROJECT: *RED LOBSTER STUFFED SHRIMP/SHROOMS*

ORIGINATION DATE: *1976/1986*

JOB NO. *RL5555317-SSS*

RED ROBIN
NO-FIRE PEPPERS

☆ ♥ ☎ ✎ ✈ ✉ ✂ ☞ ✿

Menu Description: "Full-flavored jalapeños stuffed with cool cream cheese and deep-fried in a cracker-crumb coating. Served with sweet jalapeño jelly & sour cream."

Red Robin was one of the first restaurant chains to serve No-Fire Peppers, an item which can be found on many restaurant menus today under a variety of different names. The cream cheese–filled, battered and fried jalapeño peppers are actually called Poppers by their creators, Anchor Foods, a restaurant food supply company which manufactures Poppers and a variety of other appetizers for sale to restaurant chains everywhere. According to *Restaurants and Institutions* magazine, Poppers were the #1 food item added to restaurant menus in 1995, with restaurants purchasing over 700 million of the little suckers.

It's important when you make these that you allow time for them to freeze. The freezing stage ensures that the coating stays on when the peppers are fried and prevents the cream cheese from squirting out as it heats up.

4 large, fresh jalapeño peppers
1/4 pound cream cheese
2 eggs
3/4 teaspoon salt
1 teaspoon vegetable oil
2/3 cup self-rising flour

1/8 teaspoon garlic powder
Dash of paprika
Dash onion powder
1/2 cup cornflake crumbs
Vegetable oil for frying

ON THE SIDE

Hot pepper jelly

Sour cream

1. Remove the stems from the jalapeños, then slice each one down the middle lengthwise and remove the seeds and inner membranes. Be careful to wash your hands afterward.
2. Poach the jalapeño halves in a saucepan half-filled with boiling water for 10 to 15 minutes or until tender. Drain and cool.
3. Blot with a cloth or paper towel to dry the inside of each jalapeño slice, then use a teaspoon to spread about ½ ounce of cream cheese into each jalapeño half.
4. Beat the eggs in a small, shallow bowl, then add ¼ teaspoon salt and the oil and combine with a whisk.
5. In another shallow bowl, combine the flour, ½ teaspoon salt, garlic powder, paprika, and onion powder.
6. Add the cornflake crumbs to a third shallow bowl.
7. Working one at a time, dip each stuffed jalapeño into the egg mixture, then into the flour mixture. Repeat, by again dipping the jalapeño into the egg and then back into the flour. Finally, dip the jalapeño back into the egg, then into the cornflake crumbs.
8. Put the coated peppers side by side on a plate and into the freezer for at least 2 hours. This way when the peppers are fried, the breading won't fall off and the cheese in the center won't ooze out.
9. When the peppers are frozen, heat vegetable oil in a deep fryer or deep saucepan to about 350°F. Use enough oil to cover the jalapeños when frying. Fry the peppers for 3½ to 4 minutes or until the outside is a dark golden brown. Drain on a rack or paper towels. Serve hot with pepper jelly and sour cream on the side.

- SERVES 2 TO 4 AS AN APPETIZER

TIDBITS

You can also make these ahead of time by frying them for only 1½ minutes and then refreezing them until you are ready to serve them. Then cook the frozen jalapeños in hot oil for 3½ minutes or until they are hot all the way through. You may also bake the frozen jalapeños in a 450°F oven on a greased baking pan for 10 to 15 minutes, turning them over halfway through the heating time.

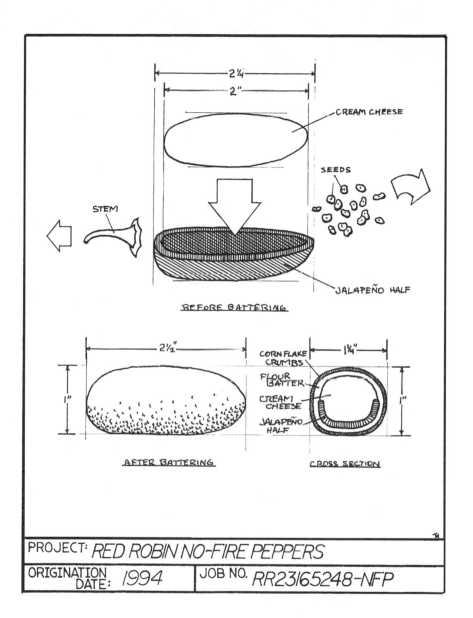

2 ¼"
2"

CREAM CHEESE

SEEDS

STEM

JALAPEÑO HALF

BEFORE BATTERING

2 ½"

1"

CORN FLAKE CRUMBS

FLOUR BATTER

CREAM CHEESE

JALAPEÑO HALF

1 ¼"

1"

AFTER BATTERING

CROSS SECTION

PROJECT: *RED ROBIN NO-FIRE PEPPERS*

ORIGINATION DATE: *1994*

JOB NO. *RR23165248-NFP*

RED ROBIN BBQ CHICKEN SALAD

☆   ♥   ☎   ✎   ✈   ⊠   ✄   ☞   ✿

Menu Description: "Breast of chicken basted in BBQ sauce & topped with cheddar cheese, tomato, fresh avocado, and black beans. Served with Ranch dressing & garlic cheese bread."

In 1969, Gerald Kingen bought a beat-up 30-year-old bar called Red Robin in Seattle across the road from the University of Washington. The pub did a booming business with the college and local crowd, but in 1973 building officials gave their opinion of the bar: Either fix it up or shut it down. Jerry not only fixed up the 1200-square-foot building, but also expanded it to three times its old size, to 3600 square feet, and added a kitchen to start making food. Red Robin soon became popular for its wide selection of gourmet burgers in addition to the designer cocktails served in kooky glasses. Jerry says he set out to create a chain of restaurants that would be recognized as "the adult McDonald's and poor man's Trader Vic's."

2 cups chopped romaine lettuce
2 cups chopped green leaf or iceberg
    lettuce
1/2 cup chopped red cabbage
1 small tomato, chopped (1/4 cup)
1 boneless, skinless chicken breast half
1/3 cup barbecue sauce (Bullseye or
    K.C. Masterpiece work well)

1/2 cup canned refried black beans
1/2 cup shredded Cheddar cheese
1/4 cup French's French Fried Onions
    (onion straws)
3 avocado slices (1/4 avocado)
1/4 cup ranch dressing

1. Toss the lettuces and cabbage together and arrange on a large plate.
2. Arrange the tomato on the lettuce mixture at the bottom of the plate.

3. Grill the chicken breast on a hot barbecue grill for 4 to 5 minutes per side or until done. Brush a generous coating of barbecue sauce over the chicken as it grills.
4. Heat the black beans in the microwave or in a saucepan over medium heat.
5. Spread the black beans over the lettuce on the left side of the plate.
6. Slice the warm chicken into bite-size pieces and arrange them neatly over the lettuce in the center of the plate.
7. Sprinkle the cheese over the lettuce on the right side of the plate.
8. Sprinkle the onion straws over the cheese.
9. Garnish the salad with 3 slices of avocado arranged side by side on the right rim of the plate. Serve with the ranch dressing and the remaining barbecue sauce on the side.

- SERVES 1 AS AN ENTREE (CAN BE DOUBLED)

TIDBITS

You can also make the onion straws yourself by following this simple recipe:

ONION STRAWS

2 cups vegetable oil	½ teaspoon baking soda
¼ cup very thinly sliced white onion	¼ teaspoon salt
½ cup all-purpose flour	⅔ cup cold water

1. Heat the oil in a wide saucepan to about 350°F.
2. Slice the onion into very thin onion rings and then cut the rings in half, making long strips or straws. Try to slice the onion as thin as possible.
3. Combine the flour, baking soda, and salt in a large bowl. Add the cold water and whisk until the batter is smooth.
4. When the oil is hot, drop the onions into the batter. Remove the onions one at a time, let them drip off a bit, and then place them into the hot oil. You will want to cook these for about 2 minutes apiece, or until you see them turn a golden brown. Drain the onion straws on a paper towel.

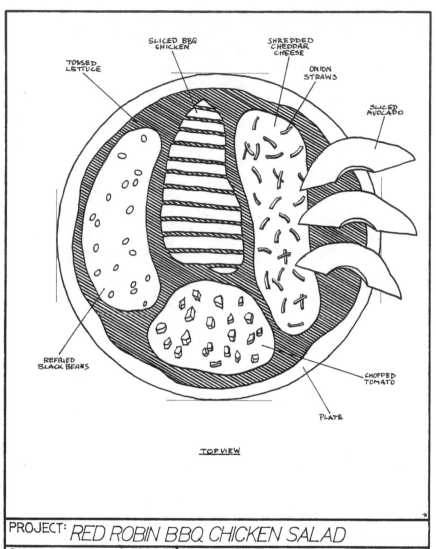

SLICED BBQ
CHICKEN

SHREDDED
CHEDDAR
CHEESE

TOSSED
LETTUCE

ONION
STRAWS

SLICED
AVOCADO

REFRIED
BLACK BEANS

CHOPPED
TOMATO

PLATE

TOP VIEW

PROJECT: *RED ROBIN BBQ CHICKEN SALAD*

ORIGINATION
DATE: 19██

JOB NO. *RR73167313-BCS*

RED ROBIN MOUNTAIN HIGH MUDD PIE

☆　♥　☎　✎　✈　✉　✂　☞　✿

Gerald Kingen is a man with a mission. In 1985 he sold his successful Red Robin chain of restaurants to Tokyo-based Skylark Co. Ltd. Unhappy with the changes the new owners were implementing, Jerry and a partner purchased a "substantial equity position" of the Irvine, California–based Red Robin in March of 1996. Now Jerry is once again at the helm of the company, with a goal of reviving old menu items and living up to the old slogan as "the world's greatest gourmet burger maker & most masterful mixologists."

A unique signature dessert item is the Mountain High Mudd Pie, which servers claim is one of the most ordered desserts on the menu. Save some room for this giant-size sundae made from chocolate and vanilla ice cream with peanut butter, caramel, and fudge sauce. There are several stages of freezing, so give yourself at least seven hours to allow for these steps. This dessert is big and serves at least a dozen, so it's good for a small party or gathering, or makes a unique birthday cake. If there's only a few of you, leftovers can be frozen in a sealed container for several weeks and enjoyed later.

6 cups chocolate ice cream
1 cup peanut butter cookie pieces
6 cups vanilla ice cream
1⅔ cups creamy peanut butter
4 chocolate-flavored graham crackers
1 cup fudge topping
One 20-ounce squirt bottle chocolate
　　topping

One 20-ounce squirt bottle caramel
　　topping
1 can whipped cream
¾ cup chopped peanuts
12 maraschino cherries, with stems

1. Soften the chocolate ice cream and load it into the bottom of a 2½- to 3-quart mixing bowl. Make sure the surface of the ice cream is smooth and leveled.

2. Spread the peanut butter cookie pieces evenly over the top of the ice cream, then cover the bowl and put it back into the freezer for at least 1 hour. (If you can't find packaged peanut butter cookies, use the recipe in "Tidbits.")

3. Soften the vanilla ice cream and spread it over the chocolate ice cream and cookie pieces. Again, be sure to smooth and level the surface of the ice cream. Cover the bowl with plastic wrap and put it back into the freezer for at least 1 hour.

4. Use a spatula to spread ⅔ cup of peanut butter over the surface of the ice cream. Be sure the ice cream has hardened before you do this or it could get sloppy.

5. Crush the chocolate graham crackers into crumbs and spread them evenly over the peanut butter. Put the bowl back into the freezer for at least 1 hour.

6. Remove the bowl from the freezer and hold it in a sink filled with warm water for about 1 minute. You want the ice cream around the edges to soften just enough that you can invert the ice cream onto a plate.

7. Turn a large plate upside down and place it on top of the bowl. Flip the bowl and plate over together, and tap gently on the bowl until the ice cream falls out onto the plate. You may have to put the bowl back into the water if it's stubborn. Once the ice cream is out, cover it with plastic wrap and place it back in the freezer for another 1 or 2 hours.

8. Without heating it up, spread the fudge evenly over the entire surface of the ice cream mountain. Put the fudge-coated ice cream back into the freezer for 1 hour.

9. When the fudge has hardened, spread the remaining 1 cup of peanut butter over the entire surface as well. Once again, back into the freezer for at least 1 hour. We're almost there.

10. Slice the ice cream with a warm knife into 12 pieces. Put waxed paper between the cuts so that when you serve it later, it is easy to divide. Then slip it back into the freezer, covered.

11. When serving, first coat a plate with a criss-cross pattern of chocolate and caramel sauce. Make three parallel lines down the

plate with the squirt bottle of chocolate sauce. Then three parallel horizontal lines made with the bottle of caramel sauce.

12. Place the slice of ice cream upright onto the plate toward the back of the design.

13. Spray whipped cream on top and down the curved edge of the ice cream slice, onto the plate over the sauces. Be generous.

14. Sprinkle about a tablespoon of chopped nuts over your creation.

15. Add a cherry to the top. Marvel at the beauty, then dig in or serve it before it melts. Repeat for the remaining slices.

• SERVES 12

TIDBITS

If you would like to make your own peanut butter cookies, rather than buying them pre-made, here is a recipe that makes about 2 dozen tasty cookies—more than enough for the ice cream dessert.

PEANUT BUTTER COOKIES

½ cup butter, softened
½ cup granulated sugar
½ cup firmly packed brown sugar
½ cup creamy peanut butter
1 egg

1 ¼ teaspoons vanilla extract
1 ½ cups all-purpose flour
1 teaspoon baking soda
½ teaspoon salt

1. Preheat the oven to 325°F.

2. Use an electric mixture to combine the butter with the sugars in a large bowl until creamy.

3. Add the peanut butter, egg, and vanilla and mix until smooth.

4. Sift together the flour, baking soda, and salt, and combine with the moist ingredients in the large bowl. Mix the dough until all of the ingredients are smooth and well blended.

5. Drop rounded tablespoons of the dough onto an ungreased cookie sheet. Press the dough flat with a fork and bake for 15 to 18 minutes, until the edges of the cookies begin to turn light brown.

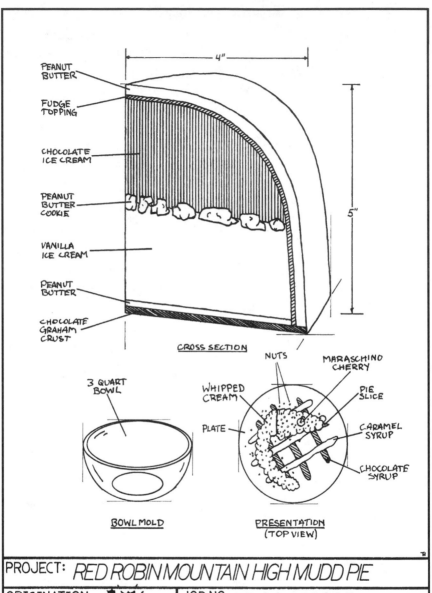

PEANUT BUTTER

FUDGE TOPPING

CHOCOLATE ICE CREAM

PEANUT BUTTER COOKIE

VANILLA ICE CREAM

PEANUT BUTTER

CHOCOLATE GRAHAM CRUST

4"

5"

CROSS SECTION

3 QUART BOWL

BOWL MOLD

NUTS

MARASCHINO CHERRY

WHIPPED CREAM

PIE SLICE

PLATE

CARAMEL SYRUP

CHOCOLATE SYRUP

PRESENTATION
(TOP VIEW)

PROJECT: *RED ROBIN MOUNTAIN HIGH MUDD PIE*

ORIGINATION DATE:

JOB NO. *RR443160265-MHMP*

RUBY TUESDAY
POTATO CHEESE SOUP

☆ ♥ ☎ ✎ ✈ ✉ ✂ ☞ ✿

Sandy Beall started managing Pizza Huts while a freshman at the University of Tennessee, to get out of fraternity house duties. It was just three years later that Sandy's boss at Pizza Hut would favor him with quite a nice gift: $10,000 to invest in a dream. With that, Sandy and four of his fraternity buddies pitched in to open the first Ruby Tuesday on the university campus in Knoxville, Tennessee, in 1972. Sandy was only 21 at the time.

Here's a great soup that can be served by the cup or in large bowls as a meal in itself. Along with the potatoes is a little bit of minced celery, some minced onion, and a small amount of grated carrot for color. An additional pinch of cheese, crumbled bacon, and chopped green onion make a tasty garnish just like on the Ruby Tuesday original.

2 large russet potatoes
2 tablespoons finely minced celery
    (½ stalk)
1 tablespoon finely minced onion
1 tablespoon grated carrot (¼ carrot)
2 cups chicken stock or broth
1 teaspoon salt
2 teaspoons white vinegar

2 tablespoons flour
1½ cups milk
1 cup plus 1 tablespoon shredded
    Cheddar cheese
1 tablespoon shredded Monterey Jack
    cheese
2 slices bacon, cooked
1 tablespoon chopped green onion

1. Peel the potatoes and chop them into bite-size pieces—you should have about 4 cups. Make sure the celery and onion are minced into very small pieces about the size of a grain of rice. The carrot should be grated into very small pieces, not shredded.
2. Combine the vegetables with the chicken, stock, salt, and vinegar in a large saucepan over medium heat. Bring the stock to a

boil, then turn down the heat, cover the pan, and simmer for 20 minutes.

3. Whisk together the flour and milk in a medium bowl.

4. Remove the saucepan of vegetables from the heat and add the flour and milk mixture. Put the pan back on the heat and simmer, uncovered, for 5 to 8 minutes or until the soup has thickened.

5. Add 1 cup Cheddar cheese to the soup and simmer until melted. By this time the potatoes should be tender and falling apart. If not, continue to cook until the soup is as thick as you like it.

6. To serve, spoon the soup into bowls. Divide the remaining 1 tablespoon of Cheddar and the Monterey Jack and sprinkle on the soup. Crumble the bacon and sprinkle it evenly on top of the cheese. Top off each bowl of soup with chopped green onion.

- SERVES 4 AS AN APPETIZER, 2 AS AN ENTREE

RUBY TUESDAY
SMOKEY MOUNTAIN
CHICKEN

☆　♥　☎　✎　✈　✉　✂　☛　✿

Menu Description: "Chicken breast topped with ham, barbecue sauce, tomatoes, scallions and cheese. Served with fries."

When the founder of Ruby Tuesday, Sandy Beall, was reviewing some early designs of printed materials for his planned restaurant, he saw that some of the art featured the faces of University of Tennessee students printed in red. At that moment Sandy knew he wanted to call the eatery "ruby something." Meanwhile, he and the four fraternity friends who joined him in the investment had been listening to lots of Rolling Stones music. One day when Sandy heard "Ruby Tuesday" come on the jukebox, he convinced his partners that they had finally found a name.

You may find a little something unusual in the name for this dish. Ruby Tuesday's menu became a victim of a common spelling error in the word "smoky." Apparently the dish is named after the Great Smoky Mountains that lie between North Carolina and Tennessee, but there's no "e" in that name or in the general spelling of the word "smoky." But, hey, what do you want: good spelling or good taste? And this dish, which combines chicken breast, ham and barbecue sauce, topped with tomatoes, scallions and cheese, tastes great no matter how you spell it. Thanks, Rubey Tuesday.

2 whole boneless chicken breasts
　　(with skin)
Vegetable or olive oil
Salt
Pinch dried thyme

Pinch dried summer savory
4 slices deli-sliced smoked ham
2 tablespoons hickory smoke barbecue
　　sauce (Bullseye is good)
2 slices provolone cheese

½ medium tomato, chopped (¼ cup)

1 green onion, chopped (2 tablespoons)

ON THE SIDE

French fries   Rice

1. Prepare the barbecue or preheat the stovetop grill.
2. Rub a little oil on the chicken, then sprinkle some salt, thyme, and savory on each chicken breast.
3. Grill the chicken on a hot, covered barbecue for 4 to 5 minutes per side, starting with the skin side up. When you flip the chicken over with the skin side down, wait a couple minutes, then put the slices of ham on the grill. This is just to heat up the ham; be careful not to scorch it.
4. When you think the chicken is about a minute away from being done, brush 1 tablespoon of barbecue sauce over the entire face-up surface of the chicken.
5. Stack 2 slices of ham on each breast, then lay a slice of provolone on top.
6. Grill the chicken until the cheese has melted, then remove the breasts from the heat.
7. Serve each breast topped with 2 tablespoons of the tomatoes and a tablespoon of green onion. Serve immediately with a side of French-fried potatoes or rice if desired.

- SERVES 2 AS AN ENTREE

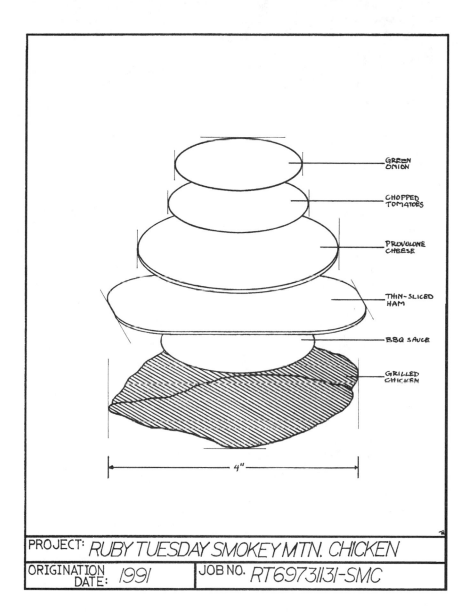

GREEN ONION

CHOPPED TOMATOES

PROVOLONE CHEESE

THIN-SLICED HAM

BBQ SAUCE

GRILLED CHICKEN

4"

PROJECT: *RUBY TUESDAY SMOKEY MTN. CHICKEN*

ORIGINATION DATE: *1991*

JOB NO. *RT69731131-SMC*

RUBY TUESDAY
SONORA CHICKEN PASTA

☆　♥　☎　✎　✈　✉　✂　☞　✿

Menu Description: "Penne pasta tossed in a spicy Southwestern cheese sauce, topped with grilled chicken, spicy black beans, scallions and more."

If you like pasta, black beans, and chicken, you'll love having it all swimming together in this spicy cheese sauce. The chicken is prepared over an open grill, then sliced before laying it over a bed of pasta and cheese sauce. The black beans and peppers give this dish a decidedly Southwestern flair.

1 pound Velveeta cheese spread (or
    one 16-ounce jar Cheez Whiz)
1/2 cup heavy cream
2 tablespoons minced red chili pepper
4 tablespoons green chili pepper
    (1/2 pepper), minced
4 tablespoons minced onion
1 clove garlic, minced
2 teaspoons olive oil
2 tablespoons water
1/2 teaspoon salt
2 teaspoons sugar
1/2 tablespoon vinegar

1/4 teaspoon cumin
One 15-ounce can black beans
Dash paprika
4 boneless, skinless chicken breast
    halves
Vegetable oil
Dash dried thyme
Dash dried summer savory
One 16-ounce box penne pasta
1 tablespoon butter
2 Roma (plum) tomatoes, chopped
2 to 4 green onions, chopped

1.　Prepare the barbecue or preheat your stovetop grill.
2.　Combine the cheese spread with the cream in a small saucepan over medium/low heat. Stir the cheese often until it melts and becomes smooth.
3.　Sauté the red chili pepper and 2 tablespoons green chili pepper,

2 tablespoons onion, and ½ clove garlic in the olive oil for a couple minutes then add the water to the pan so that the peppers do not scorch. Simmer another 2 minutes or until the water has cooked off.

4. When the cheese is smooth, add the sautéed vegetables, ¼ teaspoon salt, sugar, vinegar, and cumin. Leave on low heat, stirring occasionally, until the other ingredients are ready.

5. Pour the entire can of beans with the liquid into a small saucepan over medium heat. Add the remaining green chili pepper, onions, garlic, a pinch of salt, and a dash of paprika. Bring the beans to a boil, stirring often, then reduce the heat to low and simmer until everything else is ready. By this time the beans will have thickened and the onions will have become transparent.

6. Rub the chicken breasts lightly with oil, then season with salt, thyme, and savory.

7. Cook the breasts on a hot grill for 5 minutes per side or until done. When they have cooked thoroughly, remove them from the grill and use a sharp knife to slice each breast into ½-inch slices, so that they are easier to eat. Retain the shape of the chicken breast by keeping the slices in order with one hand as you slice.

8. As the chicken cooks, prepare the pasta in a large pot filled with 3 to 4 quarts of boiling water. Cook the pasta for 12 to 14 minutes or until tender. Drain the pasta in a colander, and toss with the butter.

9. When everything is ready, spoon one-fourth of the pasta onto each plate.

10. Pour about ⅓ cup of cheese sauce over the pasta.

11. Carefully add a sliced breast of chicken, being sure to maintain its shape as you lay the slices on the bed of pasta.

12. Spread ⅓ cup of the black beans over the chicken.

13. Sprinkle ¼ cup of chopped tomatoes on the beans.

14. Sprinkle about 1 tablespoon of green onions on the tomatoes and serve immediately. Salt to taste.

- SERVES 4 AS AN ENTREE

You can make a lighter version of this meal by using the lower fat version of the Cheez Whiz or Velveeta cheese spreads.

RUBY TUESDAY STRAWBERRY TALLCAKE FOR TWO

☆　♥　☎　✎　✈　✉　✄　☞　✿

Menu Description: "Three layers of light and airy sponge cake and strawberry mousse, drenched in strawberry sauce, topped with vanilla ice cream, fresh strawberries and whipped cream."

The Strawberry Tallcake is a signature, trademarked item for Ruby Tuesday. It's pretty big, so plan on sharing it. This copycat recipe requires that you bake the sponge cake in a large, shallow pan—I use a cookie sheet that has turned-up edges to hold in the batter. And you might find the strawberry mousse that is used to frost the cake makes a great, simple-to-make dessert on its own.

STRAWBERRY MOUSSE AND SAUCE

One 10-ounce package frozen
　　strawberries in syrup
1¾ cups water

One 3-ounce package strawberry Jell-
　　O
1 cup heavy cream

SPONGE CAKE

5 eggs, separated
1½ cups sugar
½ cup cold water
2 teaspoons vanilla

1½ cups all-purpose flour
½ teaspoon baking powder
½ teaspoon salt
½ teaspoon cream of tartar

12 to 18 scoops vanilla ice cream
　　(½ gallon)

½ pint fresh strawberries, sliced
1 can whipped cream

1. Defrost the frozen strawberries and pour the entire package, including the syrup, into a blender or food processor and purée for 10 to 15 seconds until smooth.
2. Combine the strawberry purée with 1½ cups of the water in a small saucepan over medium heat.
3. When the strawberry mixture comes to a boil, add the entire package of Jell-O, stir to dissolve, and remove the pan from the heat to cool.
4. When the strawberry mixture has cooled to room temperature, divide it in half into two medium bowls.
5. Beat the whipping cream until it is thick and forms peaks. Fold the cream into one of the bowls of the strawberry mixture until well combined. This is your strawberry mousse. Cover and chill.
6. To the other bowl, add the remaining ¼ cup of water. This is the strawberry syrup. Cover and chill this mixture as well.
7. Preheat the oven to 350°F.
8. Beat the egg yolks until they turn creamy and a much lighter shade of yellow.
9. Add the sugar and blend it well into the yolks.
10. Add the water and vanilla and combine well with the yolk mixture.
11. Sift together the flour, baking powder, and salt, and add it to the yolk mixture. Mix well until the batter is smooth.
12. In a separate bowl, beat the egg whites until smooth, then add the cream of tartar. Continue beating until the whites are stiff and form peaks.
13. Fold the egg whites into the batter and mix slowly just until well combined.
14. Pour the batter into an ungreased 17 × 11-inch cookie sheet (with turned-up edges all the way around) and bake for 25 to 30 minutes or until the top of the sponge cake is a light brown color.
15. When the cake has cooled and the mousse has firmed up, you are ready to assemble the cake. First divide the cake into three even sections by cutting down the width of the cake twice with a sharp knife. Be sure the cake has come loose from the pan. You may need to use a spatula to unstick the cake sections.
16. Divide the mousse in half and spread each half onto two sec-

tions of the cake. Carefully place the layers on top of each other so that the mousse has been sandwiched in the middle between the three layers. This cake can be stored in the refrigerator for several days until you need it.

17. When you are ready to assemble the dessert, slice the cake into 6 even sections. Put a slice into a medium-sized bowl (or a large goblet if you have one), then arrange 2 to 3 scoops of vanilla ice cream around the cake. Pour a sixth (just over ¼ cup) of the strawberry sauce over the top of the cake and ice cream, sprinkle some sliced strawberries on top, then cover the thing with whipped cream. Repeat with the remaining servings.

- MAKES SIX 2-PERSON SERVINGS

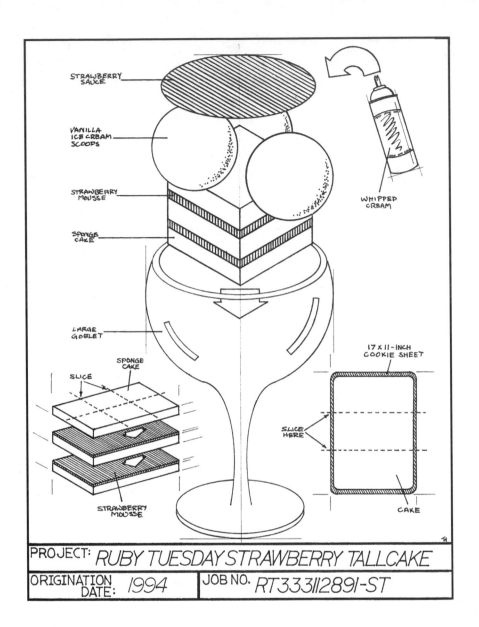

STRAWBERRY SAUCE

VANILLA ICE CREAM SCOOPS

STRAWBERRY MOUSSE

SPONGE CAKE

LARGE GOBLET

SLICE

SPONGE CAKE

STRAWBERRY MOUSSE

WHIPPED CREAM

17 X 11-INCH COOKIE SHEET

SLICE HERE

CAKE

PROJECT: *RUBY TUESDAY STRAWBERRY TALLCAKE*

ORIGINATION DATE: *1994*

JOB NO. *RT33112891-ST*

RUTH'S CHRIS STEAK HOUSE BARBECUED SHRIMP

☆　♥　☎　✎　✈　⊠　✂　☞　✿

In 1965, Ruth Fertel, divorced with two kids in their teens, was looking for a better way to support herself in her native New Orleans. Her job as a lab technician wasn't paying enough for her to send the kids to college, so she went to the classifieds to find something better. There she found a steakhouse for sale, and determined that this might be her ticket. She mortgaged her house to raise $18,000 (against the advice of her attorney) and purchased the restaurant, then called Chris Steak House. Ruth sold 35 steaks on opening day　not much for a restaurant that now sells 10,000 a day. But the restaurant would eventually become a big hit, and within the first year Ruth was making more than twice her salary at the lab.

In keeping with the New Orleans flavor of many of the Ruth's Chris dishes, this barbecued shrimp is actually Cajun-style broiled shrimp with a little kick to it.

5 to 6 large uncooked shrimp
¼ cup (½ stick) butter, melted
1 tablespoon Louisiana hot sauce
　(Frank's Red Hot or Crystal
　are good)
2 cloves garlic, pressed
¼ teaspoon salt

½ teaspoon coarsely ground or
　cracked black pepper
½ teaspoon finely chopped fresh
　parsley
Pinch dried rosemary
Lemon wedges

1. Preheat the oven to 400°F.
2. Shell and devein the shrimp.
3. In a small baking dish, combine the melted butter with the hot sauce, garlic, salt, cracked pepper, parsley, and rosemary. Stir.

4. Arrange the shrimp side by side in the baking dish and bake for 6 to 8 minutes. Immediately broil the shrimp for 2 to 4 minutes or until the shrimp are done, but not chewy. Squeeze some lemon juice over the shrimp. Serve the shrimp sizzling hot in the baking dish.

    • SERVES 2 AS AN APPETIZER

RUTH'S CHRIS STEAK HOUSE PETITE FILET

☆ ♥ ☎ ✎ ✈ ✉ ✂ ☛ ✿

Menu Description: "A smaller, but equally tender filet ... the tenderest corn-fed Mid-western beef. So tender it practically melts in your mouth."

This is the signature item for the Ruth's Chris chain. It's a delicious filet mignon that comes to your table sizzling hot and does seem to melt in your mouth as the menu claims. If you want to prepare filets the Ruth's Chris way you first need some corn-fed filets, which can be found in specialty meat markets or through mail-order outlets such as Omaha Steaks. If you can't find corn-fed beef, you can still use this cooking method with filet purchased at your supermarket, but the meat will likely not be as tasty and tender.

I've designed this recipe to duplicate the petite filet on the Ruth's Chris menu, since the larger filet is around 14 ounces. That size can be difficult to obtain unless you cut your own. Ruth's Chris uses a special broiler which reaches temperatures as high as 1800°F. It's likely you don't have such an oven, so you will have to use a conventional oven set on high broil, with the rack placed up near the top. You want to be sure the filet is about 5 to 6 inches away from the heat source, and if you have gas, be very careful to watch for flame-ups from spattering. If you begin to get flames, move the rack to a lower level so that you don't start a fire. Also, you need to have ceramic oven-safe plates to serve this meat properly sizzling. This recipe assumes that your broiler is located at the top of the oven. If not, you won't be able to use this technique until you get a new oven. Sorry.

Four 8-ounce filet mignon steaks
6 tablespoons butter, softened
Salt

Pepper
2 teaspoons chopped fresh parsley

1. Preheat the broiler.
2. Prepare the filets by drying them with a cloth or paper towel and rubbing ½ tablespoon of butter per steak over the top and bottom. Salt and pepper the filet.
3. Make sure your broiler is on high and that it is good and hot. It should have preheated for *at least* 30 minutes. Put four oven-safe ceramic serving plates on the bottom rack in the oven when you start to preheat the broiler and through the entire cooking time. Move another rack up to the top so that when you put the filets in they will be about 5 to 6 inches from the heat. You will have to check the filets periodically to be sure they haven't flamed up. Cook the meat in a broiler pan, turning halfway through cooking time for the following length of time based on your preference:

COOKING CHART

4 to 6 minutes per side—Rare
5 to 7 minutes per side—Medium Rare
6 to 8 minutes per side—Medium
7 to 9 minutes per side—Medium Well
8 to 11 minutes per side—Well

4. When the meat is done, carefully remove the ceramic plates from the oven. On each of them, place 1 tablespoon of butter. It should sizzle.
5. When the butter has melted, place a steak in the center of the plate.
6. Sprinkle a pinch of the parsley on top of the meat, and another pinch around it onto the butter.
7. Serve the dishes sizzling hot.

- SERVES 4 AS AN ENTREE

TIDBITS

Try cooking other cuts of meat using this same method—delicious! Of course, the broiling time will vary depending on the thickness of your meat.

RUTH'S CHRIS STEAK HOUSE CREAMED SPINACH

☆ ♥ ☎ ✎ ✈ ✉ ✂ ☞ ✿

"Ruth's Chris Steak House" is such a difficult name to spit out that a restaurant critic suggested it be used as a sobriety test. Surely anyone who could say the name three times fast couldn't possibly be intoxicated. But the hard-to-say name has probably worked well for the steakhouse chain; it is surely a memorable one. The name came from the first restaurant that Ruth purchased in 1965 called Chris Steak House. When she opened a second restaurant with that same name, the previous owner, Chris Matulich, tried to sue her. She won the case, but to avoid future lawsuits she put her name in front of the original and it became the tongue twister we know today.

The delicious creamed spinach served at Ruth's Chris inspired this recipe that has just a hint of cayenne pepper in it for that Louisiana zing. The recipe requires a package of frozen spinach to make it convenient, but you can use the same amount of fresh spinach if you prefer.

One 10-ounce package frozen
    chopped spinach
2 tablespoons butter
1½ tablespoons all-purpose flour
½ cup heavy cream

¼ teaspoon salt
Dash pepper
Dash nutmeg
Dash cayenne pepper

1. Cook the spinach following the directions on the package. Drain and squeeze all the liquid from the spinach when it's done.
2. Melt the butter in a saucepan over medium heat. Be careful not to burn it.
3. Add the flour to the melted butter and stir until smooth.

4. Add the cream and heat for 2 to 3 minutes or until the sauce thickens. Stir constantly so that sauce does not burn.
5. Add the spinach, salt, pepper, nutmeg, and cayenne. Cook for 2 to 4 minutes, stirring often. Serve hot.

- SERVES 4 AS A SIDE DISH

RUTH'S CHRIS STEAK HOUSE POTATOES AU GRATIN

☆ ♥ ☎ ✎ ✈ ✉ ✂ ☛ ✿

Menu Description: "In cream sauce, topped with melted sharp cheddar."

There are many ways to order potatoes from the Ruth's Chris menu including steak fries, julienne fries, shoestring fries, cottage fries, Lyonnaise, baked, and au gratin.

Here is a traditional, classic recipe for the delicious side dish inspired by the Ruth's Chris creation. You may use less of the cream and milk mixture in your version depending on the size baking dish you use and the size of your potatoes. Stop adding the creamy mixture when it is level with the sliced potatoes in the baking dish. Be sure to use a casserole dish that has a lid for the first stage of the baking.

3 to 4 medium russet potatoes,
   peeled
1 cup heavy cream
½ cup milk
1 ½ tablespoons flour
1 large clove garlic, pressed

¼ teaspoon salt
⅛ teaspoon pepper
1 tablespoon butter, softened
1 ½ cups grated Cheddar cheese
1 teaspoon finely chopped fresh
   parsley

1. Preheat the oven to 400°F.
2. Cut the potatoes into ¼-inch slices, then quarter each of those slices.
3. Beat together the cream, milk, flour, garlic, salt, and pepper by hand just until well combined.
4. Coat the inside of a large baking dish with the softened butter.
5. Arrange one-fourth of the potatoes on the bottom of the dish.

Pour some of the cream mixture over the potatoes. Repeat this layering step three more times.

6. Cover the potatoes and bake for 20 minutes. Uncover, and bake another 40 minutes or until the potatoes are starting to brown on top.

7. Sprinkle grated cheese over the top of the potatoes and continue to bake for 5 to 10 minutes or until the cheese is melted and slightly browned and the potatoes are tender.

8. Sprinkle the parsley on top and serve.

• SERVES 4 TO 6 AS A SIDE DISH

SHONEY'S COUNTRY FRIED STEAK

☆　♥　☎　✎　✈　✉　✂　☞　✿

Menu Description: "Tender steak, lightly breaded and golden fried. Smothered with country milk gravy."

Alex Schoenbaum opened the doors to his first restaurant, Parkette, a drive-in in Charleston, West Virginia, in 1947, at the start of a boom in popularity of the classic American drive-in restaurants many of us now know only from reruns of *Happy Days*. Schoenbaum's restaurant did very well and he decided, in 1951, to purchase a Big Boy franchise, the fastest growing chain at the time. In 1953, Parkette changed its name to Shoney's Big Boy.

Today Shoney's is no longer affiliated with Big Boy, but maintains a menu that features the Southern homestyle favorites that have made it so successful for so long. One of the old-time favorites is the Country Fried Steak smothered in peppered milk gravy. The technique here is to freeze the steaks after they have been breaded with flour. This way the coating won't wash off when the steaks are fried—the same technique the restaurants use.

2 cups all-purpose flour
1 tablespoon salt
1/4 teaspoon ground black pepper

2 cups water
Four 4-ounce cube steaks
Vegetable oil for frying

COUNTRY GRAVY

1 1/2 tablespoons ground beef
1/4 cup all-purpose flour
2 cups chicken stock
2 cups whole milk

1/4 teaspoon coarsely ground black pepper
1/2 teaspoon salt

1. Prepare the steaks at least several hours before you plan to serve this meal. First, sift the flour, salt, and pepper together into a large, shallow bowl. Pour the water into another shallow bowl.
2. Trim the steaks of any fat, then use your hand to press down firmly on each cube steak on a hard surface to flatten it out a bit. You don't want the steaks too thick.
3. Dredge each steak, one at a time, first in the water and then in the flour. Repeat this one more time so that each steak has been coated twice.
4. When all four steaks have been coated, place them on waxed paper and put them into the freezer for several hours until they are solid. This is the same technique used at the restaurant chain to ensure that the flour coating won't fall off when frying the steaks.
5. About 10 minutes before you are ready to cook the steaks, prepare the gravy by browning the ground beef in a small frying pan. Crumble the meat into tiny pieces as you cook it.
6. Transfer the meat to a medium saucepan over medium heat. Add ¼ cup flour and stir it in with the ground beef. Add the remaining ingredients for the gravy and bring to a boil, stirring often. Cook for 10 to 15 minutes until thick. Reduce the heat to low to keep the gravy warm while the steaks are prepared.
7. As the gravy is cooking, heat oil in a deep fryer or a deep frying pan over medium/high heat to 350°F. You want enough oil to cover the steaks when frying.
8. When the oil is hot, drop the steaks, one at a time, into the oil. Fry for 8 to 10 minutes or until golden brown, then drain on paper towels.
9. Serve the steaks with gravy poured over the top, with a side of mashed potatoes, grits, or steamed vegetables, if desired.

• SERVES 4 AS AN ENTREE

SHONEY'S SLOW-COOKED POT ROAST

☆ ♥ ☎ ✎ ✈ ✉ ✄ ☞ ✿

Menu Description: "Tender roast beef and carrots slow-simmered and served in a rich brown gravy."

Remember Mom's delicious pot roast? Shoney's tender slow-cooked entree is just as good, if not better than, many home recipes. The secret to making tender, flaky pot roast is the long slow-cooking process with frequent basting—and then cooking in the pan juices after flaking the meat. This recipe, based on Shoney's popular dish, requires 3 to 4 hours of cooking to make the meat tender. The meat is then flaked apart, put back into the pot with the pan juices and carrots, and cooked more to infuse the meat with flavor. The original recipe requires a rump roast, a tough cut of meat before cooking, which is reasonably low in fat. If you like, you can also use the more tender and less costly chuck roast. This cut of meat requires about an hour less time in the oven to tenderize it because of its higher fat content.

POT ROAST

2 tablespoons butter
One 4-pound rump roast
1 onion, chopped
2 stalks celery, chopped
1 bay leaf
1 large clove garlic, chopped
20 whole peppercorns

1½ teaspoons fresh thyme
*   (or ½ teaspoon dried)*
1½ teaspoons fresh parsley
*   (or ½ teaspoon dried)*
2 cups beef stock or canned beef broth
1 teaspoon salt
2 large carrots, sliced

2 cups beef stock or canned   ⅓ cup all-purpose flour
   beef broth   Salt and pepper to taste

ON THE SIDE

Mashed potatoes

1. Preheat the oven to 325°F.
2. Melt the butter in a large oven-safe pot or Dutch oven and sear all sides of the roast in the melted butter for 2 to 3 minutes per side, or until all sides are browned.
3. Remove the meat from the pot to a plate. Add the onion, celery, bay leaf, garlic, peppercorns, thyme, and parsley to the pot that the meat was in and sauté over high heat for 5 minutes until the onion starts to brown.
4. Put the roast back in the pot with the vegetables. Add the beef stock and ½ teaspoon salt.
5. Cook the meat in the oven, covered, for 4 hours or until the meat is tender enough to tear apart. Every half hour or so baste the meat with the broth so that it doesn't dry out.
6. When the roast is tender, remove it from the pot and strain the stock into a medium bowl. Discard the vegetables and spices, but keep the stock.
7. Using two forks, shred the roast apart into slightly bigger than bite size chunks. Put the meat back into the pot and pour the stock over it. Add the remaining ½ teaspoon salt and the carrots.
8. Put the pot back into the oven and cook for 40 to 50 minutes. This will make the meat even more tender and fill it with flavor. By this time the carrots should be tender.
9. Just before serving the pot roast make a gravy by straining the stock from the pot roast and combining it with an additional 2 cups of beef stock. Sprinkle the flour into a medium saucepan and stir in the liquid. (You should have about 3 cups of stock altogether. If not, add water until you have 3 cups of liquid.) Bring the mixture to a boil, stirring often until thick. Remove from the heat.

10. Serve the pot roast and carrots on a bed of mashed potatoes with the gravy poured over the top. Salt and pepper to taste.

- SERVES 6 TO 8 AS AN ENTREE

SHONEY'S
HOT FUDGE CAKE

☆　♥　☎　✎　✈　✉　✂　☞　✿

Menu Description: "Vanilla ice cream between two pieces of devil's food cake. Served with hot fudge, creamy topping and a cherry."

One of Shoney's signature dessert items is this Hot Fudge Cake, a dessert worshipped by all who taste it. It's such a simple recipe for something that tastes so good. To make construction of this treat simpler for you, the recipe calls for a prepackaged devil's food cake mix like that which you can find in just about any supermarket baking aisle. Bear in mind when you shop for ingredients for this recipe that the vanilla ice cream must come in a box, so that the ice cream slices can be arranged properly between the cake layers. Leftovers can be frozen and served up to several weeks later.

One 18.25-ounce box devil's food
    cake mix
3 eggs
1 1/3 cups water
1/3 cup vegetable oil
1 half-gallon box vanilla ice cream
    (must be in a box)

One 16-ounce jar chocolate fudge
    topping
1 can whipped cream
12 maraschino cherries

1. Mix the batter for the cake as instructed on the box of the cake mix by combining cake mix, eggs, water, and vegetable oil in a large mixing bowl.

2. Measure only 4 cups of the batter into a well-greased 13 × 9-inch baking pan. This will leave about 1 cup of batter in the bowl, which you can discard or use for another recipe, such as cupcakes.

3. Bake the cake according to the box instructions. Allow the cake to cool completely.

4. When the cake has cooled, carefully remove it from the pan, and place it right side up onto a sheet of waxed paper. With a long knife (a bread knife works great) slice horizontally through the middle of the cake, and carefully remove the top.

5. Pick up the waxed paper with the bottom of the cake still on it, and place it back into the baking pan.

6. Take the ice cream from the freezer and, working quickly, tear the box open so that you can slice it like bread.

7. Make six ¾-inch-thick slices and arrange them on the cake bottom in the pan. Cover the entire surface of the cake with ice cream. You will most likely have to cut 2 of the ice cream slices in half to make it all fit. Hey, it's a puzzle ... that melts!

8. When you have covered the entire bottom cake half with ice cream slices, carefully place the top half of the cake onto the ice cream layer. You now have ice cream sandwiched between the two halves of your cake. Cover the whole pan with plastic wrap or foil and pop it into your freezer for a couple hours (it will keep well in here for weeks as long as you keep it covered).

9. When you are ready to serve the dessert, slice the cake so that it will make 12 even slices—slice lengthwise twice and crosswise three times. You may not want to slice what you won't be serving at the time so that the remainder will stay fresh. Leave the cake you are using out for 5 minutes to defrost a bit.

10. Heat up the fudge either in a microwave or in a jar immersed in a saucepan of water over medium/low heat.

11. Pour the fudge over the cake slices and to each add a small mountain of whipped cream.

12. Top off each cake with a cherry stuck into the center of the whipped cream.

- SERVES 12

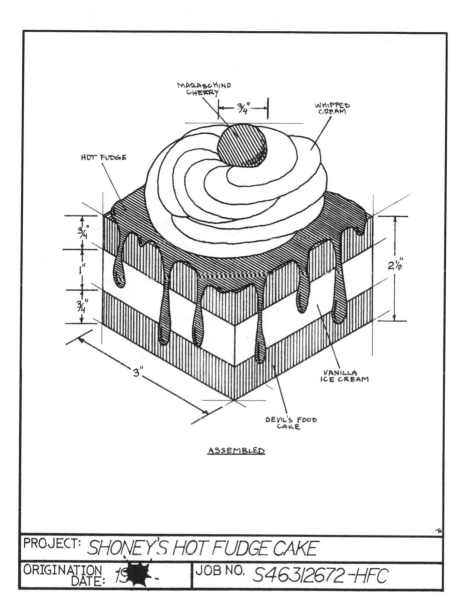

MARASCHINO CHERRY

WHIPPED CREAM

HOT FUDGE

3/4"

3/4"

1"

3/4"

2½"

3"

VANILLA ICE CREAM

DEVIL'S FOOD CAKE

ASSEMBLED

PROJECT: *SHONEY'S HOT FUDGE CAKE*

ORIGINATION DATE: *19⬛-*

JOB NO. *S46312672-HFC*

SIZZLER
CHEESE TOAST

☆　♥　☎　✎　✈　✉　✄　☞　✿

In Los Angeles in 1957, Del Johnson noticed an article in the *Wall Street Journal* about a successful $1.09 per steak steakhouse chain with locations in New York, Chicago, and San Francisco. Inspired by the article, Del decided to open his own steakhouse in L.A., but with a twist that would save him money. His idea was to develop a steakhouse where customers would order their food at a food counter and pick it up when it was ready. Doesn't sound that exciting, but the concept was a hit. After the first Sizzler was open for a year, Del decided to run a two-day, one-cent anniversary sale: buy one steak at the regular price and get a second for just a penny. Del said, "We opened at 11:00. People were lined up from 11:00 until 9:00 at night, and we sold 1050 steaks in one day and about 1200 the second day."

With every meal, Sizzler serves a slice of tasty cheese toast. It's a simple recipe that goes well with just about any entree.

4 tablespoons butter
4 slices thick-sliced French bread

4 teaspoons Kraft grated Parmesan cheese

1. Melt the butter in a small saucepan or in the microwave.
2. Use a brush to spread the butter evenly over one face of each slice of bread.
3. Sprinkle the Parmesan cheese over the butter.
4. Grill the bread, buttered side down, on a frying pan or griddle over medium/low heat for 5 minutes or until golden brown. Grill only the buttered side.

• SERVES 2 TO 4

SIZZLER
CHICKEN CLUB
SANDWICH

☆　♥　☎　✎　✈　✉　✂　☞　✿

When Del Johnson and his wife were trying to think of a name for their new restaurant concept they were looking for the perfect single-word name. "Something that would merchandise well," said Del. "In the old days, they served steaks on those sizzling platters. In a first class restaurant when you ordered a steak, they'd bring it out, put the butter on that steak and that plate was hot, it was aluminum and it would sizzle when they put it down in front of you. That's how we came up with the name. I knew we wanted to use those sizzling platters."

Eventually the restaurant would diversify the menu to include items other than the sizzling steak. One of those on the menu today is the chicken club sandwich, which you can now easily duplicate at home.

1 boneless, skinless chicken breast half	2 slices bacon, cooked
Vegetable oil	1 small slice onion, separated
Salt	2 slices tomato
1 hamburger bun	½ tablespoon Thousand Island
¼ cup chopped lettuce	dressing
1 slice Swiss cheese	

1. Prepare the barbecue or preheat the stovetop grill or broiler.
2. Lightly brush the chicken breast with oil, and grill it over medium heat for 5 minutes per side or until done. Salt the chicken.
3. Brown the faces of the bun top and bottom on the grill or in a skillet over medium heat.
4. Stack the sandwich in the following order from the bottom up:
   bottom bun
   lettuce

chicken breast
Swiss cheese
bacon slices, crisscrossed
onion
tomato slices

5. Spread the Thousand Island dressing on the face of the top bun, and top off your sandwich with it.

- SERVES 1 AS AN ENTREE (CAN BE DOUBLED)

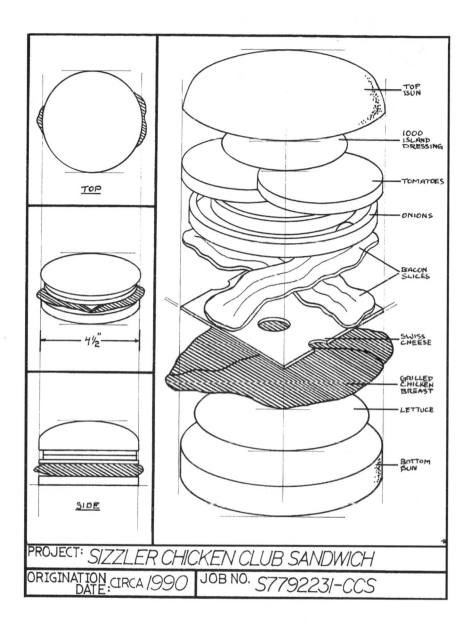

TOP

SIDE

4½"

TOP BUN

1000 ISLAND DRESSING

TOMATOES

ONIONS

BACON SLICES

SWISS CHEESE

GRILLED CHICKEN BREAST

LETTUCE

BOTTOM BUN

PROJECT: *SIZZLER CHICKEN CLUB SANDWICH*

ORIGINATION DATE: CIRCA *1990*

JOB NO. *S7792231-CCS*

SIZZLER
SOUTHERN FRIED SHRIMP

☆   ♥   ☎   ✎   ✈   ✉   ✁   ☛   ✿

One of the most popular items on the Sizzler menu is the fried shrimp, which is often offered as a belly-stuffing, all-you-can-eat deal.

12 medium shrimp (⅓ pound)
1 cup plain bread crumbs
1½ teaspoons salt
½ teaspoon dried basil, crushed fine
½ teaspoon dried parsley, crushed fine
⅛ teaspoon garlic powder

⅛ teaspoon onion powder
1 egg, beaten
½ cup milk
1 cup all-purpose flour
Vegetable oil for frying

ON THE SIDE

Lemon wedge   Cocktail sauce

1. Prepare the shrimp by removing all of the shell except the last section and the tailfins. Butterfly the shrimp by cutting most of the way through along the back of the shrimp on the side with the dark vein. Remove the vein and rinse each shrimp.
2. Combine the bread crumbs, salt, basil, parsley, garlic powder, and onion powder in a small bowl.
3. Combine the beaten egg and milk in another small bowl.
4. Sift the flour into a third small bowl.
5. Heat oil in a deep fryer or large saucepan over medium heat. You want the oil to be around 350°F and it should be deep enough to cover the shrimp.
6. Coat the shrimp one at a time, using one hand for the wet mixture and one hand for the dry stuff. First dip the shrimp into the egg and milk mixture, then drop it into the flour. Coat the shrimp with the flour with the dry hand and then drop it back into the milk mixture. When it's completely moistened drop it

into the bread crumbs and coat it again. Set each shrimp on a plate until all of them are coated.

7. Drop the shrimp into the hot oil and cook for 3 to 4 minutes or until the outside is golden. Serve with a wedge of lemon and cocktail sauce for dipping.

- SERVES 1 AS AN ENTREE, OR 2 AS AN APPETIZER

TIDBITS

This is also great with cornflake crumbs rather than bread crumbs.

STUART ANDERSON'S BLACK ANGUS CHEESY GARLIC BREAD

☆　♥　☎　✎　✈　✉　✂　☞　✿

Recent years have brought a surge in steakhouse chains across the country. But before there was Lone Star, Outback, or Ruth's Chris, a real rancher named Stuart Anderson was serving up huge cuts of delicious prime beef in his Seattle-based restaurant chain. The first Black Angus restaurant opened on April Fool's Day in 1964 and quickly became known for its huge, juicy cuts of prime rib.

Early on, Stuart Anderson's Black Angus served a signature bread dubbed "Ranch Bread" free with each meal. Around five years ago that evolved into Cheesy Garlic Bread, which is no longer free, but is still a delicious and often requested side for any meal. Try to find a large loaf of French or Italian bread for this recipe. The recipe works with just about any type of bread loaf, but to make it more like the original, bigger is better.

1 tablespoon shredded Cheddar cheese	½ teaspoon minced green onion (the white part only)
2 tablespoons shredded Monterey Jack cheese	Dash salt
2 tablespoons grated Parmesan cheese	2 tablespoons butter
1 teaspoon chopped fresh parsley	½ clove garlic, pressed
	¼ loaf French or Italian bread (see Tidbits)

1. Preheat the oven to 450°F.
2. Use finely shredded Cheddar and Monterey Jack cheese for this recipe. If you buy your cheese already shredded and it seems

coarse, use a knife to chop it up a bit before you combine it with the other ingredients.

3. Add the Parmesan, parsley, onion, and salt to the cheese blend.
4. In a large frying pan or skillet, melt the butter over low heat.
5. Add the garlic to the butter. Be sure the heat is very low or the garlic could scorch and become bitter.
6. Slice a loaf of French bread in half, then cut one of the halves lengthwise through the middle.
7. Take that quarter loaf of bread and invert it, face down, in the pan of butter. The bread will soak up some of the garlic butter. Be sure the entire face of the bread has been coated with butter.
8. Brush the crust of the bread with the butter from the pan while it sits in the pan face down.
9. Put the bread on a baking sheet and spread the cheese mixture over the face of the bread.
10. Heat the bread in the oven for 8 to 10 minutes or until the edges begin to turn brown. Give the bread a quick broil for 1 to 2 minutes just to make it crispier.
11. Slice the bread into 5 equal pieces and serve hot.

• SERVES 2 TO 4

TIDBITS

You may want to double or quadruple the recipe to use the entire loaf of bread, depending on how many are to be served.

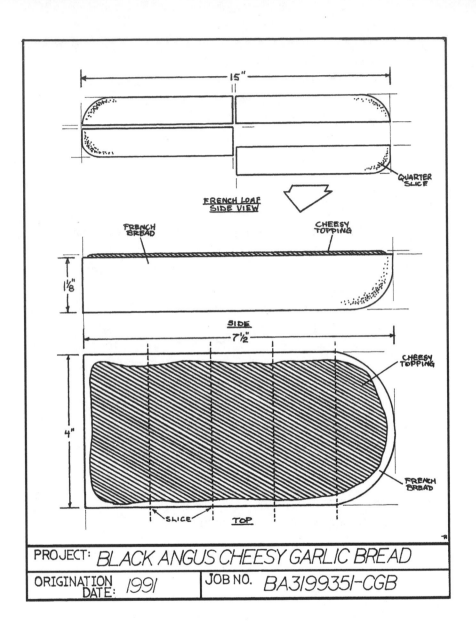

15"

QUARTER
SLICE

FRENCH LOAF
SIDE VIEW

FRENCH
BREAD

CHEESY
TOPPING

1⅛"

SIDE

7½"

CHEESY
TOPPING

4"

FRENCH
BREAD

SLICE   TOP

PROJECT: *BLACK ANGUS CHEESY GARLIC BREAD*

ORIGINATION DATE: *1991*   JOB NO. *BA3199351-CGB*

STUART ANDERSON'S BLACK ANGUS WESTERN T-BONE

☆ ♥ ☎ ✎ ✈ ⊠ ✂ ☞ ✿

Menu Description: "A huge, savory, 16 oz. bone-in U.S.D.A. choice steak, prepared with a smoky marinade and fire-grilled. Smothered with sautéed mushrooms, roasted red peppers and real smoked bacon."

"Come in for dinner and I'll do the dishes," Stuart Anderson used to promise in television ads. Stuart had a down-home appeal that worked wonders for his chain. Stuart was a rancher who raised a small number of cattle, Clydesdales, and sheep for many years, and was known for his casual, laid-back approach to just about everything. When he opened the first restaurant he built it on a "ranch-to-restaurant" philosophy, meaning that he could supply the fresh beef from his own small ranch, or at least imply that was the case. But as the dinner house's popularity exploded over the years, larger suppliers had to be called upon to deliver the beef to the growing chain. Still, the fable lived on, and it worked very well for the restaurant. Even with more than one hundred stores in the chain, customers continued to believe they were getting home-grown steaks picked by old Stuart himself—a rumor that Stuart would neither confirm nor deny.

Now you can hand pick your own T-bone steaks when you whip up this recipe for steak in a smoky marinade that clones the Stuart Anderson's Black Angus recipe. The recipe here is for T-bone steaks, but you can use the marinade and topping on any cut of steak. If you can, plan on marinating the steaks overnight for the best flavor.

SMOKY MARINADE

4 teaspoons liquid smoke
2 teaspoons salt
1 clove garlic, pressed
Dash ground black pepper

2 teaspoons vegetable oil
½ cup water
¼ teaspoon onion powder
¼ teaspoon minced fresh parsley

2 16-ounce T-bone steaks

TOPPING

2 tablespoons butter
2 cups sliced mushrooms
1 tablespoon diced roasted red pepper
    (canned is fine)
1 tablespoon diced sun-dried tomatoes
    (bottled in oil)

2 slices bacon, cooked and crumbled
Pinch chopped fresh parsley
Pinch dried thyme
Salt
½ teaspoon vinegar

1. Combine all of the ingredients for the smoky marinade in a medium bowl.
2. Pour the marinade over the T-bone steaks. You may want to use a large, sealable plastic bag for this. If you don't have one, be sure you use a covered container. Marinate the meat in your refrigerator for at least 4 hours. Overnight is best.
3. When you are ready to grill the steaks, preheat your barbecue.
4. As the barbecue heats, prepare the sautéed mushroom topping by melting the butter in a large skillet over medium heat.
5. Add the mushrooms, roasted peppers, and tomatoes to the butter. Sauté for about 5 minutes or until the mushrooms begin to turn brown on the edges.
6. Add the bacon, parsley, thyme, salt, and vinegar to the mushrooms and keep warm over low heat until the steaks are done.
7. When your grill is hot, cook the steaks for 3 to 5 minutes per side or until they are done to your liking. Salt the steaks to taste. Serve the steaks with the mushroom topping spooned over the top.

- SERVES 2 AS AN ENTREE

STUART ANDERSON'S BLACK ANGUS WHISKEY PEPPER STEAK

☆　♥　☎　✎　✈　✉　✂　☞　✿

Menu Description: "U.S.D.A. choice top sirloin, fire grilled to your liking then doused with a whiskey pepper sauce."

When the number of Black Angus restaurants had reached 117 by the early eighties, the Marriott Corporation stepped in to buy the chain from owner Stuart Anderson. Now, nearing 70, Stuart relaxes at his home on Whidby Island off the coast of Washington State, and spends his winters at his other home in warm Palm Springs, California.

Here is an easy recipe for sirloin pepper steak with a tasty whiskey sauce inspired by the popular dish served at Black Angus. Black Angus chefs probably got the idea for this dish from a classic French dish called *steak au poivre* in which the meat is covered with coarsely ground black pepper before being sautéed or broiled. Brandy or cognac is used to get the steak flaming for an elaborate presentation.

You won't have to set your steak on fire in this version. Though you will find that the flavorful sauce goes well with other cuts of steak besides the top sirloin called for here.

WHISKEY PEPPER SAUCE

1 tablespoon butter
2 tablespoons chopped white onion
2 cups beef stock or canned
* beef broth*
¼ teaspoon cracked black pepper

1 clove garlic, pressed
2 tablespoons whiskey
1 green onion, chopped
1 teaspoon cornstarch
1 tablespoon water

PEPPER STEAK

One 16-ounce sirloin steak, cut into
    two portions
2 teaspoons cracked black pepper

2 tablespoons butter
Salt

1.   Fire up the barbecue.
2.   In a saucepan or deep skillet, make the whiskey pepper sauce by sautéing the white onions in the butter over high heat. In about 3 minutes the onions will begin to turn brown.
3.   Add 1 cup of the beef stock to the onions. Add the cracked black pepper and garlic at this point as well. Continue to simmer over medium/high heat until the sauce has reduced by about half.
4.   Add the whiskey, green onion, and remaining 1 cup of beef stock to the sauce and let it simmer over low heat while you prepare the steaks.
5.   Spread ½ teaspoon of cracked pepper over the entire surface of each side of the sirloin steaks and press it into the steaks so that it sticks.
6.   Melt 2 tablespoons of butter in a large skillet over medium/high heat. Drop the steaks into the melted butter and sear each side of the steaks for 1½ to 2 minutes or until brown.
7.   When the barbecue is good and hot, grill the steaks for 3 to 5 minutes per side or until they are done to your liking. Salt the steaks lightly as they grill.
8.   When the steaks are just about done, combine the cornstarch with the tablespoon of water in a small bowl. Stir just until the cornstarch dissolves.
9.   Remove the whiskey sauce from the heat and add the cornstarch to it. Put the sauce back on the heat and continue to cook on low until the sauce is thickened to the consistency you desire. Serve the steak doused with whiskey pepper sauce.

• SERVES 2 AS AN ENTREE

T.G.I. FRIDAY'S
POTATO SKINS

☆　♥　☎　✎　✈　✉　✂　☞　✿

Menu Description: "Loaded with cheddar cheese and bacon. Served with sour cream and chives."

Perfume salesman Alan Stillman was a single guy in New York City in 1965, looking for a way to meet women who lived in his neighborhood. He figured a hip way to get their attention: buy a broken-down beer joint in the area, jazz it up, and call it "The T.G.I.F." to attract the career crowd. Within a week, police had to barricade the area to control the crowds flocking to Alan's new restaurant. The restaurant made $1 million in its first year—a lot of dough back then. Soon restaurants were imitating the concept across the country.

In 1974 T.G.I. Friday's invented an appetizer that would also be imitated by many others in the following years. Today Potato Skins are still the most popular item on the T.G.I. Friday's menu, with nearly 4 million orders served every year. The recipe has the added benefit of providing you with leftover baked potato ready for mashing or to use in another dish.

4 medium russet potatoes	¼ cup (½ stick) butter, melted
⅓ cup sour cream	1½ cups shredded Cheddar cheese
1 tablespoon snipped fresh chives	5 slices bacon, cooked

1. Preheat the oven to 400°F. Bake the potatoes for 1 hour. Let the potatoes cool down enough so that you can touch them.
2. As the potatoes are baking, make the sour cream dip by mixing the sour cream with the chives. Place the mixture in a covered container in your refrigerator.
3. When the potatoes are cool enough to handle, make 2 length-

wise cuts through each potato, resulting in three ½- to ¾-inch slices. Discard the middle slices or save them for a separate dish of mashed potatoes. This will leave you with two potato skins per potato.

4. With a spoon, scoop some of the potato out of each skin, being sure to leave about ¼ inch of potato inside of the skin.

5. Brush the entire surface of each potato skin, inside and outside, with the melted butter.

6. Place the skins on a cookie sheet, cut side up, and broil them for 6 to 8 minutes or until the edges begin to turn dark brown.

7. Sprinkle 2 to 3 tablespoons of Cheddar cheese into each skin.

8. Crumble the cooked bacon and sprinkle 1 to 2 teaspoons of the bacon pieces onto the cheese.

9. Broil the skins for 2 more minutes or until the cheese is thoroughly melted. Serve hot, arranged on a plate surrounding a small bowl of the sour cream dip.

- SERVES 2 TO 4 AS AN APPETIZER OR SNACK

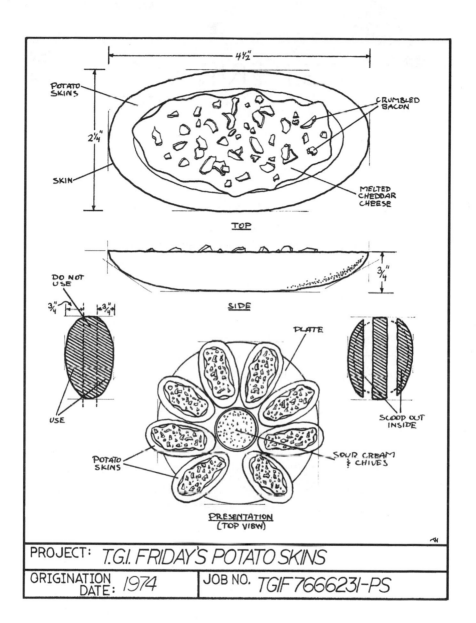

4½"

POTATO
SKINS

CRUMBLED
BACON

2¼"

SKIN

MELTED
CHEDDAR
CHEESE

TOP

SIDE

¾"

DO NOT
USE

¾"   ¾"

USE

PLATE

SCOOP OUT
INSIDE

POTATO
SKINS

SOUR CREAM
& CHIVES

PRESENTATION
(TOP VIEW)

PROJECT: T.G.I. FRIDAY'S POTATO SKINS

ORIGINATION
DATE: 1974

JOB NO. TGIF766623I-PS

T.G.I. FRIDAY'S
NINE-LAYER DIP

☆　♥　☎　✎　✈　✉　✂　☞　✿

Menu Description: "Refried Beans, cheddar cheese, guacamole, black olives, seasoned sour cream, green onions, tomatoes and cilantro. Served with tortilla chips and fresh salsa."

When the first T.G.I. Friday's opened in New York City in 1965 as a meeting place for single adults, *Newsweek* and *The Saturday Evening Post* reported that it was the beginning of the "singles age." Today the restaurant's customers have matured, many are married, and they bring their children with them to the more than 300 Friday's across the country and around the world.

The Nine-Layer Dip is one of the often requested appetizers on the T.G.I. Friday's menu. This dish will serve half a dozen people easily, so it's perfect for a small gathering, or as a snack. Don't worry if there's only a couple of you—leftovers can be refrigerated for a day or two. Cilantro, also called fresh coriander or Chinese parsley, can be found in the produce section of most supermarkets near the parsley.

⅔ cups sour cream
⅛ teaspoon cumin
⅛ teaspoon cayenne pepper
⅛ teaspoon paprika
Dash salt
One 16-ounce can refried beans
1 cup shredded Cheddar
　　cheese

½ cup guacamole (made fresh or
　　frozen, thawed)
¼ cup sliced black olives
2 green onions, chopped (¼ cup)
1 medium tomato, chopped
1 teaspoon chopped fresh cilantro

ON THE SIDE

Salsa

1. Combine the sour cream, cumin, cayenne pepper, paprika, and salt in a small bowl and mix well. Set aside.

2. Heat the refried beans until hot, using a microwave or in a saucepan over medium heat.

3. When the beans are hot, spread them over the center of a serving platter or in a shallow dish.

4. Sprinkle ½ of the cheese evenly over the beans.

5. Spread the guacamole over the cheese.

6. Sprinkle the sliced olives over the guacamole.

7. Spread the seasoned sour cream over the olives.

8. Sprinkle the green onions, then the tomatoes evenly over the sour cream layer.

9. Finish up by sprinkling the remainder of the cheese over the tomatoes, and topping the dip off with the cilantro. Serve the dip with tortilla chips and a side of your favorite salsa.

- SERVES 4 TO 8 AS AN APPETIZER OR SNACK

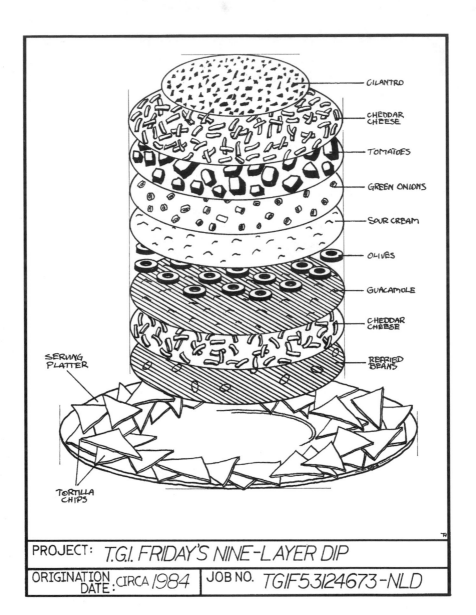

CILANTRO

CHEDDAR CHEESE

TOMATOES

GREEN ONIONS

SOUR CREAM

OLIVES

GUACAMOLE

CHEDDAR CHEESE

REFRIED BEANS

SERVING PLATTER

TORTILLA CHIPS

PROJECT:	*T.G.I. FRIDAY'S NINE-LAYER DIP*	
ORIGINATION DATE:	CIRCA *1984*	JOB NO. *TGIF53124673-NLD*

T.G.I. FRIDAY'S CALIFORNIA CHARGRILLED TURKEY SANDWICH

☆   ♥   ☎   ✎   ✈   ✉   ✄   ☛   ✿

Menu Description: "Chargrilled all-white meat turkey burger, served on a toasted whole wheat bun with lettuce, tomatoes, alfalfa sprouts, onions and avocado."

Noting the success of the first T.G.I. Friday's in New York City, a group of fun-loving Dallas businessmen opened the first franchise store. The investors decorated their Dallas T.G.I. Friday's with fun antiques and collectibles gathered from around the countryside—and now all of the Friday's are decorated that way. Six months after the opening of the Dallas location, waiters and waitresses began doing skits and riding bicycles and roller skates around the restaurant. That's also when the now defunct tradition of ringing in every Friday evolved. Thursday night at midnight was like a New Year's Eve party at T.G.I. Friday's, with champagne, confetti, noisemakers, and a guy jumping around in a gorilla suit as if he had a few too many espressos.

Here's a favorite of burger lovers who don't care where the beef is. It's an alternative to America's most popular food with turkey instead of beef, plus some alfalfa sprouts and avocado to give it a "California" twist.

HONEY MUSTARD SAUCE

¼ cup mayonnaise
1 tablespoon yellow mustard (like French's)

1 tablespoon honey
½ teaspoon sesame oil
½ teaspoon distilled vinegar

1 pound ground turkey (all-white meat
    if available)
Salt
Pepper
4 whole wheat hamburger buns
Soft butter

4 romaine lettuce leaves
½ cup alfalfa sprouts (a handful)
1 medium tomato, sliced
1 to 2 slices white onion
1 ripe avocado, sliced

1. Prepare the barbecue or preheat the stovetop grill.
2. Combine the mayonnaise, mustard, honey, oil, and vinegar in a small bowl. Cover and keep refrigerated until later.
3. Divide the ground turkey into four even portions and on wax paper pat out four ½-inch-thick patties with the same diameter as the buns.
4. Grill these patties for 6 to 8 minutes per side or until done. Be sure to salt and pepper both sides of each patty.
5. Prepare the buns by lightly buttering the face of the tops and bottoms, and then grilling them in a hot skillet until brown.
6. The sandwich is served "open face" so that the customer can put the hot side and the cold side together at the table (remember the McD.L.T?). Build the cold side of the sandwich by inverting the top bun and stacking the ingredients on it in the following order from the bottom up:
    top bun (face up)
    lettuce leaf
    alfalfa sprouts
    1 to 2 tomato slices
    2 onion rings (from the separated slices)
    2 avocado slices
7. Arrange the bottom bun on the same plate. Add the hot ground turkey patty on the face of the bun and serve with the honey mustard dressing on the side.

- SERVES 4 AS AN ENTRÉE

TIDBITS

Some tasty variations of this sandwich include adding slices of cooked bacon, or substituting barbecue sauce for the honey mustard.

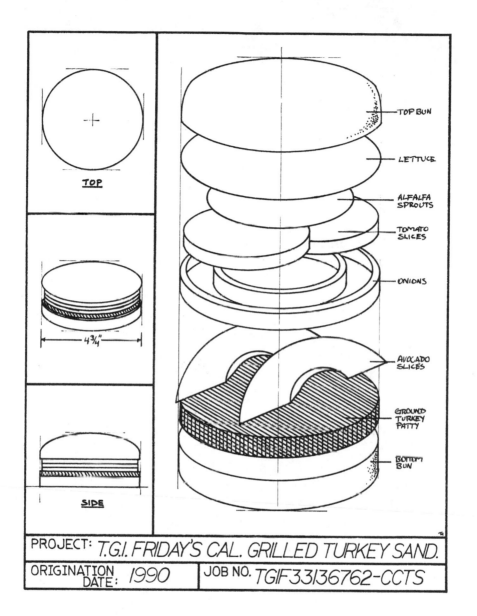

TOP

SIDE

4¾"

TOP BUN
LETTUCE
ALFALFA SPROUTS
TOMATO SLICES
ONIONS
AVOCADO SLICES
GROUND TURKEY PATTY
BOTTOM BUN

PROJECT:	T.G.I. FRIDAY'S CAL. GRILLED TURKEY SAND.	
ORIGINATION DATE:	1990	JOB NO. TGIF33136762-CCTS

T.G.I. FRIDAY'S SPICY CAJUN CHICKEN PASTA

☆　♥　☎　✎　✈　✉　✂　☛　✿

Menu Description: "Fettuccine tossed with sautéed chicken, mushrooms, onions and red and green peppers in Friday's own spicy, tomato Creole sauce."

There are over 360 T.G.I. Friday's restaurants in 44 states and 22 countries, all serving this Cajun-style chicken pasta. This dish is a bit like a jambalaya except the rice has been replaced with pasta.

Use a large pan for this recipe, and note that for the chicken stock or broth, you can also use a chicken bouillon cube dissolved in boiling water.

This recipe makes two large restaurant-size portions, but could easily serve a family of four.

4 tablespoons (½ stick) butter
1 green bell pepper, chopped (1 cup)
1 red bell pepper, chopped (1 cup)
½ white onion, sliced and quartered
    (1 cup)
1 clove garlic, pressed
2 boneless, skinless chicken breast
    halves
2 teaspoons olive oil
1 medium tomato, chopped
4 to 6 mushrooms, sliced (1¼ cup)

1 cup chicken stock or 1 chicken
    bouillon cube dissolved in 1 cup
    boiling water
Salt
¼ teaspoon cayenne pepper
¼ teaspoon paprika
¼ teaspoon white pepper
¼ teaspoon dried thyme
4 to 6 quarts water
One 12-ounce box fettuccine
2 teaspoons chopped fresh parsley

1.　Melt 2 tablespoons of the butter in a large skillet over medium/high heat.

2. Sauté the bell peppers, onions, and garlic in the butter for 8 to 10 minutes or until the vegetables begin to soften slightly.

3. As the vegetables are cooking, cut the chicken breasts into bite-size pieces.

4. Prepare a medium-size pan over high heat with the olive oil. When the pan is hot, add the chicken and cook, stirring, for 5 to 7 minutes or until the chicken shows no pink.

5. When the vegetables are soft (about 10 minutes) add the chicken to the pan.

6. Add the tomatoes, mushrooms, chicken stock, ¼ teaspoon salt, cayenne pepper, paprika, white pepper, and thyme and continue to simmer for 10 to 12 minutes until it thickens.

7. In the meantime bring the water to a boil in a large pot. If you like, add a half tablespoon of salt to the water. Cook the fettuccine in the boiling water until done. This will take 10 to 12 minutes.

8. When the noodles are done, drain them and add the remaining 2 tablespoons of butter. The butter should melt quickly on the hot noodles. Toss the noodles to mix in the butter.

9. Serve the dish by dividing the noodles in half onto two plates. Divide the chicken and vegetable sauce evenly and spread it over the top of the noodles on each plate. Divide the parsley and sprinkle it over each serving.

• SERVES 2 AS A LARGE ENTREE

TIDBITS

If you want a thicker sauce, combine ½ teaspoon arrowroot or cornstarch with 2 tablespoons of white wine in a small bowl and stir to dissolve. Remove the pan from the heat before adding this thickener, stir it in, then put it back on the heat.

T.G.I. FRIDAY'S
FRIDAY'S SMOOTHIES

☆　♥　☎　✎　✈　✉　✂　☛　✿

Menu Description: "Healthful, nonalcoholic frozen fruit drinks."
"Gold Medalist: Coconut and pineapple, blended with grenadine, strawberries and bananas."
"Tropical Runner: Fresh banana, pineapple and pina colada mix frozen with crushed ice."

From the "obscure statistics" file, T.G.I. Friday's promotional material claims the restaurant was the first chain to offer stoneground whole wheat bread as an option to its guests. It was also the first chain to put avocados, bean sprouts, and Mexican appetizers on its menu.

Also a first: Friday's Smoothies. In response to growing demand for nonalcoholic drinks, T.G.I. Friday's created smoothies, a fruit drink now found on many other restaurants' menus. Here are recipes to clone two of the nine fruit blend varieties. Great on a sizzling afternoon.

GOLD MEDALIST

8 ounces frozen strawberries (not in syrup—do not defrost)
1 banana
1 cup pineapple juice

2 tablespoons coconut cream
¼ cup grenadine
1 cup ice
2 fresh strawberries (for garnish)

1. Pour all of the ingredients except the 2 fresh strawberries in the order listed into a blender and blend on high speed for 15 to 30 seconds or until all the ice is crushed and the drink is smooth.
2. Garnish each drink with a fresh strawberry.

1 banana	*½ cup liquid pina colada mix*
One 8-ounce can crushed pineapple	*½ cup orange sherbet*
with juice	*2 cups ice*

1. Cut the banana in half and slice two ¼-inch slices from the middle of the banana and set the two slices aside for garnish.
2. Put the rest of banana and the remaining ingredients into a blender in the order listed. Blend on high speed for 15 to 30 seconds, or until the drink is smooth and creamy.
3. Add 1 banana slice to the top of each drink as a garnish.

  • EACH RECIPE SERVES 2

TIDBITS

You've probably already thought of this, but these drinks make tasty cocktails too. Just add a little rum or vodka, and about ½ cup more ice, before blending.

TONY ROMA'S
WORLD FAMOUS RIBS

☆　　♥　　☎　　✎　　✈　　✉　　✂　　☛　　✿

Tony Roma had already been in the restaurant business for many years when he opened Tony Roma's Place in North Miami, Florida, in 1972. This casual diner featured food at reasonable prices, nightly live entertainment and the house specialty—baby back ribs. Soon, customers were traveling from miles away to get a taste of the succulent, mouth-watering ribs. One rib-lover came from Texas in 1976: Clint Murchison, Jr., a Texas financier and owner of the Dallas Cowboys. After sampling the baby backs, and claiming they were the best he'd ever tasted, he struck up a deal with Tony to purchase the majority of the U.S. rights to the company and planned for a major expansion. Today that plan has been realized with nearly 150 Tony Roma's restaurants in the chain pulling in over $250 million per year.

The famous barbecue ribs served at the restaurant have been judged the best in America at a national rib cook-off and have won more than 30 awards at other state and local competitions. The secret to the tender, melt-in-your-mouth quality of the ribs at Tony Roma's is the long, slow-cooking process. Here is the *Top Secret Recipes* version of the cooking technique followed by three varieties of the famous barbecue sauce. Note that the restaurant uses pork baby back ribs for the Original Baby Backs recipe, and pork spare ribs for the Carolina Honeys and Red Hots. Of course *you* can use these sauces interchangeably on the ribs *you* like best, including beef ribs.

THE TECHNIQUE

4 pounds baby back pork ribs or
4 pounds pork spareribs

Barbecue sauce for coating (See
recipes on following pages)

1. Often when you buy ribs at the butcher counter, you get a full rack of ribs that wouldn't fit on a plate. Usually you just have to cut these long racks in half to get the perfect serving size (about 4 to 6 rib bones per rack). You'll likely have 4 of these smaller racks at about a pound each.
2. Preheat the oven to 300°F.
3. Tear off 4 pieces of aluminum foil that are roughly 6 inches longer than the ribs.
4. Coat the ribs, front and back, with your choice of barbecue sauce. Place a rack of ribs, one at a time, onto a piece of foil lengthwise and wrap it tightly.
5. Place the ribs into the oven with the seam of the foil wrap facing up. Cook for 2 to 2½ hours, or until you see the meat of the ribs shrinking back from the cut ends of the bones by about ½ inch. This long cooking time will ensure that the meat will be very tender and fall off the bone.
6. Toward the end of the cooking time, prepare the barbecue.
7. Remove the ribs from the foil and smother them with additional barbecue sauce. Be sure to save some sauce for later.
8. Grill the ribs on the hot barbecue for 2 to 4 minutes per side, or just until you see several spots of charred blackened sauce. Watch for flames and do not burn!
9. When the ribs are done, use a sharp knife to slice the meat between each bone about halfway down. This will make it easier to tear the ribs apart when they are served.

    Serve the ribs piping hot with additional sauce on the side, if desired.

- SERVES 2 TO 4 AS AN ENTREE

TIDBITS

If you've got time to marinate these ribs in advance, do it. I've found these ribs are extraordinary when they've been soaking in barbecue sauce for 24 hours before cooking. Just prepare the ribs in the foil as described in the recipe and keep them in your fridge. Toss them, foil and all, into the oven the next day, 2 to 2½ hours before you plan to scarf out.

TONY ROMA'S ORIGINAL BABY BACKS

☆　♥　☎　✎　✈　✉　✂　☛　✿

Menu Description: "Our house specialty and award-winning ribs. Lean, tender, meaty pork ribs cut from the choicest tenderloin and basted with our original barbecue sauce. So tender the meat practically falls off the bone."

This is the sauce that made the chain famous. This version of the sauce uses a ketchup base, vinegar, dark corn syrup, and a bit of Tabasco for a slight zing. The chain uses their sauce on baby back ribs and has started selling it by the bottle in each restaurant. Now you can make a version of your own that is less costly than the bottled brand, and can be used on any cut of ribs, or even chicken.

BARBECUE SAUCE

1 cup ketchup
1 cup vinegar
½ cup dark corn syrup
2 teaspoons sugar

½ teaspoon salt
¼ teaspoon garlic powder
¼ teaspoon onion powder
¼ teaspoon Tabasco pepper sauce

4 pounds baby back pork ribs

1. Combine all of the ingredients for the barbecue sauce in a saucepan over high heat. Use a whisk to blend the ingredients until smooth.
2. When the mixture comes to a boil, reduce the heat and simmer uncovered.
3. In 30 to 45 minutes, when the mixture thickens, remove it from the heat. If you want a thicker sauce, heat it longer. If you make the sauce too thick, thin it with more vinegar.

4. Use baby back ribs and the cooking technique from page 532 to complete the recipe.

- SERVES 2 TO 4 AS AN ENTRÉE

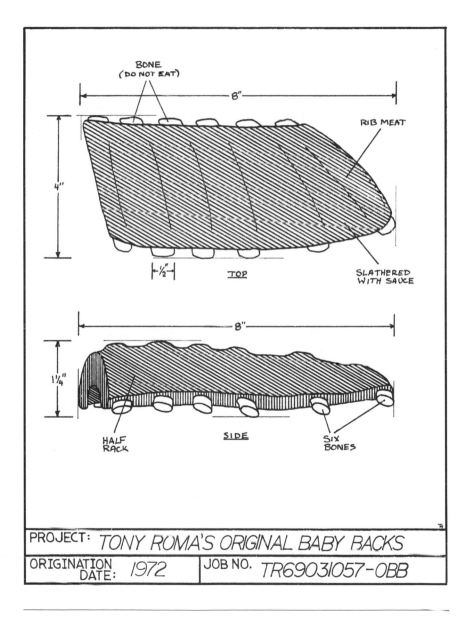

TONY ROMA'S
CAROLINA HONEYS

Menu Description: "Tender select-cut pork spare ribs basted with our special-recipe sauce. Nothing could be finer..."

This smoky sauce is perfectly sweetened with honey and molasses, and bites just a bit with pepper sauce. Smother pork spareribs with this sauce, as they do at the restaurant chain. Also use it on baby back ribs and beef spare ribs along with the slow-cooking technique. It's good with chicken, too.

BARBECUE SAUCE

1 cup ketchup	*½ teaspoon salt*
1 cup vinegar	*¼ teaspoon garlic powder*
½ cup molasses	*¼ teaspoon onion powder*
½ cup honey	*¼ teaspoon Tabasco pepper sauce*
1 teaspoon liquid smoke	

4 pounds pork spare ribs

1. Combine all of the ingredients for the barbecue sauce in a saucepan over high heat. Blend the ingredients with a whisk until smooth.
2. When the mixture comes to a boil, reduce the heat and simmer uncovered.
3. In 30 to 45 minutes, when the mixture thickens, remove it from the heat. If you overcook it and make the sauce too thick, thin it with more vinegar.
4. Use pork spareribs and the cooking technique from page 532 to complete the recipe.

  • SERVES 2 TO 4 AS AN ENTREE

TONY ROMA'S
RED HOTS

☆　♥　☎　✎　✈　✉　✂　☞　✿

Menu Description: "Some like it hot! Tender, meaty ribs basted with our spicy red hot sauce made with five types of peppers."

If you like your sauces especially spicy, this is the recipe for you. Five different peppers go into this one, including crushed red pepper, red bell pepper, Tabasco, cayenne pepper, and ground black pepper. The restaurant serves this one on pork spareribs, but you can slather it on any type of ribs, chicken, and steaks.

BARBECUE SAUCE

1 cup ketchup	½ teaspoon salt
1 cup vinegar	½ teaspoon crushed red pepper flakes
½ cup dark corn syrup	½ teaspoon Tabasco pepper sauce
2 tablespoons molasses	¼ teaspoon cayenne pepper
½ tablespoon finely diced red bell	¼ teaspoon ground black pepper
pepper	¼ teaspoon garlic powder
2 teaspoons sugar	¼ teaspoon onion powder
1 teaspoon liquid smoke	

4 pounds pork spareribs

1. Combine all of the ingredients for the barbecue sauce in a saucepan over high heat. Use a whisk to blend the ingredients until smooth.
2. When the mixture comes to a boil, reduce the heat and simmer uncovered.
3. In 30 to 45 minutes, when the mixture thickens, remove it from the heat. If you want a thicker sauce, cook it longer. If you make the sauce too thick, thin it with more vinegar.

4. Use pork spareribs and the cooking technique from page 532 to complete the recipe.

    • SERVES 2 TO 4 AS AN ENTREE

WESTERN SIZZLIN "TERIYAKI" CHICKEN BREAST

☆　♥　☎　✎　✈　✉　✂　☛　✿

Western Sizzlin is a steakhouse similar in some ways to Sizzler, but the companies are not related. Although Western Sizzlin is known for its steak, the restaurant has a nice teriyaki chicken dish that is served topped with a slice of pineapple. You'll like this recipe since it includes a great way to make a delicious teriyaki sauce that you can use as a tasty marinade for a variety of dishes. It keeps well for weeks in the fridge. For the pineapple juice in the teriyaki recipe, you don't have to buy a separate can of juice. Instead you can use the juice that comes packed in the 5½-ounce can of pineapple slices that you use as garnish on the chicken—it's just the right amount for this recipe!

TERIYAKI SAUCE

¾ cup water
½ cup soy sauce
1 slice onion, quartered (¼ inch thick)
2 nickel-size slices peeled gingerroot, halved
2 cloves garlic, quartered

⅓ cup sugar
⅓ cup pineapple juice (from canned pineapple slices)
2 tablespoons vinegar
1 tablespoon cornstarch

4 boneless, skinless chicken breast halves

4 canned pineapple slices in juice (5.5-ounce can)

1. Combine ½ cup water with the soy sauce in a small saucepan over high heat. Add the onion, gingerroot, and garlic. Bring the mixture to a boil, then reduce the heat and simmer for 10 minutes.

2. Strain off the onion, ginger, and garlic and return the liquid to the saucepan over low heat. Discard the vegetables.
3. Add the sugar, pineapple juice, and vinegar to the pan.
4. Combine the cornstarch with the remaining 1/4 cup water in a small bowl and stir to dissolve any lumps. Remove the teriyaki mixture from the heat, add the cornstarch, then put it back on the heat. Continue to simmer, stirring often, for 1 minute or so, until the mixture thickens. This will make about 1 cup of marinade.
5. When the teriyaki sauce has cooled, pour half of it over the chicken breasts arranged in a covered container or casserole dish. Keep the other half of the sauce for later to brush over the chicken while it grills, and to serve on the side as additional marinade. Marinate the breasts in your refrigerator for at least 2 hours.
6. When you are ready to cook the chicken, preheat your barbecue or stovetop grill to high. Grill the chicken on each side for 5 to 7 minutes or until done. When you flip the chicken over the first time, put a slice of pineapple on top of each breast, and brush with the leftover teriyaki sauce. When the chicken is done, serve with rice and/or steamed vegetables.

• SERVES 2 AS AN ENTREE

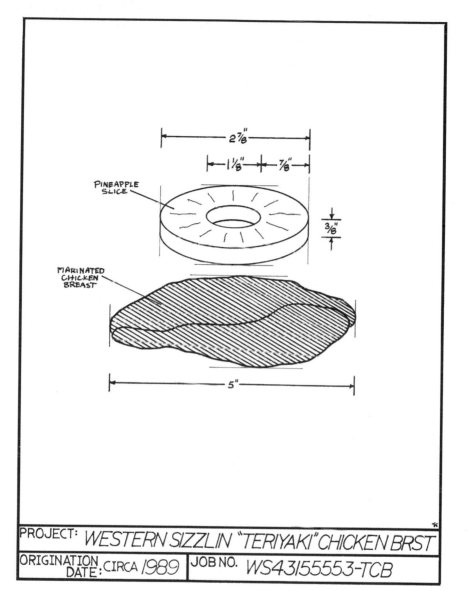

PINEAPPLE
SLICE

2⅞"

1⅛" 7⅞"

3⁄8"

MARINATED
CHICKEN
BREAST

5"

PROJECT: WESTERN SIZZLIN "TERIYAKI" CHICKEN BRST

ORIGINATION DATE: CIRCA 1989

JOB NO. WS43155553-TCB

BIBLIOGRAPHY

ANDERSON, HENRY W. *The Modern Foodservice Industry.* Dubuque, Iowa: William C. Brown Company Publishers, 1976.

BOAS, MAX, AND CHAIN, STEVE. *Big Mac: The Unauthorized Story of McDonald's.* New York: New American Library, 1976.

CATHY, S. TRUETT. *It's Easier to Succeed Than to Fail.* Nashville, Tenn.: Oliver-Nelson Publishers, 1989.

COHEN, BEN, AND GREENFIELD, JERRY. *Ben & Jerry's Homemade Ice Cream and Dessert Book.* New York: Workman Publishing, 1987.

COMPTON'S NEW MEDIA. *Compton's Interactive Encyclopedia.* Compton's New Media, Inc., 1992.

CROCKER, BETTY. *Betty Crocker Cookbook.* New York: Prentice Hall Press, 1986.

FIELDS, DEBRA. *One Smart Cookie.* New York: Simon & Schuster, 1987.

GROLIER, INC. *Grolier Multimedia Encyclopedia.* Danbury, CT: Grolier Electronic Publishing, Inc., 1995.

HAUGHTON, NATALIE. *365 Great Chocolate Desserts.* New York: HarperCollins Publishers, 1991.

HERBST, SHARON TYLER. *Food Lover's Companion.* Hauppauge, New York: Barron's Educational Series, Inc., 1990.

KROC, RAY. *Grinding It Out: The Making of McDonald's.* Chicago: Contemporary Books, 1985.

LEVENSTEIN, HARVEY. *Paradox of Plenty.* New York: Oxford University Press, 1993.

LOVE, JOHN. *McDonald's: Behind the Arches.* New York: Bantam, 1986.

PILLSBURY COMPANY STAFF. *Pillsbury Chocolate Lovers Cookbook.* New York: Doubleday, 1991.

PILLSBURY COMPANY. *Pillsbury Cookbook: The All-Purpose Companion for Today's Cook.* New York: Doubleday, 1991.

POUNDSTONE, WILLIAM. *Big Secrets: The Uncensored Truth About All Sorts of Stuff You Are Never Supposed to Know.* New York: William Morrow, 1983.

ROMBAUER, IRMA S. *The Joy of Cooking,* vol. 2. New York: New American Library, 1974.

SUNSET MAGAZINE AND BOOK EDITORS. *Easy Basics for Good Cooking.* Menlo Park, Calif.: Sunset Books, 1982.

TENNYSON, JEFFREY. *Hamburger Heaven.* New York: Hyperion, 1992.

THOMAS, DAVE. *Dave's Way.* New York: Putnam, 1991.

WARE, RICHARD, AND JAMES RUDNICK. *The Restaurant Book.* New York: Facts on File Publications, 1986.

WITZEL, MICHAEL KARL. *The American Drive-In.* Osceola, WI: Motorbooks International Publishers and Wholesalers, 1994.

WORLD BOOK, INC. *The World Book Encyclopedia.* Chicago: World Book, Inc., 1986.

TRADEMARKS

"A&W Root Beer" is a registered trademark of A&W Beverages, Inc.

"Almond Roca" and "Brown and Haley" are registered trademarks of Brown and Haley, Inc.

"Applebee's," "Pizza Sticks," "Club House Grille," and "Tijuana 'Philly' Steak Sandwich" are registered trademarks of Applebee's International, Inc.

"Arby's" is a registered trademark of Arby's Inc.

"Aunt Jemima," "Aunt Jemima Syrup," "Cap'n Crunch," and "Snapple" are registered trademarks of the Quaker Oats Company.

"Bailey's" and "Original Irish Cream" are registered trademarks of R&A Bailey & Co.

"Ben & Jerry's Ice Cream" is a registered trademark of Ben & Jerry's Homemade, Inc.

"Benihana" is a registered trademark of Benihana Inc.

"Bennigan's" and "Cookie Mountain Sundae" are registered trademarks of Metromedia Co.

"Big Boy" is a registered trademark of Elias Brothers Restaurants, Inc.

"Big Mac," "Egg McMuffin," "Filet-O-Fish," "McD.L.T.," "McLean Deluxe," "McDonald's," and "Quarter Pounder" are registered trademarks of McDonald's Corporation.

"Big Stuf," "Chips Ahoy!," "Double Stuf," "Lorna Doone," "Nabisco," "Nutter Butter," and "Oreo" are registered trademarks of Nabisco Brands, Inc.

"Blizzard," "Orange Julius," "Pineapple," "Strawberry Julius," and "Dairy Queen" are registered trademarks of International Dairy Queen.

"Butterscotch Krimpets," "Peanut Butter Kandy Kakes," and "Tastykake" is a registered trademark of Tasty Baking Company.

"California Pizza Kitchen" is a registered trademark of California Pizza Kitchen, Inc.

"Carl's Famous Star," "Carl's Jr.," "Sante Fe Chicken," "Western Bacon Cheeseburger," "Junior Western Bacon Cheeseburger," and "Double Western Bacon Cheeseburger" are registered trademarks of Carl Karcher Enterprises.

"The Cheesecake Factory" is a registered trademark of The Cheesecake Factory, Inc.

"Chesapeake," "Sausalito," and "Pepperidge Farm" are registered trademarks of Campbell Soup Company.

"Chi-Chi's" and "Mexican 'Fried' Ice Cream" are registered trademarks of Family Restaurants, Inc.

"Chick-fil-A" is a registered trademark of Chick-fil-A, Inc.

"Chili's" is a registered trademark of Brinker International.

"Cinnabon" is a registered trademark of Cinnabon World Famous Cinnamon Rolls.

"Cracker Barrel Old Country Store" is a trademark of Cracker Barrel Old Country Store, Inc.

"Cracker Jack" and "Borden" are registered trademarks of Borden, Inc.

"Denny's," "El Pollo Loco," "Scram Slam," "Moons Over My Hammy," and "Super Bird" are registered trademarks of Flagstar Cos, Inc.

"Dive!," "Carrot Chips," "Sicilian Sub Rosa," "Brick Oven Mushroom and Turkey Cheese Sub," and "Dive! S'mores" are registered trademarks of Levy Restaurants, Inc.

"Double-Double" and "In-N-Out" are registered trademarks of In-N-Out, Inc.

"Dunkin' Donuts" is a registered trademark of Dunkin' Donuts, Inc.

"Frosty," "Wendy's," and "Wendy's Single" are registered trademarks of Wendy's International.

"Hardee's" is a registered trademark of Hardee's Food Systems, Inc.

"Hard Rock Cafe" and "Famous Baby Rock Watermelon Ribs" are registered trademarks of Hard Rock America, Inc., and Rank Organisation PLC.

"Heath" and "Bits o' Brickle" are registered trademarks of L. S. Heath & Sons, Inc.

"Hooters" is a registered trademark of Hooters of America.

"Houlihan's," "Houli Fruit Fizz," " 'Shrooms," and "Smashed Potatoes" are registered trademarks of Houlihan's Restaurant Group, Inc.

"IHOP" and "International House of Pancakes" are registered trademarks of International House of Pancakes, Inc.

"J&J" and "Super Pretzel" are registered trademarks of J&J Snack Foods Corporation.

"Jumbo Jack" and "Jack-in-the-Box" are registered trademarks of Jack-in-the-Box, Inc.

"Kahlúa" is a registered trademark of the Hiram-Walker Group.

"Keebler," "Pecan Sandies," "Soft Batch," and "Toffee Sandies" are registered trademarks of Keebler Corporation.

"KFC," "Original Recipe," "Enchirito," and "Taco Bell" are registered trademarks of PepsiCo.

"Little Caesar's," "Crazy Bread," and "Crazy Sauce" are registered trademarks of Little Caesar's Enterprises, Inc.,

"Lone Star Steakhouse & Saloon" and "Amarillo Cheese Fries" are registered trademarks of Lone Star Steakhouse & Saloon, Inc.

"Long John Silver's" is a registered trademark of Jerrico, Inc.

"Marie Callendar's" is a registered trademark of Marie Callendar's Pie Shops, Inc.

"M&M/Mars," "Mars," "Mars Almond Bar," "Milky Way," "Snickers," "3 Musketeers," and "Twix" are registered trademarks of Mars, Inc.

"Mounds," "Almond Joy," and "Peter Paul" are registered trademarks of Cadbury U.S.A., Inc.

"Nestlé," "Crunch," and "100 Grand Bar" are registered trademarks of Nestlé USA, Inc.

"The Olive Garden" and "Red Lobster" are registered trademarks of Darden Restaurants, Inc.

"Outback Steakhouse," "Bloomin' Onion," "Walkabout Soup," and "Alice Springs Chicken" are registered trademarks of Outback Steakhouse, Inc.

"Peanut Butter Dream Bar" and "Mrs. Fields" are registered trademarks of Mrs. Fields, Inc.

"Perkins," and "Granny's Country Omelette" are registered trademarks of The Restaurant Co.

"Pizza Hut" is a registered trademark and "Stuffed Crust Pizza" and "Triple Decker Pizza" are trademarks of Pizza Hut, Inc.

"Planet Hollywood" and "Chicken Crunch" are registered trademarks of Planet Hollywood (Region IV), Inc., in the United States and Canada, and Planet Hollywood International, Inc., elsewhere.

"Pogen's" is a registered trademark of Pogen's Inc.

"Popeye's Famous Fried Chicken" and "Popeye's Chicken & Biscuits" are registered trademarks of America's Favorite Chicken Company, Inc.

"Poppers" is a registered trademark of Anchor Foods, Inc.

"Red Robin Burger & Spirits Emporium," "No-Fire Peppers," and "Mountain High Mudd Pie" are registered trademarks of Skylark Co. Ltd.

"Ruby Tuesday" and "Strawberry Tallcake" are registered trademarks of Morrison Restaurants, Inc.

"Ruth's Chris Steak House" is a registered trademark of Ruth's Chris Steak House, Inc.

"Sara Lee" is a registered trademark of Sara Lee Corporation.

"See's" is a registered trademark of See's Candy, Inc.

"Shoney's is a registered trademark of Shoney's Inc.

"Sizzler" is a registered trademark of Sizzler International, Inc.

"Skor," "Reese's," "Hershey," and "York" are registered trademarks of Hershey Foods Corporation.

"Stark," "Necco," and "Mary Jane" are registered trademarks of Necco Candy Co.

"Stuart Anderson's Black Angus" is a registered trademark of American Restaurant Group, Inc.

"T.G.I. Friday's" and "Friday's Smoothies" are registered trademarks of T.G.I. Friday's, Inc.

"Tony Roma's A Place for Ribs," "Carolina Honeys," and "Red Hots" are registered trademarks of NPC International, Inc.

INDEX

Page numbers in *italics* refer to illustrations.

Alfredo Pasta, Olive Garden, 416
Alice Springs Chicken, Outback
    Steakhouse, 426–27, *428*
Almond
    Bar, M&M/Mars, 106–7, *108*
    Cookies, Twin Dragon, 198, *199*
    Joy, Peter Paul, 158–159, *160*
    Roca, Brown & Haley, 35–36, *37*
Amarillo Cheese Fries, Lone Star
    Steakhouse & Saloon, 395–96,
    397
A & W Root Beer, 13, 25, 26
Appetizers
    Applebee's
        Quesadillas, 223, 240–41, *242*
        Pizza Sticks, 243–45, *246*
    Cheesecake Factory
        Avocado Eggrolls, 295–97, *298*
        Bruschetta, 292–93, *294*
    Chi-Chi's Nachos Grande, 308–11,
        309
    Dive! Carrot Chips, 345–47, *347*
    Hooters
        Buffalo Chicken Wings, 367–68,
        369
        Buffalo Shrimp, 370–71, *372*
    Houlihan's 'Shrooms, 376–79, *378*
    Olive Garden Hot Artichoke-Spinach
        Dip, 413–14
    Outback Steakhouse
        Bloomin' Onion, 417–19, *420*
        Gold Coast Coconut Shrimp,
        421–22, *423*
    Planet Hollywood Pot Stickers,
        453–54, *455*
    Red Lobster
        Broiled Bacon-Wrapped Scallops,
        459–60
        Stuffed Mushrooms, 465, *466*
        Stuffed Shrimp, 463–64, *466*
    Red Robin No-Fire Peppers, 467–69,
        469

Ruth's Chris Steak House Barbecued
    Shrimp, 489–90
Sizzler Cheese Toast, 506
T.G.I. Friday's
    Nine-Layer Dip, 522–23, *524*
    Potato Skins, 519–20, *521*
Applebee's, 220, 238
    Club House Grill, 249–50, *251*
    Oriental Chicken Salad, 247–48
    Pizza Sticks, 243–45, *246*
        "Parmesan," 243, 247–48
    Loaded, 243, 247–18
    Quesadillas, 223, 240–41, *242*
    Tijuana "Philly" Steak Sandwich,
        252–53, *254*
Arby's Sauce, 27
Artichoke-Spinach Dip, Hot, Olive
    Garden, 413–14
Aunt Jemima Maple Syrup, 28–29
Avocado Eggrolls, Cheesecake Factory,
    295–97, *298*

Bacon
    Alice Springs Chicken, Outback
        Steakhouse, 426–27 *428*
    Amarillo Cheese Fries, Lone Star
        Steakhouse & Saloon 395–96, *397*
    Cheeseburger
        Junior, Wendy's 205, *206*
        Western, Carl's Jr., 49–50, *51*
    Chicken Club Sandwich
        Big Boy, 277–78, *279*
        Carl's Jr., 41, *42*
        Sizzler, 507–8, *509*
    Country Club Omelette, Perkins
        Family Restaurants, 434–36, *436*
    Egg McMuffin, McDonald's 18, 124–26,
        125
    Potato Skins, T.G.I. Friday's, 519–20,
        521
    Quesadillas, Applebee's, 223, 240–41,
        242

Bacon (*cont.*)
   -and Scallop Skewers, Grilled, Red
      Lobster, 460–62, *461*
   The Super Bird, Denny's, 342–44,
      343
   topping for Stuart Anderson's Black
      Angus Western T-Bone, 516
   Wrapped Scallops, Broiled, Red
      Lobster, 459–60
Bailey's Original Irish Cream, 30
Baking, 23
Banana
   Cream Pie, Marie Callender's, 409–10,
      411
   Nut Pancakes, International House of
      Pancakes, 389–90, *391*
   Smoothies, T.G.I. Friday's
      Gold Medalist, 530
      Tropical Runner, 531
   Syrup, for International House of
      Pancakes, 389–90
Barbecue (BBQ)
   Burrito, Chi-Chi's Twice Grilled,
      314–16, *316*
   Chicken Pizza, California Pizza Kitchen
      Original, 280–82, *283*
   Chicken Salad, Red Robin, 470–71,
      472
   Ribs
      Hard Rock Cafe Famous Baby Rock
         Watermelon, 364–65
      Tony Roma's Carolina Honeys, 536
      Original Baby Backs, 534–35
      Red Hots, 537–38
      World Famous, 532–33
   Scallop and Bacon Skewers, Grilled,
      Red Lobster, 460–62, *461*
   Shrimp, Ruth's Chris Steak House,
      489–90
Barbecue Sauce, Tony Roma's
   for Carolina Honeys, 536
   for Original Baby Backs, 534–35
   for Red Hots, 537–38
Batter-Dipped Fish, Long John Silver's,
   103–4, *105*
Beans
   California Pizza Kitchen Southwestern
      Burrito Pizza, 288–90, *291*
   Lone Star Steakhouse & Saloon Black
      Bean Soup, 398–99

Popeye's Red Beans and Rice,
   165–66,*167*
Ruby Tuesday Sonora Chicken Pasta,
   482–84
T.G.I. Friday's Nine-Layer Dip, 522–23,
   524
Wendy's Chili, 200–201
Bean sprouts
   Benihana Hibachi Chicken and Hibachi
      Steak, 255–57
Beef
   Applebee's Tijuana "Philly" Steak
      Sandwich, 252–53, *254*
   Big Boy Original Double-Decker
      Hamburger Classic, 274–75, *276*
   Burger King Whopper, 38–39, *40*
   Carl's Jr.
      Famous Star, 43–44, *45*
      Western Bacon Cheeseburger,
         49–50, *51*
   Chi-Chi's
      Nachos Grande, 308–10, *311*
      Twice Grilled Barbecue Burrito,
         314–16, *316*
   hamburger patties, tips on, 24
   Hardee's 1/4-Pound Hamburger, 71–72,
      72
   Hard Rock Cafe Filet Steak Sandwich,
      358–59, *360*
   In-N-Out Double-Double, 76–77, *78*
   International House of Pancakes Fajita
      Omelette, 392–93, *394*
   Jack-in-the-Box
      Jumbo Jack, 79–80, *81*
      Taco, 82–83, *84*
   McDonald's
      Big Mac, 121–22, *123*
      Hamburger, 129–30, *131*
      McD.L.T., 132–33, *134*
      Quarter Pounder (with Cheese),
         135–36, *136*
   Taco Bell Enchirito, 185–86, *187*
   Ruth's Chris Steak House Petite Filet,
      491–93
   Shoney's Slow-Cooked Pot Roast,
      500–502
   Stuart Anderson's Black Angus
      Western T-Bone, 515–16
      Whiskey Pepper Steak, 517–18
   Wendy's

Chili, 200–201
Double, *209*
Junior Bacon Cheeseburger, 205,
206
Single, 207–8, *209*
White Castle Burgers, 210–11, *212*
Bell pepper
Cheesecake Factory Cajun Jambalaya
Pasta, 299–301
Chi-Chi's Twice Grilled Barbecue
Burrito, 314–16, *316*
Hard Rock Cafe Grilled Vegetable
Sandwich, 361–63, *362*
Perkins Family Restaurants Granny's
Country Omelette, 431–32, *433*
T.G.I. Friday's Spicy Cajun Chicken
Pasta, 528–29
Benihana
Dipping Sauces, 258–59
Ginger, 259
Mustard, 258
Hibachi Chicken, 255–57
Hibachi Steak, 255–57
Japanese Fried Rice, 260–61
Ben & Jerry's Heath Bar Crunch Ice
Cream, 31–32
Bennigan's
Buffalo Chicken Sandwich, 262–63,
264
California Turkey Sandwich, 265–66,
267
Cookie Mountain Sundae, 268–71,
271
Beverages
A & W Root Beer, 25, 26
Bailey's Original Irish Cream, 30
Hard Rock Cafe Orange Freeze, 366
Houlihan's Houli Fruit Fizz, 375
Julius
Orange, 155
Pineapple, 156
Strawberry, 156
Kahlúa Coffee Liqueur, 85–86
Snapple Iced Tea, 177–78
Cranberry, 178
Diet Lemmon, 177
Lemon, 177
Orange, 178
Strawberry, 178
T.G.I. Friday's Smoothies, 530–31

Gold Medalist, 530
Tropical Runner, 531
Wendy's Frosty, 202
Yoo-Hoo Chocolate Drink, 213
Big Boy, 220, 221, 236
Club Sandwich, 277–78, *279*
Cream of Broccoli Soup, 272–73
Original Double-Decker Hamburger
Classic, 274–75, *276*
Big Mac, McDonald's, 121–22, *123*
Biscuits, KFC Buttermilk, 92–93
Black beans
Lone Star Steakhouse & Saloon Black
Bean Soup, 398–99
Red Robin BBQ Chicken Salad,
470–71, *472*
Ruby Tuesday Sonora Chicken Pasta,
482–84
Blintz, Cheese, International House of
Pancakes, 385–87, *388*
Blizzard, Dairy Queen, 18, 58–59, *60*
Bloomin' Onion, Outback Steakhouse,
222, 417–19, *420*
Borden Crackerjack, 33–34
Bourbon Salmon, Sweet, Lone Star
Steakhouse & Saloon, 402–3
Bread(s) and rolls
Bruschetta, Cheesecake Factory,
292–93, *294*
Buttermilk Biscuits, KFC, 92–93
Cheesy Garlic, Stuart Anderson's
Black Angus 512–13, *514*
Cinnamon Rolls, Cinnabon, 55–56, *57*
Cornbread, Famous Golden, Marie
Callender's, 404–5
Crazy, Little Caesar's, 100–101, *101*
Eggs-in-the-Basket, Cracker Barrel,
331–32, *333*
French Toast, International House of
Pancakes, 382–83, *384*
Pizza, Planet Hollywood, 447–49, *448*
Pizza Sticks, Applebee's, 243–45, *246*
Pretzels, Super, J&J, 182–83, *184*
Brick Oven Mushroom and Turkey
Cheese Sub, Dive!, 352–53, *354*
Broccoli Soup, Cream of, Big Boy,
272–73
Broiled Bacon-Wrapped Scallops, Red
Lobster, 459–60
Brown & Haley Almond Roca, 35–36, *37*

Bruschetta, Cheesecake Factory, 292–93, *294*
Buffalo Chicken Sandwich, Bennigan's, 262–63 *264*
Buffalo Chicken Wings, Hooters, 367–68, *369*
Buffalo Shrimp, Hooters, 370–71, *372*
Burger King
    Double Whopper with Cheese, 10
    Whopper, 38–39, *40*
Burgers, White Castle, 210–11, *212*
Burgers. See Cheeseburger; Hamburger
Burrito
    Pizza, California Pizza Kitchen Southwestern, 288–90, *291*
    Twice Grilled Barbecue, Chi-Chi's, 314–16, *316*
Buttermilk
    Biscuits, KFC, 92–93
    Pancakes, International House of Pancakes, 157
Butterscotch
    Lollipop, See's, 174–75, *176*
    Krimpets, Tastykake, 189–90, *191*

Cabbage
    Applebee's Oriental Chicken Salad, 247–48
    KFC Cole Slaw, 94–95, *96*
Cajun Chicken Pasta, T.G.I. Friday's Spicy, 528–29
Cajun Jambalaya Pasta, Cheesecake Factory, 299–301
Cajun Mayonnaise Dipping Sauce, for Dive! Carrot Chips, 346
Cake(s) and Cupcake(s)
    Cheesecake Factory
        Key Lime Cheesecake, 305–6, *307*
        Pumpkin Cheesecake, 302–3, *304*
    Chi-Chi's Sweet Corn Cake, 312–13
    Chili's Peanut Buttercup Cheesecake, 325–27, *328*
    Dunkin' Donuts, 61–64, *64*
    Hostess Twinkies, 17, 73–74, *75*
    Ruby Tuesday Strawberry Tallcake for Two, 485–87, *488*
    Sara Lee Original Cream Cheesecake, 171–72, *173*
    Shoney's Hot Fudge Cake, 503–4, *505*
    Tastykake

Butterscotch Krimpets, 189–90, *191*
    Chocolate Cupcakes, 192–94, *194*
    Peanut Butter Kandy Kakes, 195–96, *197*
California Chargrilled Turkey Sandwich, T.G.I. Friday's, 525–26, *527*
California Pizza Kitchen
    Original BBQ Chicken Pizza, 280–82, *283*
    Southwestern Burrito Pizza, 288–90, *291*
    Thai Chicken Pizza, 284–86, *287*
California Turkey Sandwich, Bennigan's, 265–66, *267*
Calories, 10–11
Candy
    Brown & Haley Almond Roca, 35–36, *37*
    Heath Bar, 36
    in Ben & Jerry's Heath Bar Crunch Ice Cream, 31–32
    in Dairy Queen Blizzard, 18, 58–59, *60*
    Hershey's Skor, 36
    M&M/Mars
        Almond Bar, 106–7, *108*
        Caramel Twix Bars, 109–10, *111*
        Milky Way, 112–13, *114*
        Snickers Bar, 115–16, *117*
        3 Musketeers, 118–19, *120*
    Nestlé
        Crunch, 151–52, *152*
        100 Grand Bar, 153, *154*
    Peter Paul
        Almond Joy, 158–59, *160*
        Mounds, 158–59, *160*
    Reese's Peanut Butter Cups, 7, 168–69, *170*
    See's Butterscotch Lollipop, 174–75, *176*
    Stark Mary Jane, 179–80, *181*
    York Peppermint Pattie, 214–15, *216*
Cap'n Crunch cereal
    in Planet Hollywood Chicken Crunch, 450–51, *452*
Capocollo
    in Dive! Sicilian Sub Rosa, 348–50, *351*
Caramel
    M&M/Mars
        Almond Bar, 106–7, *108*

Milky Way, 112–13, *114*
Snickers Bar, 115–16, *117*
Twix Bars, 109–10, *111*
Nestlé 100 Grand Bar, 153, *154*
topping, for Red Robin Mountain High
    Mudd Pie, 473–75, *476*
Caribbean Salad, Chili's Grilled, 320–21
Carl's Jr., 6, 14, 18
    Chicken Club, 41, *42*
    Famous Star, 43–44, *45*
    Sante Fe Chicken, 46–47, *48*
    Western Bacon Cheeseburger, 49–50,
        51
    Double, 51
    Junior, 51
Carolina Honeys, Tony Roma's, 536
Carrots
    Dive! Chips, 345–47, *347*
    KFC Cole Slaw, 94–95, *96*
Casserole, Cracker Barrel Hash Brown,
    329–30
Cheese
    Blintz, International House of
        Pancakes, 385–87, *388*
    Fries, Lone Star Steakhouse & Saloon
        Amarillo, 395–96, *397*
    six- blend, for Pizza Hut Triple Decker
        Pizza, 444–46
    Soup
        Outback Steakhouse Walkabout
        Soup, 424–25
        Ruby Tuesday Potato, 477–78
    Toast, Sizzler, 506
    see also Cheeseburger; and specific
        types
Cheese, American
    Big Boy Original Double-Decker
        Hamburger Classic, 274–75, *276*
    Carl's Jr.
        Sante Fe Chicken, 46–47, *48*
        Western Bacon Cheeseburger,
        49–50, *51*
    Denny's Moons Over My Hammy,
        339–40, *341*
    In-N-Out Double-Double, 76–77, *78*
    Jack-in-the-Box Taco, 82–83, *84*
    McDonald's
        Big Mac, 121–22, *123*
        Cheeseburger, 130
        Egg McMuffin, 18, 124–25, *126*

McD.L.T., 132–33, *134*
Quarter Pounder (with), 135–36,
    136
Wendy's
    Double with, *209*
    Junior Bacon Cheeseburger, 205,
    206
    Single with, 207–8
    White Castle Burgers, 210–11, *212*
Cheese, Cheddar
    Applebee's
        Club House Grill, 249–50, *251*
        Quesadillas, 223, 240–41, *242*
        Tijuana "Philly" Steak Sandwich,
        252–53, *254*
    California Pizza Kitchen Southwestern
        Burrito Pizza, 288–90, *291*
    Chi-Chi's Nachos Grande, 308–11,
        309
    Denny's Scram Slam, 337–38
    International House of Pancakes Fajita
        Omelette, 392–93, *394*
    Lone Star Steakhouse & Saloon
        Amarillo Fries, 395–96, *397*
    Outback Steakhouse
        Alice Springs Chicken, 426–27 *428*
        Walkabout Soup, 424–25
    Red Robin BBQ Chicken Salad,
        470–71, *472*
    Ruby Tuesday Potato Cheese Soup,
        477–78
    Ruth's Chris Steak House Potatoes Au
        Gratin, 496–97
    Stuart Anderson's Black Angus Cheesy
        Garlic Bread, 512–13, *514*
    Taco Bell Enchirito, 185–86, *187*
    T.G.I. Friday's
        Nine-Layer Dip, 522–23, *524*
        Potato Skins, 519–20, *521*
    White Dipping Sauce, for Dive! Carrot
        Chips, 346–47
Cheese, Colby
    Cracker Barrel Hash Brown Casserole,
        329–30
Cheese, cream. See Cream cheese.
Cheese, Gouda
    California Pizza Kitchen Original BBQ
        Chicken Pizza, 280–83, *282*
Cheese, Monterey Jack
    Applebee's

Cheese, Monterey Jack (*cont.*)
    Quesadillas, 223, 240–41, *242*
    Tijuana "Philly" Steak Sandwich,
      252–53, *254*
    California Pizza Kitchen Southwestern
      Burrito Pizza, 288–90, *291*
    Chi-Chi's Nachos Grande, 308–11,
      309
    Lone Star Steakhouse & Saloon
      Amarillo Fries, 395–96, *397*
    Outback Steakhouse Alice Springs
      Chicken, 426–27 *428*
    Ruby Tuesday Potato Cheese Soup,
      477–78
Cheese, Mozzarella
    Applebee's Pizza Sticks, 243–45, *246*
      Loaded, 243, 247–48
      "Parmesan", 243, 247–48
    California Pizza Kitchen
      Original BBQ Chicken Pizza,
      280–82, *283*
      Thai Chicken Pizza, 284–86, *287*
    Pizza Hut
      Original Stuffed Crust Pizza,
      437–40, *441*
      Original Stuffed Crust Pepperoni
      and Cheese Pizza, 442
      Triple Decker Pizza, 443–45, *446*
    Planet Hollywood Pizza Bread,
      447–48, *449*
Cheese, Parmesan
    Applebee's Pizza Sticks, 243–45, *246*
      Loaded, 243, 247–48
      "Parmesan", 243, 247–48
    Sizzler Cheese Toast, 506
Cheese, Provolone
    Ruby Tuesday Smokey Mountain
      Chicken, 479–80, *481*
Cheese, Swiss
    Big Boy Club Sandwich, 277–78, *279*
    Carl's Jr. Chicken Club, 41, *42*
    Denny's
      Moons Over My Hammy, 339–40,
      341
      The Super Bird, 342–43, *344*
    Dive! Brick Oven Mushroom and
      Turkey Cheese Sub, 352–53, *354*
    Sizzler Chicken Club Sandwich, 507–8,
      509
Cheeseburger

Carl's Jr. Western Bacon, 49–50, *51*
McDonald's, 130
Wendy's
    Double with cheese, *209*
    Junior Bacon, 205, *206*
    Single with cheese, 207–8, *208*
  see also Hamburger
Cheesecake
    Key Lime, Cheesecake Factory, 305–6,
      307
    Original Cream, Sara Lee, 171–72,
      173
    Peanut Buttercup, Chili's, 325–27, *328*
    Pumpkin, Cheesecake Factory, 302–3,
      304
Cheesecake Factory
    Avocado Eggrolls, 295–97, *298*
    Bruschetta, 292–93, *294*
    Cajun Jambalaya Pasta, 299–301
    Key Lime Cheesecake, 305–6, *307*
    Pumpkin Cheesecake, 302–3, *304*
Cheesy Garlic Bread, Stuart Anderson's
    Black Angus, 512–14, *514*
Chesapeake Cookies, Pepperidge Farm,
    91
Chi-Chi's, 220
    Mexican "Fried" Ice Cream, 317–18,
      319
    Nachos Grande, 308–10, *311*
    Sweet Corn Cake, 312–13
    Twice Grilled Barbecue Burrito,
      314–16, *316*
Chicken
    Alice Springs, Outback Steakhouse,
      426–27 *428*
    Buffalo Wings, Hooters 367–68, *369*
    Crunch, Planet Hollywood, 450–51,
      452
    & Dumplins, Cracker Barrel, 334–36
    Fajita(s)
      Omelette, International House of
      Pancakes, 392–93, *394*
      for Two, Chili's, 322–24
    Flame-Broiled, El Pollo Loco, 65–66
    Fried
      Famous, Popeye's, 163, *164*
      Original Recipe, KFC, 97–98, *99*
    Hibachi, Benihana 255–57
    Nachos Grande, Chi-Chi's, *311*, *309*
    Pasta

Cajun Jambalaya, Cheesecake
 Factory, 299–301
Sonora, Ruby Tuesday, 482–84
Spicy Cajun, T.G.I. Friday's, 528–29
Pizza
 Original BBQ, California Pizza
  Kitchen, 280–82, 283
 Southwestern Burrito, California
  Pizza Kitchen 288–90, 291
 Thai, California Pizza Kitchen,
  284–86, 287
Pot Pie, Marie Callender's, 406–8
Salad
 BBQ, Red Robin, 470–71, 472
 Grilled Caribbean, Chili's, 320–21
 Oriental, Applebee's, 247–48
Sandwich
 Buffalo, Bennigan's, 262–63 264
 Chicken Club, Carl's Jr., 41, 42
 Chick-Fil-A-Chicken, 52–53, 54
 Club, Sizzler, 507–8, 509
 Grilled Fillet, Wendy's, 203, 204
 Sante Fe Chicken, Carl's Jr., 46–47,
  48
 Smokey Mountain, Ruby Tuesday
  479–80, 481
 "Teriyaki" Breast, Western Sizzlin,
  539–40, 541
Chick-Fil-A-Chicken Sandwich, 52–53,
 54
Chili, Wendy's, 200–201
Chilies
 California Pizza Kitchen Southwestern
  Burrito Pizza, 288–90, 291
Chili's Grill & Bar, 220
 Fajitas for Two, 322–24
 Grilled Caribbean Salad, 320–21
 Peanut Buttercup Cheesecake,
  325–27, 328
Chocolate
 Bennigan's Cookie Mountain Sundae,
  268–71, 271
 Chili's Peanut Buttercup Cheesecake,
  325–27, 328
 cooking tips, 20–21
 Dive! S'Mores, 355–56, 357
 Dunkin' Donuts Glazed Donuts,
  61–64, 64
 Red Robin Mountain High Mudd Pie,
  473–75, 476

Tastykake Chocolate Cupcakes,
 192–94, 194
top-selling bars, 13–14
Chocolate Chip Cookies (semisweet)
 for Bennigan's Cookie Mountain
  Sundae, 268–71, 271
 Keebler Soft Batch, 90–91
 Mrs. Fields, 3–4, 137–38, 139
  Peanut Butter Dream Bars, 140–
   41, 142
 Nabisco Chips Ahoy!, 143, 144
 Pepperidge Farm
  Chesapeake, 91
  Sausalito, 91
 in Tastykake Chocolate Cupcakes,
  192–94, 194
Chocolate chips, milk-
 Brown & Haley Almond Roca, 35–36,
  37
 Heath bar, 36
 Hershey's Skor, 36
 M&M/Mars
  Almond Bar, 106–7, 108
  Caramel Twix Bars, 109–10, 111
  Milky Way, 112–13, 114
  Snickers Bar, 115–16, 117
  3 Musketeers, 118–19, 120
 melting, 20–21
 Mrs. Fields Peanut Butter Dream Bars,
  140–41, 142
 Nestlé
  Crunch, 151–52, 152
  100 Grand Bar, 153, 154
  Peter Paul Almond Joy, 158–59, 160
  Reese's Peanut Butter Cups, 7,
   168–69, 170
 Tastykake Peanut Butter Kandy Kakes,
  195–96, 197
 type to buy, 20–21
Chocolate chips, semisweet
 Keebler Soft Batch Chocolate Chip
  Cookies, 90–91
 melting, 20–21
 M&M/Mars
  Milky Way, 112–13, 114
  3 Musketeers, 118–19, 120
 Peter Paul Mounds, 158–59, 160
 York Peppermint Pattie, 214–15, 216
Chocolate-drink powder
 Wendy's Frosty, 202

Chocolate-drink powder (*cont.*)
Yoo-Hoo Chocolate Drink, 213
Cinnabon Cinnamon Rolls, 55–56, *57*
Cinnamon Rolls, Cinnabon, 55–56, *57*
Club Sandwich
Applebee's Club House Grill, 249–50, *251*
Big Boy Chicken, 277–78, *279*
Carl's Jr. Chicken, 41, *42*
Sizzler Chicken, 507–8, *509*
Coconut
Outback Steakhouse Gold Coast Shrimp, 421–22, *423*
Peter Paul
Almond Joy, 158–59, *160*
Mounds, 158–59, *160*
Coffee Liqueur, Kahlúa, 85–86
Cole Slaw, KFC, 94–95, *96*
Convenience food, 10–19
Cookie(s)
baking tips, 23
Keebler
Pecan Sandies, 87–88, *89*
Soft Batch Chocolate Chip, 90–91
Toffee Sandies, 88
Mountain Sundae, Bennigan's, 268–71, *271*
Mrs. Fields
Chocolate Chip, 3–4, 137–39, *139*
Peanut Butter Dream Bars, 140–41, *142*
Nabisco
Chips Ahoy!, 143, *144*
Double Stuf Oreo, 148, 150
Nutter Butter, 145–46, *147*
Oreo, 148–49, *150*
Oreo Big Stuf, 150
Peanut Butter, for Red Robin Mountain High Mudd Pie, *476*
Pepperidge Farm
Chesapeake, 91
Sausalito, 91
Pogen's Gingershaps, 161–62
Twin Dragon Almond, 198, *199*
Cooking tips, 20–24, 225–26
baking, 23
and blueprints, 226
chocolate, 20–21
eggs, 22–23
hamburger patties, 24

reading recipes, 225
recipe yields, 226
using parts of recipes for other dishes, 226
yeast dough, 21–22
Corn
Chi-Chi's Sweet Corn Cake, 312–13
Cornmeal
Chi-Chi's Sweet Corn Cake, 312–13
Marie Callender's Famous Golden Cornbread, 404–5
Cottage cheese
International House of Pancakes Cheese Blintz, 385–87, *388*
Country Club Omelette, Perkins Family Restaurants, 434–36, *436*
Country Fried Steak, Shoney's, 498–99
Cracker Barrel, 220
Chicken & Dumplins, 334–36
Eggs-in-the-Basket, 331–32, *333*
Hash Brown Casserole, 329–30
Crackerjack, Borden, 33–34
Cranberry juice
Houlihan's Houli Fruit Fizz, 375
Snapple Iced Tea, 178
Crazy Bread, Little Caesar's, 100–101, *101*
Crazy Sauce, Little Caesar's, 102
Cream
Bailey's Original Irish Cream, 30
Big Boy Cream of Broccoli Soup, 272–73
Marie Callender's Banana Cream Pie, 409–10, *411*
Outback Steakhouse Walkabout Soup, 424–25
Ruth's Chris Steak House
Creamed Spinach, 494–95
Potatoes Au Gratin, 496–97
Cream cheese
Cheesecake Factory
Key Lime Cheesecake, 305–6, *307*
Pumpkin Cheesecake, 302–3, *304*
Chili's Peanut Buttercup Cheesecake, 325–27, *328*
Houlihan's 'Shrooms, 376–79, *378*
International House of Pancakes Cheese Blintz, 385–87, *388*
Olive Garden Hot Artichoke-Spinach Dip, 413–14

Red Robin No-Fire Peppers, 467–69,
469
Sara Lee Original Cream Cheesecake,
171–72, 173
Creme filling
for Tastykake Chocolate Cupcakes,
194
Creole Mustard Sauce, for Planet
Hollywood Chicken Crunch,
450–51
Crepes, for International House of
Pancakes Cheese Blintz, 385–87,
388
Crunch, Nestlé, 151–52, 152

Dairy Queen Blizzard, 18, 58–59, 60
Deli meats
Dive! Sicilian Sub Rosa, 348–50, 351
Denny's, 220, 236
Moons Over My Hammy, 339–40, 341
Scram Slam, 337–38
The Super Bird, 342–43, 344
Devil's food cake mix
in Shoney's Hot Fudge Cake, 503–5,
505
Diet Lemon Iced Tea, Snapple, 177
Dip
Olive Garden Hot Artichoke-Spinach,
413–14
T.G.I. Friday's Nine-Layer, 522–23, 524
Dipping Sauce
Benihana, 258–59
Ginger Sauce, 259
Mustard Sauce, 258
Cajun Mayonnaise, for Dive! Carrot
Chips, 346
for Cheesecake Factory Avocado
Eggrolls, 296
Creole Mustard, for Planet Hollywood
Chicken Crunch, 450–51
Marinara, Applebee's Quesadillas, 223,
240–41, 242
Marmalade, for Outback Steakhouse
Gold Coast Coconut Shrimp, 422
mayonnaise
-horseradish, for Outback
Steakhouse Bloomin' Onion,
417–19, 420
-mustard-horseradish, for Houlihan's
'Shrooms, 376–79, 378

Ranch Dressing, for Lone Star Steak
House & Saloon Amarillo Cheese
Fries, 397
White Cheddar, for Dive! Carrot
Chips, 346–47
Dive!, 220
Brick Oven Mushroom and Turkey
Cheese Sub, 352–53, 354
Carrot Chips, 345–47, 347
Sicilian Sub Rosa, 348–50, 351
S'Mores, 355–56, 357
Double, Wendy's, 209
with cheese, 209
Double-Decker Hamburger Classic, Big
Boy Original, 274–75, 276
Double-Double, In-N-Out, 76–77, 78
Double Stuf Oreos, Nabisco, 148, 150
Doughnuts
Dunkin', 61–64, 64
holes, 64
Dressing
Applebee's Oriental, 247–48
Olive Garden Italian, 412
Ranch, Lone Star Steak House &
Saloon, 397
see also Dipping Sauces
Dumplings
Cracker Barrel Chicken &, 334–36
Planet Hollywood Pot Stickers,
453–54, 455
Duncan Hines
Dark Dutch Fudge cake mix, in
Nabisco Oreo Cookies, 148–49,
150
Moist Deluxe Devil's Food cake mix, in
Tastykake Chocolate Cupcakes,
192–94, 194
Dunkin' Donuts, 61–64, 64
chocolate glazed, 62
donut holes, 64
plain glaze, 61

Eggplant
Hard Rock Cafe Grilled Vegetable
Sandwich, 361–63, 362
Eggrolls, Cheesecake Factory Avocado,
295–97, 298
Eggs
French Toast, International House of
Pancakes, 382–83, 384

Eggs (*cont.*)
-in-the-Basket, Cracker Barrel, 331–32, *333*
McMuffin, McDonald's, 124–26, *Moons* Over My Hammy, Denny's, 339–40, *341*
Omelette
Country Club, Perkins Family Restaurants, 434–36, *436*
Fajita, International House of Pancakes, 392–93, *394*
Granny's Country, Perkins Family Restaurants, 431–32, *433*
Scram Slam, Denny's, 337–38
separating, 22–22
El Pollo Loco
Flame-Broiled Chicken, 65–66
Salsa, 67
Enchirito, Taco Bell, 185–86, *187*

Fajita
Omelette, International House of Pancakes, 392–93, *394*
for Two, Chili's, 322–24
Famous Fried Chicken, Popeye's, 163, 164
Famous Golden Cornbread, Marie Callender, 404–5
Famous Star, Carl's Jr., 43–44, *45*
Famous Baby Rock Watermelon Ribs, Hard Rock Cafe, 364–65
Farmer cheese
International House of Pancakes Cheese Blintz, 385–87, *388*
Fast-food chains, 25
leading, 16–17
light or healthy fare in, 17–19
Fat, 10, 17–18
and hamburger patties, 24
Fettuccine
Cheesecake Factory Cajun Jambalaya Pasta, 299–301
Olive Garden Alfredo Pasta, 416
T.G.I. Friday's Spicy Cajun Chicken Pasta, 528–29
Filet mignon
Applebee's Tijuana "Philly" Sandwich, 252–53, *254*
Hard Rock Cafe Filet Steak Sandwich, 358–59, *360*

Ruth's Chris Steak House Petite Filet, 491–93
Fish
Lone Star Steakhouse & Saloon Sweet Bourbon Salmon, 402–3
Long John Silver's Batter-Dipped, 103–4, *105*
McDonald's Filet-O-Fish, 127–28, *128*
Flame-Broiled Chicken, El Pollo Loco, 65–66
Food additives, 7–8
French Fries
Hardee's, 68–69, *70*
Lone Star Steakhouse & Saloon Amarillo Cheese, 395–96, *397*
French's French Fried Onions in Houlihan's Smashed Potatoes, 380–81, *381*
French Toast, International House of Pancakes, 382–83, *384*
Fried Chicken
KFC Original Recipe, 97–98, *99*
Popeye's Famous Fried Chicken, 163, 164
"Fried" Ice Cream, Chi-Chi's Mexican, 317–18, *319*
Fried Rice, Benihana Japanese, 260–61
Fruit Fizz, Houlihan's Houli, 375
Fudge
in Chili's Peanut Buttercup Cheesecake, 325–27, *328*
Hot, Bennigan's Cookie Mountain Sundae, 268–71, *271*
Red Robin Mountain High Mudd Pie, 473–75, *476*
Shoney's Hot Fudge Cake, 503–4, *505*
"Full-service" restaurants, 219–22
number of, 220
top ten chains, 220

Garlic Bread
Cheesecake Factory Bruschetta, 292–93, *294*
Stuart Anderson's Black Angus Cheesy, 512–13, *514*
Ginger Sauce, Benihana Dipping Sauces, 259
Gingershaps, Pogen's, 161–62
Golden pound cake mix

Tastykake Peanut Butter Kandy Kakes,
195–96, *197*
Graham crackers
in Dive! S'Mores, 355–56, *357*
Granny's Country Omelette, Perkins
Family Restaurants, 431–32, *433*
Gravy
Country, for Shoney's Country Fried
Steak, 498–99
for Shoney's Slow-Cooked Pot Roast,
500–502
Grilled Caribbean Salad, Chili's, 320–21
Grilled Chicken Fillet Sandwich, Wendy's,
203, *204*
Grilled Scallop and Bacon Skewers, Red
Lobster, 460–62, *461*
Grilled Vegetable Sandwich, Hard Rock
Cafe, 361–63, *362*

Ham
Applebee's Club House Grill, 249–50,
251
Denny's Moons Over My Hammy,
339–40, *341*
Perkins Family Restaurants Granny's
Country Omelette, 431–32, *433*
Ruby Tuesday Smokey Mountain
Chicken, 479–80, *481*
Hamburger
Big Boy Original Double-Decker
Classic, 274–75, *276*
Burger King Whopper, 38–39, *40*
Carl's Jr. Famous Star, 43–44, *45*
Hardee's ¼-Pound, 71–72, *72*
In-N-Out Double-Double, 76–77, *78*
Jack-in-the-Box Jumbo Jack, 79–80, *81*
McDonald's
Big Mac, 121–22, *123*
Hamburger, 129–30, *131*
McD.L.T., 132–33, *134*
Quarter Pounder (with Cheese),
135–36, *136*
patties, tips on, 24
Wendy's
Double, *209*
Single, 207, *209*
See also Cheeseburger
Hardee's
French Fries, 68–69, *70*
¼-Pound Hamburger, 71–72, *72*

Hard Rock Cafe, 220, 237–38
Famous Baby Rock Watermelon Ribs,
364–65
Filet Steak Sandwich, 358–59, *360*
Grilled Vegetable Sandwich, 361–62,
363
Orange Freeze, 366
Hash Brown(s)
Casserole, Cracker Barrel, 329–30
in Perkins Family Restaurants Granny's
Country Omelette, 431–32, *433*
in Perkins Family Restaurants Potato
Pancakes, 429–30
Heath Bar, 36
Blizzard, Dairy Queen, 18, 58–59, *60*
Crunch Ice Cream, Ben & Jerry's,
31–32
Heath Bits 'o Brickle, 88
Herb Cheese Filling, for Houlihan's
'Shrooms, 376–79, *378*
Hershey's, 13
milk-chocolate bars, in Dive! S'Mores,
355–56, *357*
milk-chocolate chips, in Reese's Peanut
Butter Cups, 7, 168–69, *170*
Tastykake Peanut Butter Kandy Kakes,
195–96, *197*
Skor, 36
Hibachi Steak, Benihana, 255–57
Hollandaise Sauce
for Perkins Family Restaurants
Country Club Omelette, 434–36
Honey
Butter, for Marie Callender's Famous
Golden Cornbread, 404–5
Mustard Marinade, for Outback
Steakhouse Alice Springs Chicken,
426
Mustard Sauce, for T.G.I. Friday's
California Chargrilled Turkey
Sandwich, 525–26
Tony Roma's Carolina Honeys, 536
Hooters
Buffalo Chicken Wings, 367–68, *369*
Buffalo Shrimp, 370–71, *372*
Pasta Salad, 373–74
Horseradish
-mayonnaise dipping sauce, for
Outback Steakhouse Bloomin'
Onion, 417–19, *420*

Horseradish (*cont.*)
  -mayonnaise-mustard dipping sauce
    Houlihan's 'Shrooms, 376–79, *378*
Hostess, 13
  Twinkies, 17, 73–74, *75*
Hot Artichoke-Spinach Dip, Olive
    Garden, 413–14
Hot Fudge Cake, Shoney's, 503–4, *505*
Hot Taco Sauce, Taco Bell, 188
Houlihan's
  Houli Fruit Fizz, 375
  'Shrooms, 376–79, *378*
  Smashed Potatoes, 380–81, *381*
Howard Johnson's, 13

Ice Cream and Sherbet
  Ben & Jerry's Heath Bar Crunch,
    31–32
  Bennigan's Cookie Mountain Sundae,
    268–71, *271*
  Chi-Chi's Mexican "Fried," 317–18,
    319
  Dairy Queen Blizzard, 18, 58–59, *60*
  Hard Rock Cafe Orange Freeze, 366
  Red Robin Mountain High Mudd Pie,
    473–75, *476*
  Ruby Tuesday Strawberry Tallcake for
    Two, 485–87, *488*
  Shoney's Hot Fudge Cake, 503–4, *505*
  Wendy's Frosty, 202
Iced Tea, Snapple, 177–78
  Cranberry, 178
  Diet Lemon, 177
  Lemon, 177
  Orange, 178
  Strawberry, 178
Icing
  Buttercream, Tastykake Chocolate
    Cupcakes, 192–94, *194*
  Chocolate, Tastykake Chocolate
    Cupcakes, 192–94, *194*
Ingredients, 7–8
International House of Pancakes, 236
  Cheese Blintz, 385–87, *388*
  Fajita Omelette, 392–93, *394*
  French Toast, 382–83, *384*
  Pancakes, 157
    Banana Nut, 389–90, *391*
Irish whiskey
  in Bailey's Original Irish Cream, 30

Italian Salad Dressing, Olive Garden, 412
Italian sausage
  Applebee's Pizza Sticks, 243–45, *246*
  Loaded, 243, 247–48

Jack-in-the-Box, 6
  Jumbo Jack, 79–80, *81*
  Taco, 82–83, *84*
Jalapeño peppers
  Red Robin No-Fire Peppers, 467–69,
    469
J&J Super Pretzels, 182–83, *184*
Jambalaya Pasta, Cheesecake Factory
    Cajun, 299–301
Japanese Fried Rice, Benihana, 260–61
Julius
  Orange, 155
  Pineapple, 156
  Strawberry, 156
Jumbo Jack, Jack-in-the-Box, 79–80, *81*
Junior Bacon Cheeseburger, Wendy's,
    205, *206*

Kale
  Olive Garden Toscana Soup, 415
Keebler, 13
  Pecan Sandies, 87–88, *89*
  Soft Batch Chocolate Chip Cookies,
    90–91
  Toffee Sandies, 88
Key Lime Cheesecake, Cheesecake
    Factory, 305–6, *307*
KFC (Kentucky Fried Chicken), 15, 17, 18
  Buttermilk Biscuits, 92–93
  Cole Slaw, 94–95, *96*
  Original Recipe Fried Chicken, 97–98,
    99
Krimpets, Tastykake Butterscotch,
    189–90, *191*

Lemon, Snapple Iced Tea, 177
  Diet, 177
Lime
  Cheesecake Factory Key Lime
    Cheesecake, 305–6, *307*
Liqueur
  Bailey's Original Irish Cream, 30
  Kahlúa Coffee, 85–86
Little Caesar's
  Crazy Bread, 100–1, *101*

Crazy Sauce, 102
Lobster, Red Lobster Broiled Lobster, 456–57, *458*
Lollipop, See's Butterscotch, 174–75, *176*
Lone Star Steakhouse & Saloon
  Amarillo Cheese Fries, 395–96, *397*
  Black Bean Soup, 398–99
  Sweet Bourbon Salmon, 402–3
  Texas Rice, 400–401
Long John Silver's Batter-Dipped Fish, 103–4, *105*

Macadamia nuts
  Mrs. Fields Chocolate Chip Cookies, *139*
  Pepperidge Farm Sausalito Cookies, 91
M&M/Mars, 13
  Almond Bar, 106–7, *108*
  Caramel Twix Bars, 109–10, *111*
  Milky Way, 112–13, *114*
  Peanut Butter Twix Bars, 110
  Snickers Bar, 115–16, *117*
  3 Musketeers, 118–19, *120*
Maple Syrup, Aunt Jemima, 28–29
Marie Callender's, 220
  Banana Cream Pie, 409–10, *411*
  Chicken Pot Pie, 406–8
  Famous Golden Cornbread, 404–5
Marinade
  Chi-Chi's Twice Grilled Barbecue Burrito, 314–16, *316*
  Chili's Fajitas for Two, 323
  Honey Mustard, for Outback Steakhouse Alice Springs Chicken, 426
  Smoky, for Stuart Anderson's Black Angus Western T-Bone, 516
  Sweet Bourbon, for Lone Star Steakhouse & Saloon Salmon, 402–3
Marinara Dipping Sauce, Applebee's Quesadillas, 223, 240–41, *242*
Marmalade Sauce, Outback Steakhouse Gold Coast Coconut Shrimp, 422
Marshmallows
  in Dive! S'Mores, 355–56, *357*
Mary Jane, Stark, 179–80, *181*
Mayonnaise
  Cajun Dipping Sauce, for Dive! Carrot Chips, 346

-horseradish Dipping Sauce, for Outback Steakhouse Bloomin' Onion, 417–19, *420*
-mustard-horseradish, for Houlihan's 'Shrooms, 376–79, *378*
McD.L.T., McDonald's, 132–33, *134*
McDonald's, 14–15, 18, 236
  Big Mac, 121–22, *123*
  cost, 5–6
  taste, 8
  Cheeseburger, 130
  Egg McMuffin, 18, 124–25, *126*
  Filet-O-Fish, 127–28, *128*
  Hamburger, 129–30, *131*
  McD.L.T., 132–33, *134*
  Quarter Pounder (with Cheese), 135–36, *136*
Mexican "Fried" Ice Cream, Chi-Chi's, 317–18, *319*
Milk
  Yoo-Hoo Chocolate Drink, 213
  Milky Way, M&M/Mars, 112–13, *114*
  II, 18
Moons Over My Hammy, Denny's, 339–40, *341*
Mortadella
  Dive! Sicilian Sub Rosa, 348–50, *351*
Mounds, Peter Paul, 158–59, *160*
Mountain High Mudd Pie, Red Robin, 473–75, *476*
Mousse, Strawberry, for Ruby Tuesday Strawberry Tallcake for Two, 485–87, *488*
Mrs. Fields
  Chocolate Chip Cookies, 3–4, 137–38, *139*
  Peanut Butter Dream Bars, 140–41, *142*
Mrs. Paul's breaded fish portions
  McDonald's Filet-O-Fish, 127–28, *128*
Mudd Pie, Mountain High, Red Robin, 473–75, *476*
Mushrooms
  Benihana Hibachi Chicken and Hibachi Steak, 255–57
  Denny's Scram Slam, 337–38
  Dive! Brick Oven Mushroom and Turkey Cheese Sub, 352–53, *354*
  Houlihan's 'Shrooms, 376–79, *378*

Mushrooms (*cont.*)
  Outback Steakhouse Alice Springs
    Chicken, 426–27 *428*
  Red Lobster Stuffed, 465, *466*
  topping, for Stuart Anderson's Black
    Angus Western T-Bone, 516
Mustard
  Benihana Dipping Sauces, 258
  Creole Sauce, for Planet Hollywood
    Chicken Crunch, 450–51
  Honey Sauce, for T.G.I. Friday's
    California Chargrilled Turkey
    Sandwich, 525–26
  Honey Marinade, for Outback
    Steakhouse Alice Springs Chicken,
    426
  mayonnaise-horseradish, for
    Houlihan's 'Shrooms, 376–79, *378*

Nabisco, 13
  Chips Ahoy!, 143, *144*
  Double Stuf Oreos, 148, 150
  Lorna Doone shortbread cookies, in
    M&M/Mars Caramel Twix Bars,
    109–10, *111*
  Nutter Butter, 145–46, *147*
  Oreo Cookies, 148–49, *150*
    Oreo Big Stuf, 150
Nachos Grande, Chi-Chi's, 308–11,
  309
Nestlé, 13
  Butterscotch Morsels, in Tastykake
    Butterscotch Krimpets, 189–90, *191*
  Crunch, 151–52, *152*
  100 Grand Bar, 153, *154*
Nine-Layer Dip, T.G.I. Friday's, 522–23,
  524
No-Fire Peppers, Red Robin, 467–69,
  469
Nougat
  3 Musketeers, M&M/Mars, 118–20
Nut Banana Pancakes, International
  House of Pancakes 389–90, *391*
Nutrition, 11, 17
Nutter Butter, Nabisco, 145–46, *147*

Olive Garden, 220
  Alfredo Pasta, 416
  Hot Artichoke-Spinach Dip, 413–14
  Italian Salad Dressing, 412

Toscana Soup, 415
Olives
  Taco Bell Enchirito, 185–86, *187*
Omelette
  International House of Pancakes Fajita,
    392–93, *394*
  Perkins Family Restaurants
    Country Club, 434–36, *436*
    Granny's Country, 431–32, *433*
100 Grand Bar, Nestlé, 153, *154*
Onion
  Outback Steakhouse
    Bloomin', 417–19, *420*
    Walkabout Soup, 424–25
  Straws, for Red Robin BBQ Chicken
    Salad, *472*
Orange
  juice
    Hard Rock Cafe Freeze, 366
    Houlihan's Houli Fruit Fizz, 375
    Julius, 155
    Snapple Iced Tea, 178
  Marmalade Sauce, Outback
    Steakhouse Gold Coast Coconut
    Shrimp, 422
Oreo Cookies, Nabisco, 148–49, *150*
  Big Stuf, 150
  in Chili's Peanut Buttercup
    Cheesecake, 325–27, *328*
  Double Stuf Oreos, 148, 150
Oriental Dressing, for Applebee's
  Oriental Chicken Salad, 247–48
Outback Steakhouse, 220, 222
  Alice Springs Chicken, 426–27 *428*
  Bloomin' Onion, 417–19, *420*
  Gold Coast Coconut Shrimp, 421–22,
    423
  Walkabout Soup, 424–25

Pancakes
  International House of Pancakes, 157
    Banana Nut, 389–90, *391*
    Crepe-style, for Blintz, 385–86
  Perkins Family Restaurants Potato
    Pancakes, 429–30
Pasta
  Cheesecake Factory Cajun Jambalaya,
    299–301
  Hooters Salad, 373–74
  Olive Garden Alfredo, 416

Ruby Tuesday Sonora Chicken,
482–84
T.G.I. Friday's Spicy Cajun Chicken,
528–29
Pattie, York Peppermint, 214–15, *216*
Peanut Butter
Buttercup Cheesecake, Chili's, 325–27,
328
Cookies, for Red Robin Mountain High
Mudd Pie, *476*
Cups, Reese's, 7, 168–69, *170*
Dream Bars, Mrs. Fields, 140–41, *142*
Kandy Kakes, Tastykake, 195–96, *197*
in Mary Jane, Stark, 179–80, *181*
Mountain High Mudd Pie, Red Robin,
473–75, *476*
Nutter Butter, Nabisco, 145–46, *147*
Sauce, California Pizza Kitchen Thai
Chicken Pizza, 285
in Snickers Bar, M&M/Mars, 115–16
in Twix Bars, M&M/Mars, 110
Peanuts
in Snickers Bar, M&M/Mars, 115–16
Pecans
International House of Pancakes
Banana Nut Pancakes, 389–90, *391*
Keebler Sandies, 87–88, *89*
Pepperidge Farm Chesapeake
Cookies, 91
Pepperidge Farm, 13
Chesapeake Cookies, 91
Sausalito Cookies, 91
Peppermint Pattie, York, 214–15, *216*
Pepperoni
Applebee's Pizza Sticks, 243–45, *246*
Loaded, 243, 247–48
Pizza Hut Original Stuffed Crust
Pepperoni and Cheese Pizza, 442
Pepper Steak, Stuart Anderson's Black
Angus Whiskey, 517–18
Perkins Family Restaurants
Country Club Omelette, 220, 434–36,
436
Granny's Country Omelette, 431–32,
433
Potato Pancakes, 429–30
Peter Paul, 13
Almond Joy, 158–9, *160*
Mounds, 158–9, *160*
Pico de Gallo

Chili's Grilled Caribbean Salad, 321
Pie
Marie Callender's
Banana Cream, 409–10, *411*
Chicken Pot, 406–8
Red Robin Mountain High Mudd,
473–75, *476*
Pie crust, for Marie Callender's Banana
Cream Pie, 409–10, *411*
Pineapple
Houlihan's Houli Fruit Fizz, 375
Julius, 156
T.G.I. Friday's Smoothies Tropical
Runner, 531
Western Sizzlin "Teriyaki" Chicken
Breast, 539–40, *541*
Pizza
California Pizza Kitchen
Original BBQ Chicken, 280–83, *282*
Original Stuffed Crust, 437–40, *441*
Original Stuffed Crust Pepperoni
and Cheese Pizza, 442
Southwestern Burrito Pizza,
288–90, *291*
Thai Chicken Pizza, 284–86, *287*
Pizza Hut
Triple Decker, 443–45, *446*
Pizza Bread, Planet Hollywood, 447–49,
448
Pizza crust
California Pizza Kitchen, 284–85, 289
Original BBQ Chicken Pizza,
280–83
Pizza Hut
Original Stuffed, 437–40
Triple Decker, 443–46
Planet Hollywood dough, 447–49, *448*
Pizza Hut, 220
Original Stuffed Crust Pizza, 437–40,
441
Pepperoni and Cheese Pizza, 442
Triple Decker Pizza, 443–45, *446*
Pizza Sticks, Applebee's, 243–45, *246*
Loaded, 243, 247–48
"Parmesan," 243, 247–48
Planet Hollywood, 220, 238
Chicken Crunch, 223, 450–51, *452*
Pizza Bread, 447–48, *449*
Pot Stickers, 453–54, *455*
Pogen's Gingersnaps, 161–62

Popeye's
    Famous Fried Chicken, 163, 164
    Red Beans and Rice, 165–66,167
Pork. See Ham; Ribs
Potatoes
    Au Gratin, Ruth's Chris Steak House,
        496–97
    French Fries
        Amarillo Cheese, Lone Star
            Steakhouse & Saloon, 395–96, 397
        Hardee's, 68–69, 70
    Hash Brown Casserole, Cracker
        Barrel, 329–30
    Pancakes, Perkins Family Restaurants,
        429–30
    Skins, T.G.I. Friday's, 519–20, 521
    Smashed, Houlihan's, 380–81, 381
    Soup
        Cheese, Ruby Tuesday, 477–78
        Toscana, Olive Garden, 415
Pot Roast, Shoney's Slow-Cooked,
    500–502
Pot Stickers, Planet Hollywood, 453–54,
    455
Pretzels, J&J Super, 182–83, 184
Prosciutto
    Dive! Sicilian Sub Rosa, 348–50, 351
Pumpkin Cheesecake, Cheesecake
    Factory, 302–3, 304

Quarter Pounder (with Cheese),
    McDonald's, 135–36, 136
Quesadillas, Applebee's, 223, 240–41,
    242

Ranch Dressing, for Lone Star Steak
    House & Saloon Amarillo Cheese
    Fries, 397
Red Beans and Rice, Popeye's,
    165–66,167
Red Hots, Tony Roma's, 537–38
Red Lobster, 220
    Broiled Lobster, 456–57, 458
    Scallops and Bacon, 459–61, 462
    Stuffed Mushrooms, 465, 466
    Stuffed Shrimp, 463–64, 466
Red Robin, 238
    BBQ Chicken Salad, 470–71, 472
    Mountain High Mudd Pie, 473–75,
        476

No-Fire Peppers, 467–69, 469
Reese's Peanut Butter Cups, 7, 168–69,
    170
    in Chili's Peanut Buttercup
        Cheesecake, 325–27, 328
Restaurant companies, top ten, 237
Ribs
    Hard Rock Cafe Famous Baby Rock
        Watermelon Ribs, 364–65
    Tony Roma's
        Carolina Honeys, 536
        Original Baby Backs, 534–35, 535
        Red Hots, 537–38
        World Famous Ribs, 532–33
Rice
    Benihana Japanese Fried, 260–61
    Lone Star Steakhouse & Saloon Texas,
        400–401
    Popeye's Red Beans and, 165–67, 167
Rice Krispies
    in Nestlé Crunch, 151–52
    in Nestlé 100 Grand Bar, 153, 154
Rolls
    Cinnabon Cinnamon, 55–56, 57
Root Beer, A & W, 13, 25, 26
Rotini
    Hooters Pasta Salad, 373–74
Ruby Tuesday
    Potato Cheese Soup, 477–78
    Smokey Mountain Chicken, 479–80,
        481
    Sonora Chicken Pasta, 482–84
    Strawberry Tallcake for Two, 485–87,
        488
Ruth's Chris
    Barbecued Shrimp, 489–90
    Creamed Spinach, 494–95
    Petite Filet, 491–93
    Potatoes Au Gratin, 496–97

Salad
    Applebee's Oriental Chicken, 247–48
    Chili's Grilled Caribbean, 320–21
    Hooters Pasta, 373–74
    KFC Cole Slaw, 94–95, 96
    Red Robin BBQ Chicken, 470–71, 472
Salami
    Dive! Sicilian Sub Rosa, 348–50, 351
Salmon, Lone Star Steakhouse & Saloon
    Sweet Bourbon, 402–3

Salsa
El Pollo Loco, 67
Pico de Gallo, Chili's Grilled Caribbean
Salad, 320–21
Tomatillo, California Pizza Kitchen
Southwestern Burrito Pizza, 289
Sandies, Keebler
Pecan, 87–88, 89
Toffee, 88
Sandwich
Wendy's Grilled Chicken Fillet,
203, 204
Sandwiches
Chicken
Buffalo, Bennigan's, 262–63, 264
Chick-Fil-A, 52–53, 54
Club, Carl's Jr., 41, 42
Club, Sizzler, 507–8, 509
Sante Fe, Carl's Jr., 46–47, 48
Club
Big Boy, 277–78, 279
Chicken, Carl's Jr., 41, 42
Chicken, Sizzler, 507–8, 509
House Grill, Applebee's, 249–50,
251
Egg
McMuffin, McDonald's, 18, 124–26,
125
Moons Over My Hammy, Denny's,
339–40, 341
Fish
Filet-O-, McDonald's, 127–28, 128
Steak
Filet, Hard Rock Cafe, 358–59, 360
Tijuana "Philly," Applebee's 252–53,
254
Sub
Brick Oven Mushroom and Turkey
Cheese, Dive!, 352–53, 354
Sicilian Rosa, Dive! 348–50, 351
Turkey
Brick Oven Mushroom and Cheese
Sub, Dive!, 352–53, 354
California, Bennigan's, 265–66, 267
California Chargrilled, T.G.I. Friday's,
525–26, 527
The Super Bird, Denny's, 342–43,
344
Vegetable Grilled, Hard Rock Cafe
361–63, 362

See also Cheeseburgers; Hamburgers
Sante Fe Chicken, Carl's Jr., 46–47, 48
Sara Lee Original Cream Cheesecake,
171–72, 173
Sauce
Arby's, 27
Barbecue
Carolina Honeys, Tony Roma's,
536
Original Baby Backs, Tony Roma's,
534–35
Red Hots, Tony Roma's, 537–38
Crazy, Little Caesar's, 102
Creole Mustard, for Planet Hollywood
Chicken Crunch, 450–51
Ginger, Benihana, 259
Hollandaise, for Perkins Family
Restaurants Country Club
Omelette, 434–36
Honey
Mustard, for T.G.I. Friday's California
Chargrilled Turkey Sandwich,
525–26
-Vinaigrette Dipping, for
Cheesecake Factory Avocado
Eggrolls, 296
Hot Taco, Taco Bell, 188
Marinara, for Applebee's Quesadillas,
223, 240–41, 242
Marmalade, for Outback Steakhouse
Gold Coast Coconut Shrimp, 422
Mayonnaise
Cajun Dipping, for Dive! Carrot
Chips, 346
-horseradish, for Outback
Steakhouse Bloomin' Onion,
417–19, 420
-mustard-horseradish, for Houlihan's
'Shrooms, 376–79, 378
Mustard
Benihana, 258
Honey, for T.G.I. Friday's California
Chargrilled Turkey Sandwich,
525–26
Peanut, for California Pizza Kitchen
Thai Chicken Pizza, 285
Strawberry, Ruby Tuesday, 485–88,
488
Teriyaki, Western Sizzlin, 539–40
Tomato, Pizza Hut, 437–40, 444–46

Sauce (*cont.*)
  Whiskey Pepper, Stuart Anderson's
    Black Angus, 517–18
  White Cheddar Dipping, for Dive!
    Carrot Chips, 346–47
  See also Gravy
Sausage
  Olive Garden Toscana Soup, 415
  See also Pepperoni
Sausalito Cookies, Pepperidge Farm, 91
Scallops
  and Bacon Skewers, Grilled, Red
    Lobster, 460–62, *461*
  Broiled Bacon-Wrapped, Red Lobster,
    459–60
See's Butterscotch Lollipop, 174–75, *176*
Shoney's, 220, 236
  Country Fried Steak, 498–99
  Hot Fudge Cake, 223, 503–4, *505*
  Slow-Cooked Pot Roast, 500–502
Shrimp
  Barbecued, Ruth's Chris Steak House,
    489–90
  Buffalo, Hooters, 370–71, *372*
  Cajun Jambalaya Pasta, Cheesecake
    Factory, 299–301
  Gold Coast Coconut, Outback
    Steakhouse, 421–22, *423*
  Southern Fried, Sizzler, 510–11
  Stuffed, Red Lobster, 463–64, *466*
Single, Wendy's, 207, *209*
Sizzler, 236
  Cheese Toast, 506
  Chicken Club Sandwich, 507–8, *509*
  Southern Fried Shrimp, 510–11
Skor, Hershey's, 36
Smashed Potatoes, Houlihan's, 380–81,
  381
Smokey Mountain Chicken, Ruby
  Tuesday, 479–80, *481*
Smoky Marinade, for Stuart Anderson's
  Black Angus Western T-Bone, 516
Smoothies, T.G.I. Friday's, 530–31
  Gold Medalist, 530
  Tropical Runner, 531
Snapple Iced Tea, 177–78
  Cranberry, 178
  Diet Lemon, 177
  Lemon, 177
  Orange, 178

Strawberry, 178
Snickers Bar, M&M/Mars, 115–16, *117*
  calories and fat, 10–11
Slow-Cooked Pot Roast, Shoney's,
  500–502
Soft Batch Chocolate Chip Cookies,
  Keebler, 90–91
Sonora Chicken Pasta, Ruby Tuesday,
  482–84
Soup
  Black Bean, Lone Star Steakhouse &
    Saloon, 398–99
  Cream of Broccoli, Big Boy, 272–73
  Potato Cheese, Ruby Tuesday, 477–78
  Toscana, Olive Garden, 415
  Walkabout, Outback Steakhouse,
    424–25
Sour cream, in T.G.I. Friday's Nine-Layer
  Dip, 522–23, *524*
Southern Fried Shrimp, Sizzler, 510–11
Southwestern Burrito Pizza, California
  Pizza Kitchen, 288–90, *291*
Spicy Cajun Chicken Pasta, T.G.I. Friday's,
  528–29
Spinach
  -Artichoke Dip, Olive Garden 413–14
  Creamed, Ruth's Chris Steak House,
    494–95
Sprite, in Houlihan's Houli Fruit Fizz, 375
Squash, summer
  Hard Rock Cafe Grilled Vegetable
    Sandwich, 361–63, *362*
Stark Mary Jane, 179–80, *181*
Steak
  Burrito, Twice Grilled Barbecue, Chi-
    Chi's, 314–16, *316*
  Country Fried, Shoney's, 498–99
  Fajita Omelette, International House
    of Pancakes, 392–93, *394*
  Hibachi, Benihana, 255–57
  Petite Filet, Ruth's Chris Steak House,
    491–93
  Sandwich
    Filet, Hard Rock Cafe, 358–59, *360*
    Tijuana "Philly," Applebee's, 252–53,
      254
  Western T-Bone, Stuart Anderson's
    Black Angus, 515–16
  Whiskey Pepper, Stuart Anderson's
    Black Angus, 517–18

Strawberry
  beverages
    Julius, 156
    Snapple Iced Tea, 178
    T.G.I. Friday's Gold Medalist, 530
    Tallcake for Two, Ruby Tuesday,
      485–87, *488*
Stuart Anderson's Black Angus, 220
  Cheesy Garlic Bread, 512–13, *514*
  Western T-Bone, 515–16
  Whiskey Pepper Steak, 517–18
Stuffed Crust Pizza, Pizza Hut Original,
  437–40, *441*
Stuffed Mushrooms, Red Lobster, 465,
  466
Stuffed Shrimp, Red Lobster, 463–65,
  464
Sub
  Brick Oven Mushroom and Turkey
    Cheese Sub, Dive!, 352–53, *354*
  Rosa, Sicilian, Dive!, 348–50, *351*
Sundae, Bennigan's Cookie Mountain,
  268–71, *271*
Super Bird, Denny's, 342–43, *344*
Super Pretzels, J&J, 182–83, *184*
Sweet Bourbon Salmon, Lone Star
  Steakhouse & Saloon, 402–3
Syrup
  Banana, International House of
    Pancakes, 389–90
  Maple, Aunt Jemima, 28–29

Taco
  Jack-in-the-Box, 82–83, *84*
  Hot Sauce, Taco Bell, 188
Taco Bell, 14
  Enchirito, 185–86, *187*
  Hot Taco Sauce, 188
Tastykake, 13, 17
  availability of, 6
  Butterscotch Krimpets, 189–90, *191*
  Chocolate Cupcakes, 192–94, *194*
  Peanut Butter Kandy Kakes, 195–96,
    197
Tea, Iced, Snapple, 177–78
  Cranberry, 178
  Diet Lemon, 177
  Lemon, 177
  Orange, 178
  Strawberry, 178

"Teriyaki" Chicken Breast, Western
  Sizzlin, 539–40, *541*
Texas Rice, Lone Star Steakhouse &
  Saloon, 400–401
T.G.I. Friday's, 220, 221, 237, 238
  California Chargrilled Turkey
    Sandwich, 525–26, *527*
  Nine-Layer Dip, 522–23, *524*
  Potato Skins, 519–20, *521*
  Smoothies, 530–31
    Gold Medalist, 530
    Tropical Runner, 531
  Spicy Cajun Chicken Pasta, 528–29
Thai Chicken Pizza, California Pizza
  Kitchen, 284–86, *287*
Theme restaurants, 238–39
3 Musketeers, M&M/Mars, 118–19, *120*
Tijuana "Philly" Steak Sandwich,
  Applebee's, 252–53, *254*
Toast
  Cheese, Sizzler, 506
  French, International House of
    Pancakes, 382–83, *384*
Toffee Sandies, Keebler, 88
Tomatillo Salsa, California Pizza Kitchen,
  289
Tomatoes
  Bruschetta, Cheesecake Factory,
    292–93, *294*
  Cajun Jambalaya Pasta, Cheesecake
    Factory, 299–301
  Chili, Wendy's, 200–201
  McD.L.T., McDonald's, 132–33, *134*
  Sauce
    Crazy, Little Caesar's, 102
    Marinara Dipping, Applebee's, 223,
      240–41, *242*
    Salsa, El Pollo Loco, 67
Tony Roma's
  Carolina Honeys, 536
  Original Baby Backs, 534–35, *535*
  Red Hots, 537–38
  World Famous Ribs, 532–33
Tortillas
  Applebee's
    Quesadillas, 223, 240–41, *242*
    Tijuana "Philly" Steak Sandwich,
      252–53, *254*
  Jack-in-the-Box Taco, 82–83, *84*
  Taco Bell Enchirito, 185–86, *187*

Toscana Soup, Olive Garden, 415
Triple Decker Pizza, Pizza Hut, 443–45, *446*
Turkey
    Omelette, Country Club, Perkins Family Restaurants 434–36, *436*
    Pot Stickers, Planet Hollywood, 453–54, *455*
    Sandwich
        Brick Oven Mushroom and Cheese Sub, Dive!, 352–53, *354*
        California, Bennigan's, 265–66, *267*
        California Chargrilled, T.G.I. Friday's, 525–26, *527*
        Club, Big Boy, 277–78, *279*
        Club House Grill, Applebee's, 249–50, *251*
        The Super Bird, Denny's, 342–43, *344*
Twice Grilled Barbecue Burrito, Chi-Chi's, 314–16, *316*
Twin Dragon Almond Cookies, 198, *199*
Twinkie, Hostess, 7, 17, 73–74, *75*
Twix Bars, M&M/Mars
    Caramel, 109–10, *111*
    Peanut Butter, 110

Vegetable Sandwich, Hard Rock Cafe Grilled, 361–63, *362*
Velveeta cheese spread
    in Perkins Family Restaurants Granny's Country Omelette, 431–32, *433*
    in Ruby Tuesday Sonora Chicken Pasta, 482–84
Vinaigrette
    Dive!, 349
    Hooters, 373–74
    See also Dipping Sauce; Dressing
Vodka
    Kahlúa Coffee Liqueur, 85–86

Walkabout Soup, Outback Steakhouse, 424–25

Walnuts, Mrs. Fields Chocolate Chip Cookies, *139*
Watermelon Ribs, Hard Rock Cafe Famous Baby Rock, 364–65
Wendy's, 18
    Chili, 200–201
    Double, *209*
        with cheese, *209*
    Frosty, 202
    Grilled Chicken Fillet Sandwich, 203, *204*
    Junior Bacon Cheeseburger, 205, *206*
    Single, 207, *209* with cheese, *208*
Western Bacon Cheeseburger, Carl's Jr., 49–50, *51*
Western Sizzlin', 220
    "Teriyaki" Chicken Breast, 539–40, *541*
Whiskey
    Bailey's Original Irish Cream, 30
    Whiskey Pepper Steak, Stuart Anderson's Black Angus, 517–18
White Castle, 13
    Burgers, 210–11, *212*
White Cheddar Dipping Sauce, for Dive! Carrot Chips, 346–47
Whopper, Burger King, 38–39, *40*
    Double with Cheese, 3
Wonton wrappers, in Planet Hollywood Pot Stickers, 453–54, *455*

Yeast dough, 21–22
Yogurt cheese, for lowfat International House of Pancakes Cheese Blintz, 387
Yoo-Hoo Chocolate Drink, 213
York Peppermint Pattie, 214–15, *216*

Zucchini
    Benihana Hibachi Chicken and Hibachi Steak, 255–57
    Hard Rock Cafe Grilled Vegetable Sandwich, 361–63, *362*